ADVANCES IN OPERATIONAL RISK

SECOND EDITION

ADVANCES IN OPERATIONAL RISK

Firm-wide Issues for Financial Institutions

Second Edition

Published by Risk Books, a division of Incisive RWG Ltd.

Haymarket House
28–29 Haymarket
London SW1Y 4RX
Tel: +44 (0)20 7484 9700
Fax: +44 (0)20 7484 9758
E-mail: books@riskwaters.com
Website: www.riskbooks.com
www.riskwaters.com

Every effort has been made to secure the permission of individual copyright holders for inclusion.

© Incisive RWG Ltd 2003
First Edition 2001
This Edition 2003

ISBN 1 904339 16 6

British Library Cataloguing in Publication Data
A catalogue record for this book is available from the British Library

Managing Editor: Sarah Jenkins
Assistant Editor: Kathryn Roberts

Typeset by Mark Heslington

Printed and bound in Great Britain by Bookcraft (Bath) Ltd, Somerset.

CONDITIONS OF SALE

All rights reserved. No part of this publication may be reproduced in any material form whether by photocopying or storing in any medium by electronic means whether or not transiently or incidentally to some other use for this publication without the prior written consent of the copyright owner except in accordance with the provisions of the Copyright, Designs and Patents Act 1988 or under the terms of a licence issued by the Copyright Licensing Agency Limited of 90, Tottenham Court Road, London W1P 0LP.

Warning: the doing of any unauthorised act in relation to this work may result in both civil and criminal liability.

Every effort has been made to ensure the accuracy of the text at the time of publication. However, no responsibility for loss occasioned to any person acting or refraining from acting as a result of the material contained in this publication will be accepted by Incisive RWG Ltd.

Many of the product names contained in this publication are registered trade marks, and Risk Books has made every effort to print them with the capitalisation and punctuation used by the trademark owner. For reasons of textual clarity, it is not our house style to use symbols such as TM, ®, etc. However, the absence of such symbols should not be taken to indicate absence of trademark protection; anyone wishing to use product names in the public domain should first clear such use with the product owner.

CONTENTS

	List of panels	vii
	List of contributors	ix
	Introduction: Operational Risk Management: New Disciplines, New Opportunities Peyman Mestchian of SAS UK	xv

MANAGING OPERATIONAL RISK

1	**Operational Risk Management: The Solution is in the Problem** Peyman Mestchian of SAS UK	3
2	**Managing Operational Risk** Robert Hübner, Mark Laycock and Fred Peemöller of Deutsche Bank AG	17
3	**New Trends in Operational Risk Insurance for Banks** Brendon Young of ORRF and Simon Ashby of FSA	43
4	**Operational Risk in Bank Acquisitions: A Real Options Approach to Valuing Managerial Flexibility** Hemantha S. B. Herath of University of Northern British Columbia and John S. Jahera Jr of Auburn University	59
5	**How to Introduce an Effective Operational Risk Management Framework** Roland Kennett of BNP Paribas	73

RISK ANALYSIS, IDENTIFICATION & MODELLING

6	**Operational Risk Capital Allocation and Integration of Risks** Elena A. Medova of University of Cambridge	95
7	**Developing an Operational VAR Model using EVT** Marcelo Cruz of RiskMaths	109
8	**The Use of Reliability Theory in Measuring Operational Risk** Patrick Mc Connell of Henley Management College	121
9	**Model Selection for Operational Risk** Michel Crouhy of CIBC, Dan Galai of Hebrew University and Robert Mark of Black Diamond	145
10	**Model Error in Enterprise-wide Risk Management: Insurance Policies with Guarantees** Andrea Consiglio of University of Cyprus and University of Palermo and Stavros A. Zenios of University of Cyprus and The Wharton School	179

PRACTICAL IMPLEMENTATION

11	**Building and Running an Operational Loss Database** John Thirlwell of ORRF and BBA Global Operational Loss Database	197
12	**Reputational Risk** Peter Schofield of American Express Corporate Audit	209
13	**Corporate Reputation: Not Worth Risking** Knowledge@Wharton in association with Aon	223
14	**Moody's Analytical Framework for Operational Risk Management of Banks** Brendon Young of Moody's Investors Service Limited	227
15	**From Operational Risk to Operational Excellence** Barbara Döbeli of Swiss National Bank, Markus Leippold of University of Zurich and Paolo Vanini of University of Southern Switzerland and Zurich Cantonal Bank	239
16	**The Legal and Regulatory View of Operational Risk** Dermot Turing of Clifford Chance LLP	253
	Index	267

LIST OF PANELS

OPERATIONAL RISK: KEY THEMES AND EXAMPLES

Throughout this book special panels introduce key themes and offer illustrative examples:

Functional units 20
The Basel statement on insurance 44
Insurance in risk management 45
Risk management – spreading the load 48
Differences between banks and the decision to insure 50
A spectrum of views on basket products 53
Pros and cons of reinsurance 54
The alternatives to insurance 55
BB&T Corporation's acquisition of Bankfirst Corporation 65
The rocky path to acceptance 75
Internal capital calculation 87
Viewing operational risk from an EVT perspective 89
Real options 91
Evolution of the capital charge 96
Establishing the normal 102
Overcoming the conflicting requirements of threshold
choice and parameter estimation 106
Total capital charge reconciliation 106
Operational research and risk 123
Component reliability under stress 126
Impact of the learning period 128
Human reliability under stress 130
Calculation of VAR for a portfolio of processes 135
Quality management systems 137
The "rogue" traders' lessons 146
Example: use of OpVAR to measure Visa fraud 154
Scenario properties for financial planning 185
Loss categories in the GOLD database 200
Impact/effect categories in the GOLD database 202
Soft loss 204
Business lines in the GOLD database 205
Media damage 212
Truth will out 214
Hit it before it hits you 218
The Basel Committee's 2003 principles 254
The Basel Committee's list of operational risk events that can
result in substantial losses 255
Qualifying criteria for AMA models 257

CONTRIBUTORS

Dr Simon Ashby is currently a policy advisor at the Financial Services Authority (FSA), advising on the FSA's policy for internal control, risk management, business continuity management and outsourcing. Simon was involved in drafting the FSA's recent Consultation Paper (CP142) on operational risk systems and controls. He is also involved in drafting much of the new policy on systems and controls for the forthcoming Integrated Prudential Sourcebook. Prior to working at the FSA, Simon was a lecturer at the University of Nottingham's Centre for Risk and Insurance Studies where he taught and researched risk and crisis management.

Andrea Consiglio is an associate professor of mathematical finance at the University of Palermo. Previously he was assistant professor at the University of Calabria. He has also visited Yale University, and has been a research associate with the University of Cyprus where he is currently a fellow of the HERMES Center of Excellence on computational finance and economics. The focus of his research is on financial modelling and computational finance. He has also participated in consultant projects with the Banca della Svizzera Italiana, Switzerland and Prometeia Calcolo in Italy. He has co-authored numerous articles for various academic journals including *Mathematical Programming, Journal of Risk and Finance, Operations Research* and the *Journal of Economics Dynamics and Control*. He has a PhD in applied mathematics to finance and economics.

Michel Crouhy is senior vice president, Business Analytic Solutions, Treasury Balance Sheet and Risk Management Division, at CIBC (Canadian Imperial Bank of Commerce). His responsibilities include the approval of all pricing, balance sheet, risk and capital related models, the development of risk measurement methodologies and models for market, credit (corporate and retail) and economic capital attribution, as well as customer behaviour analytics. Prior to his current position at CIBC, Dr Crouhy was a professor of finance at the HEC School of Management in Paris, where he was also director of the MS HEC in international finance. He has been a visiting professor at the Wharton School and at UCLA. Dr Crouhy holds a PhD from the Wharton School. He is co-author of *Risk Management* (McGraw-Hill) and has published extensively in academic journals in the areas of banking, options and financial markets. He is also associate editor of the *Journal of Derivatives*, the *Journal of Banking and Finance*, and is on the editorial board of the *Journal of Risk*.

Dr Marcelo Cruz has over six years of experience in operational risk modelling and measurement and he is a globally recognised expert on the subject. Currently, Dr Cruz works as a risk management consultant to several large global financial institutions as well as to a number of regulators. His most recent position in a large organisation was in leading the operational risk methodology development at UBS AG/UBS Warburg. Prior to that, he led the operational risk quantification efforts at a large British bank and worked as a derivatives trader for major international investment banks. He is the author of the first academic article on operational risk, an application of extreme value theory in risk measurement. He has authored an extensive list of technical publications in professional and academic journals and magazines and has also written academic texts on risk management. He is the author of *Mathematical Methods in Operational Risk* (John Wiley & Sons, 2001) and has contributed to several risk management books, including *Extremes and Integrated Risk Management* (Risk Publications, 2000);and *Managing Hedge Fund Risk* (Risk Publications, 2001). He is also a member of the publishing board of GARP (Global Association of Risk Professionals) and acts as an assistant editor for numerous finance, risk management and stochastic modelling publications. Dr Cruz has been involved in the Industry Technical Working Group (ITWG) that has collaborated with the Basel Committee to define the standards for operational risk measurement in the new Basel Accord. He has also been in constant discussion with the regulators involved. Dr Cruz has chaired, coordinated and/or spoken in important industry conferences and at top Universities in numerous countries. He is a visiting professor of universities in the USA, Europe and Latin America. He holds a PhD in mathematical finance as well as a MSc, a MBA and a BSc in economics/econometrics.

Barbara Döbeli works for the Swiss National Bank (SNB) where she is in charge of coordinating and supporting knowledge transfer to transition countries. Previously, she worked at the SNB for the International Monetary Fund (IMF). Her research work focuses on moral hazard and on operational risk issues. Barbara graduated in Economics from the University of Zurich.

Dan Galai is the Abe Gray Professor of finance and business administration at the Hebrew University, school of business administration in Jerusalem. He was a visiting professor of finance at INSEAD and at the University of California, Los Angeles and has also taught at the University of Chicago and at the University of California, Berkeley. He has served as a consultant for the Chicago Board of Options Exchange and the American Stock Exchange as well as for major banks. He has published numerous articles in leading business and finance journals, on options, risk management, financial markets and institutions, and corporate finance. He is a co-author of *Risk Management* (McGraw-Hill, 2000). He was a winner of the first annual Pomeranze Prize for excellence in options research presented by the CBOE. Dr Galai is a principal in Sigma PCM which is engaged in portfolio management and corporate finance. Dr Galai holds a PhD from the University of Chicago and undergraduate and graduate degrees from the Hebrew University.

Hemantha S.B. Herath is an assistant professor of accounting in the Faculty of Business, Brock University. Previously, he was an assistant professor at University of Northern British Columbia and a consultant in the Oil and Gas Division of the World Bank. He is a recipient of a Fulbright Scholarship. Dr Herath has published articles in academic journals including, *Managerial Finance, The Engineering Economist, Corporate Finance Review* and discussion papers at the World Bank. His research won a Best Paper Award from the American Society of Engineering Education. Dr Herath's research interests are in real options, economic decision analysis and corporate governance. He received his MS and his PhD from Auburn University and is an associate member of the Chartered Institute of Management Accountants, UK.

Robert Hübner is Deutsche Bank AG's divisional operational risk officer for global corporate finance and heads the project management office for the design and implementation of Deutsche Bank's global operational risk management framework. He reports into the chief risk officer operational risk. He joined Deutsche Bank AG in November 1998, and was responsible for automation, process management and principles questions of Deutsche Bank's global new product approval process. Since early 1999 he has worked on operational risk management. He developed Deutsche Bank's operational risk framework and the top-down operational risk self-assessment (db-RiskMap). Robert, who is a lawyer, was previously engaged at BfG Bank AG (Group Credit Lyonnais), where he started as law consultant in 1992. From

1994 he introduced the quality policy (EFQM-based) and became business manager of the capital markets area in 1995. In addition he was project manager "minimum requirements for trading business" (ie, implementation of market risk management) and project manager "re-engineering FX and MM" (the whole process value chain from sales to financial accounting / regulatory reporting).

John S. Jahera Jr is the colonial bank professor of finance and interim dean of the college of business at Auburn University. He has been a member of the Auburn University faculty since 1980 and served as head of the department of finance from 1988 until 2000. In addition to administrative duties, he has taught at both graduate and undergraduate levels as well as in a number of executive education programs. Dr Jahera is the author of more than 50 articles in a variety of journals including the *Journal of Financial Research*, the *Journal of Law, Economics & Organization*, *Research in Finance*, the *Journal of Real Estate Finance & Economics* and the *Journal of Banking & Finance*. His research has focused on issues relating to the banking industry as well as corporate governance issues. Dr Jahera holds a BS, MBA and PhD from the University of Georgia.

Roland Kennett works on operational risk at BNP Paribas. He is an experienced operational risk manager with extensive knowledge of the financial services industry. He has been working at the forefront of operational risk management since 1993, developing holistic methodologies for operational risk management. He began his operational risk career at Bankers Trust, moving on to Deutsche Bank and then Barclays Bank. His focus is based on a systematic measurement and management of the related risks. Roland has built his reputation on portraying the complex issues that make up operational risk in a straightforward and accessible manner. This is combined with a pragmatic yet innovative approach to delivering value added risk management solutions to all areas of the business process. Roland is a member of several industry working groups and a regular contributor at conferences on operational risk.

Mark Laycock is a member of the group operational risk team for the Deutsche Bank Group, which he joined in 1996. In this role he is devising, with the businesses and their support functions, mechanisms for managing operational risk, and enhancing transparency. He has been involved in a number of industry initiatives associated with regulatory discussions on operational risk. Since receiving his MBA from Manchester Business School he was worked at a number of financial institutions. His jobs have included trading a variety of capital market products and market risk methodologies. Immediately prior to Deutsche Bank, he worked for the Bank of England, in banking supervision. At the Bank of England he was involved in the implementation of the Capital Adequacy Directive, and the traded markets team.

Markus Leippold is assistant professor of finance at the Swiss Banking Institute of the University of Zurich. Prior to moving back to academia he worked for Sungard, Trading and Risk Systems, and the Zurich Cantonal Bank. Markus' main research interests are term structure modelling, asset pricing, and risk management. He has been published in several journals such as *Journal of Financial and Quantitative Analysis*, *Journal of Economic Dynamics and Control*, and *European Finance Review*. He obtained his PhD in financial economics from the University of St.Gallen, Switzerland.

Dr Robert Mark is the chief executive officer of Black Diamond Inc., which provides risk management consulting and transaction services. He serves on the Board of the Fields Institute for Research in Mathematical Sciences, IBM's Deep Computing Institute and The Royal Conservatory. In 1998, he was awarded the Financial Risk Manager of the Year by the Global Association of Risk Professionals (GARP). He is the Chairperson of The Professional Risk Managers' International Association's (PRMIA) Blue Ribbon Panel.

Prior to his current position, Dr Mark was the senior executive vice-president and chief risk officer and corporate treasurer at the Canadian Imperial Bank of Commerce, partner in charge of the Financial Risk Management

Consulting practice at Coopers & Lybrand (C&L) and a managing director in the Asia, Europe, and Capital Markets Group at Chemical Bank. He is an adjunct professor and co-author of "Risk Management" (McGraw-Hill, 2000). He also served on the board of ISDA and was the chairperson of the National Asset/Liability Management Association (NALMA).

Dr Mark earned his PhD, with a dissertation in options pricing, from New York University's Graduate School of Engineering and Science, graduating first in his class. Subsequently, he received an Advanced Professional Certificate in accounting from NYU's Stern Graduate School of Business. He is a graduate of the Harvard Business School Advanced Management Program.

Dr Patrick Mc Connell is principal of Risk Trading Technology Ltd a small consulting company, which specialises in developing IT strategies for international banks. Pat has over 30 years experience in developing advanced information systems and over 20 years as a manager and consultant in banking technology. He holds a doctorate in business administration, an MSc in operational research and a BSc in mathematics. Dr Mc Connell is also an academic supervisor with Henley Management College – the UK's largest MBA school – where he is engaged in research into IT and risk management and he has published several articles on these topics.

Elena A. Medova is senior research associate at the Centre for Financial Research in the Judge Institute of Management at the University of Cambridge. She is also a director of Cambridge Systems Associates Limited. Elena specialises in stochastic system optimisation and financial risk management. Her current research implements extreme value models for operational risk management, capital allocation and methods for the integration of operational risk with market and credit risk. She has recently been involved in risk management executive education in London, New York, Moscow and Athens. Elena Medova holds an MA and a PhD in applied mathematics from Dalhousie University in Canada. She also holds a Dip Eng.

Peyman Mestchian is the director of the Risk Management Practice at SAS UK. Previously, Peyman was director of the Business Risk Consulting practice at Ernst & Young (London) and was also a member of Ernst & Young's global taskforce for developing new products and solutions for addressing business and operational risks. Over the last 15 years, Peyman has been involved in numerous board-level consulting and implementation projects establishing enterprise-wide operational risk management systems for leading banks, insurance companies and industrial organisations. His special area of interest and research is the application of information technology to risk management and he is an established thought-leader and writer on the subject. He has recently contributed to such publications as *International Risk Management*, *Derivatives & Risk Technology* and *Banking Technology*. Peyman has a Bachelors degree in computer science and a Masters degree in human-computer interaction from the University of London. He is also a qualified Member of the Institute of Risk Management (MIRM).

Fred Peemöller is the chief risk officer for operational risk of Deutsche Bank Group, which he joined in 1977. In his role, he is responsible for the development of the operational risk management framework including tools and methodology. He is chairman of the group operational risk committee and a member of the group risk committee. A lawyer by profession, he started his career in the bank as regional manager for Latin America. He acted as representative of the bank for the debt restructuring negotiations with Brazil in the late 1980s. For an extended period of time he worked as general manager of Deutsche Bank's subsidiary in Brazil. Thereafter he has held various senior positions in credit and country risk management, *inter alia* as alternate chairman of the group credit committee.

Peter Schofield has been with American Express for over 20 years and since January 2001 has been a vice president and audit leader with the American Express Corporate Audit Group, with particular responsibility for American Express Financial Advisors. His previous position was the operational risk manager for American Express Bank with responsibility for global operations policies and procedures, control self-assessment and business continuation planning. Prior to that position, he led American Express Bank's project for the implementation of the euro. He has held management positions in both line management and support functions with the bank in the USA, the UK, Greece, India, Egypt and Bangladesh. Prior to this he held various positions in Lebanon, Sri Lanka and the Republic of Congo. Peter holds an MA from Corpus Christi College at Oxford University.

John Thirlwell was, until March 2003, a director of the British Bankers' Association (BBA), which he joined in December 1996 from Hill Samuel Bank, where he had been director and head of risk. At the BBA he was responsible for risk issues, particularly operational risk, which included setting up and chairing the BBA's Global Operational Loss Database (GOLD). On credit risk he was involved, among other things, in issues concerning portfolio management, loan documentation, insolvency and trade finance. He has been heavily involved, on behalf of the banking industry, in discussions with regulators concerning the new Basel Capital Accord and integration of the FSA. John chairs the Financial Services and Insurance Committee of the International Chamber of Commerce in the UK and is a frequent speaker and writer on risk and related issues. He is a non-executive Director of SVB Syndicates Limited and Executive Director of the Operational Risk Research Forum (ORRF). John graduated from Oxford University with a degree in English.

Dermot Turing is a partner in the Financial Institutions, Risk Management and Regulation Group at Clifford Chance. He advises on risk and regulatory issues covering a wide range of financial institutions and products, including derivatives, regulatory capital, securities, netting, collateral and EU directive implementation. He is the author of the "Risk Management Handbook" (2000). He has also authored chapters in other works on the EU Settlement Finality Directive as well as on the subject of netting.

Paolo Vanini is assistant professor of quantitative finance at the University of Southern Switzerland, Lugano, and deputy of corporate risk control, Zurich Cantonal Bank, Zurich where he is in charge of credit and operational risk on the group level.

His main research interests are credit risk, operational risk and asset liability management. He publishes on a regular basis in refereed journals such as the *Journal of Economic Dynamics and Control*, the *European Finance Review* and *European Financial Management*. Paolo is an author of the article "Operational Risk: A Practitioner's View", which appears in the *Journal of Risk*. He graduated from ETH Zurich in mathematical physics.

Brendon Young is Chairman of the *Operational Risk Research Forum (ORRF)*, an internationally recognised independent organisation endorsed by regulatory authorities, academic institutions and leading firms within the financial services sector. Currently, he holds the position of Operational Risk Specialist with Moody's Investors Service Ltd, Banking Team. In addition to developing *Moody's Analytical Framework for Operational Risk Management*, he is undertaking operational risk assessments (ORA) of leading European banks, hence facilitating benchmarking and future operational risk ratings. Previously, he was a director of the University of Central England Business School where his research interests included risk management and business development. Prior to academia he spent eight years as a venture capitalist, having previously worked in the City as a management consultant with PKF and Deloitte & Touche. He has also developed an operational risk programme for the Dutch National Bank and has created, in association with the British Library, a leading operational risk website (*www.orrf.org*). He has lectured widely and has authored numerous papers including a co-authored international award winning research paper on insurance as a mitigant for operational risk. Brendon is qualified as a chartered engineer and a chartered management accountant.

Stavros A. Zenios is professor and Rector at the University of Cyprus, the director of RiskLab at the Cyprus International Institute of Management, and a senior fellow at the Wharton School at the University of Pennsylvania. He is also the director of HERMES on computational finance and economics, which has been selected by the European Commission as a European Center of Excellence. Dr Zenios is known internationally for his work in computational finance and financial services, high-performance and parallel computations, and operations research. In his career he has authored two books, edited 12 books and journal issues, and (co)authored over 130 scholarly articles in some of the premier journals in the field. He holds two US patents on financial engineering methods. His book with Yair Censor Parallel Optimization received the 1999 ICS prize of the Institute of Operations Research and the Management Sciences. His article on banking services with A. Soteriou in Management Science received a Best Paper Award from the Decision Sciences Institute in 1999. In 2000 he was a Marie Curie Fellow of the European Commission.

INTRODUCTION

Operational Risk Management: New Disciplines, New Opportunities

Peyman Mestchian

SAS UK

The management of risk is one of the biggest challenges faced by an organisation. Hazards and threats and their associated risks can be managed in order to reduce the likelihood and impact of loss from risk events (downside risks) and to increase the probability and size of rewards from business opportunities (upside risks). This "risk–reward" balance is at the heart of all risk management activity.

Most large and medium-sized firms carry out risk management activities to varying degrees and risk management is implicitly or explicitly a strategic component of any organisation's survival and performance. This is reflected, for example, in firms employing directors of risk or CROs (chief risk officers) and making significant investments in setting up and maintaining risk management departments and functions. Furthermore, a multi-million pound industry has emanated from audit and consulting firms, insurance firms and software companies providing a proliferation of tools, techniques and solutions for risk management. Finally, recent legislation and national/international standards on corporate governance and risk management have brought the subject of risk further up the corporate agenda and given it greater visibility.

In the financial services industry, the areas of market risk and credit risk management are well developed and are supported by established tools and techniques. Financial firms have made significant investments in sophisticated systems and technology to ensure that the activities of their traders (market risk) and lenders (credit risk) do not jeopardise their existence and meet the requirements of the regulators. However, a string of high profile financial disasters (Barings, Sumitomo, Orange County, etc) have given rise to an increased awareness of the need to develop a more effective and efficient approach to the management of operational risk. Furthermore, The Basel Committee on Banking Supervision has introduced new requirements for banks to hold extra capital for this risk.

What is operational risk?
"Operational risk is the risk of loss resulting from inadequate or failed internal processes, people and systems or from external events."[1]

Poor management of operational risk can have a negative impact on the achievement of business objectives and, ultimately, shareholder value. This can materialise in a number of ways:

1. *Direct loss*: assets stolen (client, employees or competition), physical damage, litigation costs, human error resulting in irrecoverable asset or fund transfer, unexpected staff costs, regulatory penalties, project failures.
2. *Indirect loss*: brand erosion, loss of market share, key staff leakage, loss of key customers, increased insurance costs.
3. *Opportunity costs*: lack of innovative product development, forgone opportunities to enter new markets, missed opportunity to leverage the latest technologies and gain a competitive edge.

What is operational risk management?

Operational risk management is a subtle, complex and often qualitative concept. A review of the literature shows that there are a variety of different theoretical and practical approaches to operational risk measurement and management. Despite the variety of analysis and lack of standards, there are four key factors that are central to most research on operational risk management. These are:

1. Operational risk management is a process.
2. Operational risk management belongs to everyone in the firm.
3. Operational risk management requires qualitative and quantitative data.
4. Operational risk management needs sponsorship from the top.

At a more detailed level, operational risk management is about the effective use of resources through improved process efficiency, establishment of a sound system of internal controls (including removing redundant and ineffective controls), the sharing of knowledge and good practice, leveraging of technology to collect and analyse internal and external data, and prioritisation of effort. Like any other significant business process, operational risk management needs to be supervised and reviewed.

Ultimately, operational risk management is the same as good business management.

Key challenges

In spite of the overall industry consensus to tackle operational risk and recent developments in this discipline, financial institutions are faced with a multitude of practical challenges on the way to developing effective organisational systems and functions for operational risk management.

The fundamental question of definition has been partially addressed by the new Basel requirements. It is clear that operational risk is a broader concept than "operations" or back-office risk. The inclusion of people, process, technology and external events in the definition means that, unlike market and credit risk, which tend to be isolated in specific areas of the business, operational risks are inherent in all business processes.

Data remains as the single greatest obstacle to effective operational risk management. The sources of operational risk data include internal loss data and exposures collected from within the organisation, qualitative opinions based on self-assessment by management, key risk indicators derived from internal operation and performance systems. Even if a financial institution were able to capture all relevant data generated from its own operations, it would still lack data on low-probability high-severity events. Such information can only be collated by organisations pooling data on major losses and near misses – but this needs to be achieved in a way that protects the confidentiality of the data provider. The inherent problem here is that, unlike credit and market risk, operational risk events often occur behind closed doors and their communication to the outside world may have an adverse effect on the most valuable asset of a financial firm, its reputation.

People and culture issues around operational risk are significant. By definition, operational risk is often caused by human factor failures including human error, fraud and lack of knowledge. Similarly, in order to address operational risk its management needs to be embedded into all business processes and operational activities. This requires accountability, responsibility and empowerment for each individual within the organisation to identify, assess and treat the risks within their sphere of control. Ultimately, the best policies, procedures and systems in the world will not be enough for managing operational risk unless the people within the organisation understand their importance and are motivated to use them.

This book

This book is a collation of several papers written by leading practitioners and thought-leaders in the field of operational risk management. The first part, "Managing Operational Risk", focuses on defining the problem and presenting practical solutions. These include strategy, process, technology, insurance and real options.

The second part, "Risk Analysis, Identification and Modelling", covers some of the tools and techniques for tackling operational risk assessment. The chapters discuss some of the latest thinking in this area and present to the reader a range of best-practices.

The final part, "Practical Implementation", looks at some of the specific issues that need to be addressed as part of an operational risk management programme. These include legal, technical and reputational issues.

Although operational risk management in the financial services industry is relatively immature, there is a growing industry. By understanding the advances in operational risk management, financial institutions can enhance their ability to achieve their objectives and improve their processes, technology and business practices leading to improved shareholder value.

1 *Source: Basel Committee on Banking Supervision.*

BIBLIOGRAPHY

Basel Committee on Banking Supervision, 2001, "The New Basel Capital Accord", Bank for International Settlements, January.

Operational Risk and Financial Institutions, 1998, (London: Risk Books).

MANAGING OPERATIONAL RISK

1

Operational Risk Management: The Solution is in the Problem

Peyman Mestchian

SAS UK

"There are risks and costs to a program of action, but they are far less than the long-range risks and costs of comfortable inaction", John F. Kennedy

During the last few years there has been growing interest in the need for firms within the financial services industry to have in place robust systems for managing operational risk. This systematic approach to operational risk management requires a comprehensive control structure that is designed to address the full spectrum of risks faced by firms. The increasing level of interest in operational risk management has been stimulated by a variety of factors:

❏ the increasing complexity of financial products and trading mechanisms, particularly with the development of derivative products;
❏ the introduction of further requirements by banking and securities regulators and supervisors with the particular focus on the mechanisms for the "regulatory capital" calculations;
❏ the acceptance of senior executives that the systems supporting operational risk management have been, and in many cases still are, inadequate, and that good quality risk management requires significant improvement in processes and technologies that are now available for effective operational risk management; and
❏ the increase in knowledge and expertise in the practical application of statistical techniques to the operational risk management challenge.

The problem

There now appears to be a consensus forming that the definition of operational risk is:

the risk of loss resulting from inadequate or failed internal processes, people, and technology or from external events.[1]

To understand the problem further we need to decompose this definition:

Process risks: These include inefficiencies or ineffectiveness in the various business processes within the organisation. These include value-driving processes (front-office) such as sales and marketing, product development and customer support, as well as value-supporting processes (back-office) such as IT, HR and operations.

People risks: These include employee errors, employee misdeeds, employee unavailability and inadequate employee development and recruitment.

Technology risks: These include system failures caused by breakdown, data quality and integrity issues, inadequate capacity and poor project management.

External risks: These include the risk of loss caused by actions of external parties such as competitor behaviour, external fraud, regulatory change, and macro- and socio-economic events.

The interaction of these risks is shown in Figure 1.

THE COMMON FACTOR: DATA
The lack of available or suitable data, especially for larger and unexpected loss events, insufficient statistical samples and the incomplete statistical relationship between cause and effect or control variables all prove that there is significant room to improve data collection and correlation analysis. Successful risk practitioners have recognised this and are working towards alignment of operational risk measures to those of market and credit risk, if only at the level of common language.

The conceptual foundations for modelling operational risk shown here have been given most attention and a case can be made for all of them.

Economic pricing models: These base forecasts on economic models. One such operational risk model uses the capital asset pricing model (CAPM) to suggest a relative distribution of pricing of operational risk among other price determinants for capital.

Scenario analysis/subjective loss estimate models: Used to capture diverse opinions, concerns and experience/expertise of managers and represent them in matrix and graphic form.

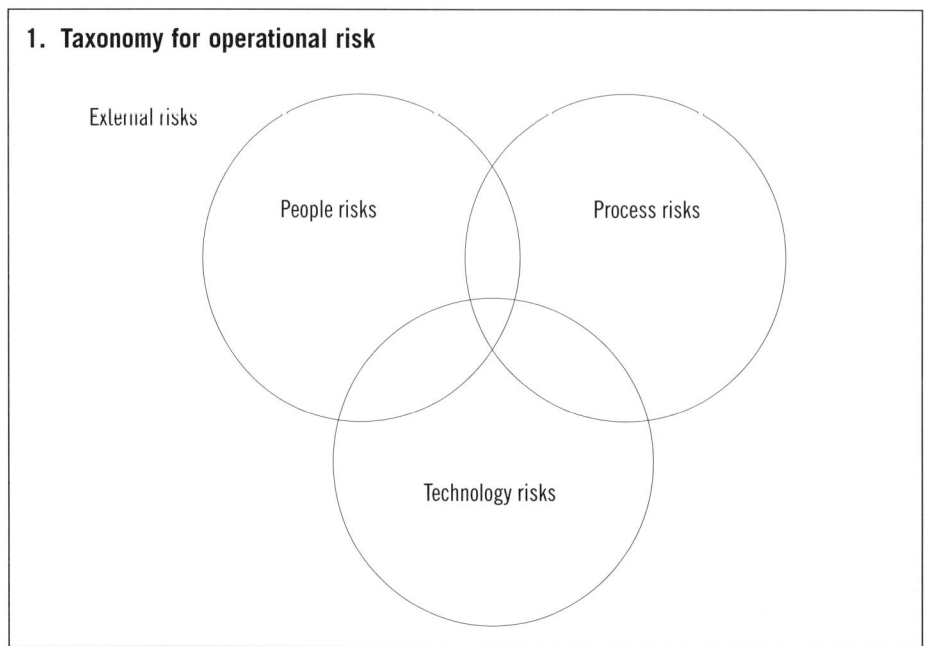

1. Taxonomy for operational risk

Statistical/actuarial/loss distribution loss models: Actual loss data are used to construct data representations of loss frequencies and severities in the form of statistical probability distributions in modelling expected losses for the future.

Factor-driven models: Apply loss and/or causal factors to build a bottom-up prediction of loss expectancies. For instance, these models are being applied in operations and processing units in conjunction with Bayesian Belief Networks and value-at-risk.

The solution

As discussed above, the key elements of operational risk are:

- process;
- people;
- technology; and
- external events.

In this chapter we suggest that the key components of successful operational risk management are an exact reflection of these four elements. The one common factor between the four solution areas is the need for a data-driven approach. This data is required for modelling risk as well as ensuring a continuous cycle of performance improvement.

THE PROCESS SOLUTION TO OPERATIONAL RISK

The key steps in an effective operational risk management process, as shown in Figure 2, are:

Step 1 *Setting policy*: Effective operational risk management policies set clear direction for the organisation to follow. They contribute to all aspects of business performance as part of a demonstrable commitment to continuous improvement. Responsibilities to people and the business community are met in ways that fulfil the spirit and letter of the law. Stakeholders' expectations in the activity (whether they are shareholders, employees, or their representatives, customers or society at large) are satisfied. There are cost-effective approaches to preserving and developing tangible and intangible assets, which reduce financial losses and liabilities.

Step 2 *Establishing the organisation*: An effective management structure and arrangements are in place for delivering the policy. All staff should be motivated and empowered to work safely and to protect the long-term success of the firm. The arrangements are:

- underpinned by effective staff involvement and participation; and
- sustained by effective communication and the promotion of competence which allows all employees and their representatives to make a responsible and informed contribution to the operational risk management effort.

There is a shared common understanding of the organisation's vision, values and beliefs. A positive risk management culture is fostered by the visible and active leadership of senior managers.

Step 3 *Implementation*: There is a planned and systematic approach to implementing the operational risk management policy through an effective operational risk management system. The aim is to minimise risks. Risk assessment methods are used to decide on priorities and to set objectives

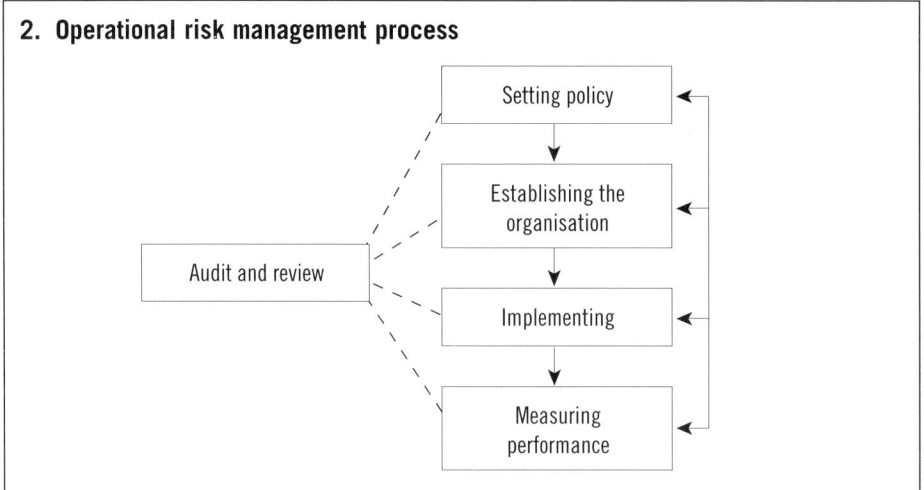

2. Operational risk management process

for eliminating hazards and reducing risks. Wherever possible, risks are treated through selection and design of appropriate controls. If risks cannot be controlled internally then various risk transfer methods are considered. The overall capital adequacy is reviewed taking into account the overall operational risk profile of the firm. Performance indicators are established and used for measuring risk. Specific actions to promote a positive operational risk culture are identified and implemented.

Figure 3 illustrates the key elements of the implementation process.

❑ *Define / review risk categories and risks*: The first step is to agree and capture the common definitions for risk categories, risks, events and their interdependencies. This is a top-down approach, where risks are tied to loss events. A process view can be taken, where conflict and inefficiencies are isolated and categorised.
❑ *Assess risks*: Some form of initial assessment of all risks based on impact and probability is needed to create a common view of the most significant risks. These can be visualised using risk maps.
❑ *Define risk strategy*: For the most important risks, based on agreement on acceptable levels of each risk.
❑ *Key risk indicators (KRIs)*: KRIs are used to track risks as they move toward the target acceptable levels. Thresholds are assigned, above which alerts and escalation procedures are triggered.
❑ *Define strategic actions and mitigation*: To ensure that KRI values move towards defined tolerance levels and stay there, strategic actions have to be defined. KRIs typically measure the probability level of risk. At the impact level, actions to mitigate risks need to be defined.
❑ *Monitor risk progress and environment*: Reporting on the progress of KRIs highlights critical areas where thresholds are breached and require actions. Periodic re-assessment of the risks via self-assessment allows the firm to identify changes in the environment and the impact on the risks.

The above strategic view is supported with tactical activities. To ensure that line managers and staff across the wider organisation participate in the risk management process, the following should be carried out.

❑ *Set targets for KRI*: The first step of such a cascade is to select the risks and KRIs applicable to a given organisational unit and to set appropriate targets or thresholds for these KRIs.
❑ *Monitor KRI progress*: The time intervals for monitoring KRIs at the tactical level

OPERATIONAL RISK MANAGEMENT: THE SOLUTION IS IN THE PROBLEM

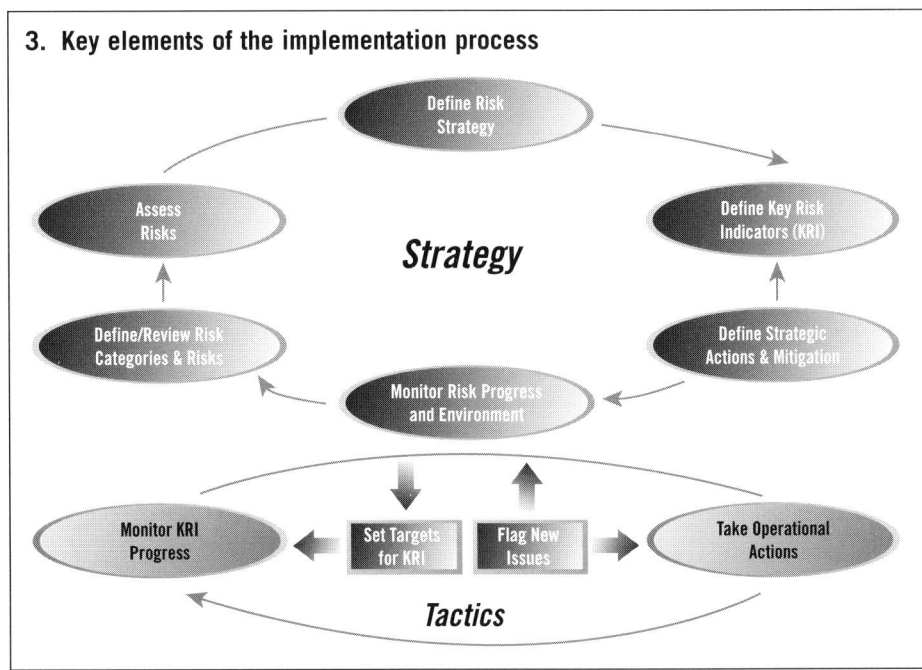

3. Key elements of the implementation process

are shorter (eg, weekly intervals), while top level monitoring can be monthly or quarterly.
- *Take operational actions*: By implementing shorter time intervals for monitoring operational actions a business unit manager can address risks before they escalate to higher levels. Consequently, top management can focus attention on wider and more important issues.
- *Flag new issues*: New loss events, near-misses, or simply changes in the environment make it essential that managers flag issues to senior management using the risk management process.

Step 4 *Measuring performance*: Performance of the operational risk management system is measured against standards to reveal when and where improvement is needed. Proactive self-monitoring reveals how effectively the operational risk management system is functioning. This looks at both internal and external risk factors. If controls fail, reactive monitoring discovers why, by investigating risk events that could cause loss. The objectives of active and reactive monitoring are:

- to determine the immediate causes of sub-standard performance; and
- to identify the underlying causes and the implications for the design and operation of the operational risk management system.

Step 5 *Auditing and reviewing*: The organisation learns from all relevant experience and applies the lessons. There is a systematic review of performance based on data from monitoring activities and from independent audits of the whole risk management system. These form the basis of self-regulation and of complying with various national and international standards. There is a strong commitment to continuous improvement involving the constant development of policies, systems and techniques of risk measurement and control. Performance is assessed by:

- internal reference to key performance indicators; and
- external comparison with the performance of business competitors and best practice.

Finally, the feedback loop is an essential aspect of the operational risk management process. This is not a one-off activity and an ongoing continuous improvement cycle is critical to the success of the overall system.

THE PEOPLE SOLUTION TO OPERATIONAL RISK

Loss events are seldom random events. They generally arise from failures of control and involve multiple contributory factors. The immediate cause may be a human or technical failure, but they usually arise from organisational failings which are the responsibility of management. Successful policies aim to exploit the strengths of employees. They aim to minimise the contribution of human limitations and fallibilities by examining how the organisation is structured and how jobs and systems are designed.

Firms that are good at managing operational risk create an effective framework to maximise the contribution of individuals and groups. Operational risk objectives are regarded in the same way as other business objectives. They become part of the culture and this is recognised explicitly by making operational risk a line management responsibility. The approach has to start at the top. Visible and active support, strong leadership and commitment of senior managers and directors are fundamental to the success of operational risk management. Senior managers communicate the beliefs which underlie the policy through their individual behaviour and management practice. Operational risk is a boardroom issue and a board member takes direct responsibility for the co-ordination of effort. The whole organisation shares the management perception and beliefs about the importance of operational risk and the need to achieve the policy objectives.

Figure 4 shows the interaction of the human factors that affect operational risk.

Organisational factors: These have a major influence on individual and group behaviour, yet it is common for them to be overlooked during the design of work and when investigating loss events. Organisations need to establish their own risk management culture that promotes employee involvement and commitment at all levels. This culture should emphasise that deviation from established risk management standards is unacceptable.

Job factors: These directly influence individual performance and the control of risks. Tasks should be designed according to sound financial and operational principles to take into account the limitations of human performance. Mismatches between job requirements and individuals' capabilities increase the potential for human error. Matching the job to the individual ensures that people are not overloaded; this contributes to consistent performance. This involves taking into account the

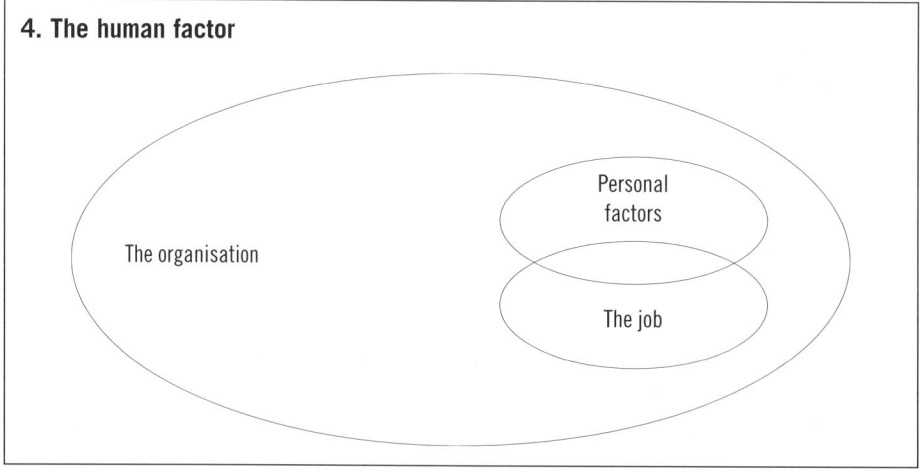

4. The human factor

individual's information and decision-making requirements as well as his or her perception of the task. Mismatches between job requirements and the individual's capabilities increase the potential for human error.

Personal factors: The attributes that employees bring to their jobs may be strengths or weaknesses in relation to the demands of a particular task. They include attributes such as habits, attitudes, skills and personality, which influence behaviour in complex ways. Negative effects on task performance cannot always be mitigated by job design solutions. Some characteristics, such as skills and attitude, can be modified by training and experience; others, such as personality, are relatively permanent and cannot be modified within the work context. People therefore need to be matched to their jobs through appropriate selection techniques.

THE TECHNOLOGY SOLUTION TO OPERATIONAL RISK AND MEETING THE DATA CHALLENGE
It goes without saying that technology solutions for operational risk management are the least developed element of the risk management infrastructure. However, recent developments in the definition of operational risk together with advances in risk quantification and data management technology have led to the development of a number of key technological components for an enterprise-wide operational risk management system.

Figure 5 describes some of the key elements of the operational risk technology developed by SAS.

Self-assessment of risks
It is generally accepted that in many organisations there is a need for an initial assessment ('health check') of operational risks, taken from a wide and geographically dispersed selection of individuals across the firm. The most effective – and repeatable – process to support such an exercise is to make it easy to capture the results and store them in a robust database that reliably manages them and allows them to be analysed with ease. Some firms prefer a more interactive, regular "group workshop" approach to gathering data, but whatever approach is taken, the key task is to capture and store the data in a standard manner.

The proposed SAS solution includes fully web-enabled, highly configurable questionnaires that are distributed selectively to any or all of the target individuals and groups responsible for any number of risk categories. The process includes approvals and escalation levels to ensure that responses are consolidated and consistent as the key summary data is filtered up the organisation. Lastly, the process can also be automated and scheduled with ease, making it possible to conduct these reviews on a regular basis.

Each risk has a questionnaire dynamically linked to it. By selecting any of the assigned topics for risk assessment, the user can assess the risk based on impact (severity, qualitatively or quantitatively) and probability (frequency), specify root causes, assign specific amounts to impacts, indicate whether risks are acceptable and indicate that if risks are unacceptable, what measures or controls are in place to mitigate those risks.

The content of questionnaires is configurable and can be extended to include more complex elements, qualitative and quantitative impacts. The entire process can be managed from a single location with relative ease and distributed via intranet.

Risk maps
Having captured the results of risk self-assessments, SAS provides the capability to generate sets of dynamic, multi-dimensional views of the risks showing the responses submitted by each user and reflecting impacts and probabilities. Risk maps are

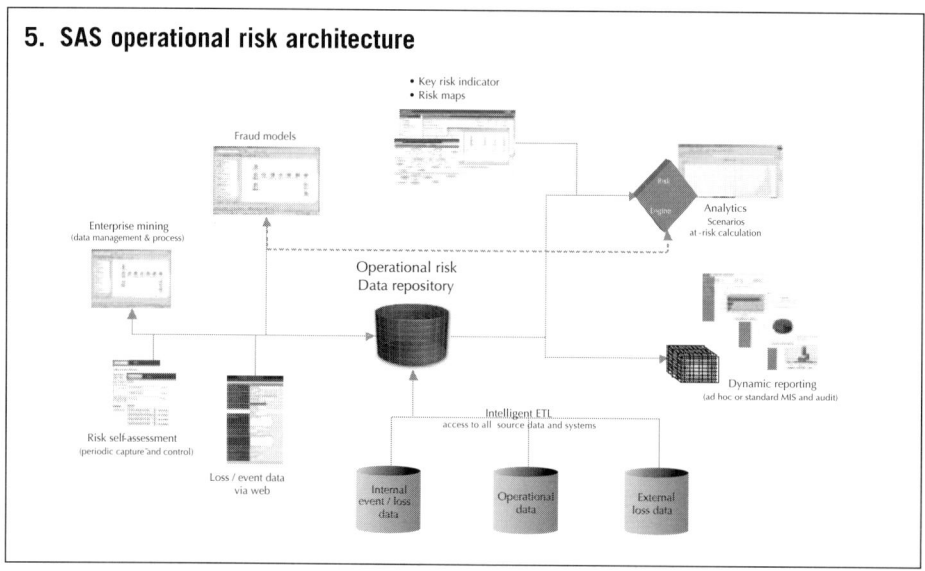

5. SAS operational risk architecture

particularly useful at a senior level of the organisation, where it quickly becomes clear what the key areas of risk – or opportunity – are.

Users can view the data at any level of detail or aggregation and can also select categories (highest, lowest, top 10, etc). Group managers can select the specified risks of a business unit to see how each user rates the risk, or select a specific risk and view its ranking. The value of the risk map is its ability to isolate those risks (or opportunities) that give the firm a clear perspective on where to act.

Data access
The primary data sources for an operational risk system are:

- self assessment data (discussed above);
- internal event / loss data;
- operational data; and
- external loss data.

A key requirement for any solution is for users to be able to select blocks of loss data for analysis from multiple databases holding loss data. Each of these data sources is reviewed below and data management issues are then discussed.

Internal event / loss data
To facilitate the process of feeding the internal event/loss data model, users have secure access to a web-based application, similar to the self-assessment and scorecard modules. A series of configurable input screens allow assigned users to capture all relevant data associated with specific events and losses, such as:

- event category;
- general information (eg, event id, status flag, regulatory flag);
- categories (four-dimensional, multi-level, event-type, cause-type, effect-type, insurance policy);
- descriptions;
- status:
  - event dates (eg, start, end, reported, booked, last update);
  - process (eg, detected by, reported by, reported to, open/closed);
- organisational structures:
  - country, region, branch, division, area, product group, regulatory business line;
- loss amounts:

- actual loss, potential loss, recoveries;
- currency;
❑ correlated events; and
❑ exposure indicator.

Operational data

The SAS system can act as the ultimate integrator of operational risk information and needs access to operational data to feed its early warning indicators and to assign the right level of detail to loss events. For example, when faced with a sporadically failing IT system, one would want to know the system's details, the number of hours the problem has persisted, and so on. This data can be manually captured in the risk scorecard or ideally sourced from operational databases already in use. Accessing this data in an automated, rapid and user-friendly manner is crucial to the risk warehouse.

External loss data

Regulators welcome the inclusion of external loss data, but these databases are in their infancy. The best-known initiative is the ORX pool set-up by major global banks. The British Bankers' Association has also established a data pool known as GOLD. However, these data pools will only contain losses above a certain threshold.

Only 10 data fields are captured. External loss data cannot be integrated directly into the internal loss database and needs to go through a scaling process where the loss is transformed to correctly reflect the profile of the client's own organisation. No standard market method exists for scaling data; almost every bank uses its own algorithms.

Data management

All successful risk management projects share a strong emphasis on complete management of input data and computed results. The SAS solution includes data management tools to manage the data repository and supports complete definition and management of the entire inflow process, including the risk model. All metadata is documented and every step of the ETL (Extract–Transform–Load) process can be visualised graphically.

Also included in the solution is support for full creation of dynamic HTML documentation, including hyperlinks and deep drill-down capabilities that use all of the metadata in the environment. This is especially useful to provide valid and current documentation to anyone who needs to understand the model.

Risk analysis

The first level of analysis starts from the operational risk data repository. Using the available statistical analysis tools within the risk engine, a user can determine the best fit of:

❑ frequency distributions of loss events, such as poisson, negative binomial, binomial, hyper geometric and geometric; and
❑ severity distribution of loss events, such as log-normal, Pareto, exponential, gamma, beta and Weibull.

Using the maximum likelihood estimation (MLE) and other similar techniques, a user can fit a curve of data points to two or more combinations of these distributions and then perform Monte Carlo simulation(s) using the joint distribution.

Monte Carlo simulations include using either the expected loss frequency or a user-defined frequency to define the arrival rate of losses, and either the fitted severity distribution or the empirical distribution of losses to define the severity of each loss. The process combines frequency and severity distributions to generate the combined loss distribution. The number of trials required, the time period to be covered (eg, one year) and reports of these results are all user-defined, eg, expected (mean) loss, median loss, minimum loss, maximum loss, 99% confidence level and user-specified confidence level (eg, 99.75%). Users can also include or exclude zero and negative losses (ie, gains) from the analysis; if zero losses are included, the system forms a composite distribution, which includes a probability of the loss being zero, and a severity distribution contingent on the loss being non-zero.

Monte Carlo simulations can be run simultaneously using data sets that apply to a number of different lines of business, each of which has had frequency and severity distributions fitted. Results can be reported for each of the data sets individually, for the combination of all data sets, and for all intervening levels of the line of business hierarchy, with some of the results being additive up the hierarchy and others not.

A second – optional – level of analysis focuses around fraud models, by exploring and modelling fraud behaviour by mining through transaction data to uncover previously unknown patterns. The resulting models are fed into the risk engine, which then computes capital-at-risk – a measure that expresses how much one can potentially lose, within a timeframe and with a specified confidence level – and performs scenario / stress analysis.

Result presentation
The scorecard is an ideal presentation layer for operational risk, an approach that integrates "top-down" and "bottom-up" perspectives. Scorecards present graphic cause–effect flows, as illustrated in Figure 6 for an operational risk environment.

The scorecard is also an ideal communication channel to link causes with the actions to be taken by those affected by or responsible for actions. As a result, every employee in the organisation is brought into the process.

This approach brings together the early warning indicators, capital at risk figures, self-assessment and loss data. Advanced reporting features allow risk managers, senior management and others to access and communicate risk measures across the entire enterprise, fuelling better decision-making. The risk scorecard makes it possible for management to retain a strategic vision without losing sight of, or access to, the details.

Performance tracking
Key risk indicators (early warning indicators) are used to track the risk exposures linked to each of the defined risks. These can be viewed at the global framework level, or for a particular business unit. As with the risk maps, the loss event database can be presented in a variety of ways in the form of views, graphs and diagrams. In these cases the user has complete control over both the display of loss event types and what information to display in the views. In Figure 6, the view has been configured to show only the internal scores and comparison against external scores. Using advanced analytics and reporting a user can drill-down through the scorecard data for more detailed analysis. For example, it would be possible to drill-down on IT failure rates to get a standard report on system down times, generated from the risk data details. Integrating the qualitative and quantitative measures into the scorecard is achieved simply by configuring it to pick up the result calculations from the risk engine.

Event (loss) analysis
As with the risk maps, the loss event database may be presented in a variety of ways in the form of views, graphs and diagrams.

Users have the ability to graph loss events over time (at a detailed or summary level). Users can also comment on (or review comments on) loss events, in the same manner as outlined earlier.

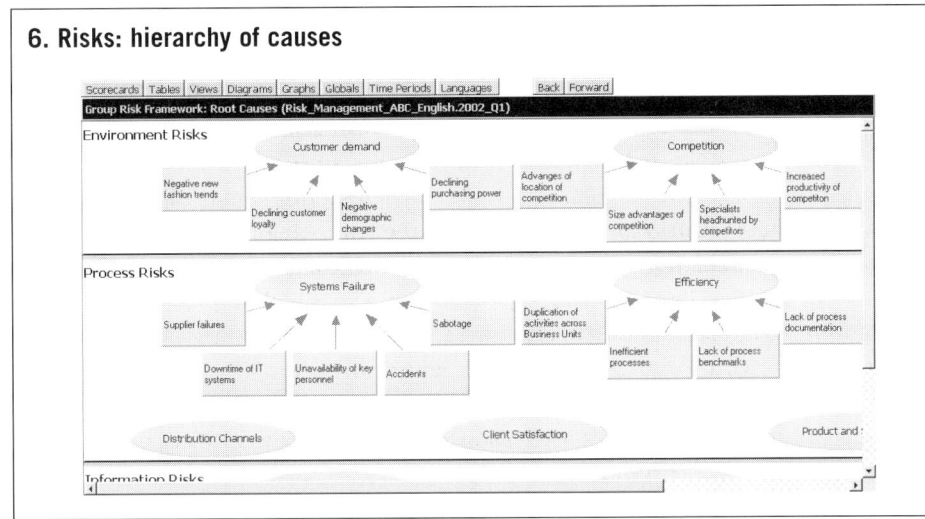

Finally, due to the dynamic nature of risk management, it is important for any technology solution not only to meet today's requirements, but also be flexible enough to evolve and meet the future expectations of regulators, risk managers and top management.

To be successful, firms must establish a link between qualitative and quantitative risk measures and build a process with which they can leverage this knowledge.

THE EXTERNAL SOLUTION TO OPERATIONAL RISK
So far in the discussion we have focused on the use of various internal mechanisms, namely people, process and technology, for managing operational risk. However, where appropriate, organisations do have access to external sources of operational risk management.

Insurance
In recent times financial services firms have invested significant amounts of time and money to identify ways of managing and hedging market and credit risk. This includes instruments such as credit derivatives used for hedging against counterparty default. These instruments are often supported by sophisticated information systems used for modelling and managing exposures.

The attention of hedging experts has now turned to operational risk. A key tool here is insurance. Elements of operational risk have been insured for some time. Examples include property coverage, fire, workers compensation, employer's liability and professional indemnity. Insurance provides financial services firms with the means of taking risk off their balance sheet and avoiding the significant costs of capital associated with the provisions for risk.

Demand for traditional insurance coverage has increased dramatically in recent times as senior executives wake up to the potential horrors presented by various operational risks, and the insurers are responding; there has been a move toward multi-risk coverage programmes comprising of multi-billion dollar limits. Moreover, the market for alternative risk transfer has been growing in recent years. Multi-year, multi-line coverage whereby the various lines of coverage are bundled into one complete package and spread over five to 10 years as opposed to the traditional annually renewable policy have become more popular. This gives both premium and transaction savings to the client as well as wider coverage.

One way to look at the decision-making process for operational risk insurance is to categorise by severity and frequency on a risk map, as shown in Figure 7.

It should be noted that as multinational firms have increased in size and capital it has become more attractive for them to self-insure by setting up internal

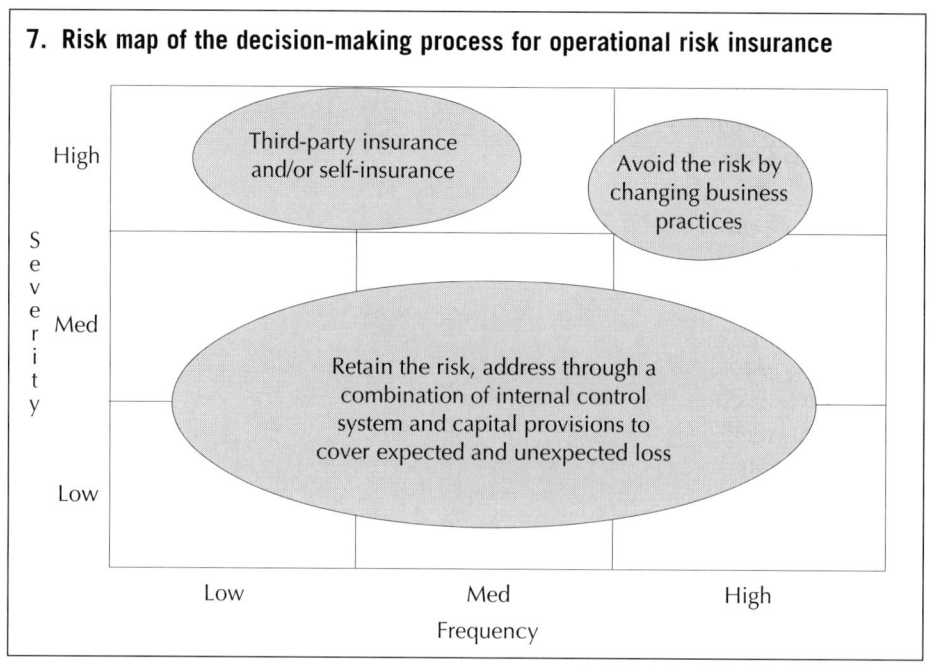

7. Risk map of the decision-making process for operational risk insurance

investment funds. This has the advantage of avoiding the regular two-way transaction costs of making claims and paying premiums on a regular basis as well as reduction in the actual premium. For a large organisation the savings can amount to several million dollars. Moreover, by setting up these funds in the form of offshore captives, large organisations can benefit from additional financial and tax advantages.

Outsourcing
Another method for transferring risks to an external entity is outsourcing. Essentially, this allows financial institutions to select the various business processes or functions that are non-core and high risk to a third party. Recent examples of this have been the outsourcing of non-core back-office functions such as IT and/or HR. The third-party firms often benefit from economies of scale and specialisation and can pass on cost savings as well as quality improvements to the client. The critical success factor is the nature of the relationship and the service level agreement between the two companies. The management of this interface has its own operational risks but, if managed effectively, it can be an elegant mechanism for transferring risk.

In addition to transferring risk, outsourcing has several other business benefits. These include:

❏ cost control;
❏ access to best-practice tools and methodologies;
❏ freeing up capital and resources to focus on core business; and
❏ reduction in bureaucracy and administrative burden.

The future
Each solution area covered in this chapter has its own direction in future development. In many cases, these future developments will address gaps in current thinking and clarify ambiguities in current understanding.

Two main driving forces will influence the direction of operational risk management.

Firstly, the application of existing business management approaches to operational risk management will gain pace over the next few years. For example, operational risk management tools and techniques have been developed and established within non-financial organisations for many years. These have been around for decades in safety-critical industries such as energy, defence, aviation and transportation. Many of the methods and tools developed in these sectors can be applied to managing risks in the financial services sector. Some of the leading management tools applicable to operational risk management are:

❑ *Reliability-centred management*: This is comprised of a set of methods and techniques by which an organisation can use process, equipment and control failure data to develop a flexible and cohesive operational maintenance and resilience capability.
❑ *Behaviour-based management*: This applies the principles of total quality management coupled with the latest thinking in organisational behaviour and statistical techniques to the issue of unsafe behaviours and attitudes by employees. It has had several decades of success in the manufacturing and industrial sectors.
❑ *Knowledge management*: In recent years many leading organisations have invested in the latest systems and processes for managing their intangible assets. It has been shown that individual and organisational knowledge can be utilised to create more efficient and effective business processes. This has direct relevance to operational risk management as existing knowledge management systems can be used to identify potential risk events as well as assist in the communication of risk prevention initiatives and best-practices. Of particular relevance is the application of the latest text-mining technology. This technology allows organisations to scan and interrogate unstructured data (ie, data that is not in any specific database) and identify clues about risk events before and/or after their occurrence. Research has shown that 80% of all organisational data is in an unstructured format (eg, Word documents, spreadsheets, presentations, reports, emails and intranet). Therefore, a systematic approach for identifying operational risk events can only be complete when this data is utilised.
❑ *Activity-based management*: Activity-based costing and activity based management systems became prevalent in the 1990s. The aim of these systems is to achieve greater accuracy in cost allocation and provide "true" economic information to management and help them make decisions to satisfy customers and improve profits. This activity-based view of the business is highly relevant to operational risk management as it assists in decisions concerning pricing, product mix, costs reductions, process improvement, process or product redesign, and planning or managing activities. Moreover, this approach can be directly linked to the risk scorecard and key indicator approaches described earlier in the technology section.

The second key driving force for further development of operational risk management as a discipline is new regulatory requirements focusing on adequacy of capital allocation and implementing sound systems of internal control. A significant gap in current understanding is the link between backward-looking historical risk event data which can be modelled using well established statistical methods and the forward-looking self-assessment and risk indicator data, which is derived from input by key personnel and operational databases. It is not yet clear how these three sets of data can be mathematically aggregated to arrive at a single economic capital calculation. It is envisaged that more advanced mathematical techniques such as Bayesian analysis and fuzzy logic may be applied to this problem. This is an area that requires further research.

Ultimately, regulatory compliance is not the best reason for implementing operational risk management systems and processes. A purely regulatory view will in general lead to firms implementing the minimum possible to achieve compliance and not realising the full business benefits of effective risk management. Thinking

OPERATIONAL RISK MANAGEMENT: THE SOLUTION IS IN THE PROBLEM

beyond Basel II and focusing on the significant and unquestionable returns on investment that can be derived from effective operational risk management will move this discipline into the next phase of development and embed it as part of the day-to-day activity of every business unit within a financial services organisation.

1 *Basel Committee on Banking Supervision 2001.*

2

Managing Operational Risk

Robert Hübner, Mark Laycock and Fred Peemöller
Deutsche Bank AG

Managing operational risk is not a new idea. What is new is the organisation of the components of operational risk components into a coherent, structured framework. The relative novelty of the framework however, is one of the factors that has contributed to the difficulty of the discussions with regulators on how best to devise and implement it. In this chapter we will discuss the driving forces behind the management of operational risk along with the skills and attributes that are required to conduct a programme effectively.

Why manage operational risk?
The rationale and driving forces behind these organising efforts include:

❏ shareholder value and competition;
❏ senior management and corporate governance issues; and
❏ regulatory and rating agency focus.

To manage the different aspects of operational risk, firms need access to skills in areas such as IT security, human resources, legal matters, compliance and many others. These will be discussed in detail later in the chapter. This is the other element of innovation in operational risk – the effort to integrate these skills into a risk management framework. "Templates" for such a framework can be borrowed from the risk management processes already in place for credit and market risk management and we will attempt to apply these tried and tested frameworks to operational risk.

The rising importance of the various stakeholders in a firm – particularly shareholders – means that they can influence the way the firm conducts its affairs, affecting, among other things, its competitiveness. For example, if an operational risk management framework is to be effective, it is desirable to have the stakeholders' endorsement as such a framework may significantly affect the firm's competitiveness. For the firm capital has many roles, one of which is to absorb losses arising out of the considered and deliberate taking of unexpected risk. In particular, capital is required to cover unexpected losses falling between the 50% confidence interval and stress or catastrophic losses. In compensation for taking on these possible losses the shareholders require a return. In this context, operational risk management helps senior management to identify the risks and, as with credit and market risk, provides a basis for deciding the appetite for specific risks, such as the euro in 2002 and for more generic day-to-day risks. Our experience is that the quality of the service provided to customers and clients is reflected in a firm's competitiveness in the financial services sector (an obvious example is that a firm with a continued tendency to make settlement errors is unlikely to win many custody mandates) and that some of the drivers that influence this service relate to operational risk and related activities.

Decisions on risk appetite (the level of exposure to a risk with which a firm feels comfortable) and the support required to make them contribute to the obligations of senior management in respect of corporate governance. These obligations have increased in specificity and scope with the publication of papers by the Basel Committee on Banking Supervision and, in the case of Deutsche Bank, the issuance of the firm's own corporate governance statement. For some, the image of operational risk management may be that it is a reactive and fire-fighting activity, but an objective in formalising this function should be to promote a more proactive attitude among its practitioners as well as more widely inside the firm.

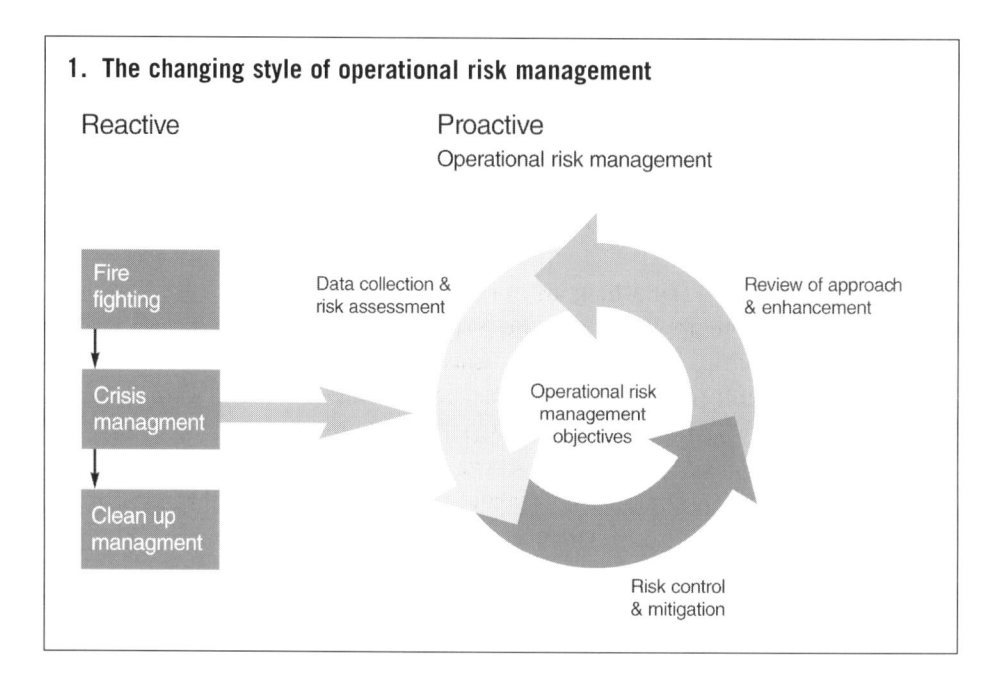

1. The changing style of operational risk management

Reactive
- Fire fighting
- Crisis managment
- Clean up managment

Proactive
Operational risk management

- Data collection & risk assessment
- Review of approach & enhancement
- Risk control & mitigation

Operational risk management objectives

The regulators too are taking a greater interest in this area, partly because of the changing risk profile of the financial services sector – as seen, for example, in the growth in e-business operations – and the increasing intensity of and reliance on technology.

At the time of writing the industry has received a number of consultative papers from the Basel Committee and a draft new Capital Adequacy Directive (CAD3) from the EU Commission. These papers indicate that banks and, in EU jurisdictions, securities firms and asset management companies, will have a capital requirement for operational risk. This regulatory focus has been emphasised by the recent publication of "Sound Practices for the Management and Supervision of Operational Risk" in February 2003.

The topics addressed in the rest of the chapter include, in the next section, roles and responsibilities. This section comments on guidelines, risk management and risk ownership, operational risk management activities at group level, risk ownership and functional units, and committees. A later section describes risk management processes – in particular risk control and mitigation activities. Such risk management processes require data and information, and these are discussed in a section on information requirements, which considers the types and "dimensions" of information and how they can be integrated. The fact that operational risk management takes place within a firm means that the firm's "culture drivers" should not be ignored insofar as they may influence its risk management activities. The chapter concludes with some comments on successfully tested steps through which operational risk management can be expected to evolve.

Roles and responsibilities

Having defined roles and responsibilities for specific risk that compose operational risk is not a new feature. What is new is the objective of providing a structure and a

MANAGING OPERATIONAL RISK

transparency that are comparable to those seen in credit and market risk management. The lag in developing integrated operational risk management compared with other risk management activities has largely been due to the need to bring together information from a range of existing functional units and the resources required to achieve this. A contributing historical factor has simply been the lack of an organisational label (ie, "operational risk management") under which these activities could be grouped. This section discusses some issues that need to be considered in establishing such an operational risk management structure and, in particular, the allocation of roles and responsibilities.

Managing operational risk itself is an activity that firms have always undertaken; they have always had specialists who managed such risks, and their counterparts today are integral to the development and functioning of an operational risk management framework. Almost from the first moments of a corporation's existence, before the first loan has been made or a single market risk taken, lawyers and other legal specialists are involved in managing legal risk. Figure 1 gives brief descriptions of the functional units.

One of the aims of establishing an operational risk management function is to help to coordinate the application of these specialist skills to banking and trading activities. Coordination should, in turn, encourage greater communication and transparency, hopefully reducing the number of hard lessons that have to be learnt and identifying any gaps between the expertise of the various specialists. The overriding objective is to provide proactive support for the company, and the businesses of which it is composed, in taking the operational risks that it wishes to and the extent to which they are taken.

GUIDELINES
Any risk management framework needs a set of guidelines or a policy statement. Such documents outline the various roles that have to be filled and by whom, adding to the transparency of the framework. In the case of credit and market risk many of these features are embedded in the fabric of the firm, but for the emerging operational risk frameworks it is necessary to explicitly define the issues, the various elements of the framework and the interactions between them. As can be surmised from a definition or description of operational risk, the diversity of its scope is one feature that distinguishes it from the relatively narrowly defined credit or market risks, which are also more widely understood and appreciated as risk types. This diversity of scope and application within the firm means that formal documentation is needed to support understanding and communication. This documentation would include, for example, definitions, terminology in support of consistent communication, categories, responsibilities and reporting requirements.

The last item on this list is integral to such guidelines, for without reporting and formal communication, corporate governance becomes very difficult. The financial industry may be experiencing an increased interest in operational risk from the banking regulators, but there are others who focus on issues of corporate governance – for example, the stock exchanges, through their reporting requirements. Although the diversity of operational risk, ranging from legal to technological to behavioural concerns, makes it difficult to limit the number of dimensions required to describe it, as has been done for market risk with value-at-risk, (VAR), the difficulty must not prevent reporting from taking place. This aspect is explored in more detail below.

Establishing clear guidelines for operational risk management enables senior management to provide leadership through clear communication of their expectations. Such expectations, clearly expressed, provide a sense of discipline, consistency of direction, and act as a source of motivation and empowerment.

A danger with having to cover so many aspects in one set of guidelines is that local effort and initiative may be stifled. Part of the art in constructing guidelines at the

MANAGING OPERATIONAL RISK

> ### PANEL 1
>
> ### FUNCTIONAL UNITS
>
> Most firms have access to the knowledge and expertise embodies in the functions described below, either internally or externally. In addition, the departmental labels often differ between firms. It is not possible to fully describe the range of activities and responsibilities in such a brief commentary.
>
> - Business continuity planning – a diverse range of activities from risk assessment to coordinating responses to an inability to access corporate assets, whether buildings or networks or corporate data etc
> - Change management – legal entity committees; new product approval; IT project governance; client adoption processes; in/out-sourcing processes; restructuring/cost containment programmes
> - Compliance
> - Management and financial accounting – often responsible for management information collection; information analysis and reporting
> - Corporate purchasing – contractual terms; out-sourcing
> - Corporate real estate services – buildings and property management; utilities
> - Corporate security – protecting corporate assets from harm in the form of physical and IT security; provisions for senior executives; reacting to civil disruption; access infrastructures ranging from buildings to data
> - Group development – strategy and business portfolio management
> - Group marketing and investor/public relations – this category not only supports external communications but also internal as well as responsibilities including brand management and a role in crisis management
> - Human resources – tactical and strategic issues ranging from background checks on new staff to skill shortages and training in discrimination issues etc
> - Insurance – this function assists the firm in identifying those risks that it wishes to keep and those whose financial impact could usefully be transferred elsewhere. This activity is expected to grow as the diversity of the type and amount of operational risks becomes more transparent
> - Legal – contractual issues such as the choice of law, jurisdiction and drafting to ensure that the desired commercial effects are enforceable; intellectual property issues such as trademarks, copyright, patents, trade secrets and protection of those owned by the firm and protection against infringement
> - Quality management – across processes with effects upon issues such as data quality
> - Tax
> - Treasury – increasingly involved in performance assessment through mechanisms such as economic capital, RAROC etc
> - Audit – a valuable and necessary independent review function. While largely focused on upon the internal function, the external auditors also have a role in connection with the accounts and in some cases with responsibilities imposed by banking regulators

group level is to strike a balance between describing the overall intent and establishing group standards while also catering for local circumstances and requirements by defining appropriate local operational risk guidelines that are nevertheless consistent with the group standards.

Irrespective of how well guidelines are crafted, they can only be implemented by providing adequate resources to do so throughout the organisation. Adequate in this sense means not just quantity but also quality in terms of the experience and perspectives that are available. As already indicated, many of the highly technical skills relevant to operational risk already exist in the firm within the functional units. These functions, since their approach is proactive, may already have a number of initiatives in various stages of development. Hence, one way in which the operational risk management framework can be developed and extended is to coordinate, support and encourage interaction between the various initiatives already under way. Support can take the form of promoting the transfer of know-how between functions and/or locations, developing common standards or even contributions to budgets. Supporting existing initiatives not only allows resources to be devoted to filling gaps, but it also helps to contain costs by avoiding the duplication of efforts.

WHO "OWNS" OPERATIONAL RISK?
In the broadest sense, risk management must be integrated into the activities of the risk-takers in the company. However, for an independent risk management structure to operate there has to be an oversight activity that operates independently of the risk-takers. In the case of credit and market risk there is, as the result of many years of experience, a well-established concept of how such an activity should function. For operational risk the issue is a little more complex as it raises the question of who "owns" or is responsible for the risk. One possible answer is that the business lines own it, in which case ownership of operational risk is aligned with the profit centre and the risk-takers. This is intuitively obvious for credit and market risk with their transaction-related focus as the profit centres are aligned with "front-office" activities. The same approach can be applied to operational risk even though some operational risks are not related to transactions but are environmental.

An instructive example of external operational risk, is the one that arises when there is a change in the interpretation or implementation of banking regulatory requirements, even if the published requirements themselves have not changed.

Within the current regulatory proposals for the New Basel Capital Accord and CAD3 there is a capital calculation, the Standardised Approach, for operational risk, that requires mapping the gross income to regulatory specified business lines. These regulatory-specified business lines are organised around profit centres. For the Advanced Measurement Approach, an alternative approach for firms to determine their operational risk regulatory capital, there is a requirement to be able to map their losses to these regulatory business lines. This regulatory view appears to support the assumption that the businesses own operational risk and are responsible for its day-to-day management.

Nevertheless, the risk-takers also manage the risks. Most formally this arises in the budgeting and planning processes, where risk–return decisions may be made by the risk owner in connection with investment budgets and the generation of returns on risk-based capital. These decisions are similar to those made in connection with credit and market risk – for example, the return available from lending to a particular counterparty at one point in time. The risk owners, therefore, have a significant input into resource allocation, which means that risk-return considerations are part of the decision making process for credit, market and operational risks.

While settlement failures can be due to operational risk events and are transaction-related, other quite different internal matters are also considered to be sources of operational risk. Some of these, such as staff-related issues, apply throughout an organisation. For example, all business and functional units have some degree of exposure to problems of employee discrimination. As a result, on one level, functional units assist in the oversight and control of operational risk and on another they are exposed to operational risk themselves. This situation cannot be avoided, even if every task had an associated independent control function or activity as that independent function would also have exposure to operational risk. If every control had an additional independent set of controls then the firm could end up being excessively controlled and out of profitability. In reality the situation is not so dire as the human resources function, depending on its remit, operates throughout the firm with regard to discrimination cases and managers oversee their subordinates.

In summary, while the credit risk management function does not have market risk and the market risk management function may have a limited amount of credit risk implanted in its products, they both have operational risk embedded in their activities and processes, eg, data quality.

From a different perspective, operational risk is not limited to the operations function – the settling of transactions – but is found across the entire organisation, including the operational risk management function as it also has data and staff. This situation is not unique to operational risk management in the financial sector but also applies to the corporate sector – for example, Boeing, Marks & Spencer, Shell, Hoechst and many others. For these firms, operational risk is often their dominant risk and they have appropriate supporting functions, whether these be product testing, health and safety at work or many others – where these functions themselves have operational risk such as the staff issues mentioned above. Despite these complexities, an independent oversight function can be established to monitor the material risks and reduce exposure to a level that is in line with the risk appetite of the firm.

Operational risk management activities at group level

As indicated above, one of the key tasks of a group-level function is to produce guidelines that establish standards, a sense of direction and clear communication of roles and responsibilities. However, as with the credit and market risk management functions, the task of operational risk management does not end with the production and review of guidelines. In particular, as with those functions, an important and ongoing activity is determining what levels of operational risk are acceptable, or the "risk appetite". In the case of credit and market risk a wide range of methods can be used to determine or in some manner quantify such levels, or limits, ranging from risk concentrations to VAR-type calculations. At present, it is not possible to set up a formal structure of limits across operational risk because the calculation methodologies are still at an early stage of development and the lack of detailed data means that the results are not sufficiently detailed.

Those responsible for credit and market risks can call on years of industry experience in establishing their respective risk appetites at the group and lower organisational levels. The tools (procedures, methodologies and data collection) for these functions, and for communication about risk appetite, are now very sophisticated and risk-sensitive, considering issues such as stand-alone risk and the contribution to the risk portfolio both within and across risk types. Possibly more important even than the tools, is the communication process that is required to arrive at a common understanding of risk appetite for the group and how it is distributed throughout the firm. The tools and processes needed to determine the appetite for operational risk are less well developed than for credit and market risk, and it will be some time before operational risk limits similar to those for credit or market risk, can be derived and discussed with the same level of clarity. This is partly due to the sheer diversity of the topics that come within the scope of operational risk, ranging from staff fraud to acts of God to intellectual property issues. Even if a tool could be devised to quantify a particular aspect of operational risk, the complexity of the issue would mean that there would need to be a specific education on the tool and how to interpret its output.

This does not mean, of course, that, pending the development of such tools, discussions cannot take place with regard to the implications and interconnectedness of particular operational risks and how the perceived level of risk can be adjusted to the desired level. At this point in time, one role for the operational risk manager is to propose levels of risk tolerance to serve as the basis for discussion between the board and the risk owners. Initially this might take the form of a description of a particular risk and the costs involved in its avoidance, reduction, transfer or acceptance.

At the group level and in conjunction with the discussions on risk appetite, the operational risk management function is in a good position to support group-wide risk programmes – for example, integrating insurance activities more closely with the operational risk appetite. From this level, the management function may also may be in a good position to reinforce messages about risks for which there is zero tolerance or near-zero tolerance. These might be the lack of a business continuity plan or a disaster recovery process for a crucial file server. These low levels of tolerance to specific operational risks may apply to the "expected" or extreme levels of risk as identified from a stress test. The introduction of the physical euro is another, prominent, example of risks that cannot be avoided or ignored and must be managed. By comparison, using the RAROC (risk-adjusted return on capital) tool in isolation would imply that any risk could be taken if the return is high enough. Although RAROC – or comparable methods – is becoming more widely used, it is still used as one element of a suite of tools and processes that may restrict the range of risk owners' activities; for example, there may be counterparts for whom no credit exposure is desired, irrespective of the potential return.

RISK OWNERS AND FUNCTIONAL UNITS
As noted earlier, the owners of operational risk are often deemed to be the businesses. The business units are involved in discussions on risk appetite and risk-return expectations and they have a significant influence on the allocation of resources for the supporting functional units. The interaction between the risk owners and the functional units can be constructed in many ways, but it can often involve delegation. However, delegation does not mean giving up all responsibility for the matter but implies that the delegator – in this case the risk owner – is responsible for ensuring that any instructions are carried out on the risk owner's behalf.

In practice, these functional units conduct activities on behalf of the risk owners and also act as advisors. The relationship is not limited to being reactive but also includes proactive support of the business units (for example, assessing the possible consequences of US patents being granted for business processes and complying with the possible future enforcement of those patents in Europe rather than waiting to be pursued for the unlicensed use of a patent). Nevertheless, only the business unit can take certain decisions once the individual risks and their potential consequences are known. A representation of this relationship is shown in Figure 2.

This simple representation also illustrates a potential corporate governance activity that exists between the functional units at group level and the board. In addition it indicates how issues are often communicated up the hierarchy within the business and functional unit channels.

The formalisation of the operational risk management process means that there needs to be clarity over the interaction between the risk owners and the functional units. Interaction at the lower levels is expected by local management and by the home and host-state regulators. Although the operational risk management function may be delegated, these local management groups also need to be involved and actively participate in decisions, as with credit and market risk. This is shown in Figure 3.

One of the roles of the operational risk management function is to support the communication process – for example, by contributing to discussions on the budgeting process or being present on operating committees managed by the

MANAGING OPERATIONAL RISK

2. Relationship between business units and functional units

	Business Division		Functional Unit
Global		↔	
Regional		↔	
Local		Request / Advise	

Reporting flows upward from Local → Regional → Global → Group Board on both the Business Division and Functional Unit sides.

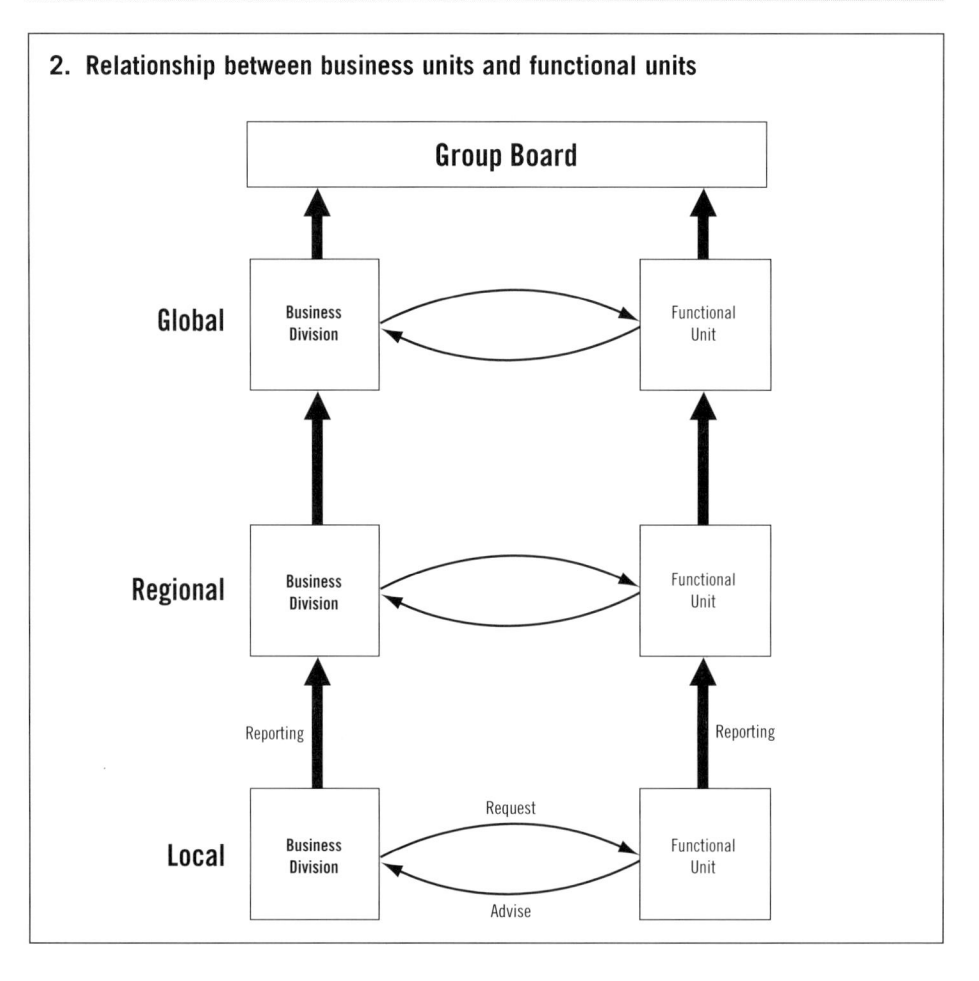

3. Relationship between operational risk, business units and functional units

At each level (Global, Regional, Local): Business Division ← Specialist Function ↔ Specialist Function, with Reporting flowing upward to the Group Board. At the Local level: Request / Advise between Specialist Functions, and Reporting & Advise from the local Specialist Function back to the Business Division.

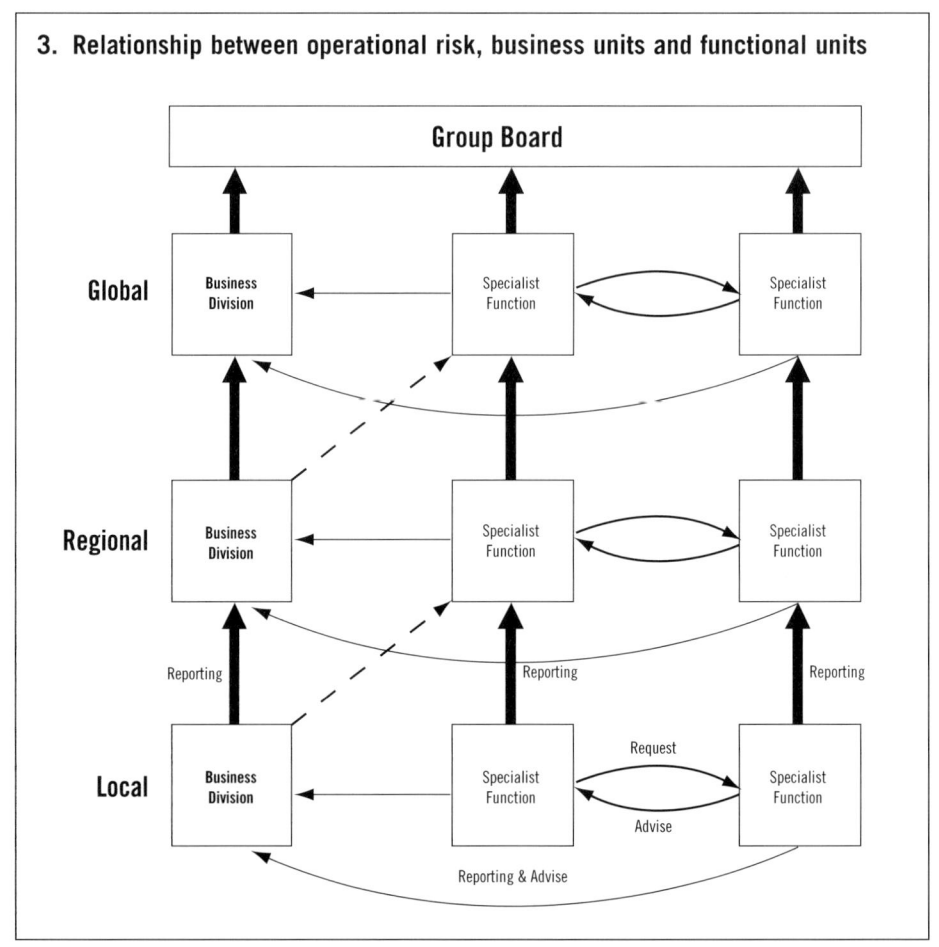

businesses. This support is intended to minimise gaps, duplication or overlap between the functional units. Another role of operational risk management is to ensure that certain risks, such as those related to intellectual property rights, are not overlooked. It also seeks to ensure that the issues identified and addressed are seen in the context of the overall operational risk-taking environment and, where appropriate or even feasible, promote some degree of consistency of risk tolerance across functional units. This requires the functional units to communicate with operational risk management as well as with the business units

Committees
Committees can perform a number of roles in relation to operational risk management, but there are some traps to watch out for.

Although committees can be a good way of exchanging information, this aspect is becoming less important in the age of the Internet. The informal communication network is also hard to beat once individuals are plugged in. However, committees are useful for conducting a dialogue among a group and their use can reduce the volume of chain-letter e-mails.

Other drawbacks of committees include a lack of clarity or focus concerning their tasks and responsibilities, a problem that can be exacerbated as the committee gets larger: too many topics can result in none getting the attention they need. Another trap relates to the accountability, responsibility and empowerment of the committee: is it advisory, can it require action and to whom is it accountable? Often committees do not have their own budgetary resources, though they may have some degree of access to those of individual members.

The risk management process
In order for the operational risk management framework to enable a firm to adjust its risk profile ("the risks it actually takes") in line with its risk appetite, a number of processes need to be present and working. These processes, outlined in Figure 4, are consistent with those in operation for credit and market risk – but there are some differences, most notably in the risk control and mitigation tools.

Risk management cycle diagrams take more than one form but they tend to show similar features or stages. Figure 4 shows that after setting out the risk objectives and standards, the next phase is risk identification. A satisfactory level of risk

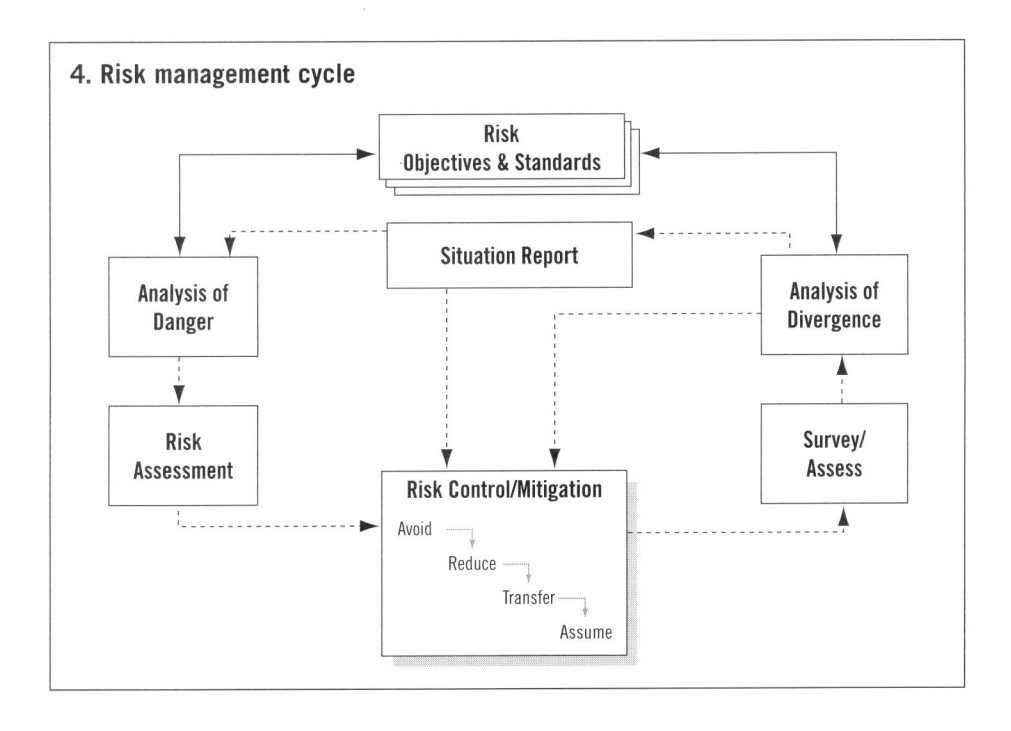

4. Risk management cycle

identification can often be achieved by talking with the experts who live with the risks on a daily basis. These may be found in the supporting functional units or in the business itself.

RISK ASSESSMENT

The next stage is risk assessment. In some circumstances it is possible to consider the probability of an event separately from its severity. Nevertheless, on many other occasions the assessment may be limited to estimating the risk of loss as high, medium or low. Unlike credit and market risk assessment, operational risk assessment is not yet equipped with a sufficiently broad range of tools to make confident estimates of frequency and severity in all situations.

RISK CONTROL/MITIGATION

When a risk has been identified and assessed there are a number of choices in terms of the action that needs to be taken to control or mitigate risk. Generally there are four options: avoid, reduce, transfer or assume the risk.

Avoid
Avoiding the risk can be quite difficult and may raise questions about the viability of the business in terms of the risk-return relationship. On occasions, the risk-return results for an activity may lead to its de-merger so that the firm is in a stronger position to focus on core competencies.

Reduce
Reduction tends to have the form of risk control efforts as it can involve tactics ranging from business re-engineering to staff training as well as various less extensive staff and/or technical solutions. Reducing risk can raise a number of issues, including not only the prospective risk-reward relation of the activity but also the availability of resources as even a technical solution will require programmers. To provide support in this area, firms may use cost-benefit tools to assist in structuring decisions and to prevent the business from being controlled out of profit. Although money saved in the form of a loss reduced or avoided is valuable, the economics of the business have to be taken into account. Here the issue is whether the cost of reducing a loss exceeds the saving achieved, and whether this is a fixed or variable cost can also affect the equation. Depending on the reduction mechanism, the risk profile of the activity could be transformed from a large number of small losses into rare large losses, and this can also influence the desirability of a particular course of action.

Transfer
In the case of operational risk, the objective of transfer is to transfer the activity, as in the case of outsourcing, or to transfer the financial consequences in the case of insurance. In transferring a specific operational risk, other operational risks may arise through the transfer mechanism. In the cases of outsourcing and insurance legal risk tends to arise. A firm may decide that it can manage the risks that arise in the transfer process so that it achieves an overall net reduction in its risk profile. In exchange for this risk reduction the firms will be paying insurance premiums and meeting other contractual requirement in the case of outsourcing, so firms have to consider the economics in addition to the change in risk profile.

As noted above, the transfer of risk may also involve transformation of the original risk into other types of risk. This transformation between risk types is not new: consider hedging market risk with derivatives contracts. In the case of operational risk acquiring an insurance contract transfers some of the risk, but at the same time it may give rise not only to legal risk but also to contingent credit risk – ie, will the insurer pay when required?

Assume
The final choice is to take on the risk – either through proactive decision or by default. The decision to do so may be made during the first iteration of the risk management cycle or it may be applied to the residual risk during a later iteration. When a risk is taken on it is supported by the firm's capital. Many banking regulators are currently moving to requiring the assumed operational risk to be explicitly supported by regulatory capital (see endnote 4).

Most of these choices are also found in credit and market risk management cycles. For example, the reduction activity may require daily margin or collateral calls, whereas transfer is often affected by hedging.

In practice a firm is likely to use combinations of the reduction, transfer and assume actions when dealing with operational risk. Figure 5 provides an indication of which control mechanism could be used and when.

SURVEY/ASSESS AND ANALYSIS OF DIVERGENCE
The next stage of the cycle, survey and assess, involves measurement of the risk remaining after the risk controls and mitigation choices have been employed. In the final step, analysis of divergence, the amount of risk that remains is compared with the level the risk controls and mitigation were expected to achieve and also with the risk standards and objectives.

ITERATION OF THE RISK MANAGEMENT CYCLE
A firm may often have to go through the risk management cycle several times to arrive at a residual risk position that matches its risk standards and objectives (see Figure 6). In some cases these iterations are necessary because of the complexity of the causes and various contributory factors. In others, changes in the internal and/or external environment increase the residual risk above the risk standards or objectives, requiring another iteration of the cycle. Such changes could be related to volumes of transactions, a legal decision, stakeholder expectations or many other factors.

Compared to credit and market risk, the culture of operational risk management is currently less well understood within firms and is less sophisticated as a discipline. The rate at which sophistication is achieved is an underlying influence on the risk management cycle as the activities, for operational risk, have to be applied to such diverse elements across the firm. Developments that are aimed to address this situation, based on lessons learnt from the credit and market risk frameworks,

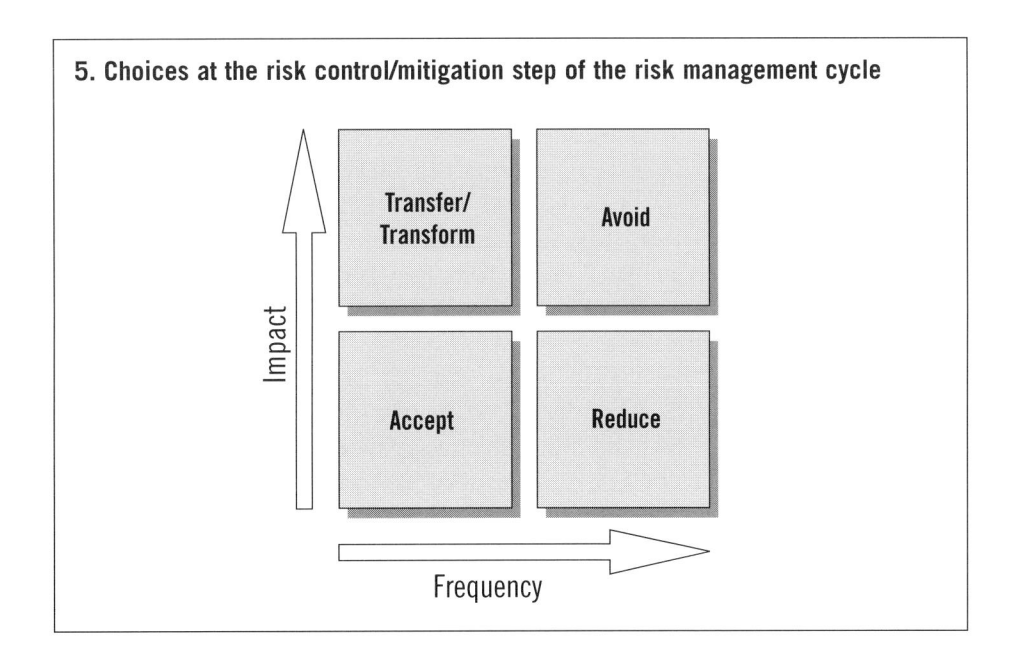

5. Choices at the risk control/mitigation step of the risk management cycle

	Low Frequency	High Frequency
High Impact	Transfer/Transform	Avoid
Low Impact	Accept	Reduce

include tools to support risk identification and measurement and decision-making aids like cost–benefit analysis. For an operational risk management function to operate efficiently it is necessary to achieve a level of awareness of this function throughout the organisation and of its elements through training and education programmes. Such programmes also help to remove some of the corporate cultural barriers surrounding operational risk.

Information requirements

A basic assumption is that even though operational risk has been managed inside banks since the beginning, the development of comprehensive systematic oversight is still at an embryonic stage. Discussion in regulatory circles has made considerable progress in arriving at industry standards for the types of information required and the relevant dimensions.[4] However, these standards will remain "moving targets" while the industry gains a better understanding of the different types of operational risk to which it is exposed. The improved validation of collected data by cross-referencing is a considerable aid as, with few absolute measurement techniques available, some degree of triangulation helps to ensure consistency, ie, if the risk figure for operational risk was 99% on a 12-month horizon, we would have to wait 100 years to find out if we had the right answer. In this way, identifying dependencies, correlations and typical patterns of association that are required to build a basis for scenario analysis, greatly improves operational risk management capabilities. Achieving these aims requires an integrated framework of operational risk information collection tools and processes. These are discussed in more detail below.

TYPES OF INFORMATION

For a number of reasons operational risk management cannot be solely based on a VAR or VAR-like figure. First, models for operational risk VAR calculation have been developed, although questions remain about the interpretation of the results and the judgement and scaling required to combine internal and external loss data to generate a top-down result and one that is both robust and flexible. Another set of scaling mechanisms is required to provide a risk-sensitive allocation between the business units or risk owners; here the development of solutions is at an early stage. (Within the proposed regulatory operational risk framework the allocation

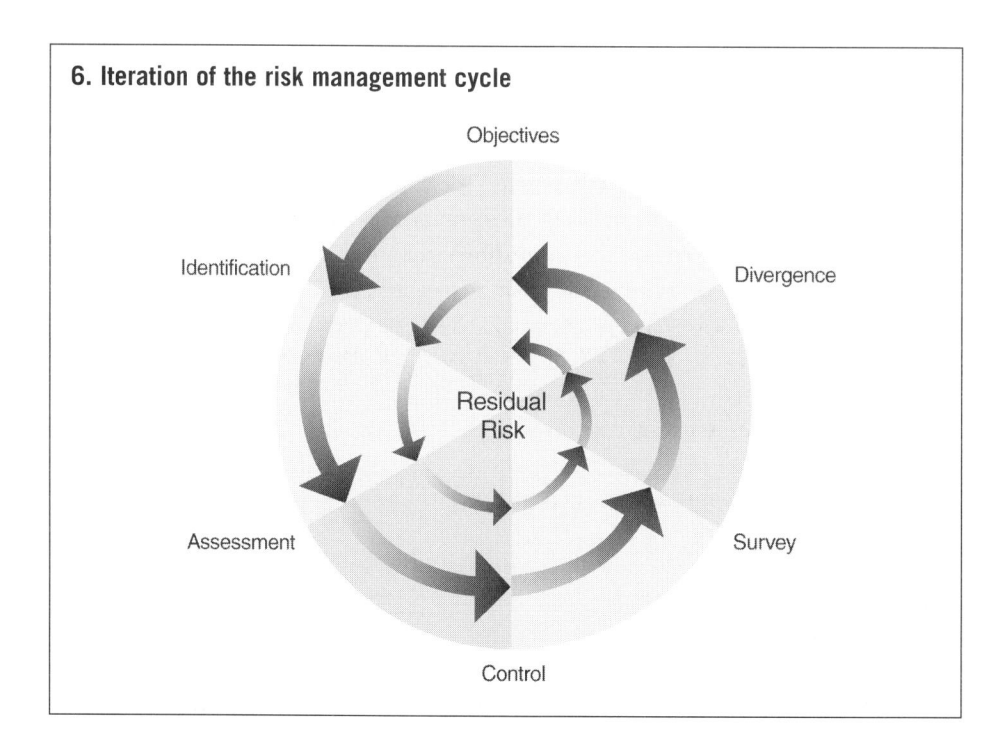

6. Iteration of the risk management cycle

Objectives · Divergence · Survey · Control · Assessment · Identification

Residual Risk

mechanism revolves around exposure indicators, which are often based on size – not risk.) Another problem is that VAR figures provide an indication of the amount of risk but not of its form (eg, legal risk as opposed to technology risk). These missing dimensions in the operational risk VAR figures make it difficult to focus on specific exposures and manage them. Although some of these issues also apply to credit and market risk VAR results, experience in their use has helped to overcome certain shortcomings.

A recent development is insurance contracts or hedging options to match the overall operational risk exposure, the bridge between operational risk and insurance is quickly developing, for example influencing the nature of insurance coverage. However, the pricing of such contracts and options has to be based on experience and estimates of various specialists as a validated statistical model has yet to be devised and constructed. VAR as a measure of exposure can only be an important summary figure.

To ensure that the exposure to operational risk is under control, loss data, risk indicators, risk self-assessments and other information are required to provide the "granularity" that is missing from a pure VAR number. This additional granularity, or specificity, should facilitate historical analysis and projections into the future – eg, in scenario analysis. The usual way of dealing with past events is through loss data. The future is a more difficult topic. Expert opinion provides one way of predicting the future, risk indicators another. However, proper analysis and some judgment are required to interpret opinions and indicators as they are collected.

Expert opinions are based on their experience and their ability to monitor the horizon – the ability to spot trends, developments or events at an early stage. Expert opinions will therefore include subjective components, which should be validated and discussed as occurs with the opinions of financial analysts. An efficient way of achieving this is via structured and moderated self-assessment workshops. Such workshops should call upon the know-how of the respective business unit and their related supporting functional units, preferably in one room. To ensure proper validation, the experts' opinions should be challenged with historic loss data, audit reports and developments or changes in risk indicators.

Our experience is that a short questionnaire is a useful way of preparing for workshops, especially as their results can be used to structure the discussion. Clearly the number of questions is potentially huge (we have seen questionnaires with several thousand) but too many can, apart from anything else, inhibit discussion and validation. For example, it is difficult to maintain a reasonable cost–benefit relation if hundreds of questions have to be answered and discussed before topics for discussion can even be agreed; and acceptance by those involved of the need to participate in such a demanding process would have to be gained. These issues are emphasised when considering that these risk assessments must take place on a regular basis if they are to reflect environmental and organisational changes. Presently, our strategy is to ask a few questions, then try and focus on potential high impacts, hot spots, action points and priorities, try to keep the discussion short (less than one day) and, at this stage, not to ask for quantification. At this time, it is difficult for the functional units to provide the basis for a mathematical calculation of the exposure.

Our questionnaire currently focuses on:

❏ Contractual specifications and documentation.
❏ Project management:
  ● project risk; and
  ● change management.
❏ Employees:
  ● errors due to lack of training;
  ● unintentional employee errors and errors due to operating environment; and

- unauthorised activities.
- ❏ Information technology:
  - system unreliability and underperformance; and
  - development or technology deficiencies.
- ❏ Non information technology:
  - disasters; and
  - infrastructure failures.
- ❏ External influences:
  - legal, regulatory;
  - suppliers; and
  - criminal activities.
- ❏ Customer relationships:
  - customer relationships; and
  - external distribution channels.

One outcome of the workshop is the identification of priority risks and risk indicators to monitor – directly or by inference – the changes in these risks. Risk indicators are not confined to operational risk management and some functions within firms have highly developed key performance indicators, which may also serve as risk indicators; for example, the tracking of outstanding aged reconciliations by the operations department; a technical benchmark in operations.

Normally risk indicators are based on existing information as the creation of new reporting requirements is very expensive and most reports can be used for more than one purpose. Moreover, experience shows that it is difficult to identify meaningful risk indicators. Indicators are used for different purposes and in any case most of the commonly available indicators are performance indicators (eg, volume of transactions), while some are historic indicators (eg, settlement breaks). With many of these indicators there may be a limited relationship to the frequency or severity of operational risk. One goal, reflected in the "basic indicator approach" presently proposed by Basel, is to identify universal risk indicators that represent the common operational risk issues across the whole bank. The current proposal is for that universal risk indicator to be gross income. However, discussions in banking industry bodies have revealed serious doubts about the risk sensitivity of a limited set of indicators representing the operational risk of an entire firm. From industry discussions it is very difficult to identify a limited set (less than five) of universal risk indicators that are truly risk-sensitive and so the cost of production of the indicator increases in importance. A single indicator will not accurately reflect operational risk across an entire firm, but may be an acceptable compromise.

It is interesting to compare the use of this universal indicator with the situation for indicators of individual operational risks, for example, settlement failures. Although the absolute value of a specific risk indicator may not in itself be particularly informative (eg, five settlement breaks per year), relative figures – between units or for one unit across time – can be very useful. Some analysis can also aid the interpretation; for example, two or more relative figures are combined into a basket or index – say, the daily increase in brokerage transactions multiplied by the change in the number of the operation's staff (both figures expressed as percentages). It should be noted that this type of data and analysis can indicate changes in the frequency of loss events but not their severity. In part this reflects the banks' ability to control the causes of events that affect them. However, the ability to influence the severity of an event is limited, although this is possible (through business continuity plans or crisis management).

Many types of external data are an important source of information as well, although their validation is not an easy task. Due to the complexity and near-permanent state of change of modern banking organisations and processes, nobody can identify all pitfalls in advance. Nevertheless, one does not have to learn every lesson on their own, they can profit from the experience of others. The negative experiences of others can be used as a guide in the operational risk management effort. That is why Deutsche Bank uses external loss data and is continually reviewing the horizon, and the transfer of experience from one firm to another may also be a reason why consultancy continues to grow. Potential drawbacks of these approaches are that the experiences of others might not be transferable because the organisation or the training has been set up differently, and external experts can have their own agenda (eg, pitching for additional projects or selling software). Nevertheless, access to external information is better than being unaware of the operational risk linked to the behaviour of your outsourcing partners, suppliers or distribution partners.

DIMENSIONS OF INFORMATION

One important advance in the rapidly improving understanding of operational risk is that the disaggregation and classification of operational risk is being put on a more rational footing. All efforts to define, analyse and interpret operational risk are based on making collections of risk types and the losses associated with these risks. Disaggregation involves separating out the different components of a risk cluster into irreducible categories. While this may be the long-term objective, the current process is to promote consistency in terminology, eg, to support risk assessment. The disaggregation does not just have to be in terms of cause, it could also be grouped by location within the firm where events materialise. Including a list of these various categories in support of an explanation of operational risk helps to promote discussion and facilitates further data collection. Then, as soon as the practical business of managing these risks begins, the question of consistency arises. If the disaggregation of risks (or events) into categories is to be consistent, the classification used must have a clear logical structure.

The information we need to understand operational risk has a number of possible "dimensions" but a common choice is causes, events and effects. For example, a settlement failure eg, a failure to make an interest payment on time, is an event. The causes of a settlement failure could be human error, poor data quality or computer system failure. The effects of a settlement failure could be legal fees, regulatory fines, compensation payments for lost interest and even write-downs. The dimensions can then be used as the basis for risk classification systems – eg, a cause-based classification system. From a risk management perspective causes are very important. However, a single event – like the settlement failure – can have many contributory causes, and it can also lead to more than one effect.

An initial industry standard for a cause-based classification can be found in Basel's definition of operational risk (see Basel Consultative paper on the New Basel Accord). However, event- and effect-based regulatory classifications also appear in various Basel papers including the Quantitative Impact Study 3, which was released to major banks in October 2002 and the final consultative paper on revisions to the 1998 Basel Accord.

The logical reasons for the three dimensions of cause, event and effect are clear and easy to understand. Every operational risk manager who wants to know how to reduce an exposure needs a causal disaggregation to identify areas where management actions will have the desired effect – ie, of avoiding the cause altogether, or of reducing the influence of the cause on the frequency or severity of the resulting events. As losses can have many causes, they (the losses) must be analysed to identify each contributing cause. This may not be simple as there may be a multiplicity of causes, which is one reason why the event-based classification has been developed. An event-based classification makes the operational risk manager's task easier as losses can be considered to "materialise" in an event.

To ensure that collection of loss data for a particular event is reasonably complete a reconciliation is needed. A logical process would be a reconciliation between effects and how they are reflected in the financial accounts, but this is not a straightforward matter. As an event can have several effects, entries in different general ledger accounts and losses/costs from other sources are also booked into accounts. Hence it may not be appropriate to use losses identified solely on the basis of an effect-classification as the basis for a regulatory framework.

Two other ways of dividing or categorising operational risk into manageable units have been proposed by the Basel Committee, and these are according to regulatory-specified business lines or functional units. However, from the banks' point of view these are not very satisfactory. The structure of regulatory business lines for the Standardised Approach does not reflect the way in which banks are structured or managed. Very few banks will find that their organisational structure matches the regulatory business lines or will use that structure to allocate economic capital. Every bank has arrived at its own unique current organisational structure as a result of its history and its main line of business (eg, product and/or customer focused). In contrast, the regulators are trying to arrive at a framework that will fit the whole range of banks and firms. Moreover, it would be inappropriate for a bank to change its organisational structure to match the regulatory business lines. The mapping of a sophisticated bank's more than 1,000 product lines to these regulatory business lines, is time-consuming and difficult and will be done solely for regulatory purposes. Also, the need to collect data in a manner that reflects an externally imposed structure will only add to the expense of compliance.

An alternative classification structure based on responsibility or the functional units is very specific to an individual firm. What is covered by the labels in such a categorisation, eg, the "Legal department", can be expected to vary between firms due to their history and internal environment. In addition, in the same firm these labels may vary between countries in response to local legal requirements (eg, the tasks of compliance functions are comparable in Anglo-American legal systems but are different in continental European legal systems). Nevertheless, there is clear added value in using this categorisation as such disaggregation empowers and encourages the functions to monitor and manage risk on a structured basis. This could have huge cultural implications as it emphasises the role of these functions as providers of proactive, rather than reactive, risk management support to the risk owners.

Another, very useful, tool for analysis is the "segmented transaction value chain". The transaction value chain includes all aspects of customer/counterparty-related product/business transactions throughout their life cycle (pre-commitment, commitment, processing, maintenance, expiration). This is a valuable basis for explicitly pricing operational risks into the products. Currently this pricing of operational risk happens implicitly via cost allocation for some elements of the transaction value chain. For example, the processing element can contribute data relating to historic loss experiences – eg, credit card processing, securities and cash settlement – to the pricing algorithms as they tend to capture such data even if they do not directly give rise to the event.

An integrated data requirements framework

Once the types and dimensions of information have been decided, the ground is ready for the next stage: specifying the methods and tools that will be needed for data collection, validation and analysis.

LOSS DATABASE

A prime requirement is a loss database. Initially, defining and specifying its form might seem an easy task as the data dimensions have already been identified. The first difficulties appear as the data collection process has to be capable of adapting to changes in the organisational structure of the firm. A mechanism needs to be developed to split the old business units and merge the historic organisational units to form the new business units. Using the general ledger accounts as a source for these data is not always successful for reasons already discussed in relation to event- and effect-based classifications. The only way forward is to set up a separate loss database with manual entry and description of the losses, including details of the various categories. This does not have to be an additional task as often there are several existing manual reporting lines into business and functional units (such as audit, compliance and insurance broker units) and they use closely related data. Replacement of these various reporting tools with a technical solution can generating sufficient added value to justify the effort. This experience provides useful illustration of why a workflow and reporting capability – that takes into account the flexibility needed for both decentralised and centralised entries, approvals, reporting and analysis – should be put in place to operate in conjunction with a central loss database.

Nevertheless, there are some difficult elements that call for judgement in balancing different interests. To manage the operational risks reflected in losses we would all like as much information as we can get, down to detailed information on a case by case basis. However, legal considerations – for instance data protection requirements and data secrecy relating to customers or staff – restrict the level of detail permissible. Moreover, there is a need to check the legal situation in different geographical locations to ensure that the loss database itself does not become an operational risk and influence the severity of losses in certain instances.

RISK INDICATORS AND SCORECARDS
The tracking and monitoring of indicators has been conducted in other areas of the banking business for quite a long time, the use of balanced scorecards to monitor the implementation of strategy being one example. Software is available to support these efforts. Scorecards can be viewed as simple databases with a customised structure and the main workload here is in defining the structure. This should be more or less identical to that of the loss database. It should reflect the organisational structure and cater for any organisational changes that may occur. One option is to use the same organisational description and data dimensions as for the loss database – ie, the reporting and aggregation lines from products to group level and the cause/ event/effect classifications. This will reduce the cost of maintenance and improve consistency. As some of the data are already available in the firm's computer systems (eg, processing systems or human resource systems), it is important to identify possible automated interfaces. There is a danger in having to transfer data manually from one system to another as this can result in process breaks and data errors – a source of operational risk in itself. Sometimes using automated interfaces will reduce the information available for operational risk monitoring, as any changes to the specifications of the existing source database, for example in human resources will increase costs. There is a need for manual entry of those indicators that are not held in existing systems or where those systems cannot provide an automated interface.

One important element of an integrated operational risk management framework is the checking of correlation between losses and risk indicators to confirm the value of collecting and analysing the latter. As a result, there is some justification in creating a single, common database for losses and indicators with a shared administrative layer and report generator and two workflow components for the loss data collection and indicator work.

As indicators tend to be more qualitative than quantitative (even though they may be in the form of numbers), any aggregation along causal/effect or business lines is a challenging task. This problem is usually overcome by using the scores (weights) generated by scorecards. It would be a great benefit to the discipline of operational risk management if practical and academic research could provide statistical techniques to arrive at these scores. Until these techniques are available, one valid source of weights is the ranking of identified risks and their causes, which can be generated by risk assessment.

RISK ASSESSMENT WORKSHOPS

The main task of a risk assessment workshop is to identify and rank material risks (although both the risks identified and their ranking will differ from unit to unit and from location to location). The workshop includes a review of the information given in response to a short questionnaire. Some of the analysis applied to the results (involving a simple database using a workflow tool such as Lotus Notes) enables aggregates to be generated, and it has the further benefits of supporting the ranking process and promoting the production of results and their regular review. An automatic interface with the indicator collection tool or scorecard will both reduce the work involved in maintaining the relative weighting of the scores and it can support the regular review process by producing reminders notifying those involved that a review is due. The organisational map should use the same source data as the other operational risk data collection tools, such as the loss database and the scorecard.

The main purpose of the questionnaire used by the workshop is to identify critical issues, specific areas requiring immediate attention, useful tracking instruments and possibilities for risk mitigation. Once issues and problems have been identified, they need to be tracked in a much the same way as audit findings. Alternatively, a project management tool or similar instrument could be used to check whether issues have been addressed within the agreed time frame. The cheapest solution may be to take whatever tool the internal audit department uses and adapt it. The challenge is to align the identified issues with the different dimensions of operational risk; structuring the audit findings along these dimensions will simplify the comparison and aggregation of both internally and externally identified issues.

It would be highly beneficial if audit departments could be persuaded to classify their findings in the same way as operational risk. This would allow the disaggregation of all relevant information into the dimensions of operational risk, increasing transparency and facilitating quick management decisions at both decentralised and centralised levels.

ECONOMIC AND REGULATORY CAPITAL

Using the risk indicators and internal and external loss data, a risk engine, such as a Monte Carlo simulator, can be used to calculate the group level economic capital (taking into account mitigation through insurance and any incentive structures). In the future the engine could be adapted to calculate regulatory capital. At present, validation of the calculated economic capital is not very sophisticated, and much of the validation has to be based on the experience of senior risk managers and this management experience should be part of the process for allocating economic capital across the business units for RAROC-based and other performance measures. Until there is a single industry-standard internal model for the calculation of capital for operational risk there are many good reasons for tolerating differences between the economic and regulatory capital calculated by different organisations. One is that the current diversity and exploration of techniques should provide a useful basis for defining an industry standard in the future.

Build or buy?

In implementing an integrated data requirements framework, a critical decision for any institution is whether to build or buy. Two aspects influencing the decision are: the desirability of developing internal skills in this rather new discipline and, the resources and skills required to develop, enhance and maintain such a framework. Alternatively, one can buy a black box and this implies outsourcing the know-how to consultants. This, however, will restrict flexibility and could force the management and reporting processes to follow externally imposed standards; these might not fit the bank's practices and therefore either require changes in the way the bank is managed or lead to inappropriate operational risk management. Deutsche Bank decided to build.

Cultural drivers

Experience of implementing credit and market risk management frameworks suggests that operational risk management will in time become an intrinsic part of a company's culture as well as of the financial industry as a whole. As incorporating an awareness of operational risk into an organisation's culture is an important part of prevention, we now consider a number of steps that can be taken to promote this process.

Devising and publicising a framework and its supporting policies are only a portion of the investment needed; the rest comes in the form of empowering and motivating individuals and groups to support its implementation. The questions that are often raised in this context are those of resources and costs. One response is that operational risk management can be a source of competitive advantage. It appears that this aspect will gain more prominence in the future as operational risk events are related to capital on which an explicit return to shareholders has to be generated.

Not only are regulators well on the way to devising a capital framework for operational risk, including disclosure requirements but, as we and other firms are experiencing, the rating agencies and analysts are increasingly asking questions on this aspect of how a financial services firm conducts itself. Part of this focus arises out of the perception that firms are increasingly dependent on technology for their infrastructure and product delivery and in response to spectacular failures of the recent past, like Barings and Sumitomo, or the recent hype and collapse of e-commerce. Although such events are linked to the culture of an organisation and its consistency, other contributing factors include the growing complexity of activities and the effort required to maintain oversight in an international organisation.

A problem that arises with operational risk is the unwillingness to talk openly about certain issues. Few expect a trader to generate positive revenue all the time, or a loan officer never to have a bad loan. However, it appears to be difficult to get individuals and firms to take the same view of operational risk. Possibly this is due to the perception that operational risk is "one-way" – that it only results in losses. This is, of course, an important part of the argument for embedding operational risk into the company corporate culture. Engaging the organisation in facing the issues can help to tackle the problems. Another part of the argument is that appropriate management of operational risk should provide competitive advantage in the medium to long term; for example, product pricing in custody will increasingly be dependent on the amount of regulatory capital charged for operational risk. This means that part of the dialogue within the firm has to be about risks, events, and the trade-off between risk and return. There is a need, for example, to explain that any strategic decision to open a new discount broking line carries with it an implicit acceptance that the move will entail a certain amount of operational risk along with the additional revenue. Important aspects of the post-mortem after an unfavourable event are the lessons to be learnt and, where appropriate, the amendment of processes and controls so that the firm does not have to repeat the experience. Hence the need to discuss issues of operational risk and, through this communication, increase its profile in the company culture.

One place where this risk-return trade-off can be seen is in the RAROC process or structure. The performance of a business line or unit is judged on the basis of its return on capital, where the capital is based on estimates of the risk being taken. Because of RAROC, if a business decides to take some operational risk it should be required to support it with capital. The more risk a business has, the more capital it should be allocated. The more capital it has, the higher the absolute return must be to meet a portfolio hurdle rate of return after taking into account operational risk losses. Currently, arriving at a risk-sensitive amount of capital for operational risk is a difficult process, but one that is fast developing. Alternatively, if costs are incurred to alter the operational risk control environment of the business (eg, by introducing an additional check), these should be offset by a reduction in its capital requirement.

MANAGING OPERATIONAL RISK

If the additional control leads to a reduction in the business's absolute amount of losses, then the absolute amount of earnings required to meet the same portfolio hurdle rate of return can also be reduced.

In reality these investment decisions are not easy to make, especially if they are based solely or mainly on a VAR figure.[7] At one extreme is the prospect of over-controlling the business to the extent that it is difficult to generate a profit and at the other, is a complete lack of control, with operational risk losses consuming the revenue.

TOOLS

A few firms are devising tools and techniques to support decision-makers in such discussions of risk-return considerations for operational risk. Some of the tools relate to cost-benefit analysis, where the aim is to support discussion on the balance of costs with the benefits gained and the resulting impact on the profit stream. The objective of using these tools and techniques is to optimise the conversion of

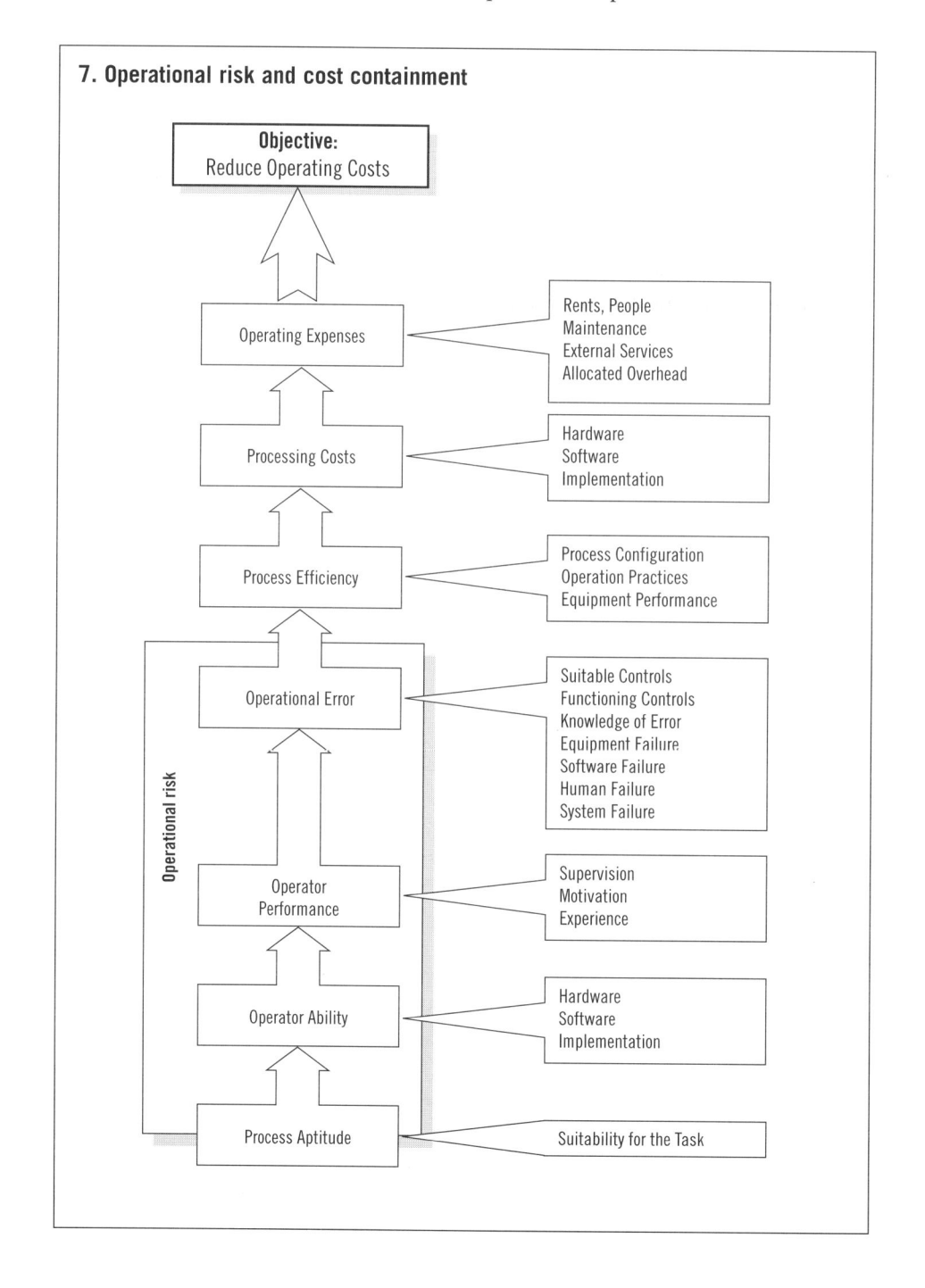

7. Operational risk and cost containment

Objective: Reduce Operating Costs

↑

Operating Expenses — Rents, People / Maintenance / External Services / Allocated Overhead

↑

Processing Costs — Hardware / Software / Implementation

↑

Process Efficiency — Process Configuration / Operation Practices / Equipment Performance

↑

Operational Error — Suitable Controls / Functioning Controls / Knowledge of Error / Equipment Failure / Software Failure / Human Failure / System Failure

↑

Operator Performance — Supervision / Motivation / Experience

↑

Operator Ability — Hardware / Software / Implementation

↑

Process Aptitude — Suitability for the Task

(Operational risk encompasses from Process Aptitude through Operational Error)

revenue into profit so that a loss foregone becomes a contribution to the bottom line.

Firms have experiences of these issues and the benefits that accrue, but the difficulty is often in being able to demonstrate their overall economic impact with the necessary degree of rigour. Functional units can often provide examples of a process change that was implemented with an expected life of several years but which has paid for itself through losses and costs avoided in a matter of months.

Other tools may relate to quality and efficiency aspects of the production process. For both there are tools used in other circumstances that can be adopted and/or adapted for the financial sector. For example, issues of data quality are not unique to the financial sector. Improving data quality is a general issue and may call for a proactive approach to data cleaning or the redesign of processes to limit the likelihood of poor-quality data. The alternative is to fix the data after the event, leaving no choice but to incur the cost. Settlement failures are an example where "good value" may be paid in compensation for the late settlement of funds or securities, with additional costs in the form of work done on reconciliation and for processing transactions at least twice.

One argument for operational risk management is – in the widest sense – the role it can play in containing costs, thereby improving the firm's competitive position. Figure 7 summarises some of the issues involved. It is evident that some of these relate not only to the immediate economics of a transaction, such as the failure of a trade to settle, but that they can also have consequences for the ability to attract transactions in the first place. Getting a reputation as a counterparty with the ability to "get it right first time" is likely to attract business from others for whom good value compensation if the deal goes wrong does not cover all of their costs. Plan sponsors are increasingly raising this kind of concern when soliciting bids for custody mandates.

EDUCATION AND TRAINING

While the comments above describe the cultural issues and some of the means that can be used to put operational risk and its management into context, education and training also play an important role. Because operational risk is present across the entire firm, everybody should be made aware of the issue and related management processes. However, this does not mean that everybody needs to reach the same degree of understanding. One of the first tasks in implementing an education programme is to divide up the internal "market" on the basis of needs and then decide for each sector how long education or training should last and how it should be conducted. Some individuals may be able justify devoting two days of their time, but for others this is not warranted. In addition, a distinction should be made between the initial educational programme and the continuing updates that will be required to keep people appraised of developments, such as the availability of new tools to support operational risk management processes.

As illustrated in Figure 8, individuals at the lowest level need to be made aware of the concept of operational risk and that the company has a framework for its management. They should also be told who to go to within the firm for additional expertise and that the regulators have an interest in the subject. It is interesting to note that employees with no direct connection with credit and market risk management are expected to have a basic understanding of the risk management processes concerned. Part of the essential message to be given at this level is that operational risk exists, that it is understood and that it can be managed.

The next sector is composed of those who are directly concerned with operational risk. This group includes many of the functional units mentioned in Figure 1 and also the credit and market risk functions. Communication with these functions should cover their role in the context of overall operational risk management. Furthermore, in their role as specialists they are well placed to provide feedback on the changing operational risk profile of the firm. For example, the legal specialist can identify whether or not intellectual property associated with a business process has the potential to become a significant issue. Equally, compliance is in a good position to comment on the changing implications of "know your client" when products are distributed via e-commerce channels.

In terms of the active participants in operational risk management, it is important to ensure that they understand how their roles and responsibilities influence the firm's overall operational risk environment. As part of the operational risk management framework they should also understand, to the level required by their responsibilities, the tools in use and the process of disaggregating operational risk losses.8 Of particular interest to chief operating officers will be the effect on competition, shareholder value and RAROC figures, as well as the use of some of the tools mentioned above.

The next sector, labelled in Figure 8 as the "OR champions", is likely to involve individuals within the functional units. These have the additional role of supporting their departmental colleagues in relation to operational risk – for example, by moving problems out of their functional unit up into the operational risk management framework. For others, such as project managers, operational risk is such a key element in determining the success of their projects that additional expertise in this discipline may be required.

The last sector comprises the specialist staff of the operational risk management functions. This group must have a full understanding of quantification tools and techniques and of regulatory requirements. Some members will be on the cutting edge of their practice and may even be developing such tools and techniques. However, it is vital that time is devoted to effective departmental cross-fertilisation to avoid the danger of individuals or small groups becoming isolated or operating at a tangent to the main effort.

As indicated earlier, a number of methods can be used to achieve the desired level of awareness. For some segments focused briefings are appropriate, while for others information can be broadcast (via web pages, internal magazines and newsletters) and sessions held in departmental workshops. Operational risk staff should be given time to access various resources that are available outside the financial industry – for example, to learn about techniques used by NASA or the hazard identification and analysis that is often an element of industrial "operational" risk management. The use of a range of communication channels can reinforce the message and is less time-

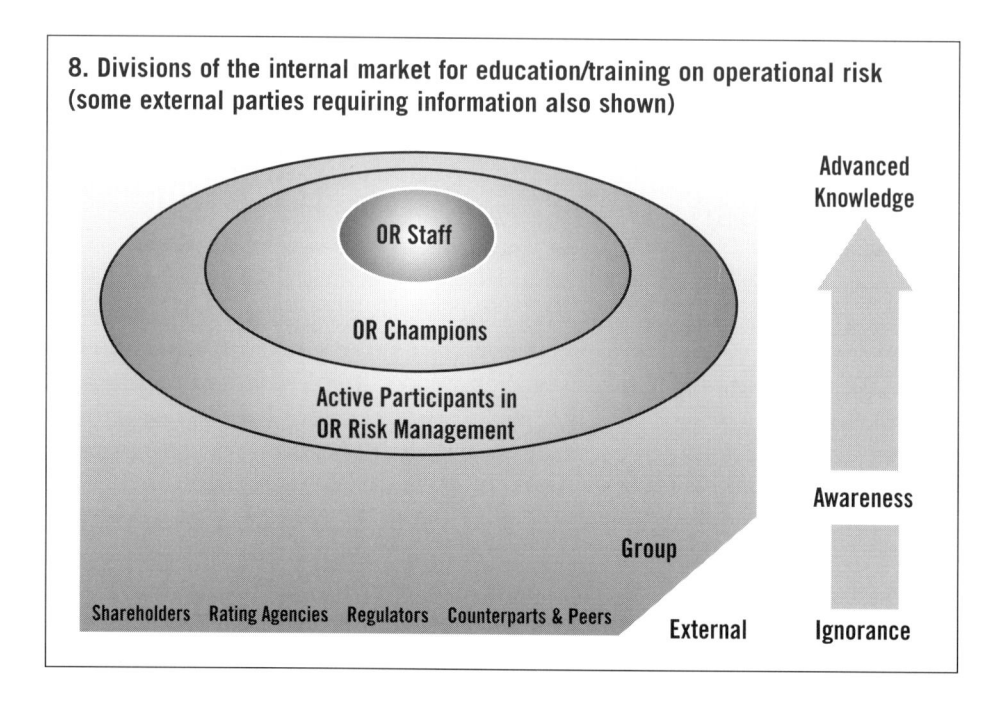

8. Divisions of the internal market for education/training on operational risk (some external parties requiring information also shown)

- OR Staff
- OR Champions
- Active Participants in OR Risk Management
- Group
- Shareholders, Rating Agencies, Regulators, Counterparts & Peers — External

Ignorance → Awareness → Advanced Knowledge

consuming than face-to-face communication alone, so reducing the cost of the exercise.

With the probable regulatory requirement for public and private firms to disclose more about operational risk, the greater the range of stakeholders that will also need education on the topic. Most fundamentally, stakeholders must appreciate that, unlike credit and market risk, operational risk is not a matter of choice although the degree of exposure can be controlled to a greater or lesser extent. Therefore, if operational risk management is to become widely accepted and effective in firms, employees will have to undergo education and training appropriate to their position within the hierarchy. Such education programmes should be followed up by the ongoing provision information and updates. Through these efforts the implications, practicalities and benefits of operational risk management can be made more tangible to all.

Conclusion
STAGES ON THE PATH TO MATURITY

Much of this chapter is based on the development of an operational risk management framework at one firm – Deutsche Bank. Other firms, however, will be going through similar processes. A detailed description of the stages in developing such a framework can be found in "Operational Risk – The Next Frontier". The analysis given there is still valid, although firms introducing an operational risk management programme will not necessarily implement the stages in the order shown in Figure 9.

Support for the development and implementation of a framework will be influenced by the bank's business priorities. If the bank's focus is on ensuring future revenues (eg, through the expansion of its business activities), those responsible for this may be reluctant to support the kind of initiatives that are needed to set up such a framework. This is because there is a tendency to associate operational risk management with the bank's control environment and as such, the framework may be seen as a source of additional bureaucratic burden. If the bank's focus is cost-cutting, the emphasis tends to be on short-term gains and not on the medium-term loss reductions, which operational risk management can achieve. In these situations

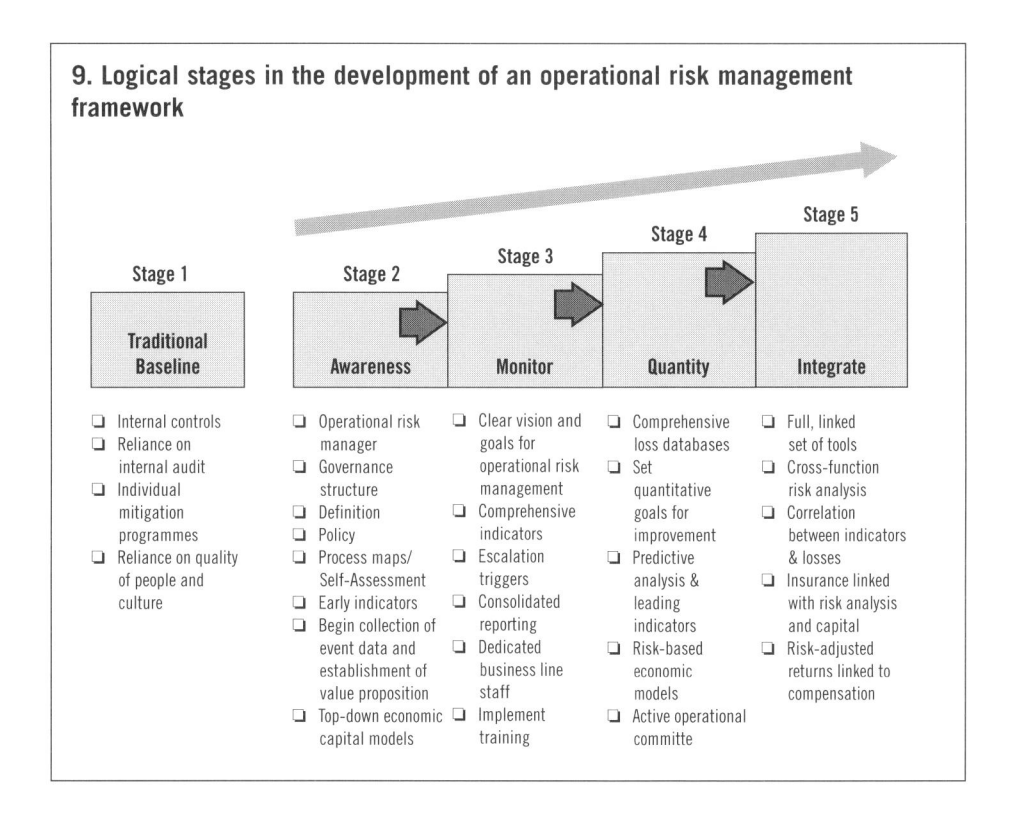

9. Logical stages in the development of an operational risk management framework

Stage 1	Stage 2	Stage 3	Stage 4	Stage 5
Traditional Baseline	**Awareness**	**Monitor**	**Quantity**	**Integrate**
❏ Internal controls ❏ Reliance on internal audit ❏ Individual mitigation programmes ❏ Reliance on quality of people and culture	❏ Operational risk manager ❏ Governance structure ❏ Definition ❏ Policy ❏ Process maps/Self-Assessment ❏ Early indicators ❏ Begin collection of event data and establishment of value proposition ❏ Top-down economic capital models	❏ Clear vision and goals for operational risk management ❏ Comprehensive indicators ❏ Escalation triggers ❏ Consolidated reporting ❏ Dedicated business line staff ❏ Implement training	❏ Comprehensive loss databases ❏ Set quantitative goals for improvement ❏ Predictive analysis & leading indicators ❏ Risk-based economic models ❏ Active operational committe	❏ Full, linked set of tools ❏ Cross-function risk analysis ❏ Correlation between indicators & losses ❏ Insurance linked with risk analysis and capital ❏ Risk-adjusted returns linked to compensation

it is difficult to make an attractive business case for funding operational risk management. The key to success, therefore, is to find a suitable balance between the additional investment required on the one hand and, on the other, the benefits of an improved control environment and incentives in the form of added value for the business and for the sponsors whose backing is sought.

One way of getting the matter of incentives right is to include operational risk in performance measurement and in the basis for bonus calculation (eg, via economic capital). Performance measurement is probably the most powerful source of incentives, but it is also a tricky one to handle. Performance measurement will appear to be a stick rather than a carrot if business units cannot influence the capital charge through qualitative adjustments based upon their operational risk management actions. If operational risk management is viewed only as a stick then this view poses a huge risk of creating resistance to any development and funding of an operational risk management function. However, now that Basel is preparing to introduce a regulatory capital charge for operational risk (see Basel Committee consultative paper, 2001) the pace is being set by an external agent. This represents a real opportunity for those in charge of developing and implementing a bank's operational risk management framework in that it is very likely that the internal operational risk management framework will influence the regulatory capital charge – the more sophisticated the framework, the more risk-sensitive the capital charge will be.

The other important element of implementation mentioned above is to ensure the support of sponsors. The main sponsors are the business line management because they own the operational risk and have to provide the budget.

One way of gaining this support is to promote the perception of operational risk management as a discipline ranking alongside credit and market risk management and one that is necessary for an integrated risk management framework. However, to have clear responsibilities within the integrated framework there must be clear borders between operational risk on one side and credit and market risk on the other. Any ambiguity might influence the relationship between the different groups of risk managers, especially as the size/importance of operational risk within a bank tends to remain "undiscovered" while its contribution to the minimum capital requirements is being determined. Balancing this difficult relationship is a major challenge for the operational risk management programme manager. Clarity will only appear once valid historic loss data collection has been established and the results are made available.

While operational risk capital is viewed as percentage of credit and market risk, this simplistic approach can give a very distorted result to specialist firms who may have little credit or market risk.

As with every project, support will increase with improved credibility. Ways of gaining credibility include:

❑ achieving results in the short term or quick wins (eg, initial operational risk reports or "heat maps" providing an overview of the perceived risks and their distribution around the firm);
❑ establishing champions and communicating their involvement;
❑ commenting on events and lessons learnt (extraordinary loss experiences); and
❑ describing and preparing for external pressure (eg, regulators reviewing progress towards implementing an operational risk framework). Some Asian and North American regulators have been enquiring about progress since 2000 and 2001 at several banks. Another source of external pressure is the rating agencies such as Moodys, and financial analysts who are beginning to ask some detailed questions of bank management.

Existing initiatives can provide the material for an operational risk report. Early initiatives might include quality assurance or process management and their key indicators, such as isolated loss data collections in the audit and the review or processing of claims by the insurance management units. It is probably more difficult to start with the financial accounting data as the book entries often do not provide sufficient background information, making the identification and management of operational risk rather difficult.

As the term "operational risk" is already in common use, many firms have set up initiatives that have not been originated by an operational risk function to address aspects of this risk. If, as is usual, the label operational risk is used to promote the credibility of such initiatives or projects, it is necessary to allocate responsibility for leading the integration of the projects into a formal operational risk framework and for taking the oversight role. Independence of the oversight function might be an important consideration in any decision on project ownership. Independence also ensures that the oversight role is not used to promote one specific risk management initiative to the detriment of others. Many projects and initiatives across the firm will be required to establish control over operational risk – this protean new kid on the block.

At Deutsche Bank the foundation of the project was an important step in reinforcing the credibility of the exercise to integrate its operational risk management initiative into routine risk management activities and the behaviour of staff. Important milestones in achieving this formalisation were:

❑ the creation of an operational risk committee to bring together existing initiatives,
❑ the risk managers of the business units and some functional units with operational
❑ risk management units; and, operating as a steering committee, to hold regular
❑ meetings to review the progress of implementation;
❑ the involvement of the chief risk officer in the regulatory debate;
❑ approving operational risk management guidelines setting out core definitions and responsibilities;
❑ establishing balanced incentives;
❑ the involvement of financial accounting and risk managers in the Basel's Committee's Quantitative Impact Studies; and
❑ involvement of the members of the operational risk committee in the creation of an initial operational risk report.

Our experience of planning and implementing an operational risk management framework at a major bank leads us to the view that there are many possible starting points for such a project. Momentum is built up and reinforced by showing early results, which also enhance the credibility of the exercise and increase awareness of operational risk management. A firm may start with a top-down estimate of operational risk, but the framework created to manage such risks requires bottom-up involvement and support for it to be sustainable.

1 *Basel Committee on Banking Supervision (September 1999); "Enhancing Corporate Governance for Banking Organisations".*
2 *Deutsche Bank (March 2001); "The Corporate Governance Principles of Deutsche Bank".*
3 *For further details the reader is referred to www.bis.org, where the latest publications can be found as well as to Chapter 16 of this volume where Jeremy Quick discusses regulatory aspects of operational risk.*
4 *See note 3 and www.bis.org/bcbs/cacomments.htm – in particular the comments from the International Institute of Finance Working Group on Operational Risk.*
5 *See note 4. Banking industry bodies that have taken part in discussions on Basel's basic indicator approach include the Institute of International Finance, the*

International Swaps and Derivatives Association, the Industry Technical Working Group (ITWG), the Bundesverband deutscher Banken (BdB) and the British Bankers' Association.

6 See note 3.

7 See the section "Information requirements".

8 See the section "Information requirements".

9 A study of operational risk management initiated by the British Bankers' Association, the Risk Management Association and the International Swaps and Derivatives Association and conducted by PricewaterhouseCoopers. The evolutionary stages are described on p. 14.

BIBLIOGRAPHY

Basel Committee, 2003, "Sound Practices for the Management and Supervision of Operational Risk", February.

British Bankers' Association, International Swaps and Derivatives Association, Robert Morris Associates, 1999, "Operational Risk – the Next Frontier" (London).

Cruz, M. G., 2002, *Modelling, Measuring and Hedging Operational Risk* (John Wiley & Sons).

Frost, C., D. Allen, J. Porter and P. Bloodworth, 1999, *Operational Risk and Resilience* (Butterworth Heinemann).

Hoffman, D. G., 2002, *Managing Operational Risk: 20 Firmwide Best Practice Strategies* (John Wiley & Sons).

Kaplan, R. S., and D. P. Norton, 1996, *The Balanced Scorecard* (Harvard Business School Press).

Kaydos, W., 1999, *Operational Performance Measurement: Increasing Total Productivity* (CRC Press).

King, J. L., 2001, *Operational Risk Measurement and Modelling* (John Wiley & Sons).

Marshall, C., 2001, *Measuring and Managing Operational Risks in Financial Institutions* (John Wiley & Sons).

Olave, N-G., J. Roy and M. Wetter, 1997, *Performance Drivers: A Practical Guide to Using the Balanced Scorecard* (John Wiley & Sons).

Reason, J., 1997, *Managing the Risks of Organisational Accidents* (Ashgate Publishing).

Simons, R., 2000, *Performance Measurement & Control Systems for Implementing Strategy* (Prentice Hall).

3

New Trends in Operational Risk Insurance for Banks

Brendon Young and Simon Ashby

ORRF; FSA

Operational risk has been defined by a number of key banking organisations as "the risk of direct or indirect loss resulting from inadequate or failed internal processes, people and systems or from external events" (RMA, BBA, ISDA and PricewaterhouseCoopers 1999; Basel Committee on Banking Supervision 2001). Thus it would seem that a bank's operational risks only have a downside. In fact, operational risk events can have a significant negative effect on the financial position of a bank through the loss of valuable assets (eg, buildings, computers, investments etc), increased liabilities (primarily via lawsuits or other compensation payments) and damage to its reputation.

Operational risk has become an area of growing concern in banking. The failures of banks such as Barings, Daiwa and Sumitomo, coupled with increases in the sophistication and complexity of banking practices (eg, outsourcing, securitisation and new technology) have raised the industry's awareness of the need for effective operational risk management. Moreover, these developments have brought the management of operational risk to the attention of 'Basel', the international banking regulator (see Basel Committee on Banking Supervision 1999, 2001) and a number of domestic banking regulators (such as the Financial Services Authority in the UK, see Quick, 2000).

In the light of this increased interest in the banking sector's operational risks, the question for insurers is: to what extent can they contribute towards improving the practice of operational risk management within a bank? Insurers have, for decades, played a role in financing the banking industry's operational risks by providing products such as the 'Banker's Blanket Bond' (ie, Fidelity), 'Director's and Officer's Liability' and 'Professional Indemnity' cover. However, whether these products go far enough in the current operational risk-aware environment is open to debate. Key criticisms have come from the regulators. In particular, although recognising the potential of insurance as a mitigant for the financial effects of operational risk, the Basel Committee on Banking Supervision (2001) has expressed doubts about the effectiveness of existing products, stating, "it is clear that the market for insurance of operational risk is still developing".

This article aims to review the effectiveness of three interesting developments in operational risk insurance for banks: basket insurance products, pre-claim settlement cash advances and securitisation. It is argued that these developments offer banks the chance to improve the financial management of their operational risks. However, it is also suggested that there are many supply-side issues that need to be resolved before their full potential can be realised and they can be accepted by both the banks and their regulators as viable operational risk management solutions. Conclusions about these developments are drawn for not only insurers, but also the banks and the regulators.

NEW TRENDS IN OPERATIONAL RISK INSURANCE FOR BANKS

Multi-peril basket insurance products

WHAT IS BASKET INSURANCE?

Traditional insurance products are sold on a peril-specific basis, with each product offering cover against losses that are the result of a limited set of causes. In the banking sector it is common for banks to purchase the following types of peril-specific operational risk insurance product:

PANEL 1

THE BASEL STATEMENT ON INSURANCE

The use of insurance as a potential tool for the mitigation of operational risk has been recognised for some time now by the Basel Committee (see Basel Committee, 2001). This has now culminated in a Committee proposal to allow banks using the Advanced Measurement Approach to take account of the risk mitigating impact of insurance in their capital calculations. However, this is subject to a number of conditions. In brief the substance of these conditions are as follows:

- The recognition of insurance will be limited to 20% of a bank's total operational risk capital charge.
- Banks must use insurance providers that are at least 'A' rated (to ensure that these insurers have sufficient resources to pay any claims).
- To be recognised an insurance policy must have an initial term of at least one year. In addition there must be a minimum notice period for cancellation or non-renewal of the contract. (These requirements ensure that banks do not suddenly find themselves without cover.) Policies with a residual term of less than one year or those with unfavourable cancellation and non-renewal terms must be discounted accordingly (although it is not clear by how much).
- A recognised insurance policy must not include any exclusions or limitations based upon regulatory action or for the receiver or liquidator of a failed bank.
- Banks must map their insurance coverage directly to their actual operational risk exposures (this is to ensure that they have a properly structured insurance strategy that achieves the right level of cover for the right risks). Where there is a mismatch between a bank's insurance cover and its actual operational risk exposures it will have to discount the value of its insurance cover accordingly.
- The insurance must be provided by a third party entity. Therefore, 'transfers' to Captive Insurance Companies will not count unless exposures are laid off to an independent third party through reinsurance or some other mechanism. It is not clear whether transfers to open market and group captives (ie, captives that provide cover on the open market and that are owned by more that one parent) will count.
- Banks must provide and document a well-reasoned framework that outlines its strategy for the use of insurance.
- Banks must discount the value of their insurance cover to reflect any uncertainties regarding payment.
- Finally banks must disclose the extent to which its operational risk capital charge has been reduced by insurance.

Full details of the Committee's proposals are available in its "Third Consultative Paper" which was published recently (Basel Committee, 2003, pp. 129–30). The Committee is seeking comments on this paper by June 31, 2003 and aims to complete its proposals for insurance (along with the rest of the Accord) by the fourth quarter of 2003.

- Fidelity/bankers' blanket bond – this is designed to protect an employer against losses caused by dishonesty or default on the part of an employee as well as those that are caused by fraud and forgery. In addition, it may cover accidental damage to assets (whether this occurred in an office or in-transit), losses due to counterfeit currency and certain types of trading losses.
- Electronic computer crime – this provides cover against losses due to computer failure, viruses, data transmission problems, forged electronic funds transactions, etc.
- Professional indemnity – this typically covers liabilities to third parties for claims arising out of employee negligence while providing professional services (eg, investment advice) to clients.
- Director's and officer's liability – this covers the personal assets of directors and

---

PANEL 2

INSURANCE IN RISK MANAGEMENT

Insurance is a well-established risk management tool that has been used by the banking sector for many decades to provide protection in three main areas: legal liability, crime and property damage. Peril-specific policies offered by insurance companies include:

- *Fidelity/banker's blanket bond* protects an employer against dishonesty or default by an employee as well as fraud and forgery. It may also cover on-premises losses such as office damage, in-transit loss, counterfeit currency and some forms of trading loss.
- *Electronic computer crime cover* against computer failure, viruses, data transmission problems, forged electronic fund transactions, etc.
- *Professional indemnity* typically covers liabilities to third parties for claims arising from employee negligence while providing professional services (eg, investment advice) to clients.
- *Directors' and officers' liability* covers the personal assets of directors and officers against the expenses that might be incurred due to legal actions arising from the performance of their duties.
- *Employment practices liability* covers liabilities that might arise due to breaches in employment law, such as harassment, discrimination, breach of contract.
- *Non-financial property* covers the usual range of property risks (fire, weather damage, etc).
- *Unauthorised trading* is a relatively new product that offers financial protection against unauthorised trading that is either concealed or falsely recorded.
- *General and other liability* public liability, employer's liability, motor fleet, etc.

Multi-peril "basket" products

Increasingly, a number of multi-peril basket insurance products are being offered to banks. Examples are all-risks operational risk insurance and organisational liability insurance, which is a limited multi-peril product that covers losses arising from internal and external fraud, rogue trading and many other forms of general liability. An advantage of these products is that they may provide a bank with more comprehensive cover, helping to eliminate any gaps or overlaps that might exist between peril-specific products. Moreover, by allowing insurers to take into account correlations across losses, the price of a basket product may be lower than the sum of the equivalent peril-specific products (Culp, 2001, p. 562).

> **Depositor protection schemes**
>
> Many Western countries protect policyholders from both operational and non-operational risks faced by banks by requiring banks to purchase depositor protection insurance. Such schemes are usually government-run. In the UK the Deposit Protection Scheme provides partial cover against losses that arise out of bank insolvency. Banks that are incorporated outside the EEA (European Economic Area) may also be covered in respect of deposits taken by their UK offices. The scheme is financed on a compulsory basis by the banking industry but is effectively controlled by the state (Hadjiemmanuil, 1996).
>
> *Advantages*
> The main advantage of these schemes is that when all else has failed they act as a failsafe for depositors against bank insolvency. In addition, their use provides regulators with the option to refuse to bail out ailing deposit-taking institutions, particularly if they are small or new (Hadjiemmanuil, 1996). Thus, deposit insurance is not linked to specific causes; instead, all that is required is the total failure of the bank to trigger the payment of compensation. This means – at least for small depositors – that the banks are already in effect purchasing fully comprehensive (though not full-cover) all-risks insurance, providing much of the financial security they need. Obviously, this leaves other stakeholders unprotected.
>
> *Disadvantages*
> Full-cover deposit protection insurance does have its problems. The high rate of "Savings and Loan" failures in the USA in the 1980s has been attributed to the use of non-experience-rated, full-cover deposit protection schemes (Karels and McClatchey, 1999). The primary reason for this is moral hazard. In the case of deposit protection insurance, moral hazard is manifested as the incentive for insured depositors to place their funds in banks that take large risks in an attempt to offer high returns (Hadjiemmanuil, 1996). Depositors are drawn to high-risk organisations because their deposits are guaranteed by the state.

officers against the expenses that might be incurred due to legal actions arising from the performance of their duties.
- Employment practices liability – this covers liabilities that might arise due to breaches in employment law, such as harassment, discrimination, breach of contract, etc.
- Non-financial property – this covers the usual range of property risks (fire, weather damage, etc).
- Unauthorised trading – this is a relatively new product that offers financial protection against unauthorised trading losses that were either concealed or falsely recorded.
- General and other liability – public liability, employer's liability, motor fleet, etc.

In its simplest form, basket operational risk insurance for a bank would involve an insurer bundling some or all of the above peril-specific policies into a single product.[1] There is, though, another and arguably more revolutionary approach to basket insurance. This is where payment is conditional on the broad effects of exposure to a risk (for example, a loss in earnings or simply a loss of assets/increase in liabilities, see Roberts, 2000), rather than the presence of a specific cause or combination of causes. In the banking sector only a very small number of insurers are claiming to offer effect-based cover. This claim is justified on the basis that they are offering cover against any operational losses that a bank might incur. However, these insurers are quite careful about how they define an operational loss, for example, one basket provider defines operational risk as: relationship risks, people risks, technology risks, physical asset risks and external fraud. Moreover these policies still exclude some potential causes of operational loss (eg, pollution, terrorism, insolvency, errors in computer programming, etc).

THE ADVANTAGES

Just because basket insurance for operational risk is available does not mean that a bank should buy it. In fact the established market for peril-specific products already offers high levels of quality cover against quite a wide range of operational risks. Basket products are not just gimmicks though. If designed and used correctly they can help to improve the cost effectiveness of a bank's operational risk financing programme. Key advantages include the following.

Elimination of gaps and overlaps

One key advantage of basket operational insurance products is that they may provide a bank with more comprehensive cover, thereby helping to eliminate any gaps or overlaps that might exist between peril-specific products (see Butler 2000).

The elimination of gaps helps to improve the value of insurance as a risk financing tool by ensuring that money is available to finance a wider set of losses than before (see Figure 1). Basket products are especially valuable if they provide cover against losses that are typically excluded from standard peril-specific policies (eg, losses that cannot be attributed to a specific cause). Where this is possible insurance can increasingly be seen as a substitute (at least in part) for the self-financing of operational risk and perhaps even as a substitute for Basel's proposed capital charge (Basel Committee on Banking Supervision, 2001). Currently the only way that most banks can be sure that finance will be available for all operational risks is to hold some of their own liquid assets in reserve (since the use of retained funds need not be contingent on specific causes).

The presence of overlaps means that a bank may be paying for more cover than it actually needs. Overlaps exist where two or more similar peril-specific insurance products offer cover against the same loss event (eg, fidelity and computer crime products may both offer protection against certain types of employee fraud). Another problem with overlaps is that they could lead to delays in the payment of claims if insurers argue over which of them is responsible for financing a particular loss.

Compliments 'enterprise-wide' risk management

'Enterprise-wide' or as it is sometimes termed 'integrated' risk management is based around the notion that a firm can benefit by managing all of its risks (irrespective of their origin) together.[2] The rationale behind this approach is that the piece-meal management of individual risks can lead to inefficient risk management decisions. In part this may be because by not managing its risks as a portfolio a firm may overstate its exposure to risk (and hence spend too much on risk management), since it is not taking into account the effects of diversification (see Miller, 1998; Doherty, 2000, Chapters 1 and 4). In contrast a firm that fails to take account of the fact that certain losses could all happen at once, may underestimate its exposure to risk. For example, as shown by Barings the combination of unauthorised derivatives trading, poor management systems and fraud in a bank can lead to financial collapse.

By providing a broad level of cover, basket operational risk insurance products fit very well into the principles of enterprise-wide/integrated risk management. A bank that purchases cover against a wide range of operational risks protects itself against the possibility of losses caused by the interaction of multiple perils. In addition, basket policies do not disrupt a bank's attempts to exploit the diversification benefits of its multiple exposures to risk. For example, a bank that purchases a basket insurance product may find that it does not need as much insurance as it thought it did when it bought insurance on a peril-specific basis and ignored the effects of diversification.

Basket insurance products that provide cover against, not only operational risks, but also, say, financial, credit, strategic and reputational risks would further enhance the degree to which insurance could compliment the practice of enterprise-wide risk management in a bank. Non-banks have purchased insurance products that span broad risk groupings (such as the weather, economic downturns and unfavourable currency movements – see Sclafane 1999; Roberts 2000). Whether such products become available to firms in the banking sector remains to be seen.

Diversification benefits
This 'advantage' is far from straightforward. In theory an insurance company that underwrites a large number of different perils in a basket product can create what is in effect a pool of pools and further exploit the benefits of diversification.[3] For example, an insurance company might use the profits earned from underwriting one particular peril (where claims are lower than expected) to subsidise the losses of another. As such, even where the losses on one peril exceed the value of its allocated pool of funds, an insurance company may be able to cross-subsidise, using funds

---

PANEL 3

RISK MANAGEMENT – SPREADING THE LOAD

Although most banks have some in-house expertise in operational risk management, an insurer may well have a far greater wealth of resources and expertise, gained from a wide range of clients in various sectors. A bank that transfers its operational risks to an insurer can utilise these resources and expertise, appropriating the following benefits.

Service efficiencies
The core business of every insurer is assessing, controlling and financing risk. Thus, large insurance companies may have an advantage over all but the largest banks may be at an advantage in terms of access to data, experience and economies of scale. A bank may therefore find it cost-effective to outsource elements of its risk management programme to an insurance company. In particular, insurers may offer loss adjustment and assessment services together with legal advice, as well as administrative services such as the payment of claims (Mayers and Smith, 1982; Main, 1982; Doherty and Smith, 1993).

Monitoring
It is possible that particular stakeholder groups, including consumers, governments and shareholders, will require a bank's managers to invest more in operational risk management than they might otherwise wish to do. These stakeholders, though, may find it difficult and expensive to monitor the behaviour of management and ensure compliance. One possible solution is for stakeholders to demand the purchase of insurance and then use the insurer to perform the monitoring role (Holderness, 1990; Skogh, 1989, 1991; Grillet, 1992).

It is important to note that, effectively, the monitoring activities of insurers support the functioning of market forces. Risk is a commodity like any other that can be traded. Problems can arise when certain stakeholder groups, like managers, exploit their position and expose other stakeholders to risks for which they are not properly compensated.

It has been argued that the correction of market forces is a key regulatory role and, therefore, that the presence of an efficient insurance market could be regarded both as a support and a substitute for regulation (Katzman, 1985; Freeman and Kunreuther, 1996).

from elsewhere. The net result of this is that the more perils an insurer underwrites in a basket product, the lower could be the necessary premium. Alternatively, the insurer could provide a higher level of cover, via a lower deductible or a higher policy limit.

However, diversification benefits are far from guaranteed. Consideration needs to be given to the possibility that the losses from some risks might be positively correlated or that several uncorrelated losses might simply all happen at the same time. Particular care also needs to be taken when an insurer includes a risk in a basket product that it has not underwritten before, especially when this risk is very different from those that it usually deals with. This is because any change in the composition of an insurer's portfolio of risks may have the effect of increasing the overall risk of this portfolio. This can occur when the standard deviation of the new risk is substantially greater than those risks that are already in the portfolio (see Doherty, 2000, Chapter 4).

SOME KEY ISSUES TO OVERCOME
Although basket operational risk insurance products offer a number of advantages over the traditional peril-specific route there are a number of major issues that need to be overcome before they can be seen as a truly viable alternative for the majority of banks. However, the advantages of basket products are such that insurers and banks should not underestimate their potential. There is a need, therefore, to find and implement solutions to the problems that are listed below.

Lack of critical mass
The market for multi-peril basket operational risk insurance lacks a critical mass of both insurers and banks. A large number of insurers are necessary to achieve a viable re-insurance market for the spreading of risk. Similarly, a critical mass of banks is necessary to provide a pool of risks that is large enough to ensure accurate premium calculations.

Given that there are insufficient banks and insurers participating in the basket operational risk insurance market to achieve critical mass, there will be an initial period of high risk for those insurers offering multi-peril operational risk products. This risk may well explain the reluctance of many insurers to offer such products. However, as more insurers enter the market and more banks buy basket products, things should improve. Consultations with a number of insurance/banking industry experts yielded the following estimates for critical mass:

❏ On the demand-side there is a need for between 10 to 20 major banks to purchase basket operational risk insurance policies.
❏ On the supply-side there is a requirement for at least 10 'A' or better-rated insurers to act in concert. This would give insurers the ability to provide basket cover of around US$1 billion per bank. However, more insurers than this would be better, in order to ensure a competitive market. In addition, the more insurers there are, the easier it will become for a bank to find basket cover (since no one insurer or small group of insurers would be able to underwrite every bank).

Data and risk classification
Data is important to the underwriting of all insurance products since it facilitates the quantification of risk and consequently allows insurers to calculate premiums accurately (and thus avoid making losses). Data is especially vital though for multi-peril basket products. In part this is because of the inclusive nature of many basket products, where cover is not always restricted to specific, named perils. This means that insurers need to do all they can to find out about any unknown or non-quantifiable risks that they may be insuring. In addition basket insurers need to understand the interrelationships between risks. For example a multi-peril insurer

will need to know whether the occurrence of one insurable loss is likely to lead to another (a situation that could lead to an expensive 'run' of claims). Similarly a basket insurer should be aware of the possibility that large operational losses are frequently the result of multiple causes (as in the case of Barings). Where insurance is offered against only one cause (or a very limited sub-set) it may be possible for an insurer to legitimately deny liability for a large loss event that had multiple causes. However, where the included set of proximate causes is large this may not be possible.

Currently, data on the operational risks of banks is limited, although efforts are being made to correct this problem. In fact data collection is ongoing in a variety of quarters (eg, the banks, insurers, rating agencies, industry associations and the regulatory authorities). Of particular interest are the industry-wide loss databases that have been established by the Basel Committee on Banking Supervision, the British Bankers' Association (BBA) and the MorExchange. The benefits of initiatives like these are that they should increase the availability of operational risk information and should help in the creation of a standardised approach towards the classification and demarcation of operational risks. However, cross-sectional industry level data like this needs to be used with caution as it is not always readily transportable in time and place (Young, 2000), especially when it is aggregated or where it is used to provide information on low frequency events. This is because many operational risks, especially low frequency ones, may be a direct consequence of the individual attributes of particular banks (as in the case of Barings, see for example Waring and Glendon, 1998). Moreover, given the dynamic nature of the banking industry, even when data is recorded accurately and comprehensively its 'shelf life' can be short.

PANEL 4

DIFFERENCES BETWEEN BANKS AND THE DECISION TO INSURE

Whether a bank decides to purchase operational risk insurance will depend on its particular circumstances, as these determine both the scale of potential benefits and the extent of insurability problems. Key issues are set out below.

Bank size

Whether a bank is large or small can have a major influence on its decision to insure. The differences arise because bank size affects the scale of many of the insurance benefits and insurability problems outlined in the main text.

It is difficult to say whether large or small banks have the most to gain from insurance. Small banks generally have much less capital and free cashflow and may, as a result, be more vulnerable to operational losses. Also, they often do not have the spread of risks or level of resources needed to replicate the pooling and risk management benefits of insurance (Williams, Smith and Young, 1998). In contrast, the largest banks should be able to replicate many of the pooling and risk management benefits of insurance.

Despite being able to replicate many of the functions of insurance, a large bank might still want to use insurance to protect its earnings from less common, larger-impact operational risks, especially where such events could damage investor confidence or lead to a takeover. For larger, less common risks an insurer who can pool the risks of many banks is almost always likely to be able to achieve greater benefits than an individual bank. In addition, a large bank may find it cost-effective to pass the day-to-day administration of some of its more common smaller risks to an insurer, especially when the insurance market for such risks is competitive.

> Interestingly, this strategy of outsourcing the management of small-impact risks has already been adopted by British Petroleum (Doherty and Smith, 1993).
>
> ### The bank's risk profile
> Basel has suggested that the level and types of risk found in different product lines may vary (Basel Committee, 2001). These differences are likely to affect the insurability of the risks associated with a product line (due to the availability of data or the scale of losses, for example). Thus, as well as affecting its capital charge, a bank's risk profile is likely to influence its ability to buy good-quality, cost-effective operational risk insurance cover.
>
> ### Time horizons of managers/shareholders
> The benefits of insurance often take time to materialise. In fact, a bank that cancels an insurance policy is likely to be better off in the short run because it will save money on its premium payments. Whether a bank is prepared to go through the immediate expense of paying a premium for insurance cover that is only likely to provide benefit in the long run depends on the time horizons of its managers and shareholders (Mayers and Smith, 1982). Managers and shareholders with longer-term horizons will be much more inclined to purchase insurance than those with short-term horizons.
>
> ### Attitude of stakeholders to risk
> In general, the more risk-averse a bank's stakeholders are, the more they will demand the bank to purchase insurance. There is already some empirical evidence to suggest that the presence of risk-averse stakeholders influences a bank's risk management strategy (Schrand and Unal, 1998).
>
> ### Credit rating
> The higher a bank's credit rating, the lower will be the cost of debt finance. A bank with a good rating may therefore decide to finance its losses through the use of debt rather than insurance. This does, however, presuppose that credit will be made available to a bank that has just experienced a large loss which it could have insured. Doherty (2000) discusses the use of debt as a risk-financing tool.

Using data – quantification and risk assessment
Even where data is available an insurer will need to process it correctly in order to ensure that it has an accurate picture of the operational risk exposures of a bank. This task can prove to be very difficult and possibly expensive for an insurer supplying basket products because of the range of possible eventualities that such a product may cover. For example, imagine a case in which a bank insures 10 assets, each of which has four final loss states. If each of these assets were insured through separate contracts then there would be only 40 potential insurance claims that need to be assessed. In contrast if a single basket contract was offered for all these risks, there will be more than one million (ie, 4^{10}) potential claims to consider (see Gollier and Schlesinger, 1995).

Given these issues it is doubtful whether traditional underwriting methods should be used to quantify the risks inherent in a basket operational risk insurance product. Indeed it will be interesting to see whether the banking industry's insurers have properly quantified the risks included in the basket operational risk products they are selling. One possible alternative is to adopt techniques like those used by risk-rating agencies, which typically consist of three separate activities, these being:

1. A business risk assessment in which all operating divisions are reviewed, with factors such as the quality of management, strategy and competitive position being considered.

2. A financial risk assessment which includes a review of the financial history of the organisation together with an assessment of the future projections, in addition to comparison of 60 to 80 industry average ratios.
3. An overall assessment by the risk committee, which also considers the potential impact of external factors before awarding the final rating index.

A similar system is adopted by the venture capital industry, with quantification signified by the internal rate of return on investment, which is then enhanced by the applied terms and conditions.

Moral hazard
Moral hazard occurs when, after purchasing insurance, an insured consciously or unconsciously reduces expenditure on loss prevention and loss reduction, since part of the benefit from these activities will now accrue to the insurer. Moral hazard can best be prevented where an insurer is able to monitor the risk management activities of an insured (something that insurers are very skilled at doing). This will only be fully effective though, if the insurer is able to assess the types and scale of risk faced by the insured. However, for multi-peril basket products this may prove to be difficult, especially when they offer cover against currently unknown or non-quantifiable risks. It is hard for an insurer to monitor the operational risk management performance of a bank when some of its operational risks are not properly understood in the first place. In addition, where multiple losses occur at the same time or where a particular loss is the result of multiple causes it may prove difficult and possibly expensive for an insurer to look into every eventuality.

Because of the problem of moral hazard it is likely that basket operational risk insurance products will only be made available to those banks that can prove they adopt high standards of operational risk management. Effectively this restricts cover to the larger banks who have both the resources and the incentives (in terms of consumer and regulatory scrutiny) to invest in the effective management of operational risk.

Another consequence of the potential for moral hazard in basket products is the tendency of insurers to specify comparatively high deductibles. This leaves a substantial burden with the insured and thus provides them with a strong incentive to management risk. One major basket operational risk insurer to the banking sector has already gone down this route, specifying a deductible of £100 million. Obviously this strategy reduces the scope for moral hazard, however it does prevent banks from using basket insurance to cover their smallest losses (see below).

USING BASKET OPERATIONAL RISK INSURANCE
The way in which a bank might use operational risk insurance will depend on the presence of any general supply-side problems, coupled with its own particular requirements and circumstances. As such it is hard to make firm recommendations about the role of basket insurance in a bank's risk financing programme. A number of general scenarios can be established though.

Replace all peril-specific with basket insurance
Where the advantages of basket insurance are very high a bank might decide to replace all of its peril specific insurance policies with a single basket policy (see Figure 2). However, given that basket operational risk insurance is still in a very early stage of development, and that there are many issues about its supply that need to be overcome, this is not a viable strategy for most banks at the current time. This situation may well change in the future though.

Start with peril-specific insurance, but buy basket cover for larger, more infrequent losses

A bank adopting this strategy would purchase peril-specific cover for some of its more day-to-day operational losses, while retaining others. In addition it would buy a blanket protection policy against larger, more damaging losses (see Figure 3).

The theoretical advantages of basket insurance mean that it should be particularly effective against larger risks. For example the diversification benefits of insuring a bank's entire portfolio of operational risks could allow an insurer to offer high levels of cost-effective cover. Additionally basket insurance is good at dealing with losses that have multiple causes, a feature common to many large losses.

However, due to the lack of critical mass in the basket insurance market and data problems, very large amounts of basket operational risk cover are not yet available. The effective limit at the moment is US$250 million. It is expected that this limit will increase though, to around US$1.35 billion (see Butler, 2000), as more insurers enter the market and the quality and amount of operational loss data improves.

Start with basket insurance, but buy extra peril-specific cover for some losses

The final strategy is to use basket insurance for small to medium losses that tend to be more frequent (see Figure 4). In this strategy a basket policy would be purchased to finance a bank's day-to-day losses. The bank would then identify specific risks that it feels it needs additional cover for and buy peril-specific policies to cover them.

A major advantage of this approach is that it is flexible. A bank that decides it needs US$1 billion of liability cover, but only US$200 million for its other operational risks does not want to have to go to the expense of purchasing the full US$1 billion for them all.

Pre-claim settlement cash advances or 'pay now, argue later'

One of the Basel Committee's key objections to the use of operational risk insurance is that delays in claim payment can, if the associated loss is large enough, threaten

---

PANEL 5

A SPECTRUM OF VIEWS ON BASKET PRODUCTS

All members of the IWG felt that traditional loss-specific insurance products had a role to play in transferring and mitigating the financial impact of a bank's operational risks. However, views differed on the viability of the new multi-peril basket products. These views can be categorised into three groups.

- *Scepticism* – where it is questioned whether multi-peril products will ever be a viable solution for operational risk.
- *Indifference* – basket operational risk insurance is considered as merely an additional product along with other existing forms of insurance. For this group, such insurance will only be accepted when it has been proven to add value.
- *Enthusiasm* – where action has already been taken. This group is comparatively small but very active. It consists of insurers and brokers who are already underwriting and selling basket operational risk insurance together with banks that are using it.

This spread is typical of the S-shaped curve for the adoption of new products. The curve consists of three groupings: laggards, followers and early-adopters. Given that all participants have access to the same information, their views are primarily dependent on their predisposition to risk.

the financial stability of a bank. One major cause of delay is the need for an insurer to establish whether a claim is legitimate (ie, whether a loss is covered by the policy on which it is being claimed). In addition it can take time before the true scale of a claim can be determined accurately (as in the case of many liability losses, for example). Finally long delays may arise where the insured and insurer fail to agree on the amount, time, place and cause of loss or where a peril is covered by more than one insurance policy (placed with multiple insurers) as this can lead to disputes over responsibility.

Recently though, an interesting solution to the problem of delays in operational loss claim payments to banks has emerged. This solution involves providing claimants with an up-front advance for any potential operational loss, before the exact cause of this loss, and hence validity of any claim, has been established. The advantage of this approach is that a bank is able to get the finance it needs to make good its losses quickly. As such this strategy helps to make operational risk insurance a much closer substitute to holding liquid capital (giving a bank near instant access to cash).

There are though problems with this approach. One is the possibility that a bank

---

PANEL 6

PROS AND CONS OF REINSURANCE

It is standard practice in the insurance industry for an insurer to pass on part of the risks it has underwritten to a reinsurer (or co-insurer), who may in turn lay off a part of that risk to another reinsurer, and so on. This is a long-established and highly effective practice that enables non-specialist reinsurers to increase the capacity of specialist insurers in a variety of insurance market sectors. The practice also helps to spread risk and mitigate the problem of catastrophic losses.

Recently, however, critics have suggested that reinsurance creates a lack of transparency in the insurance market and can result in circularity. A bank making an operational risk insurance claim finds itself dependent on the weakest link. This can result in:

❑ The slowing down of a claim payment because an insurer or reinsurer may only be willing or able to meet its obligation after it has secured funds from the immediate reinsurer in the chain. In some circumstances, though, a reinsurer may have recourse to a precedent which states that it need only pay out once the insurer has paid the claim. This can lead to liquidity problems for the insurer.
❑ The addition of further terms and conditions to the original insurance contract. A reinsurer might therefore refuse to pay a claim that is technically covered under the original contract.
❑ The creation of counterparty risks with reinsurers that may not be known to the bank itself. Should a reinsurer fail, the bank would still have legal recourse against its original insurer. However, if this insurer failed, the bank would have no recourse against the reinsurer.
❑ A concentration of risk with an unknown counterparty that might be unacceptable on a known basis.

Nevertheless, it is true to say that reinsurers provide some of the highest-rated security in the insurance industry. Insurers would argue that reinsurance plays a major role in reducing volatility and adds stability to the insurance process. For example, the chance that an A-rated reinsurer will fail is considered to be almost insignificant.

may either refuse or simply be unable to pay back the up-front advance. Another is that by providing immediate finance an insurer could lose several months (or even years) of investment income. As such this feature is only likely to be a practical proposition for select banks (ie, those that can not only pay for it, but also demonstrate their ability to repay an up-front advance as necessary).

Securitisation
Although securitisation is not strictly a type of insurance, the convergence of insurance and financial risk management means that the boundaries are becoming blurred. Insurance products can now be purchased to cover financial risks. Similarly it is possible to buy derivative products against risks that have traditionally been insured (eg, the risk of weather related losses).[4]

Cruz (1999) has already discussed the possibility of securitisation acting as a substitute for conventional operational risk insurance products. The advantages of securitisation are linked to the fact that it provides banks with the potential to transfer operational risk to investors in the global capital markets. Therefore, compared to conventional insurance products, the scope for risk spreading and the availability of financial resources are much greater, thereby reducing counterparty risk (ie, the risk of an insurer defaulting on valid claim payments) and increasing cover limits.

One possible means of securitising operational risk is via issuing a bond similar

---

PANEL 7

THE ALTERNATIVES TO INSURANCE

Several members of the IWG commented on alternative methods of providing protection against operational risk, although opinions on their viability were divided.

Mutual self-insurance pools
Mutual self-insurance pools usually require a large number of contributors to be cost-effective. IWG members estimated that a banking pool for operational losses would need at least 30 members.

Discussions have taken place between a number of banks, with involvement from the British Bankers' Association, on the establishment of a mutual insurance company for the industry. As several IWG members pointed out, since most bank executives believe their bank to be better run than the competition, it is unlikely that many would risk their bank's capital to cover the operational failures of a rival.

Securitisation
IWG members considered that, currently, securitisation has limited potential – a key reason being that investors are not ready for such unconventional investment products. Some also stated that data on operational losses were still too limited to price bonds properly, with the result that investors would demand too high a rate of return to make them cost-effective. The working group speculated that at the present time securitisation costs could be up to five times higher than insurance costs for low-frequency, high-severity risks.

Finite risk plans
Finite risk plans merely provide a way of helping a bank to structure the financing of its retained risks and do not transfer risk. As such they are by no means a perfect substitute for insurance. Such plans are controversial, some critics suggesting that their benefits are illusory (Williams, Smith and Young, 1998).

to the new style of catastrophe bonds. For example, a bank could issue a bond whose value is related to certain pre-specified operational losses. The purchaser of the bond would expect to receive a high yield. However, if one of the operational events described in the bond occurred, the purchaser would lose some or all of the principle and interest.

Despite its potential, securitisation is unlikely to make much of an impact on the insurance market, at least currently. One key reason for this is that many investors (except perhaps insurance companies) are simply not ready for such unconventional investment products. In addition, so long as their remains insufficient data on operational losses (especially for low frequency, high severity losses) it will be difficult to price an operational risk bond accurately. As a result it is likely to be some time before investors demand a rate of return for operational risk bonds that is low enough to make them a cost effective alternative to insurance.

Conclusions
THE REGULATORS
Although the operational risk insurance market may, in the eyes of the regulators, be "still developing", it is important for them to remember that it has a lot of potential. New developments such as basket insurance, "pay now, argue later" and securitisation offer banks the chance to substantially improve their management of operational risks.

It is imperative that the regulators do not underestimate the potential of insurance to help manage a bank's operational risks or hinder in any way new product development. The regulators could even take an active role by helping to develop the market for operational risk insurance. One of the ways in which they are attempting to do this is by offering banks that buy suitable insurance products a reduction in the proposed capital charge for operational risk (see Basel Committee, 2003). Additionally the regulators could work with insurers to help improve their ability to supply new operational risk insurance products. For example, the effectiveness of basket insurance could be improved if the regulators were to help insurers collect appropriate and accurate loss data.

The insurers
The involvement of certain insurance companies and brokers in new product development for a bank's operational risks indicates that the insurance marketplace is far from stagnant. However, there still appears to be a degree of reluctance from many in the insurance industry to embrace these new developments. Perhaps this is because many insurance companies and brokers are waiting to see how the pioneers of these new products fair. Although this may seem a sensible strategy, it does little to help develop the potential of insurance as an operational risk management tool. The increasing rate of change within the financial services sector means that insurers and brokers must be more responsive to the demands of their clients, providing products that clearly add value through enhancing operational risk management. Insurers and brokers that fail to respond may find that their products have become marginalised and that their more innovative and dynamic rivals have superseded them.

The banks
The demand for basket operational risk insurance products remains very low. Similarly, few banks are using securitisation to manage their operational risks or taking advantage of features like cash advances. One obvious reason for this is that there are currently too many supply-side problems for these developments to be truly viable for all but a small number of the larger banks. Another could be that many in the banking industry are presently unaware of the potential of these new developments.

It is recommended therefore that risk/insurance managers in the banking industry carefully assess the benefits of these new developments for their firms. In particular these managers should remember that the purpose of risk management is to add value to a firm. Thus where new insurance products provide potential cost savings or help to increase the effectiveness of a bank's risk management programme they should be given careful consideration. Innovative use of operational risk insurance could directly benefit bondholders thus reducing the bank's cost of capital.

1 *One limited example of policy bundling in the banking sector is organisational liability insurance. This is a limited multi-peril product that covers losses arising from internal and external fraud, rogue trading and many other forms of general liability.*
2 *For example see Dowd (1998), who defines enterprise-wide risk management as "the management of overall institutional risk across all risk categories and business units".*
3 *Note that an insurer that sold many different peril-specific insurance products might also be able to exploit the benefits of diversification. However, where an insurer includes risks in a basket product that it has not insured in the past, the potential diversification benefits are greater.*
4 *See Skipper (1998, p. 132) for a number of examples of convergence.*

BIBLIOGRAPHY

Basel Committee on Banking Supervision, 1999, "Capital Requirements and Bank Behaviour: The Impact of the Basel Accord", Working Papers No.1, April.

Basel Committee on Banking Supervision, 2001, *Consultative Document: Operational Risk*, (Bank for International Settlements).

Basel Committee on Banking Supervision, 2003, New Basel Capital Accord Third Consultative Paper (CP3), April.

Botosan, C., 1997, "Disclosure Level and the Cost of Equity Capital" *The Accounting Review* 72(3), pp. 323–49.

Butler, D., AON Group Limited, Financial Institutions and Professional Risks, 2000, "The Role of Insurance in Operational Risk Mitigation" Bank Treasury Operational Risk Conference, London, 27/28 September.

Cruz, M., 1999, "Taking Risk to Market" *Risk, Special Report on Operational Risk*, November, pp. 21–4.

Culp, C., 2001, *The Risk Management Process: Business Strategy and Tactics* (New York: John Wiley & Sons).

Deming, W., 1988, *Out of Crisis* (Cambridge University Press).

Doherty, N., 1985, *Corporate Risk Management: A Financial Exposition* (New York: McGraw-Hill).

Doherty, N., 2000, *Integrated Risk Management: Techniques and Strategies for Reducing Risk*, (New York: McGraw-Hill).

Doherty, N., and C. Smith, 1993, "Corporate Insurance Strategy: The Case of British Petroleum", *Journal of Applied Corporate Finance* 6(3), pp. 4–15.

Dowd, K., 1998, *Value at Risk: The New Science of Risk Management*, (London: Wiley).

Freeman, P., and H. Kunreuther, 1996, "The Roles of Insurance and Well-Specified Standards in Dealing with Environmental Risks", *Managerial and Decision Economics* 17, pp. 517–30.

Froot, K., D. Scharfstein and J. Stein, 1993, "Risk Management: Co-ordinating Corporate Investment and Financing Policies", *The Journal of Finance* 48(5), pp. 1629–58.

Gollier, C., and H. Schlesinger, 1995, "Second-Best Insurance Contract Design in an Incomplete Market", *Scandinavian Journal of Economics*, 97(1), pp. 123–35.

Grillet, L., 1992, "Corporate Insurance and Corporate Stakeholders: I. Transactions Cost Theory", *Journal of Insurance Regulation* 11(2), pp. 232–51.

Hadjiemmanuil, C., 1996, *Banking Regulation and the Bank of England* (London: LLP).

Holderness, C., 1990, "Liability Insurers as Corporate Monitors", *International Review of Law and Economics* 10(1), pp. 115–29.

Johnson, G., 2000, "Organisational Culture & Strategy", presented to the Sixth Meeting of the Operational Risk Research Forum, 18 May; also available at URL: http://www.orrf.org.

Kane, E., and R. Hendershott, 1996, "The Federal Deposit Insurance Fund that Didn't Put a Bite on U.S. Taxpayers", *Journal of Banking and Finance* 20(8), pp. 1305–27.

Karels, G., and C. McClatchy, 1999, "Deposit Insurance and Risk-Taking Behaviour in the Credit Union Industry", *Journal of Banking and Finance* 23(1), pp. 105–34.

Katzman, M., 1985, *Chemical Catastrophes: Regulating Environmental Risk Through Pollution Liability Insurance* (Illinois: Richard D. Irwin, Inc).

Main, B., 1982, "Business Insurance and Large, Widely Held Corporations", *The Geneva Papers on Risk and Insurance* 7(24), pp. 237–47.

Mayers, D., and C. Smith, 1982, "On the Corporate Demand for Insurance", *Journal of Business* 55(2), pp. 281–96.

Oldfield, G., and A. Santomero, 1997, "Risk Management in Financial Institutions", *Sloan Management Review* 39(1), pp. 33–46.

Quick. J., 2000, "A Regulators View on Managing Other Risks in Banking", *Risk Management: An International Journal*, 2(3), pp. 15–21.

RMA, BBA, ISDA and PricewaterhouseCoopers, 1999, *Operational Risk: The Next Frontier*, (Philadelphia: RMA).

Roberts, S., 2000, "Top Priority on Bottom Line", *Business Insurance*, (34)12.

Schmit, J., 1986, "A New View on the Requisites of Insurability", *Journal of Risk and Insurance* 53(2), pp. 320–29.

Schrand, C., and H. Unal, 1998, "Hedging and Co-ordinated Risk Management: Evidence from Thrift Conversions", *Journal of Finance* 53(3), pp. 979–1013.

Sclafane, S., 1999, "Bottom-Line Coverage Moves Closer to Reality", *National Underwriter*, (103)43.

Shapiro, A., and S. Titman, 1985, "An Integrated Approach to Corporate Risk Management", *Midland Corporate Finance Journal* 3, pp. 41–56.

Skogh, G., 1989, "The Transactions Cost Theory of Insurance: Contracting Impediments and Costs", *Journal of Risk and Insurance* 56(4), pp. 726–32.

Skogh, G., 1991, "Insurance and the Institutional Economics of Financial Intermediation", *The Geneva Papers on Risk and Insurance: Issues and Practice* 16(58), pp. 59–72.

Stultz, R., 1996, "Rethinking Risk Management" *Journal of Applied Corporate Finance* 9(3), pp. 8–24.

Theodore, S., 2001, "Moody's Bank Analysis and European Bank Outlook", presented to the Tenth Meeting of The Operational Risk Research Forum, 2 May; also available at URL: http://www.orrf.org.

Turnbull, N., *et al*, 1999, *Internal Control: Guidance for Directors on the Combined Code* (The Institute of Chartered Accountants in England and Wales).

Waring, A., and I. Glendon, 1998, *Managing Risk* (London: Thomson Business Press).

Williams, C., M. Smith and P. Young, 1998, *Risk Management and Insurance*, Eighth Edition (New York: Mc-Graw Hill International).

Young, B., 1999, "Raising the Standard", *Risk, Special Report on Operational Risk*, November, pp. 10–12.

Young, B., 2000a, "Data Days", *Futures & OTC World* 348, May, pp. 24–5.

Young, B., 2000b, "Developing a Standard Methodology for Operational Risk: A Market Value Maximisation Approach", presented at the Risk Waters OpRisk Conference; also available at URL: http://www.orrf.org.

4

Operational Risk in Bank Acquisitions: A Real Options Approach to Valuing Managerial Flexibility

Hemantha S. B. Herath and John S. Jahera Jr
University of Northern British Columbia; Auburn University

As the banking industry becomes increasingly consolidated, a number of issues have arisen in regard to the structure of acquisitions. From an accounting perspective, bank mergers and acquisitions have been completed using either the pooling or purchase method. One area that has yet to receive much attention is that aspect of operational risk that results from the specific terms of an acquisition. We contend that explicit valuation of managerial flexibility in setting the final terms of an acquisition may enhance value in the process. We demonstrate, using an example, how real options may be used to value such managerial flexibility and thus be used to enhance shareholder value for the acquiring bank. The real options methodology provides a mechanism whereby the value of such flexibility can be measured and accounted for in the acquisition process.

Operational risk and banking

The issue of operational risk in banking has become of greater concern in recent years, as bank supervisory agencies have come to recognise its importance. In 1998, bank consideration of operational risk and how to measure and monitor such risk, was in its infancy (Basel Committee on Bank Supervision, 1998). Since then, the Basel Committee has continued to develop principles to guide appropriate management and supervision of operational risk. More recently, the Basel Committee (2003) offered further research in this regard noting that even the definitions of operational risk may differ within the banking industry. The 2003 Basel Committee report states that "... failure to properly manage operational risk can result in a misstatement of an institution's risk profile and expose the institution to significant losses". This current report provides specific principles for sound management of operational risk. The general principles are encompassed within four broad areas:

1. development of an appropriate risk management environment;
2. the identification, assessment, monitoring and control of operational risk;
3. the role of supervisory authorities; and
4. the role of disclosure.

From a research perspective, there are many elements of operational risk for banks, which makes measurement of such risk even more difficult. The Basel report even

OPERATIONAL RISK IN BANK ACQUISITIONS: A REAL OPTIONS APPROACH TO VALUING MANAGERIAL FLEXIBILITY

notes that the definition of what exactly comprises operational risk remains unclear. One view is that operational risk is more of a residual risk element covering anything not already captured in traditional market and credit risk measures. Certainly, regardless of how one defines operational risk in banking, there are dependencies among market, credit and operational risk.

A number of articles have attempted to address operational risk in banking (see Blount, 2001; Cumming and Hirtle, 2001). Bethell-Jones (2001) discusses the Basel Capital Accord that recommends a portion of regulatory capital cover operational risk elements. He notes that operational risk may be defined as including losses that result from external events. One area in which operational risk can arise is in the process and structure of a merger/acquisition between banks (see Herath and Jahera, 2002). Given the many uncertainties between the initial negotiation and agreement and the final consummation of the acquisition, conditions can change and result in adverse effects to either the acquirer or the acquired institution. This chapter focuses on the use of real options to assess the operational risk that can arise in the process and structure of an acquisition.

Mergers and acquisitions – some considerations

Between the initial negotiation and agreement and the completion of a merger or acquisition, conditions that appeared fixed at the outset may alter. Such changes can affect either party to the process in ways that may be unfavourable.

ACCOUNTING METHODS

To understand how operational risk can be impacted in the merger/acquisition process, we first need to understand the accounting aspect. The alternative approaches to account for business combinations are the pooling method and the purchase method. The consideration (price paid) for a merger or acquisition transaction can be either a cash deal, a stock deal or a combination. Stock deals are accounted for by the pooling method and the cash deals by the purchase method. From this accounting perspective, the two methods deal with such transactions quite differently. In the pooling method the balance sheet of the acquiring company and the target company are combined and treated as if they were a single company. The pooling method avoids creating goodwill and thus ignores intangible assets created in a business combination transaction. Applying this method involves adding the book values (net assets at historic costs) of the target firm and the acquiring firm. No effort is made to identify all the acquired assets and liabilities or to measure their fair market value. From an accounting context, the pooling method is more attractive because goodwill is not created and so its value does not lower the reported earnings of the firm created by the merger or acquisition.

The purchase method is used when the consideration is cash or assets other than stock. In this method goodwill *is* recorded. In order to record the goodwill, fair market value of the net tangible and identifiable assets are compared with the purchase price of the acquisition. Goodwill is the excess of the purchase price over the fair market value of the net assets that are acquired. Using the purchase method means the acquiring firm records, as its costs, the assets of the target company, resulting in amortisation of goodwill lowering reported earnings. The goodwill is written off as a non-tax-deductible expense over a period not exceeding forty years.

MANAGERIAL FLEXIBILITY

The rest of this chapter does not address the accounting aspects of either method in bank mergers and acquisitions. Rather, our interest is that one should consider the value of managerial flexibility in acquisition decisions. Hence our objective is to value the flexibility that may be available to an acquiring firm in the time between the announcement and closing of an acquisition. Managerial flexibility is particularly important, if stock prices of the target and the acquiring firm are are highly volatile and there is a considerable lapse of time (eg, several months) between the initial announcement and completion.

If the deal is based on a fixed stock exchange ratio – which is usually the ratio at the outset of the acquisition process – the shareholders of the acquiring firm may have to pay a premium for the net assets of the target firm if the latter's stock appreciates in value over this time. The premium results from the increase in deal value. If the target firm's value does increase, an acquiring firm should have a right – which it does not have at present – either to swap stock or to pay the fair market value of the net assets of the target when the deal is closed. A deal may be closed at any point within a few months after announcement.

The value of managerial flexibility to optimise a deal is all too often ignored in the traditional acquisition valuation process, but it can be significant. The premium to target firm shareholders is a hidden loss to the shareholders of the acquiring firm, representing value of managerial flexibility that is forgone. A better approach in structuring an acquisition is to also consider the value of managerial flexibility to switch between alternate purchase considerations – swap stock or pay the fair market value of net assets. More importantly, how much extra would an acquiring firm be willing to pay for the flexibility to offer either its stock in exchange for net assets of the target firm or pay the fair market value of those assets? We use real options analysis to value this flexibility.

The real options model

Valuation plays an important role in bank acquisitions. The bidding (acquiring) bank has to decide on a fair market value for the target bank. The target bank has to determine a reasonable value for its net assets before accepting or rejecting the offer. The fair market value of the net assets, (E), is assumed known and agreed by both parties. The deal is structured such that the acquiring bank can pay a price equal to the fair market value of the net assets or swap its own stock for those assets according to an exchange ratio, (F), that is fixed at the time the deal is announced.

Let S_A and S_B denote the stock prices of the acquiring bank and the target bank, respectively, at the announcement of the deal. The time between the announcement of the deal, (t_0), and the closing of the deal, (t_1), is $t = t_1 - t_0$. Over time (t), the economic impact on the acquisition value can be quite significant, especially if both the target bank's and the acquiring bank's stocks are highly volatile. We measure the volatility of a stock as the standard deviation of log returns using historic stock price data. Let σ_A and σ_B represent stock price volatility of the acquiring bank and its target, respectively. The short-term interest rate, (r_f), and stock volatility are assumed to remain constant throughout the analysis.

We use the binomial lattice approach to value the exchange real option. The time (t) is divided into periods of length Δt, which may be measured in weeks or months. The stock price of bank i, S_i, follows a random walk: it takes one of two values one period from now – value S_i^+ (or $S_i u_i$) with probability q_i, or value S_i^- (or $S_i d_i$) with probability $(1 - q_i)$. In order to develop the binomial lattices to price the exchange real option, we use the well-known formulae to compute the risk-neutral probability, (p_i), and determine the values for u_i and d_i.

More specifically,

$$u_i = e^{\sigma_i \sqrt{\Delta T}}$$
$$\text{and } d_i = e^{-\sigma_i \sqrt{\Delta T}}$$
$$\text{and } p_i = \frac{e^{r_f \Delta T} - d_i}{u_i - d_i},$$

where σ_i is the stock price volatility of bank i and ΔT is the length of time. Using the above parameters, we develop the binomial lattices for the movement in stock prices of the acquiring and target bank.

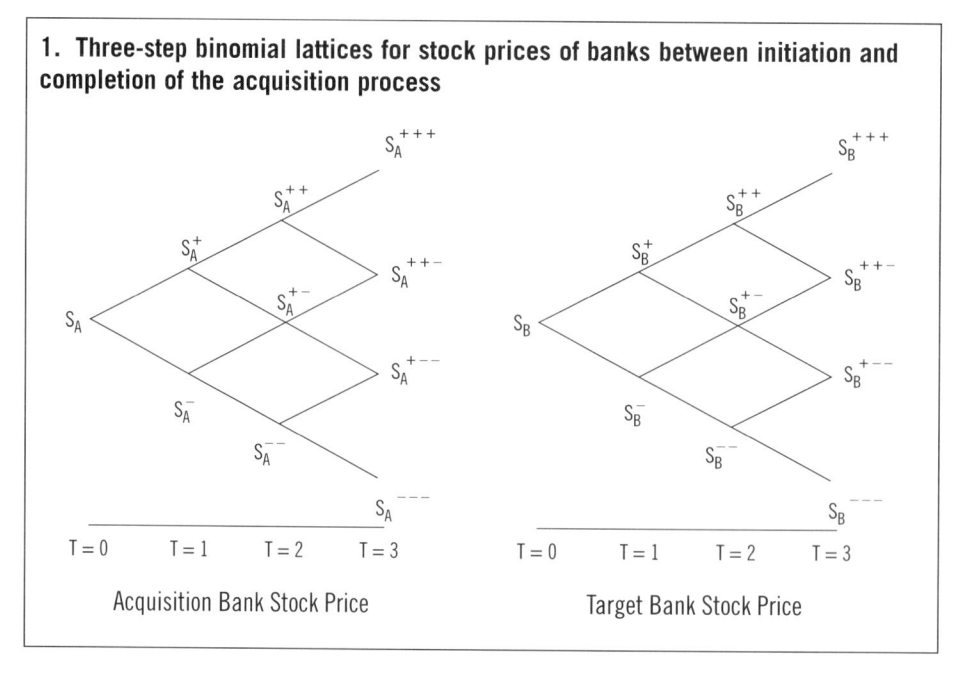

1. Three-step binomial lattices for stock prices of banks between initiation and completion of the acquisition process

Acquisition Bank Stock Price (left lattice, $T=0$ to $T=3$, nodes S_A, S_A^+, S_A^-, S_A^{++}, S_A^{+-}, S_A^{--}, S_A^{+++}, S_A^{++-}, S_A^{+--}, S_A^{---})

Target Bank Stock Price (right lattice, $T=0$ to $T=3$, nodes S_B, S_B^+, S_B^-, S_B^{++}, S_B^{+-}, S_B^{--}, S_B^{+++}, S_B^{++-}, S_B^{+--}, S_B^{---})

Assume that there are four decision points ($T = 0, 1, 2, 3$) pertaining to when the deal may be closed since its announcement. We assume that the deal is not closed immediately. We divide the time period (t) into three equal periods of length $\Delta T = t/3$. Over the time (ΔT), the stock price of bank i, S_i, takes one of two values, S_i^+ (or $u_i S_i$) or S_i^- (or $d_i S_i$), at $T = 1$. In the next period S_i^+ takes one of two values: S_i^{++} (or $u_i^2 S_i$) and S_i^{-+} (or $u_i d_i S_i$). Similarly, S_i^- takes one of two values, S_i^{-+} (or $d_i u_i S_i$) and S_i^{--} (or $d_i^2 S_i$), at $T = 2$. Hence, at $T = 2$ there are three nodes with the values S_i^{++}, S_i^{-+} and S_i^{--}. At $T = 3$, S_i^{++} takes one of two values: S_i^{+++} (or $u_i^3 S_i$) and S_i^{-++} (or $u_i^2 d_i S_i$). Similarly, S_i^{-+} takes one of two values: S_i^{-++} (or $d_i u_i^2 S_i$) and S_i^{-+-} (or $u d_i^2 S_i$). Finally, S_i^{--} takes one of two values, S_i^{--+} (or $d_i^2 u_i S_i$) and S_i^{---} (or $d_i^3 S_i$), at $T = 3$. Hence, at $T = 3$ there are four nodes, corresponding to the values S_i^{+++}, S_i^{-++}, S_i^{-+-} and S_i^{---}. The three-step binomial lattices for the acquiring and target banks are shown in Figure 1.

The combined value of managerial flexibility available to an acquiring bank to either pay in stock based on the fixed exchange ratio (F) or the fair market value of net assets of the target bank (E) is the sum of three real options. More specifically, the managerial action to close the acquisition deal can be viewed as a real option to offer either stock or the fair market value of net assets at the end of each period $T = 1, 2$ or 3.

Assume that an acquiring bank offers stock in exchange for the assets of the target bank. The value, V_T^k, to be paid by the acquiring bank at any period T in state k can be calculated as follows:

$$V_T^k = F n S_A^k$$

where the number of common stock issued by the target bank is denoted by n. As per our notation, the state variable k would be either + or − and F is the fixed exchange ratio of the stock swap.

Note that an option to switch between the two payment considerations $V_{(T)}^{(.)}$ and E depends directly on whether $V_{(T)}^{(.)}$ is less than or greater than E. It does not depend directly on the ratio of the projected stock price of the acquiring bank and the target bank under each state k and time T. However, this ratio is important as it provides an indication of whether the shareholders of the target bank will receive a premium or a discount. We refer to the variable exchange ratio as the *critical exchange ratio* defined by f^k, where$

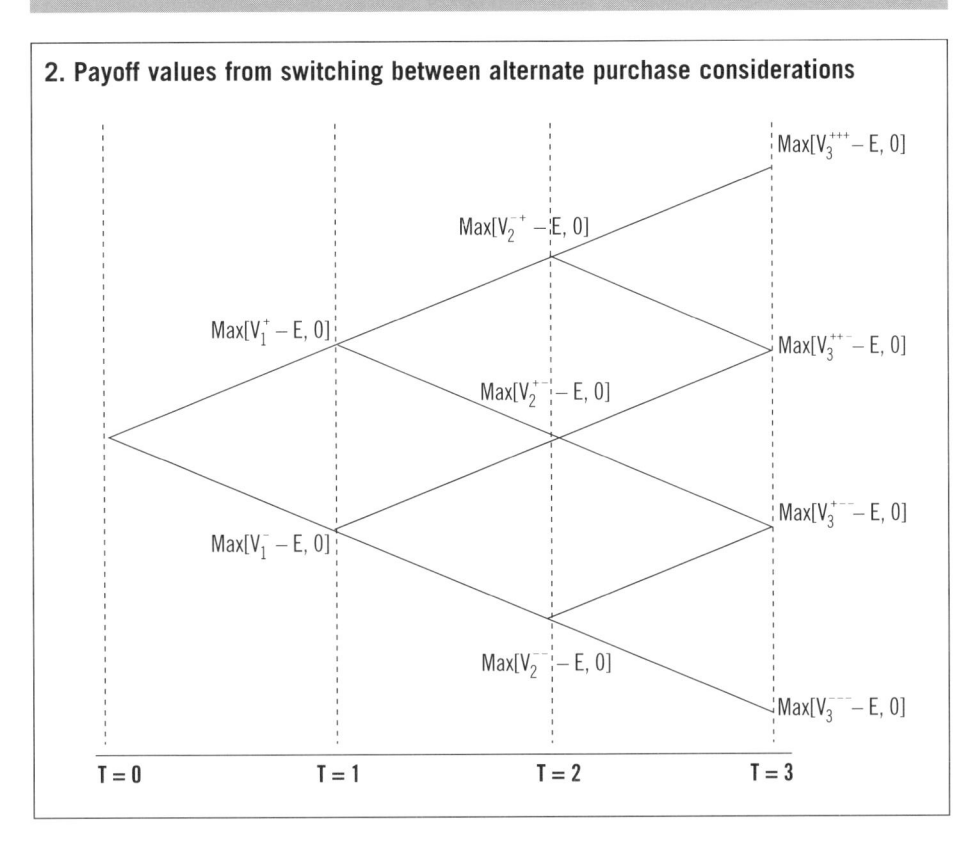

2. Payoff values from switching between alternate purchase considerations

$$f^k = \frac{S_B^k}{S_A^k}$$

If the critical exchange ratio, f^k, is less than the fixed exchange ratio F, the shareholders of the target bank receive a premium above the projected closing price of the deal. On the other hand, the stockholders of the target bank receive a discount if $f^k > F$. The valuation rules that combine exchange ratios with the flexibility to pay either stock or the fair market value of net assets are summarised as follows:

1. If $f^k < F$, the shareholders of the target bank receive a premium over the projected closing price. If $f^k > F$, the target bank's stockholders receive a discount. If $f^k = F$, the target bank's shareholders receives neither a premium nor a discount.
2. If $V_T^k > E$, the acquiring bank's shareholders pay a hidden premium if it swaps stock based on a fixed exchange ratio. Therefore, a better alternative is to pay the fair market value E; ie, min $(V_T^k, E) = E$. The premium that is saved is $\max[V_T^k - E, 0] = V_T^k - E$ since $V_T^k > E$.
3. If $V_T^k < E$, the acquiring bank's holders receive a much more profitable deal if the bank offers stock; min $(V_T^k, E) = V_T^k$. The premium saved is $\max[V_T^k - E, 0] = 0$.

By applying the above rules one can determine the payoffs, C_T^k, to an acquiring bank that has an option either to swap stock based on a fixed ratio or to pay the fair market value of the net assets in each period T and state k. More specifically, the payoff values can be calculated as

$$c_T^k(V_T^k \to E) = C_T^k = \max[V_T^k - E, 0]$$

The payoff values in each state k and time T are shown in Figure 2. Note that each of the three real options is priced using the risk-neutral approach, which is consistent with financial option pricing models, as it is done below.

OPERATIONAL RISK IN BANK ACQUISITIONS: A REAL OPTIONS APPROACH TO VALUING MANAGERIAL FLEXIBILITY

Option to switch at the end of period 1

The real option to switch from a stock swap to pay the fair market value in period 1 is a one-period European-type real call option denoted by $C_1(V_T^k \to E)$. The real call C_1 is valued by computing the terminal payoff values at $T = 1$, C_1^+, C_1^-, and discounting one period. This is done by first multiplying the terminal payoff values by the risk-free probabilities and discounting using the short-term interest rate over one period. For the terminal payoffs we calculate

$$C_1^+ = \max[V_1^+ - E, 0]$$

$$C_1^- = \max[V_1^- - E, 0]$$

Using the standard binomial approach, we next compute the value of $C_1(V_T^k \to E)$ by risk-neutral discounting. More specifically,

$$C_1(V_T^+ \to E) = e^{-r_f \Delta T}[p_A C_1^+ + (1 - p_A)C_1^-]$$

Option to switch at the end of period 2

Alternatively, an acquiring firm should have the option to switch from a stock swap to pay the fair market value of the target in period 2 if it is beneficial to do so. This would amount to a two-period European-type real call option denoted by $C_2(V_T^k \to E)$. The real call C_2 is valued by finding the terminal payoff values at $T = 2$, C_2^{++}, C_2^{-+}, C_2^{--}, and discounting two periods. For the payoffs at $T = 2$ we obtain

$$C_2^{++} = \max[V_2^{++} - E, 0]$$

$$C_2^{-+} = \max[V_2^{-+} - E, 0]$$

$$C_2^{--} = \max[V_2^{--} - E, 0]$$

Using the standard binomial approach, we next find the values of C_2^+ and C_2^- at the end of period 1 by risk-neutral discounting.
Specifically,

$$C_2^+ = e^{-r_f \Delta T}[p_A C_2^{++} + (1 - p_A)C_2^{-+}]$$

$$C_2^- = e^{-r_f \Delta T}[p_A C_2^{-+} + (1 - p_A)C_2^{--}]$$

Then, by applying risk-neutral discounting once more, we compute the value of the real call, $C_2(V_T^k \to E)$.

$$C_2(V_T^k \to E) = e^{-r_f \Delta T}[p_A C_2^+ + (1 - p_A)C_2^-]$$

Option to switch at the end of period 3

Finally, the acquiring firm should have the flexibility to switch from a stock swap to pay the fair market value in period 3 if it is beneficial to do so. Now we have a three-period European-type real call option denoted by $C_3(V_T^k \to E)$. The real call C_3 is found by applying the risk-free discounting procedure recursively as already illustrated.

VALUE OF MANAGERIAL FLEXIBILITY IN AN ACQUISITION

The value of the flexibility available to an acquiring bank to either swap stock or pay the fair market value of net assets is the combined value of the flexibility denoted by $C(V_T^k \to E)$. More specifically,

$$C(V_T^k \to E) = C_1(V_T^k \to E) + C_2(V_T^k \to E) + C_3(V_T^k \to E)$$

The value attached to flexibility in an acquisition can be significant, especially when stock prices are volatile and if it is a long time between the announcement date and the closing date. In a well-structured acquisition managers should have the flexibility to select the alternative that maximises the value of the deal to the acquiring bank's shareholders. Consequently, this value should be added to the value of the deal that is agreed between the two parties at time $T = 0$ given by $V_0 = FnS_A$. Therefore, the value of an acquisition that takes into account the flexibility to offer alternative purchase considerations can be calculated as:

$$V = V_0 + C_1(V_T^k \to E) + C_2(V_T^k \to E) + C_3(V_T^k \to E)$$

Next, we will illustrate, using the data and history given in Panel 1, how one can value the managerial flexibility available to an acquiring firm using real options analysis.

PANEL 1

BB&T CORPORATION'S ACQUISITION OF BANKFIRST CORPORATION

On 23 August 2000, BB&T Corporation announced that it was to acquire BankFirst Corporation (BKFR) for US$149.7 million in stock. Based on the BB&T's closing price of US$26.81, BKFR, with US$848.8 million in assets, was valued at US$12.21 per BankFirst share. The closing price of BKFR on the announcement day was US$11.50. The exchange ratio was fixed at 0.4554 BB&T stock for each share of BankFirst Corporation.

The deal closed on 28 December 2000, for US$216.2 million in stock. Accordingly, on a per share basis the deal was valued at US$17.42 per BKFR share based on the BB&T closing price of US$38.25. Note that, over the four-months from announcement to closing, the value of the deal increased by US$66.6 million – an increase of 44%. Theoretically, the increase is a hidden loss to the shareholders of the acquiring firm as they are effectively paying more for almost the same net assets as if the deal had closed at the original value of US$149.7 million. Note that the fundamental economics of the acquisition do not change because the actual cashflow that is expected will be the same. The prices paid in a stock swap are real prices and, as such, there is greater dilution of the equity interest of the acquiring firm's shareholders. From a purely accounting perspective, however, the increase in deal value would make no difference as the transaction would be recorded using the pooling method, ie, using the historic book values of net assets.

What would have been the dilution of value to BB&T shareholders if its management had the flexibility to offer the lower of a stock swap or the fair value of BKFR's net assets? How much would that flexibility be worth? The data for our model were obtained from company annual reports and through the Internet (at http://finance.yahoo.com). The volatility of BB&T stock was estimated using the stock price data for the relevant period (August 1998 to December 2000). BankFirst Corporation went public in August 1998, and so stock price data for the period (August 1998 to December 2000) were used to estimate the volatility of BKFR stock. The data for the model are summarised as follows. The stock price data for the period August 1998 to December 2000 for BBT and BKFR and the volatility estimates are given in Table 5 in the Appendix.

OPERATIONAL RISK IN BANK ACQUISITIONS: A REAL OPTIONS APPROACH TO VALUING MANAGERIAL FLEXIBILITY

- BB&T Corporation annual stock price volatility, σ_A, estimated using historic data is 35.7%. BankFirst Corporation annual stock volatility, σ_B, using historic data is 33%. The binomial lattices for BB&T and BKFR along with the actual stock prices (highs for period) are presented in Figure 3. The parameters for constructing the lattices and the four period lattices in tabular form are given in Table 6 in the Appendix. The volatility is measured as the standard deviation of log returns of stock price over the period.
- A constant risk-free rate, $r_f = 6\%$, is assumed.
- Fixed exchange ratio is F = 0.4554 BB&T stock for each BKFR share.
- Fair market value of BankFirst Corporation net assets is E = US$149,500,000.
- Number of BKFR common stock outstanding is n = 12,260,500 shares.
- The time from announcement to closing is t = 4 months. Thus t is divided into four periods of equal length ΔT (ΔT = 1 month or 0.0833 years).

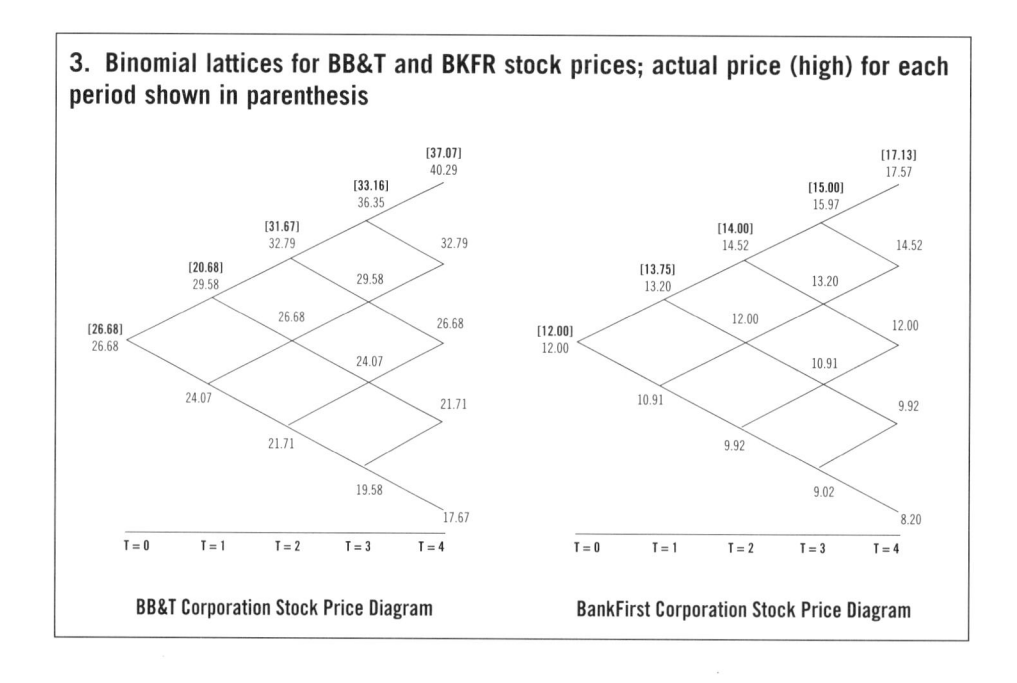

3. Binomial lattices for BB&T and BKFR stock prices; actual price (high) for each period shown in parenthesis

BB&T Corporation Stock Price Diagram

T=0	T=1	T=2	T=3	T=4
				[37.07] 40.29
			[33.16] 36.35	
		[31.67] 32.79		32.79
	[20.68] 29.58		29.58	
[26.68] 26.68		26.68		26.68
	24.07		24.07	
		21.71		21.71
			19.58	
				17.67

BankFirst Corporation Stock Price Diagram

T=0	T=1	T=2	T=3	T=4
				[17.13] 17.57
			[15.00] 15.97	
		[14.00] 14.52		14.52
	[13.75] 13.20		13.20	
[12.00] 12.00		12.00		12.00
	10.91		10.91	
		9.92		9.92
			9.02	
				8.20

In order to value the exchange real option, it is necessary to develop binomial lattices for the movement of the two banks' stock prices.[1] Using the binomial model formulae we compute the following parameters: upside potential, $u_{(.)}$, downside potential, $d_{(.)}$, and the risk-neutral probabilities, $p_{(.)}$, for both BBT and BKFR stock. Table 1 summarises the binomial parameters that are required to develop the lattice for each stock.

Table 1. Binomial lattice parameters

	BB&T stock	BKFR stock
Initial stock price	S_A = US$26.68	S_B = US$12.00
Volatility	σ_A = 35.7%	σ_B = 33%
Upside potential	$u_A = e^{0.357\sqrt{0.0833}} = 1.109$	$u_B = e^{0.33\sqrt{0.0833}} = 1.099$
Downside potential	$d_A = e^{-0.357\sqrt{0.0833}} = 0.9021$	$d_B = e^{-0.33\sqrt{0.0833}} = 0.9091$
Risk-free probability of upside change	$p_i = \dfrac{e^{0.06(0.0833)} - 0.9021}{1.1086 - 0.9021} = 0.499$	$p_i = \dfrac{e^{0.06(0.0833)} - 0.9091}{1.0999 - 0.9091} = 0.502$

Using the binomial parameters, we develop the lattices pertaining to each stock as displayed in Figure 3. The procedures to develop the lattices are as follows: for

Table 2. Variable exchange ratio of BKRF/BBT stock price (f^k)

T = 0	T = 1	T = 2	T = 3	T = 4
0.4498	0.4463	0.4428	0.4394	0.4360
	0.4533	0.4498	0.4463	0.4428
		0.4568	0.4533	0.4498
			0.4604	0.4568
				0.4640

BB&T the initial stock price is S_A = US$26.68, therefore, the two values that the stock can take at T = 1 are S_A^+ = 26.68(1.109) = 29.58 or S_A^- = 26.68(0.9021) = 24.07. This procedure is repeated for the next three periods and for BKFR stock. The actual stock prices (the highs for each period T) of the two banks are shown in parenthesis in Figure 3.

Once we have developed the binomial trees for each stock, we compute the variable stock exchange ratio, f^k, for each state k. For example, the variable stock exchange ratio at T = 0 is computed as f = 12/26.68 = 0.4498.

The variable exchange ratios are presented in Table 2. In this format an upward movement is shown directly to the right and a downward movement is shown directly to the right but one step down. The ratios (in boxes) indicate when a shareholder of the target bank would receive a premium above its projected closing stock price. Note that one would not know the actual future stock price.

In order to compute the payoff values at each state k and time T we must first compute the value, V_T^k, to be paid by the acquiring bank at period T in state k under the stock swap. The swap value at state + and time T = 1 is V_1^+ = 0.4554 × 12,260,500 × 29.58 = US$165.16 million. One can compute the payoff values at each state k and time T directly by applying the switching rules in (2) and (3) listed earlier. Since $c_1^+(V_1^+ \to E)$ = min($V_1^+ - E$, 0), the payoff at state + and time T = 1 is $c_1^+(V_1^+ \to E)$ = min(165.16 − 149.5, 0) = US$15.66 million. Since the payoff is not zero, it is better to pay the fair market value of net assets. Alternatively, if min($V_1^+ - E$, 0) = 0, it is better to swap stock rather than pay the fair market value of net assets. The payoffs, C_T^K, from either paying with stock based on a fixed exchange ratio or paying the fair value of the net assets in each period T and state k are given in Table 3.

Table 3. Payoffs in US$ (000) from switching payment modes

T = 0	T = 1	T = 2	T = 3	T = 4
(stock) 0	15,637	33,563	53,436	75,465
	(stock) 0	(stock) 0	15,637	33,563
		(stock) 0	(stock) 0	(stock) 0
			(stock) 0	(stock) 0
				(stock) 0

Using the formulae developed in the preceding section, we next calculate the values of the four real call options.

Option to switch at end of period 1
The value of this option is computed by finding the expected terminal payoff values using the risk-free probabilities and discounting by the short-term interest rate. More specifically,

$C_1(V_T^+ \to E) = C_1 = e^{-(0.06)0.0833}[0.499(15.636) + (0.501)(0)] = US\$7.756$ million

Option to switch at end of period 2
The option to offer stock or pay the fair market value in period 2 is computed as a two-period call. The real call C_2 is valued by finding the terminal payoff values at T = 2 and applying the risk-free discounting procedure for two periods. The value of the real call option to switch payment modes at the end of period 2 is found to be C_2 = US\$8.259 million.

Option to switch at end of period 3
Similarly, by applying risk-neutral discounting recursively for three periods, we can value the flexibility to switch at the end of period 3 as C_3 = US\$12.282 million.

Option to switch at end of period 4
Similarly, we compute the value of the flexibility that should be available to the acquiring firm to offer the lower of stock or fair market value at the end of period 4 as C_4 = US\$12.745 million.

The value of each of the four real call options to switch between payment modes and the combined value of this flexibility is shown in Table 4. Note that there is relatively less incremental value in switching at the end of period 1 or period 2 and at the end of period 3 or 4. The combined value of operating flexibility in the acquisition to the acquiring firm is US\$41.04 million.

If the deal is structured as proposed, the total cost to the shareholders of the acquiring bank is the deal value at the time of announcement plus the combined value of managerial flexibility to offer the lower of stock or the fair market value of the target bank's net assets. The value of the deal when the value of managerial flexibility is included is US\$149.5 + US\$41.042 = US\$190.5 million. This is still US\$25.7 million less than the actual closing value of the stock deal of US\$216.2 million. Thus, if a market-based approach is used to value the acquisition of BankFirst Corporation by BB&T Corporation, including the managerial flexibility to make the best offer at each decision point, the dilution in value to stockholders of BB&T corporation would have decreased by 17%.

Table 4. Real call option value of switching payment modes

Option C_1	7,756,657	15,636,900			
		–			
Option C_2	8,258,709	16,649,003	33,563,274		
		–	–		
Option C_3	12,281,888	20,889,168	34,308,909	53,435,638	
		3,847,676	7,756,657	15,636,900	
		–	–	–	
Option C_4	12,745,689	21,573,653	35,183,782	54,181,273	75,465,239
		4,096,718	8,258,709	16,649,003	33,563,274
		–	–	–	–
				–	–
					–
Combined	41,042,942				

Conclusion

As demonstrated, when valuing acquisitions, decision-makers should structure the deal such that it takes into consideration the flexibility to offer the lower of a stock swap or the fair market value of net assets. As we have demonstrated, this managerial flexibility can be valued using a market-based approach using real options that are consistent with risk-free arbitrage pricing conditions. Certainly, the lack of such flexibility creates an element of operational risk that cannot be ignored. Traditional valuation approaches ignore the value of flexibility, which may be significant.

In certain instances, as demonstrated, while incorporating the value of managerial flexibility would increase the deal value, it may reduce the dilution of value to the shareholders of the acquiring company.

In summary, we have offered an argument for the use of the real option approach to explicitly consider the value of managerial flexibility in the acquisition process. This approach can serve to mitigate the effects of operational risk that are inherent when flexibility is neither considered nor valued. There are indeed many elements of operational risk and this represents just one that, in today's environment of banking consolidation, is of significant importance in the decision-making process.

1 *For more on switching real options, see Trigeorgis (1996).*

Appendix
DATA AND COMPUTATIONS

Table 5. Monthly stock prices and returns for BBT and BKFR (August 1998 to December 2000)

Month	BBT Stock		BKFR Stock (Target)	
	Closing Price $	Return r_i(%)	Closing Price $	Return r_i(%)
1	26.23	–	12.00	–
2	28.05	0.0669	11.38	–0.0535
3	33.70	0.1835	11.00	–0.0335
4	34.82	0.0327	9.75	–0.1206
5	38.00	0.0874	8.94	–0.0870
6	35.75	–0.0611	10.31	0.1431
7	35.87	0.0033	10.81	0.0473
8	34.27	–0.0456	10.00	–0.0782
9	37.99	0.1032	10.00	0.0000
10	34.72	–0.0900	9.22	–0.0813
11	34.90	0.0051	9.31	0.0101
12	33.73	–0.0342	9.00	–0.0342
13	32.05	–0.0509	8.88	–0.0140
14	30.97	–0.0342	9.50	0.0681
15	35.02	0.1226	9.00	–0.0541
16	31.05	–0.1204	9.38	0.0408
17	26.35	–0.1639	8.63	–0.0834
18	27.29	0.0349	8.38	–0.0294
19	22.80	–0.1797	8.00	–0.0458
20	27.23	0.1774	7.31	–0.0898
21	26.02	–0.0454	8.63	0.1650
22	28.65	0.0962	7.75	–0.1070
23	23.33	–0.2052	8.25	0.0625
24	24.58	0.0519	9.13	0.1008
25	26.68	0.0824	12.00	0.2739
26	29.69	0.1066	13.75	0.1361
27	31.67	0.0646	14.00	0.0180
28	33.16	0.0460	15.00	0.0690
29	37.07	0.1115	17.13	0.1325
Mean return		0.0123		0.0127
Standard deviation		0.1030		0.0971
Annual standard deviation		35.7%		33.6%
Annual mean		14.8%		15.2%

OPERATIONAL RISK IN BANK ACQUISITIONS: A REAL OPTIONS APPROACH TO VALUING MANAGERIAL FLEXIBILITY

Table 6. Binomial parameters and stock prices in the four-step lattice

Binomial Parameters		BBT		BKFR	
Risk-free rate (rf)		6%		6%	
Volatility (σ)		35.7%		33%	
Subinterval (T)		0.0833		0.0833	
Proportion of upward movement (u)		1.1086		1.0999	
Proportion of downward movement (d)		0.9021		0.9091	
Growth rate during period T (a)		1.0050		1.0050	
Risk-free probability (p)		0.499		0.502	

Lattice for BBT

	T = 0	T = 1	T = 2	T = 3	T = 4
	26.68	29.58	32.79	36.35	40.29
		24.07	26.68	29.58	32.79
			21.71	24.07	26.68
				19.58	21.71
					17.67
Actual Stock Price	26.68	29.68	31.67	33.16	37.07

Lattice for BKFR

	T = 0	T = 1	T = 2	T = 3	T = 4
	12.00	13.20	14.52	15.97	17.57
		10.91	12.00	13.20	14.52
			9.92	10.91	12.00
				9.02	9.92
					8.20
Actual Stock Price	12	13.75	14	15	17.13

BIBLIOGRAPHY

Basel Committee on Banking Supervision, 1998a, "A Framework for Internal Control Systems in Banking Organizations," September.

Basel Committee on Banking Supervision, 1998b, "Report on Operational Risk Management", September.

Basel Committee on Banking Supervision, 2003, "Sound Practices for the Management and Supervision of Operational Risk," February.

Bethell–Jones, R., 2001, "Basel Committee Tries to Come to Terms with Operational Risk", *International Financial Law Review*, March, pp. 10–12.

Blount, E., 2001, "Bankers & Supervisors Prepare for Operating Risk Changes", *ABA Banking Journal*, January, pp. 32–4.

Copeland T. E., and P. T. Keenan, 1998a, "Making Real Options Real", *The McKinsey Quarterly*, (3), pp. 128–41.

Copeland T. E., and P. T. Keenan, 1998b, "How Much is Flexibility worth?", *The McKinsey Quarterly*, (2), pp. 38–49.

Copeland T. E., T. Koller and J. Murrin, 1996, *Valuation: Measuring and Managing the Value of Companies* (John Wiley & Sons).

Cumming, C. M., and B. J. Hirtle, 2001, "The Challenges of Risk Management in Diversified Financial Companies", *Economic Policy Review*, Federal Reserve Bank of New York, March, pp. 1–17.

Dixit A. K., and R. S. Pindyck, 1994, *Investment Under Uncertainty* (Princeton University Press).

Herath H. S. B., and C. S. Park, 1999, "Economic Analysis of R&D Projects: An Options Approach", *The Engineering Economist* 44(1), pp. 1–35.

Herath H. S. B., and J. S. Jahera Jr., 2002, "Real Options: Valuing Flexibility in Strategic Mergers and Acquisitions as an Exchange Ratio Swap", *Managerial Finance*, 28(12), pp. 47–64.

Herath H. S. B., J. S. Jahera Jr and C. S. Park, 2000, "Deciding Which R&D Project to Fund", *Corporate Finance Review* 5(3), pp. 11–22.

Kester, W. C., 1994, "Today's Option for Tomorrow's Growth", *Harvard Business Review*, March–April, pp. 153–60.

Kulatilaka, N., 1993, "The Value of Flexibility: The Case of a Dual-Fuel Industrial Steam Boiler", *Financial Management*, Autumn, pp. 271–80.

Leslie, J. K., and M. P. Michaels, 1997, "The Real Power of Real Options", *The McKinsey Quarterly*, (3), pp. 4–22.

Luehrman, T. A., 1997, "What's it Worth: A General Manager's Guide to Valuation", *Harvard Business Review*, May–June, pp. 105–115.

Luehrman, T. A., 1998a, "Investment Opportunities as Real Options: Getting Started on the Numbers", *Harvard Business Review*, July–August, pp. 51–67.

Luehrman, T. A., 1998b, "Strategy as a Portfolio of Real Options", *Harvard Business Review*, September–October, pp. 89–99.

Mason S. P., and R. C. Merton, 1985, "The Role of Contingent Claim Analysis in Corporate Finance", in E. Altman and M. Subrahmanyam (eds), *Recent Advances in Corporate Finance*, (Irwin Publications).

Myers, S. C., 1977, "Determinants of Corporate Borrowing", *Journal of Financial Economics* 5(2), pp. 147–76.

Myers, S. C., 1994, "Financial Theory and Financial Strategy", *Interface* 14, January–February, pp. 126–37.

Myers, S. C., 1996, "Fischer Black's Contribution to Corporate Finance", *Financial Management* 25(4), Winter, pp. 95–103.

Park, C. S., and H. S. B. Herath, 2000, "Exploiting Uncertainty – Investment Opportunities as Real Options: A New Way of Thinking in Engineering Economics", *The Engineering Economist* 45(1), pp. 1–36.

Ross, S. A., 1995, "Uses, Abuses, and Alternatives to the Net-Present-Value Rule", *Financial Management* 24(3), Autumn, pp. 96–102.

Trigeorgis, L. and S. P. Mason, 1987, "Valuing Managerial Flexibility", *Midland Corporate Financial Journal* 5(1), pp. 14–21.

Trigeorgis, L., 1996, *Real Options* (MIT Press).

5

How to Introduce an Effective Operational Risk Management Framework

Roland Kennett

BNP Paribas

Over the last few years, operational risk has matured into a discipline in its own right. This maturing has not been straightforward and we are probably only in the difficult adolescent stage but progress has, and continues to be, undoubtedly made. In the early days the pioneers, a bit like runaway children, were continually pushing hard against the limits of their methodologies and the limits of organisational authority. Just as operational risk looked like it might be a delinquent, a disciplinarian arrived in the guise of the Basel Committees to give structure in the form of the proposal on a new Capital Accord. This has focused the potentially wayward child and since then the operational risk management community (and several other interested parties) have been involved in lengthy and on-going discussions about the future regulatory environment, while at the same time starting to implement a risk management framework. These discussions have led, directly or indirectly, to changes in the regulatory proposals (eg, the introduction of the advanced measurement approach (AMA)).

With the Basel proposals giving some guidance on how the regulatory environment will probably look (the final version will not be available until late 2003), operational risk managers started in earnest in establishing an operational risk management framework. This is a very complex undertaking indeed, far more so, I believe, than for either credit or market risk and they are certainly far from simple themselves. The breadth of the subject matter, the fact that it is already managed, and has been since the year dot, the lack of almost all types of data, the fact that it affects the whole firm and the fact that a lot of the tools and techniques are more bleeding edge that cutting edge are just some of the reasons why it is very difficult.

The following pages will consider some of the issues facing the operational risk manager, (such as among other things, operational risk tools, capital calculation, granularity and management support) as he or she looks to establish an operational risk framework. The objective is not to say "Here is one I developed earlier" because each firm will have to design one that fits their culture, business profile and risk management approach. Although there will be common concepts there will also be a good deal of individuality about operational risk frameworks going forward.

What I will be trying to do is focus on areas of contention look at some industry wide issues, and share some personal experiences of having been an operational risk manager since the baby was born.

We must not loose sight of the big picture. Reducing losses directly affects the bottom line positively and that must be our ultimate goal. To achieve that we need

HOW TO INTRODUCE AN EFFECTIVE OPERATIONAL RISK MANAGEMENT FRAMEWORK

to understand what drives the risk, what our current levels of losses are, how we can track risk, how to incentivise good risk management, how to use capital to name but a few.

Operational risk management must become embedded in the culture of the firm. Every decision and action, whether it is over a large-scale investment or a more mundane matter, must involve an explicit review of the operational risk involved. Over time it must become an automatic part of every decision-making process.

If we cannot provide this then we will have failed because the business will not be better off than it is today.

So what are the generic issues facing the operational risk manager. I will split them in three sections. The first will reflect on the management of the framework building process, the second will consider generic framework issues and the third will look at the issues surrounding some of the tools that are being developed.

Managing establishing an operational risk framework

SENIOR MANAGEMENT BUY-IN

It is a very rare success indeed when any institution, let alone an international bank, radically changes its management approach without explicit senior management support. Introducing an operational risk management framework will not buck that particular trend, in fact, quite the opposite. Senior management support is essential and without it the operational risk team will plough a lonely and ultimately unsuccessful furrow.

The basic requirements of an operational risk framework all have certain characteristics in common. They all tend:

❑ to require investment;
❑ to involve other areas of the bank in additional work;
❑ to take time to develop; and
❑ to deliver their benefit as a potential reduction in costs – never quite as attractive an option as an increase in revenue when fighting for limited resources.

With these characteristics the business needs an incentive to participate. Reasonably, they will do what is best for their own business. Why then should any business get involved?

One of the key reasons is because senior management actively supports their operational risk management team in the effort. This has to be done both financially and visibly. Financially, by giving the team the wherewithal to develop the necessary tools, and, critically, to start to collect basic data and visibly by ensuring operational risk management becomes part of the bank's management culture. Visibly, this can be done by ensuring among other things that it is part of the appraisal process and is highlighted as one of the key areas of focus for the firm over then next few years etc

At this level, it is very much a battle for hearts and minds. First of all, senior management need to be persuaded that an operational risk framework will deliver value and ultimately reduce or control losses, as well as meet any regulatory requirements. If the rest of the bank can then see that senior management is supporting and funding the activity then they will respond positively. If, on the other hand, they see the reverse or if they doubt senior management commitment, then they will concentrate on whatever they perceive as more "popular" objectives.

As a note of caution having senior management support is a bit like having the stake money in a casino. It is absolutely essential to have it if you want to play but it does not guarantee a win. Senior management support does not guarantee success, you still have to deliver value added tools to the business etc but it certainly does allow you to sit at the table.

HOW TO INTRODUCE AN EFFECTIVE OPERATIONAL RISK MANAGEMENT FRAMEWORK

> **PANEL 1**
>
> ## THE ROCKY PATH TO ACCEPTANCE
>
> Why was operational risk such a hard sell? The other risk management disciplines where well accepted so why not operational risk? The roots of this problem are based in the way operational risk developed in most institutions. Operational risk Management is a relatively new discipline and even six years ago no bank had an operational risk team but in the meantime most banks have established just such a department. These have tended to have their origins in audit, insurance, internal control, risk management, facilities management and more or less any other department in the bank. This variety of backgrounds highlights the fact that most banks initially, at any rate, "reversed" into operational risk management.
>
> By "reversed" I mean that the establishment of an operational risk department was not always a positive sign of an intention to improve the management of these risks. Rather, it was an indication that banks knew they should be moving in the direction of overt operational risk management but were not really sure how to do it.
>
> So, feeling they should be doing something but not entirely sure what, banks did the sensible thing and decided not to invest too much. Far better, the argument went, to let someone else do the cutting-edge stuff than do it ourselves, we can always catch up later. So a typical thought process might have been
>
> > "John in Audit's a good guy, understands internal controls, lets ask him to set up an operational Risk team."
>
> Alternatively, it was seen as a bit of a "House of Lords". A distinguished career is rewarded by a promotion to manage the operational risk function. People who the bank did not know what to do with were put in charge of operational risk, as a sort of last chance saloon. Of course there were also some talented people who had a vision!!
>
> As with most things in life you get what you pay for. If you do not give your operational risk managers the tools to do the job then the chances are they will fail. This becomes a bit of a Catch 22 – operational risk cannot prove it adds value because it is under-funded, and because it is fails to add value no more additional funding is forthcoming.
>
> The way out of the viscous circle came in the guise of Basel Committees proposal to introduce a charge for operational risk. Here was a definite value added proposition. The operational risk department can deal with the Basel regulations ensuring that the bank gets as little capital as possible. Suddenly OR starts to get the senior management support and through that the budgets and the profile. Operational is no longer the country cousin of market and credit but a sophisticated discipline in its own right.

MANAGE EXPECTATION

What is expected now that support is in place and a budget available? Operational risk managers have to be very careful in managing the expectations of senior management and the rest of the firm. Having dipped into their pocket and put their credibility on the line management will want to see something in return. The list will include, among others, low regulatory capital, reduced losses (immediate impact on the bottom line), improved risk awareness, and the ability to risk price. All sound like great objectives but none are easy to achieve.

As those conference attendees among you will be aware, banks have been advertising how advanced they are in operational risk management for at least the last five or six years. Claims of loss databases, capital models allocating capital in a

HOW TO INTRODUCE AN EFFECTIVE OPERATIONAL RISK MANAGEMENT FRAMEWORK

sophisticated way to each business and causal analysis have been reasonably commonplace. Yet it is only now that these are becoming a reality across the industry and there are still some institutions that are only just beginning the process.

This overselling has meant that internal management (conveniently ignoring the low investment they have given to operational risk!) may expect significant results and quickly. However, if you have set up your loss data collection process as of today, it will take you three years to collect three years worth of data and three years is thought of as the minimum. The Basel proposals indicate that at least three years worth of loss data will be a minimum requirement for use of the AMA and from an internal risk measurement perspective; although modelling techniques are continually improving (eg, advances in extreme value theory), two to three years' worth of data is probably required to give the necessary level of confidence in the output.

Although benefits of a comprehensive operational risk framework will feed through more quickly than this, they may be soft and difficult to measure. If you only just started tracking operational risk losses and do not have a database of historic losses to compare against, it is difficult to show that the severity and/or frequency of losses has reduced. In fact quite the reverse is true as losses that were previously not recognised or identified as such are suddenly included in the loss picture immediately making the position appear worse.

In order to avoid disappointing both management and the business they should be well briefed on the long-term nature of the project and given realistic objectives and timescales. Obviously, a bit of common sense is required here as you do not want to be seen as too downbeat on deliverables but certainly do not be too gung-ho.

The same is true for your regulator. They are keen to see banks improve their operational risk management techniques and encourage them to do so. However, they will expect to see progress in line with what they are told. Do not make life unnecessarily hard for yourself by setting unrealistic deadlines. Keep them abreast of the process and make sure that the timeframes and objectives are achievable.

Organisation structure
Once senior management support is in place and a team has been established with the necessary credibility they need to decide how to fit into the organisation to deliver the most value and what their role should be.

The first question that should be addressed is:

Should the operational risk management team actually manage the risks?

This is a crucial question that goes to the heart of how the operational risk team will fit into the organisation. To become involved in the detail of operational risk around a large international firm requires a cast of thousands. It also comes with a large degree of moral hazard. If a business does not feel responsible for managing a certain risk then why would they invest anything in it?

This grandiose approach might be attractive but is full of pitfalls. It may be instructive to compare it to other areas of risk management. Typically, credit risk employs a considerable number of people spread around the globe wherever there is a credit exposure. If the same were done with OR, which exits in many guises in every location, the cost of running the team would be excessive (possibly leading to a loss of that hard won senior management support!). Surely, far better to link into the structures that are already in place. This reflects a subtle difference between OR and credit or market. Credit and market tend to be control functions with the power to force positions to be unwound because of the overall levels of risk. OR on the other hand is more of a collaborative effort between the OR team and the business to ensure that the business is aware of the risk they are running and taking steps to reduce it where they are not happy.

It is important to remember that banks were effectively managing their OR way before the advent of operational risk management teams. Ever since they first opened their doors as banks operational risk has been at the forefront of their activities. Most firms have managed this risk pretty effectively over the years, although there are obvious exceptions but the fact they we can all recall them shows how rare (and spectacular) they are.

Given this, it would appear sensible to accept the current risk management arrangement with the ownership, and therefore, the management of the risk remaining very much the responsibility of the business. The operational Risk team should concentrate on providing tools that give the business' management a better chance of managing the operational risks that they own.

However, the Operational Risk team does also need to develop a method of keeping in touch with what is happening around the firm. To assist in this, an "operational risk membrane" of people with an interest in operational risk should be developed.

There are departments in all Banks that contain specialists (legal, compliance, IT Security to mention a few). These areas should be bought into the overall risk framework, discussing issues, reporting data, preaching about consistent data definitions and so on. To be effective the operational risk "membrane" should have contacts in every area of the bank and, crucially, this should extend to operational risk managers in the businesses themselves. This membrane allows a small centralised operational risk team to monitor operational risk across tens of thousands of employees based in multiple business lines in countries all over the globe.

There are, however, areas of a bank, particularly with the audit function, where there is a perceived overlap of responsibility. The dynamic between operational risk and audit is interesting. Audit can feel threatened by the Johnny-come-lately operational risk team, who in turn can view audit as out of touch and not adding

1. Operational risk membrane

much value. In most cases neither is true but any uncertainty about who is responsible for what will confuse the business and reduce the effectiveness of both audit and the operational risk team.

In an ideal world audit and operational risk should be complementary functions working together to ensure that the bank knows what risks it is running and that it is managing them effectively.

Common framework issues

Before I get into discussing specific aspects of the framework there are some generic issues that cut across all facets of the framework.

GRANULARITY

Granularity is the biggest of these issues. Whether you are looking at risk indicators, losses or doing a risk assessment you need to decide at what level to do your analysis. Is it at the firm level, at business level, or product level etc?

Typically the more granular the data the more expensive it is going to be to gather. Most banks are still in the early stages of the process of data gathering and that means that a lot of the required data is well hidden and will require quite a lot of unearthing.

For example, to gather some transaction volume data at a relatively high level of the organisation will probably need to aggregate information from three or more different systems, possibly each using a different definition. This then becomes very much a manual aggregation process. Not only is manual expensive it is also plagued by human error.

To drill down lower will make the process that much more complex and consequently expensive. The growth in cost may be exponential, as increasingly more resource will need to be applied as the level of granularity increases.

The reverse side of the cost coin is value added. If it is helpful to the business to start monitoring data at an increasingly granular level then a cost benefit analysis can be done to establish whether or not the additional detail is worth the cost.

TERMINOLOGY

The industry is still moving, albeit slowly, towards a standard definition of Operational risk. However, if one reads the annual reports of a variety of banks they all have slightly different definitions. Is this a problem?

From an internal perspective consistency in this area is vitally important, as it is the foundation for everything else that risk managers do. Within an organisation there needs to be absolute clarity about any term used and so one single OR definition that is well understood and fits in with the rest of the risk universe (market, credit, liquidity etc) is essential. This is an area where operational risk managers tend to be ahead of their market and credit risk colleagues. Market and credit risk are often not that well defined.

Without this clarity of definition, confusion reigns. If a loss involves operational risk and credit risk how should it be categorised? Inevitable some losses will be double counted and some not counted at all.

This need for consistency is also evident when trying to define risk categories and key control indicators. If different people use different terminology within the same firm or interpret the same terminology in vastly different ways then the data that is collected is nearly meaningless. For the whole process to work consistent definitions need to be applied consistently.

When we step outside into the market place there is more latitude. The regulators have set up a variety

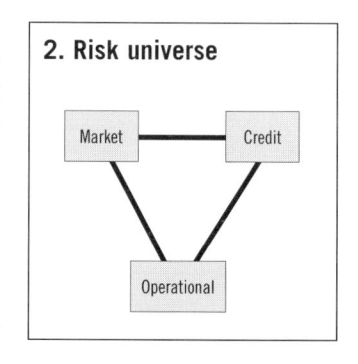

2. Risk universe

Market — Credit
   \   /
  Operational

of categories (ie, event types and loss types) for data reporting and they will expect data to be submitted in the appropriate categories. However, as long as you can map your own data to their categories there will be no issues.

The same is true for any loss consortia. Each consortium will require data submitted in a certain form in certain categories. Again this should not represent a problem as long as your data can be mapped.

However, a word of caution. This does not mean that mapping is any easy process. Far from it, as those involved in the various QIS processes know only too well. It is a complicated, painstaking and very time consuming manual exercise. Although the situation was better during the QIS3 process conducted in 2003, it was still a cumbersome and manual process for the vast majority of banks. However, it does allow an individual firm to collect and collate data to fit in with its own management approach and not be forced down a particular route by regulators.

Operational risk building blocks

Having considered the management process of introducing a framework and some generic issues we can now concentrate on the building blocks that have to be in place. These building blocks will from the foundations of the framework and are vital to its success.

LOSS DATABASES

Loss databases are a key area of development for operational risk management. Our colleagues in market and credit risk have ample examples of data (for example in market risk many years of cable rates are available and in credit risk the rating agencies have years of data) but in terms of operational risk, even several years into the process in 2003, we are still very much at the beginning of the data gathering process.

The first questions that the business always asks when are confronted with the additional cost of collecting loss information are.

❏ Do we have to collect data? or
❏ Do we really need to do this? After all we have been managing this business for years and have never really had a need to collect this type of data before so why do we have to do it now?

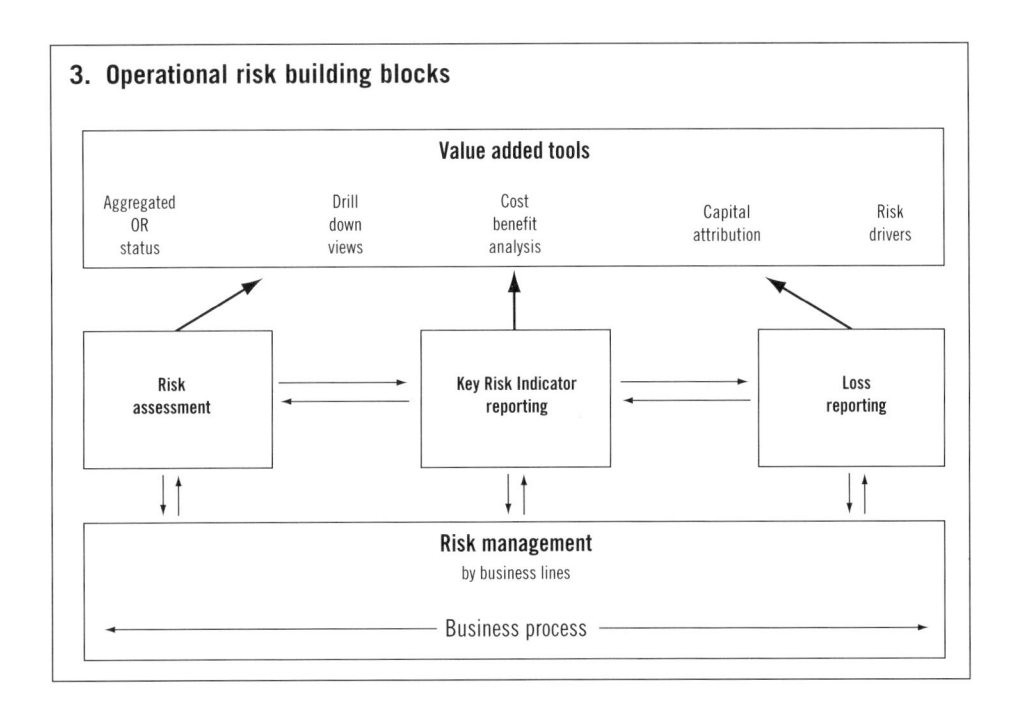

3. Operational risk building blocks

Value added tools

Aggregated OR status — Drill down views — Cost benefit analysis — Capital attribution — Risk drivers

Risk assessment — Key Risk Indicator reporting — Loss reporting

Risk management
by business lines

Business process

HOW TO INTRODUCE AN EFFECTIVE OPERATIONAL RISK MANAGEMENT FRAMEWORK

The easy answer to both is the Basel recommendations look like they will insist on it.

"Banks must begin to systematically track relevant operational risk data, including material internal loss data, by business line." [Standardised approach]

"Banks must track internal loss data according to the criteria set out in this section. The tracking of internal loss event data is an essential prerequisite to the development and functioning of a credible operational risk measurement system." [Advanced measurement approach]

(Draft Rules Document The New Basel Capital Accord Issued by Basel Committee on Banking Supervision August 2002)

The only question left is at what level of granularity do we need to collect data. Basel is less forthcoming on that particular subject, giving only the following.

"A bank must have an appropriate de minimis gross loss threshold for internal loss data collection, for example US$410,000"

(Draft Rule Document Issued by Basel Committee on Banking Supervision August 2002)

Different business may well have different requirements. Investment banking business will probably be only interested in losses over US$50,000 (possibly higher) whereas a credit card business will probably be interested in every loss.

Most institutions already have some type of loss reporting procedure in place where losses are reported on a periodic basis to a central team. In addition some losses may have to be reported to more than one central function. These procedures tend to be ignored because the business does not see any value in reporting, just the cost, and whoever receives the data does not follow up on missing returns. Here is the key to winning over the business, concentrate on the value added that the business is getting, including a reduction in required reporting (each loss only has to be reported once and once only).

Far better surely to demonstrate that there are plenty of actual benefits to the business from tracking losses as opposed to focusing purely on the regulatory angle. Use the carrot as much as possible knowing that you have the stick if necessary. Take the business with you by selling the loss database process (understanding your loss history allows causal analysis, better pricing, better control, leading to a reduction in the level of losses as well as less reporting) rather than forcing compliance by threatening the regulators.

So having persuaded the business of the benefits of tracking losses how and what do you actually collect? Many areas will already collect data – credit card businesses, as I mentioned, will tend to have a number of years worth of loss data whereas other areas will have nothing. Needless to say the majority of business will be somewhere in between.

Applying different reporting thresholds to different businesses is sensible. The one-size fits all approach will not win support as managers in investment banking are going to wonder at the value of trying to report every loss no matter how small yet their retail counterparts have been tracking that level of data for years.

The real question is what level makes sense for each area? Too high and an important part of the loss distribution is lost and too low and the cost of collection far outweighs the potential benefit. The final decision needs to bear in mind both the cost and the benefit. Empirical evidence based on discussions with a variety of managers who have started to receive reports on loss data for the first time suggests that the information is of such great value (even to those in investment banking) that

4. Simplifying loss reporting

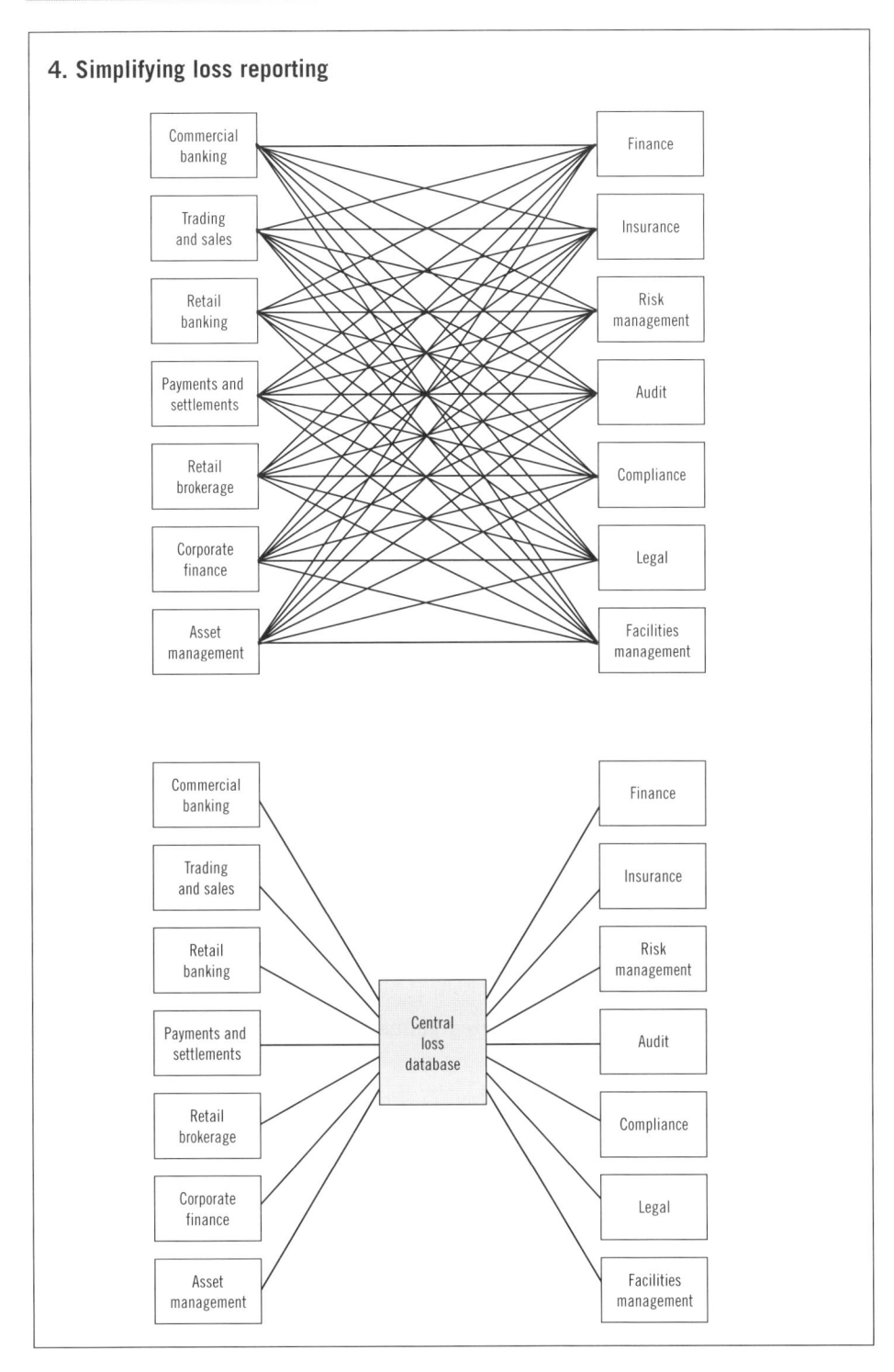

[Diagram: Top panel shows business lines (Commercial banking, Trading and sales, Retail banking, Payments and settlements, Retail brokerage, Corporate finance, Asset management) each connected to all support functions (Finance, Insurance, Risk management, Audit, Compliance, Legal, Facilities management) with many crossing lines. Bottom panel shows the same business lines and support functions each connected to a Central loss database in the middle.]

there is more interest in lowering the threshold for reporting than in having it raised. The cost implications of lowering the threshold certainly need to be explored, but the fact that these managers were interested is fascinating. Interestingly, operational risk managers at other firms have had the same experience.

Whatever the result of the threshold discussion ensuring that all losses above the threshold are reported is important. A best-efforts basis drastically reduces the value of the database, as it cannot be used in any statistical analysis. Similarly, if the data collected is not consistent ie, the reporting threshold is ignored, there is more than one definition of what constitutes a loss or what contributes to the severity of the loss varies (ie, do you include legal or consultantcy fees, do you give any value for insurance claims etc) then it also loses most of its value.

Consistency is particularly difficult to achieve when merging existing databases. Any individual business that has developed a loss database will define what they required internally. The problem comes when a central database is set up and requires these existing databases to be merged. A great deal of work needs to be done to converge what is reported and ensure it is consistent.

It may, also, be difficult to persuade a business to amend an existing loss database. After all, they had the foresight to start monitoring these losses and they know what data they want so why should they change.

The solution in these cases is to try and accommodate the business wherever possible. Try to make it possible to upload existing databases, or parts of them, into the central one. As long as (you will be surprised to hear) the data is consistent and double counting (same loss is entered twice from two different sources) or no counting (loss is not entered at all) can be controlled.

In many respects it is easier to set up a database totally form scratch without the need to incorporate existing sources of data but that is an unlikely as most banks will have something somewhere.

Even re-reading what I have written I can envisage a massive global project to set up a database with dedicated people all over the world reporting and inputting losses. That will not tend to find favour in the organisation. Somehow, a tool has to be developed that can facilitate a streamlined approach to reporting much in the same way the membrane resolved the small central team or large dispersed tem argument.

The solution to this problem lies in where losses should be reported. Should there be a local hierarchy of reporting into regional centres who collate the data and send it on to the central team? For example, a branch in Delhi reports losses to its main office in India, who collates all losses and then passes them on to Asia regional office, who then collates and passes on to the core operational risk team.

The alternative is to allow local input of losses directly into the global database. This has the advantage of leaving the responsibility of reporting to those who work where the loss occurred. Local reporting means that the detail should be more accurate as it is first hand and not subject to two or three series of Chinese whispers.

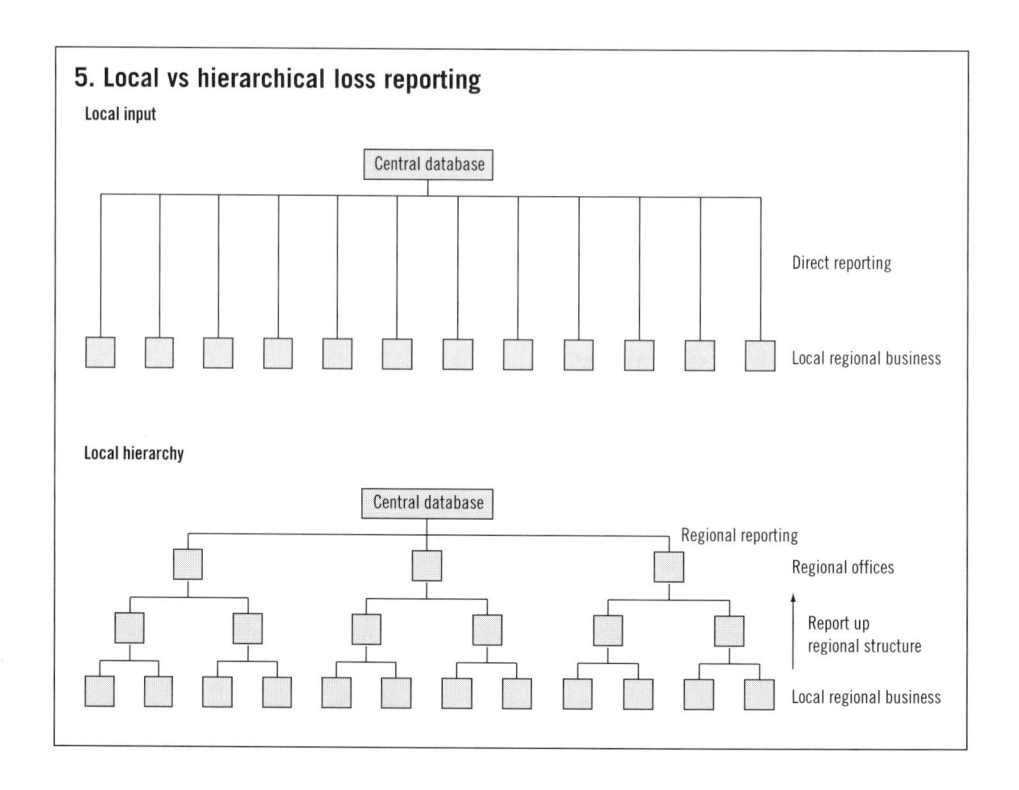

5. Local vs hierarchical loss reporting

Updates can be made easily and the data should be available more quickly. Obviously controls need to be in place to ensure compliance and data integrity.

The concept of local reporting also builds on the theory of the operational risk membrane. Instead off having an army of dedicated resource the operational risk team can utilise existing resource to cover all business in all parts of the world.

Having looked at where reporting should be done we can move onto how the reporting is done. The web offers the easiest way to deliver a standard tool to a business anywhere in the world and would support the local nature of reporting discussed above. The lower tech solution is to develop a template as a spreadsheet and have them submitted on a periodic basis and uploaded in a central database. This would support the more hierarchical reporting. Going forward, with the analytics that banks will want to run it is hard to imagine that a series of spreadsheets will be adequate.

I talked about controls and validation; both are essential to the loss reporting process.

Control would be via the four eyes principle (or something similar) but validating losses is a far more complex matter.

As I mentioned earlier having complete data is important. It is possible that someone might try to hide a loss so it is necessary to ensure that all losses are reported or more likely a procedural problem will mean that some looses are missed. Apart from having detailed procedures on reporting, an effective reconciliation between the loss database and the books of the bank will ensure that all losses are reported in a timely fashion.

Operational losses tend to be booked in a number of ways in the accounts – some have a dedicated line in the accounts, some are booked directly against P/L, there maybe timing difference etc I know it is boring but, there needs to be consistency in the way losses are booked. This is not as straightforward as it sounds. It may be easy for losses that occur in operations but some other losses, such as a commission refund, are much harder to standardise. An agreement needs to be reached with the Financial Accounting area (another member of the operational risk membrane!) on how losses are to be booked and how a reconciliation back to the loss database can be performed.

The loss database is a core tool of the operational risk team and ensuring that it is effectively established with the buy-in of the business is essential if the overall framework is to be a success.

KEY RISK INDICATORS

Loss databases are backward looking tools. They tell us where and how much we have lost in the past but they do not tell us what our losses will be or what are our current risks. This is, obviously, very interesting information but something is required to give data on how we are managing risk today. Key risk indicators (KRIs) offer the operational risk manager that view.

A KRI is a statistic or piece of data that indicates the level of risk in a particular part of the business. Some examples are:

❏ staff turnover – percentage of staff that have left in the last 12 months;
❏ system uptime – percentage of contracted time a particular system is available; and
❏ business continuity plan – does a plan exist and has it been tested.

It is not that hard to identify a large number of potential indicators on a bank-wide basis. The problem, as with loss data, is to start collecting it. There will be areas, typically operations and IT where lots of data already exists.

Operations will hold a lot of performance data (how many trades are being processed) and some risk data (eg, Nostro break data). Although the operational risk manager will be most interested in the risk data the performance data can also be used. Performance and risk data can often be combined into risk ratios ie, volumes processed is a performance data indicator but put it in conjunction with number of errors made and we have an interesting risk ratio: errors as a percentage of volumes.

Where there are pockets of operations data we are confronted with our old sparring partner consistency. If operations in London counts volume in a certain way (say number of legs per trade) and in New York they do it in a totally different way (say number of trades) then the data is incomparable. Somehow consistency has to be introduced.

This is even harder to achieve than it sounds (and I think it sounds hard). These types of statistics have arisen because individual businesses in various locations see some management value in collecting them. The only central reporting might be a consolidation of indicators from various locations. Yet, if data is to be centrally reported as part of the operational risk framework then there has to be consistent definitions. The operational risk team has to lead the standardisation debate. The business will require some persuading but it is a prerequisite of success. As with the loss database, the value-added aspects of standardising data need to be highlighted to the business, as opposed to the stick approach. The value-added may include the ability to compare like with like across the organisation, a detailed view of how risk is currently being managed or an increase in the understanding of what is driving risk in part of the organisation and how it can be managed.

Other areas of the bank will have little or no data. This may well include some central functions (ie, not directly part of a business) where you might have expected some. Human Resources, as an example, sometimes struggles to supply accurate data on absenteeism or number of contractors/temps.

Other areas where problems may exist are typically where historically they have not thought they ran any operational risk or were not perceived as being an area where performance is an issue. Finance teams or sales and marketing teams often have little or no data yet can run very large operational risk indeed.

Finance tends to operate with hundreds, if not thousands, of spreadsheets to get information from a variety of systems covering an endless list of products into a monthly set of figures.

While on the marketing side one of the hardest risks to control is what the salesman is telling clients or potential clients. Bankers Trust suffered greatly when it was found that it had not been seen to operate in the best interest of its clients. There are also examples of members of staff, just prior to defection, trying to persuade clients that their new employer would be a better place to be.

So having begun to identify KRIs we are confronted with the question of whether or not the same data should be used across the bank. Having argued, you may have noticed, for consistency I am now going to confuse you and say NO the same data does not have to be tracked across the firm.

Not only are Investment banking and retail banking totally different and so require different types of indicators but sales and marketing and finance within Investment Banking are also very different and so they require different data as well. You may also find that on a global basis there is a requirement to collect different data in the US, say to Hong Kong.

In order to reflect these very divergent risks it will be necessary to allow each business to track whatever it feels reflects its risk. However, there must be certain guidelines here. Not collecting data should not be an option and certain controls need to ensure that consistent definitions of each indicator are used throughout the firm.

Just to return to consistency, there will be of course some be indicators that are applicable to all businesses in all locations. Staff turnover is one of those examples which could apply just as much to retail banking in Trieste as asset management bin New York.

However, most indicators will be "bespoke" ie, specifically designed for a particular business. An example of a "bespoke" indicator for the retail business might be automatic teller machine (ATM) uptime.

Once all these indicators have been identified the next step is to start to gather the actual data. In the first instance, it is certainly far easier to concentrate on data that already exists! However, needless to say these indicators do not offer the same value to the business as new indicators. The business has already had that data for some time! Risk assessment (see below) deals with how KRIs can be identified.

How many KRIs should be tracked? It is very easy to start collecting an awful lot of data. Not only is that very time consuming and costly but it does not necessarily improve your risk management. There is a definite risk of paralysis of analysis. Far better to focus on a limited number of key indicators that provide an overall view of risk.

Most banks have developed a number (usually between four and six) of risk categories. In order to get the coverage there should be at three KRIs in each category but there should be more in the area where the risk is perceived as greatest. Overall I do not think that more than 25 indicators is viable, or else the amount of data generated and requiring process will be excessive.

KRIs will change over time. New risks will emerge requiring new KRIs and existing risks will mutate. In addition as risk managers become more sophisticated so they will want to move up the causal chain. Say we think that Nostro Breaks are a good KRI today. Soon we will want to know what actually causes the Nostro break and will then identify KRIs to track that. This is an iterative process and will eventually lead to far more precise indicators.

In terms of actually gathering the data the same issues apply as with the loss database. Should it be locally generated data that is fed directly into a central database or reported and aggregated locally and then submitted? Generally the same answers apply but, as mentioned above, the level of complexity is much higher.

RISK ASSESSMENT
Another popular tool is the risk assessment. Risk assessments are carried out all over every organisation. They may vary from the informal (a brief chat over a particular activity) to the very highly formalised (a full day meeting using a specific risk assessment methodology with particular outputs). Whatever the level of formality the risk assessment is undertaken to understand the risks that exist in a process, whether the control environment is adequate for the identified risks and, in some methodologies, the likelihood of a loss being incurred and its severity.

Risk assessments can produce fascinating information. They can highlight specific risks and the measures required to combat them and can show the trend over time in management perception. They can also be used to define KRIs thus providing a link to the KRI tool and can be used to cross-validate the tools in the framework.

KRIs can be tracked against losses to see whether or not they are effective at monitoring the levels of risk. If, for example, the risk assessment identified Nostro breaks are as a KRI for a particular process and they remain low but losses in fact surge then it may not be a good KRI for this process.

Additionally, the level of losses can be compared to predicted levels of losses in the risk assessment. If the risk assessment indicated a maximum loss for the year of US$1million and at the end of June the figure is US$750,000 then the risk assessment needs to be reviewed. The numbers of risk assessments that are done voluntarily reflect the value that the business perceives in them and this should be encouraged.

There are plenty of valid risk assessment methodologies each with a specific objective (high level review of an organisation to distil the ten biggest threats, a detailed review of a process to capture the range and severity of risk etc).

To be an effective and helpful risk management tool the right type of risk assessment must be used. In trying to do a high-level risk assessment of a complete organisation you do not want to be using techniques that were designed to identify risks in a specific process at a very granular level. However, as a risk manager what can we learn from the risk assessment process? Can we, for example, as some firms want to, use risk assessment as part of a capital calculation?

Where a risk assessment is most effective is where it leverages on the experience of those taking part. It utilises the combined knowledge, expertise and skills of the participants and their diverse backgrounds to evaluate the risks in a certain area. This can be very powerful and very informative. If, however, the risk assessment deals with issues outside their combined experience it cannot hope to be as effective. Fortunately, there is not enough experience within most organisations of large-scale losses to allow accurate predictions of how losses might accumulate in the once in 25-year loss let alone the one in a hundred years.

It is helpful to look at another industry for an example of how difficult it is to predict the extremes of a loss distribution. There is a train that runs to a ski resort in Austria that was designed to have a close to zero risk of fire. Yet, over a hundred and 50 people died as a fire destroyed the train in November 2000. Engineers, by the nature of their training, are skilled in predicting the limits of their designs. If they are able to get it so tragically wrong is it reasonable to expect people with little or no experience of large losses to be able to accurately predict what can happen at the extremes of their business.

By way of another example, I know of a risk assessment where maximum potential losses were predicted as part of a risk assessment on a business. The aggregate total was so low it hardly covered existing average annual losses. This maybe explained as a one off but I think that the process is flawed.

Other issues with risk assessment surround how to keep the process fresh. If risk assessments are done regularly there will be a tendency for the participants to just rubberstamp what their views were the last time round. This happens particularly after the third or fourth iteration. Risk assessment fatigue means the process will become less and less informative the more often it is performed.

One way round that is to involve different people in the process. The watchword here is our old friend, consistency. With different people involved there is a concern that risk assessments become individual events and should not be correlated to risk assessments in the past. The inevitable change in participants can, if not controlled, mean losing the trend generated by successive risk assessment, which would be a significant loss. The controls relate to hoe the risk assessment is performed, and how it is reported (ie, the output). Consistency here will keep the trend valid.

Risk assessment can be a very useful tool but it has to be kept fresh and should be treated with caution when being directly involved in estimating capital for the firm.

REGULATORY CAPITAL

The regulatory process appears to be in its final stages. The next set of papers will be issued in May 2003 with the final regulatory papers being issued later in the year. There is now a great deal more clarity around what the regulators will require, especially in terms of the AMA, although a number of key issues are still outstanding (eg, home host issue). The range of options now available under the current Basel proposals allow, at their most advanced, an incentive-based risk management framework that continues to reward improvements in the management of operational risk and encourages developments in this area.

For operational risk there has been unprecedented coverage of the topic since the Basel committee first indicated a desire to include it explicitly in the charge. As I mentioned earlier this has certainly kept operational risk in the limelight and has allowed the risk manager to show specific value added to management for the first time.

The Basel process has also forced the industry as a whole to focus on operational risk and a number of initiatives have got off the ground as a result, like loss data sharing which I touch on elsewhere. These initiatives, along with the immense amount of work done in responding to the Basel committee proposals themselves, mean that a great deal of progress has been made in developing the intellectual basis. Banks have co-operated, shared ideas and developed initiatives across the industry.

PANEL 2

INTERNAL CAPITAL CALCULATION

Internal capital modelling for operational risk is not new. Bankers Trust under the leadership of Doug Hoffman started to look at this in the early to mid 1990s. Using capital to manage the business is now an accepted part of the management. However, is it realistic for operational risk or is it more cost than benefit.

The first issue to address is a capital calculation feasible from an operational risk point of view. The answer is an unswerving yes, it certainly is possible. If the question was is it easy, the answer would be an unswerving no. So why is it so problematic?

The first problem is the lack of data. Notwithstanding the claims of some banks to have comprehensive loss databases, most do not currently have enough to construct a distribution. As I said earlier there is a certain amount of data required to do this, typically 2–3 years' historic loss data. So if you have not yet started to collect data it will be three years before your calculation is reliable.

Are there any short cuts? The loss consortia I mentioned earlier certainly represent one way of getting additional loss data. The consortia are owned by the member Banks who submit complete (ie, all losses that have occurred) loss data in a standardised form (standard business categorisation and standard loss categorisation). These losses are then "annonymised" (they remove evidence of who submitted each loss so guaranteeing confidentiality) and scaled and then made available to member banks.

These losses can be added to your own loss data to fill out your distribution. However, other firms will not exactly match your own control environment or necessarily be relevant to your company and, in addition, scaling is an inexact science. However, if there is not enough internal loss data then they could be used but they must be treated with extreme caution.

On the quantitative side the firm will set its own level of confidence. This is often set for all capital calculations (market and credit) and based on the credit rating of the firm (ie, AAA or a bank desiring to get to AAA would use a confidence of 99.98%, a AA firm would use 99.97%). The main problem here is that very high levels of confidence mean that the capital figure is driven by extreme events. The 99.98% figure means that operational risk losses will only exceeded the level of the capital figure twice in 10,000 years. The difference in using the different confidence level can be seen in this example looking at one business line using a log normal distribution:

Confidence (%)	Capital (€ 000s)
95	632
99	1,872
99.97	10,910

These very high levels of confidence will produce a correspondingly high capital figure. This then presents a problem when explaining the figure to the business. They are suddenly confronted with a very large capital figure, which they can do little to affect in the short term. If their level of expectation has not been set accurately, all the good work that has been done in the rest of the framework could be lost. The capital figure tends to be the highest profile part of the operational risk framework and if the figure that comes out is so far outside of the business' experience then confidence in the whole process could be lost. Using very high levels of confidence runs that risk. If possible, do some detailed analysis of what confidence levels can do to your capital charge before making the decision.

Another issue that the business may raise relates to losses they have suffered in the past but have taken remedial action thus preventing them from, supposedly, happening again.

A large loss, say, an option was not exercised, occurs. There follows a very detailed review of processes and people, the regulators may be involved as well as external consultants. With all that attention it is unlikely the same loss will recur (not impossible but unlikely). In reality the controls environment has probably gone too far in the other direction and the process is now over-controlled.

While the capital figure is meant to reflect all losses that can be suffered in the future and not just a repetition of what has gone before, it is still a valid question. One possible way to proceed is to remove these data points from the database but the criteria required to make that decision would be difficult to define.

Capital is a very blunt instrument, one that the business can find very hard to affect quickly. If it is based on several years worth of loss data then, even if the business could reduce losses to close to zero, it would take time for that to dramatically reduce the capital figure.

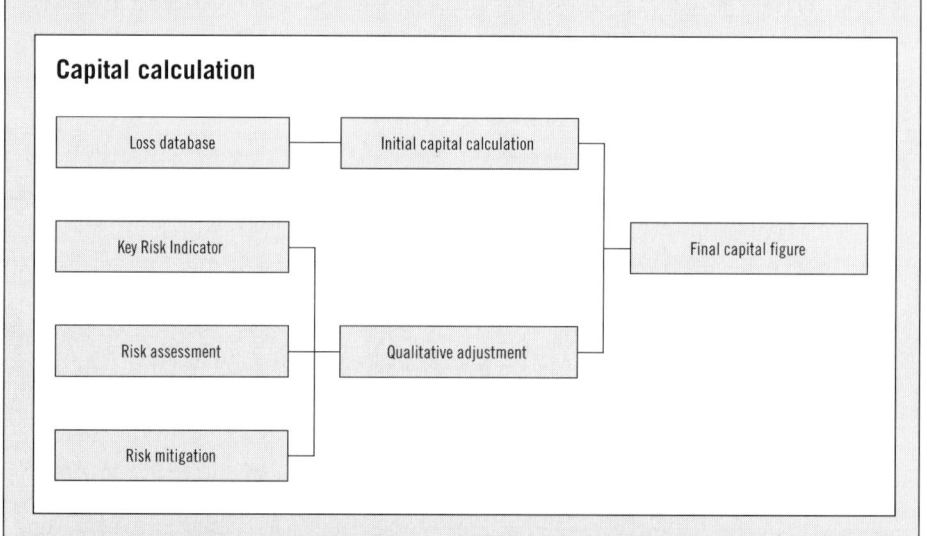

Capital calculation

Loss database → Initial capital calculation → Final capital figure

Key Risk Indicator ↘
Risk assessment → Qualitative adjustment ↗
Risk mitigation ↗

In order to make the capital process as incentive based as possible a qualitative adjustment needs to be introduced. All the risk management information that is available in the firm (KRIs, risk assessment, risk mitigation projects, insurance coverage etc) needs to be synthesised into an adjustment factor.

This is certainly one of the great challenges to the operational risk manager. How to ensure that the business is incentivised to manage their risks through the capital framework and yet and still maintain the credibility of the process.

For the adjustment to be effective it must be transparent. There is no point in using smoke and mirrors to come up with the adjustment as the business will not know how to respond. Transparency allows the business to manage their capital better. They will now what is driving it and what they need to do to reduce it. The whole process will be incentivised.

However, with even a transparent adjustment there is the opportunity for the business to try and game the process and controls (Audit will need to review the whole process) will need to be in place to protect against this.

One of the biggest concerns is that in forcing the business to manage their risk through the capital you are forcing them to focus on certain risks. In an ideal world the framework would capture the full extent of the businesses exposure but there is a

> chance that by focusing on the capital the business might be blindsided by a loss that has not been picked up. Only diligence, monitoring market trends, continual review of the risks picked up in the framework will address this risk.
>
> If these issues can be resolved then capital will help to embed operational risk management in the firm. Everyone will be judged on how they do in relation to capital and this focus (and the financial benefits that goes with it) will start to raise standards.

This is all positive for individual risk managers as they can point to what is happening elsewhere and claim a need to keep pace with external developments.

With the decision by Basel to introduce the AMA, banks have been encouraged to develop their own internal methodologies. This has led to an explosion of activity in the amount of development work being done throughout the industry, both within individual banks and in industry-wide groups like the International Institute of Finance (IIF) and the Industry Technical Working Group (ITWG)). Working through these groups ensures that banks are aware of what is going on in the rest of the industry and the research and development costs are shared across a wider group. Also, when it comes to lobbying the regulators, the more banks that have developed a position, the more likely it is that the regulators will listen.

It would appear that the regulator's idea of allowing the industry to experiment widely on methodology with the view that the best models will be adopted by the

---

PANEL 3

VIEWING OPERATIONAL RISK FROM AN EVT PERSPECTIVE

An area of considerable interest for operational risk modelling is Extreme Value Theory (EVT). EVT is officially used by UK and Dutch engineers to measure the behaviour of waves against sea defences. EVT is also employed by the insurance industry to calculate the price of catastrophe insurance. Primarily it is the robust mathematical principles underlying the theory that have established it as a reliable risk management tool amongst the professions of reliability engineering, weather forecasting and actuarial science. It is about making the best use of tail events in the sample. So given an empirical distribution of operational losses, our aim is to accurately estimate the tail where material operational losses usually occur, and hence manage extreme risks effectively.

Thus, EVT holds promise for advances in the management of low-frequency high-impact operational risks. Historic loss data enables the estimation of the severity and frequency distributions of extreme events. For the frequency distribution, the usual assumption is a Poisson process, whereas for the severity distribution there is a wider choice of candidate parametric distributions (eg, log-Gaussian, Generalised Extreme Value, Generalised Pareto distribution etc). Using the simulated distribution (based on an appropriate parametric assumption) one can calculate VAR-type and supplementary risk measures in the hope that historic loss information will reflect the firm's potential exposure.

Sources:
Kyriacou, M.N., and E.A. Medova, 2001, "Measuring risks by extreme values", *Operational Risk Newsletter*, Aug/Sep.

Kyriacou, M.N., and E.A. Medova, 2001, "Operational Risk Measurement", in *Value at Risk and Beyond*, (Cambridge University Press).

industry is happening already. Although there are differences of emphasis on how the operational risk framework will operate, in practice the industry seems to be developing in a consistent approach (Lepus Growing Importance of Operational Risk, London February 2003).

The future

An article on operational risk would not be complete without a peep into the future. Is there a place for an integrated risk management structure combining market, credit, operational, liquidity, business and the rest? This is viewed as the Holy Grail for risk management but what would it deliver? Combining the risk management frameworks of the individual risks into a single all encompassing framework would deliver massive value to any business that can achieve it. Knowing exactly what your risk profile is across all risks would allow unprecedented accurate pricing.

HOLISTIC RISK MANAGEMENT
Currently there are distinct independent areas within each firm that cover market risk, credit risk and operational risk. There is perceived value in trying to integrate all the risk management functions together.

At the moment this would be an entirely virtual change with each group remaining independent and the reporting lines just changing. However, there are synergies available. Logically this could begin with joint ventures.

An example might be to look at the benefit to the firm of understanding the complete impact of a Tokyo earthquake. The market risk managers would consider the effects of such an event on market conditions, the credit risk officers would view the impact it would have on the creditworthiness of firms exposed to Japan while their operational risk managers colleagues would consider the implications of that same earthquake on the firm itself. Although the tools and techniques used by each branch of risk management would differ substantially, a far more complete picture of how the firm would be affected by an earthquake in Tokyo would arise.

This type of joint venture will establish, I believe, a positive correlation between an event such as an earthquake in Tokyo and increase in operational and market risk. Such a correlation will prompt attempts to arrive at a single into a single absolute methodology for risk management possibly involving real options.

The advantages of such an approach are manifold. All decisions could be made with a complete range of risk information available. This does not mean mistakes will not be made but the concept of risk and return will be better understood.

From an operational risk perspective there is a tendency to over control. As we do not currently have enough loss or KRI data management tends to be conservative and add in controls. However, this may be inefficient. What is required is a control environment that reflects the absolute level of risk that the firm wants to take. The development of an holistic approach to risk will allow firms to understand more fully the risk dynamics in their organisation and effectively manage that risk according to the risk appetite that have.

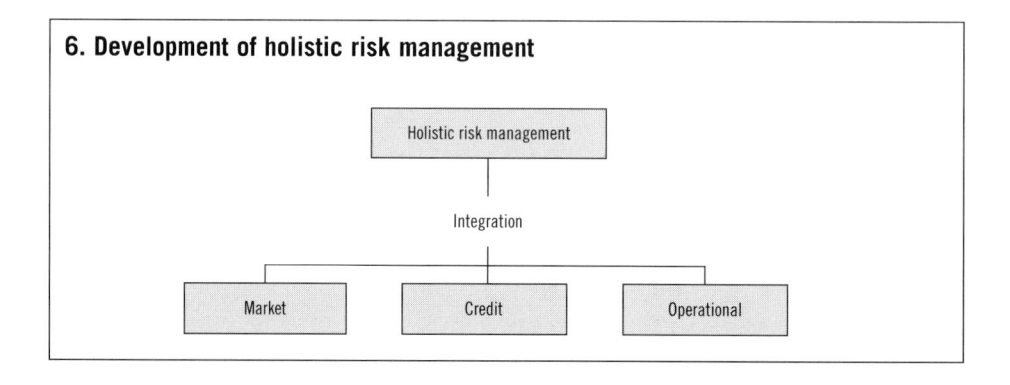

6. Development of holistic risk management

```
            Holistic risk management
                    |
                Integration
         _____|_____
        |           |           |
      Market      Credit    Operational
```

> **PANEL 4**
>
> **REAL OPTIONS**
>
> Real options aim to bring the flexibility and control of financial options to non-financial decision making. As Martha Amram and Nalin Kulatilaka note in their book *Real Options – Managing Strategic Investment in an Uncertain World*, real options unite cost benefit analysis with sound management process and allow decisions to be made that aim to maximise corporate strategy.
>
> There are very large similarities between the objectives of real options and those of capital calculation for operational risk. Both try to enfranchise managers to adjust strategy as the risk environment changes. Invest and divest decisions, re-assessing projects to ensure that they are still delivering the expected value are some of the common objectives to risk capital and real options. The philosophy is the same whether one is considering investing in a new refrigeration plant (where real options would be used) or whether one is trying to identify whether a new computer system will produce the necessary reduction in risk (where the capital calculation would help).
>
> Real options are very flexible. In terms of risk management, they could be the foundation for a holistic risk framework that would aggregate risk (market, credit and operational) and provide a method to manage the combined exposure. This is vital information for senior management trying to establish a strategy to meet their goals and for business managers who are maybe aware that they have a certain level exposure but find it impossible to substantiate. A lot of work has to be done but the potential is there.
>
> For more information on this subject refer to specific literature on the subject of which the above-mentioned book is recommended, as is *Real Options and Energy Management: Using Options Methodology to Enhance Capital Budgeting Decisions*, edited by Ehud I. Ronn (Risk Books, 2002).

Conclusion

Operational risk is still a fast developing field and the rate of development will continue as the Basel deadlines grow closer. Banks will be deciding on their individual responses to the Basel proposal and will begin to implement the operational risk framework that will deliver their objectives. As we have seen the challenges that currently face the operational risk manager are numerous and complex. However, as we address them we must remember that that the operational risk management function must, as a prerequisite, deliver value to the institution. Confusion in this most vital of areas will dramatically hinder the managers ability to make progress, a reality we have already seen. In fact, if the operational risk team fails in this, then, ultimately, it will not survive. So the need to add value should never be far from our minds.

On the positive side the benefits can be great. The operational risk team will help the institution understand the risks it runs, what drives these risks and how they can be managed. With that knowledge the firm can decide precisely how much risk it is willing to take and set its risk appetite accordingly.

Internally, the whole control environment can be shaped according to the actual levels of risks. Controls on high-risk areas can be strengthened while those in low risk areas can be reduced or abolished totally. The whole control infrastructure will be more focussed and, consequently, more effective and more efficient.

An operational risk framework should engender a more risk aware culture. Everyone will be aware of the risk that they are running at any time. They will have the information to make more informed decisions. As this data becomes more and

HOW TO INTRODUCE AN EFFECTIVE OPERATIONAL RISK MANAGEMENT FRAMEWORK

more standard so the culture of the firm will change. Risk management will become embedded in each decision making process with potentially dramatic effects.

Externally, operational risk management will deliver effective risk pricing. The price of a product will include an accurate estimation of the operational risk being run in delivering that product (at the moment it is no more than a guestimate). This will highlight where opportunities exist (a product that is priced by the market far above its risk price) or where the current price charged does not cover the risk price. Related to this is the affect that operational risk will have on strategic thinking. Decisions on where to invest/divest can be made on absolute understanding of risk (they are too risky, do not contain enough risk etc) and not just gut feel.

These are the types of benefits that can ensue if an effective operational risk framework is built. However, to do this the risk manger has to confront the issues discussed earlier. Senior management support must be harness, a cost effective manner of gathering data most be established, decisions must be made on loss databases, KRIs, risk assessment and capital and so on. These issues represent the foundations of the risk framework. If they are not resolved appropriately, then these foundations will be unstable and the whole risk management framework will be at risk. Address them and the benefits will become attainable, not guaranteed, but definitely attainable.

BIBLIOGRAPHY

Amram, M., and N. Kulatilaka, 1999, *Real Options – Managing Strategic Investment in an Uncertain World* (Harvard: Harvard Business School Press).

Basel Committee on Banking Supervision, 2001, *Consultative Document the New Basel Capital Accord*, January.

Basel Committee on Banking Supervision, 2001 *Quantitative Impact Study (QIS)* – April.

Basel Committee on Banking Supervision, 2001 *Quantitative Impact Study2 (QIS2)* May.

Kyriacou, M. N., and E. A. Medova, 2001a, "Operational Risk Measurement", in Dempster, M.A.H. -, *Risk Management Beyond Value at Risk* (Cambridge: Cambridge University Press), pp. 247–74.

Kyriacou, M. N., and E. A. Medova, 2001b, "Measuring Risks by Extreme Values", *Operational Risk Newsletter*, Aug/Sep, pp. 12–15 (Also published in *Risk*, Nov 2000)

Kennett, R, 2000, "Towards a Grand Unified Theory of Risk", Operational Risk (*Risk Professional*)

Risk Analysis, Identification & Modelling

6

Operational Risk Capital Allocation and Integration of Risks

Elena A. Medova

University of Cambridge

In September 1998, in a special address to the Credit Risk Modelling Conference held in London, W. McDonough, Basel Committee chairman and chief executive of the Federal Reserve Bank of New York, turned the attention of delegates to operational risk, reminding them of the events at Barings and Daiwa banks (McDonough, 1998). Ironically, at the very same time the biggest bail-out of our time was being discussed in New York – that of Long Term Capital Management (LTCM) – although this was known to only a handful of the conference participants. The consequences for global financial stability of LTCM's subsequent near failure raised the concern of regulators at the international level.

As a reaction to that and many other highly publicised events, all of which have involved "mismanagement" such as fraud, unauthorised trading or erroneous long-term views, the Basel Capital Accord specifically defines operational risk. For the first time banks will be required to reserve capital against risks other than credit and market. The Basel Committee proposes three approaches for the calculation of operational risk capital, but all three lack specifics and require the availability of appropriate – and increasingly detailed – data for the quantification of operational risks. All three approaches follow a simple actuarial methodology similar to the risk-based capital rules outlined in the 1988 Basel Capital Accord. Whether use of these rules will result in serious under- or overestimation of the losses caused by criminal activity or technological failure remains an open question.

But a still more serious question must be asked: does the proposed approach have flaws in its formulation and application that will limit current and all future innovation for credit and market risk management?

The new operational risk charge – regulatory response to major risk mismanagement

This section presents a brief review of the current Basel proposals along with some of the critical response. Probably the strongest criticism is that of the American Banking Association:

> *The inclusion of an operational risk capital charge ... is arbitrary, undeveloped and not capable of being implemented.* (BIS, 2001b)

The need for clarification of the new Basel proposals for the quantification of operational risk is obvious. The complexity of its originating causes, the "rare event" nature of significant losses and the desire to integrate capital provision for operational risk with that for market and credit risks all lead us to rules for capital

OPERATIONAL RISK CAPITAL ALLOCATION AND INTEGRATION OF RISKS

allocation based on results from extreme value theory (EVT).[1] The application of EVT to operational risk modelling is the principal objective of regulation:

A real concern of supervisors is the low-probability, high-severity event that can produce losses large enough to threaten a financial institution's health. (McDonough, 1998)

The theory of extreme events tells us that expected severity is a linearly increasing function of a specified threshold (see Equation 7). Therefore regulatory operational risk capital will have to be increased to higher and higher levels, and this is why extreme operational risk should be monitored but only *partially* covered by economic capital at the discretion of an institution. The lender of last resort can be considered to grant a form of put option on the uncovered extreme risk whose premium is, in effect, regulatory capital.

The fact is that no data now exist that would enable us to evaluate operational risk events similar to those experienced by Barings, Daiwa or LTCM. few, if any, and certainly not the named institutions, have consistently recorded the appropriate data and even if such internal data existed the comparability problem remains open. Furthermore, the possibility of pooling such data across institutions seems unrealistic for many years to come and would be statistically invalid without much further research. What is required by the new Basel proposals is equivalent to benchmarking such operational risks as "standard fraud" or "average technology breakdown".

In the method presented in this chapter the only data used for operational risk assessment are the *internal* data of a firm's trading and banking books. The presence of "extremes" will indicate that some operational risks exist since the "normal" markets assumption (ie, losses being not too far from their mean) is then violated. The question of the precise choice of appropriate level of capital allocation – whether economic or regulatory – is left for the industry and regulators to decide in the future. We attempt here only to provide an appropriate methodology.

Definitions of operational risk are based on the identification of causes whose consequences are often not measurable. The current definition of operational risk replaces earlier long lists of everything that could go wrong (British Bankers' Association, 1997) with the shorter classification summary:

The risk of loss resulting from inadequate or failed internal processes, people and systems or from external events.

Thus, at present, the earlier debate on the definition of operational risk has evolved into the current debate on the amount of regulatory capital required to cover it. However, lack of agreement on a definition of this risk (or its component types) may lead to irreconcilable differences between the results given by quantitative models.

PANEL 1

EVOLUTION OF THE CAPITAL CHARGE

The banking industry responded to the 1988 Basel Accord by investing in research and development of internal risk models for market and credit risks based on the value-at-risk (VAR) paradigm. The 1996 amendment (BIS, 1996) allowing the banks to use their own internal VAR models for market risk management and the current acceptance of elements of internal credit models is an admission that carefully specified VAR models can deliver a more accurate measure of risk. It has also led to practical reductions in the capital charges of leading institutions. In its new proposal (BIS, 2001a) the Basel Committee has responded by imposing a regulatory capital charge related to operational risk.

Overall, the operational risk charge will represent some fixed percentage of the minimum regulatory capital bank capital ratio (BIS, 2001d).[2] A bank's total capital ratio – the minimum figure for which is 8% – will be measured by (BIS, 2001a, point 63, p. 12):

$$\frac{\text{Total Capital}}{\text{Credit risk} + 12.5(\text{Market Risk} + \text{Operational Risk})}$$

Equivalently, total regulatory capital must be at least the sum of the assessment of 8% of credit risk, all of market risk and all of operational risk ie,

$$\text{Total capital} = 0.08 \times \text{Credit risk} + \text{Market risk} + \text{Operational risk}$$

Three options have been proposed for calculation of the operational risk charge options. In all three the amount of regulatory operational risk capital for an institution is proportional to some exposure indicator, EI, which is an accounting measure of bank activity.

Option 1 – The basic indicator approach
Gross income is proposed as an exposure indicator and is measured by a rolling three-year average. The charge, or operational risk capital, is equal to a fixed proportion, α, of the gross income ie,

$$\text{Charge} = \text{EI} \times \alpha.$$

Due to delay in publication of the third Quantitative Impact Study and possible changes to the operational risk charge, the calibration results for the value of α are not yet released at the time of this book's publication.

Option 2 – The standardised approach
A bank is divided into standard business lines. Regulators for each business line specify an exposure indicator to serve as a proxy for the area's activity (see Table 1). The charge for each business line equals a standard risk indicator or exposure indicator of the business line multiplied by an individual factor, β_i. The level of the factors β_i will be calculated to reflect the different weightings of business lines (from a given broad range of standard weightings) of business lines and the institution's EI values. With the standardised approach, then, the *charge equals the sum of the business line charges*.

The difficulties in calibrating β became apparent from the results of the second Quantitative Impact Study. The unresolved question remains whether we can really distinguish different β values across business lines (BIS, 2002).

Table 1. The standardised approach: division of an average bank into business lines

Business line	Exposure indicator
Corporate finance	Gross income
Trading and sales	Gross income
Retail banking	Annual average assets
Commercial banking	Annual average assets
Payment and settlement	Annual settlement throughput
Asset management	Total funds under management
Retail brokerage	Gross income

Option 3 – The internal measurement approach
This approach involves a more detailed view of operational losses in that it considers a number of operational risk types for each business line. The classification in Table 2 presents the current view of risk types, business lines and exposure indicators. For each business line/risk type, a bank provides an exposure indicator – which is a proxy

for the size of the risk exposure – an (expected) frequency of loss events given by the probability of a loss event, PE, and an (expected) severity of loss given by a loss given event, LGE, value. Expected loss, EL, by business line and loss type is a product of EI, PE and LGE:

$$EL = EI \times PE \times LGE \quad (1)$$

The charge by business line and loss type equals EL multiplied by an individual factor, γ, which will be determined by supervisors on the basis of industry-wide data. The industry-wide loss distribution and the regulatory specified gamma term are supposed to capture the differences in the risk profiles of individual banks.

Each option of the new proposal is viewed as a "progressive step" in the management of operational risk at "increasing levels of sophistication". Yet option 3 lacks any clarity in its formulation of the problem. In spite of a vague proposal (the γ factor) to calibrate the operational risk charge on the basis of expected and unexpected losses, the charge is proportional to *expected* loss.

Let us try to define an expected operational loss for option 3 and compare this definition with an expected credit loss. Assume long-term stationarity of the environment of an institution and – using discrete modelling for conceptual simplicity – define:

❑ *Losses* $l_k \in L$, $k = 1, \ldots, K$, occurring with probability $P(l_k)$; and
❑ *Risk-type events* $e_{ij} \in E$, business lines $i = 1, \ldots, n$, loss types $j = 1, \ldots, N$, occurring with probability $P(e_{ij})$ or PE.

Table 2. Business lines, loss types and exposure indicators

Business line	Event Type Category			
	Write-downs due to theft, fraud, unauthorized activity; loss of recourse; restitution; regulatory and compliance penalties; legal liabilities		Employment practices and workplace safety	Damage to physical assets
	EI – Financial statement-based	EI – Transactional value-based		
Corporate Finance	Gross income	Value of deals		
Trading & sales	Gross income	Value of trades		
Retail banking	Gross income/ total assets	Value of retail transactions		
Commercial banking	Gross income/ total assets	Value of com. bank. trans.	Total compensation OR Total number of employees	Book value of physical assets
Payment & settlement	Gross income	Value of trans. settled & payments made		
Agency services	Gross income/ assets under management	N/A		
Asset management	Gross income/ Funds under management	N/A		
Retail brokerage	Gross income	Value of transactions		

Then the expected loss is given by

$$E(L) = \sum_k P(l_k)l_k$$

$$= E(E(\mathbf{L} \mid \mathbf{e})) = \sum_{i,j} P(e_{ij} \mid E(\mathbf{L} \mid e_{ij}) = \sum_{ij}\sum_{k} l_k P(l_k \mid e_{ij})P(e_{ij}) \quad (2)$$

The loss given event, LGE, occurs with the conditional probability of the loss $\mathbf{L}$ being at level l given the realisation of event e. Such operational risk events belong to the set E and are indexed by the numbers of business lines and risk types. In previous work (Medova, 2000) I proposed the collection of data across business lines and risk types as in the cells of Table 3 below.

A fundamental concept of actuarial modelling is the distinction between unconditional and conditional event probabilities. Assuming that the unconditional probability of the (i, j)th event $P(e_{ij})$ is its expected frequency (empirical or subjective), the conditional probability of the event $P(e_{ij} \mid l_k)$ is its probability if we knew what the realised value, l_k, of the loss would be. The unconditional probability of the event e_i is the average value of its conditional probabilities across all realisations of losses possible from this event:

$$P(e_{ij}) = \sum_k P(e_{ij} \mid l_k)P(l_k)d$$

By Bayes' theorem the probability of the loss given event e_i is

$$P(l_k \mid e_{ij}) = \sum_k \frac{P(e_{ij} \mid l_k)P(l_k)}{\sum_{i,j} P(e_{ij} \mid l_k)P(l_k)}$$

where $P(l_k)$ is the unconditional probability of a loss of severity l_k from any source, and the expected loss given event e_{ij} is given by

$$E(\mathbf{L} \mid e_{ij}) = \sum_k l_k P(l_k \mid e_{ij}) \quad (3)$$

the inner sum of Equation 2. Thus the simplification of Equation 2 embodied in Equation 1 is to specify a *single* (representative) expected loss severity for each risk type and business line loss event occurring with the corresponding probability PE.

Given the lack of operational risk data, it is a non-trivial task to reconcile the calculation of total expected losses across all business lines and risk types for an individual bank. The final step – adjusting by individual factors γ and exposure factors EI to define total unexpected loss (indicating that the detailed considerations are *not* institution-specific) – is doubtful owing to the limited availability of operational risk data for the cells of Tables 2 and 3 and their current limited relevance across the industry.

The expression for the calculation of operational expected loss, EL, borrows notation from expected loss calculations in credit models (see, for example, Chapter 4 of Ong, 1999):

Expected loss = Exposure × Loss given default × Probability of default

For most purposes a credit loss arises only in the event of obligor default – hence "loss given default". But for default events the conditional probabilities are driven by systematic risk factors:

The conditional default probability is defined across all possible realizations of some systematic risk factors X which are identified with some specific observable quantities such as macroeconomic variables or industrial sector performance

Table 3. Firm-wide matrix of operational losses

Event Type Category 1, ..., N Business Line 1, ..., n	Technology failure 1	...	Fraud j	...	External event N	Total
1	L_1^1		L_1^j		L_1^N	$L_1^1, L_1^2, ..., L_1^N$
2	L_2^1		L_2^j		L_2^N	$L_2^1, L_2^2, ..., L_2^N$
...						
i	L_i^1		L_i^j		L_i^N	$L_i^1, L_i^2, ..., L_i^N$
...		...		...		...
n	L_n^1		L_n^j		L_n^N	$L_n^1, L_n^2, ..., L_n^N$
Firm-wide	$L_1^1, L_1^2, ..., L_1^N$	...	$L_1^j, L_2^j, ..., L_1^N$	...	$L_1^N, L_2^N, ..., L_n^N$	$L_1^1, L_1^2, ..., L_1^N$

indicators, or may be left abstract. Regardless of their identity, it is assumed that all correlation in credit events is due to common sensitivity to these factors. (Gordy, 2001)

Do systematic risk factors driving operational risks exist and, if so, what is an "industry-wide loss distribution"? Perhaps an even more important question is: how does an operational risk charge (based on such factors or not) relate to market and credit risk management? If any of the options proposed by Basel are used, the unfortunate answer is that with gross income – or any other size-related exposure indicator – a potential increase in gross income through successful market and credit risk management will be *penalised* by the operational risk charge.

The industry's dissatisfaction with the proposed operational risk capital allocation may be summarised by the following extract from the British Bankers' Association's (1997) comments:

Using proxies for the size of operational risk is an admission that measurement of operational risk does not lend itself to the approaches which have been developed for market and credit risk. Indeed, the proxy proposed is simpler than the use of risk weighted assets in the current credit regime or the use of the market value of positions in the standard market risk evaluations.

Overwhelming criticism of the New Accord proposals has been heard from the financial services industry and, hopefully, other options for the evaluation of operational risk will be considered. We propose some alternatives here.

Integrated risk capital framework

The industry hue and cry surrounding the operational risk charge is matched by the confused state of operational risk modelling. Everything from scorecards to fuzzy logic, Bayesian networks, neural networks and extreme value theory, or a hybrid of these, has been proposed for application to operational risk management. The new Basel proposal (BIS, 2001a) has mainly been influenced by actuarial models – probably because Basel's definition of operational risk is based on lists of loss events. But since it is not clear where the boundary between operational risk and market and credit risks lies and what, indeed, a meaningful industry-wide operational loss distribution might be, it is difficult to compare or evaluate most of the proposed methods.

Effective operational risk management for an individual bank or business unit in a given situation requires correct identification of the risk factors responsible for operational losses. Since both internal *and* external causal factors are included in the definition, not only may the bank's own operations give rise to operational risk but so may any financial information received from external sources. Some out-of-the-ordinary events cause significant losses. Examples of these include natural disasters and major social or political events. Statistical analysis of data that include such rare events requires special techniques that lie outside the assumption of normality. We term the related risk factors *external*. Then, processing incoming information and taking decisions at different levels of the bank may lead to further losses caused by *internal* factors, and these are reflected in increased business costs (ie, operations risks). Causes of these may be human or technological error, lack of control to prevent unauthorised or inappropriate transactions, fraud or faulty reporting. The relation between those two classes of causal factors – internal and external – and their importance for a particular business unit should be reflected in any strategic view of the risks involved.

Statistical patterns of loss data attributed to these external and internal types of causal factors can be very different. For example:

❏ mistakes in accounting, transaction errors and other human errors generate loss distributions that are usually normal;
❏ natural disasters give distributions with fat or long tails;
❏ fraudulent activity, which can be observed in trading data subject to market risk, also leads to heavy tails in the trading profit and loss (P&L) distribution;
❏ similar P&L distributions are seen when trading futures or government bonds in emerging markets through times of political crisis.

In general, losses may be classified into two categories: those which are low in value but occur frequently; and those of significant size but rare in occurrence. Modelling each category requires specific techniques, but more important from the viewpoint of data collection is to identify losses that have already been accounted for by the existing risk management process.

With the view that control procedures can be developed to reduce the frequent, low-value losses and that the cost of such control procedures will be accounted for in the operations budget, we assume here that only the rare losses of large magnitude are considered for operational risk capital provision. The aim of operational risk capital is to ensure that a bank can continue to operate (because it has sufficient economic capital) in an adverse environment or when its internal operations have caused large unexpected losses.

Operational risk may be hidden in a number of different accounts for balance sheet reporting, both in banking and trading books. To ensure an appropriate control environment, the first step in operational risk management should be a careful analysis of all available data to identify the statistical patterns of losses related to identifiable risk factors.

The model

The inclusion of operational risk in the regulatory framework requires a revision of accepted market and credit risk management practice. Standard VAR provides a measure of the market risk due to adverse market movements under *normal* market conditions, with back-testing performed to assess the accuracy of the implemented VAR models over time (usually a year). Similarly, credit provision corresponds to normal credit conditions with an indicative worst-case portfolio credit loss at some confidence level, calculated over a (one-year) time horizon.

Thus, one might naturally ask how the definition of "normality" relates to operational risk and to the problem of internal bank controls and external supervision. These questions are critical – particularly in the case of extreme losses, since market, credit and operational risks become entangled when losses are very

OPERATIONAL RISK CAPITAL ALLOCATION AND INTEGRATION OF RISKS

large. Double counting is potentially the most serious problem for all major business units involved in trading, investment and lending. Reporting integrated market and credit value-at-risk can rectify such a problem. But how can operational risk capital charges be differentiated from market and credit allocation while keeping an integrated view of risk management?

Recall a simple definition of operational risk that has been adopted in practice:

All risks that are not market or credit risk are operational risks. (Jameson, 1998)

This definition of operational risk as complementary to market and credit risk allows us to derive a capital charge for operational risk from internal operational risk measurement. To make it consistent with existing credit and market risk models, one can use as a starting point the construction of an historical profit and loss distribution for the level of the organisation of interest (Panel 2). Profit data must be included in the analysis, as they position the actual P&L distribution by defining its mean and median. The presence of large or extreme losses in the period of data collection will indicate that something has gone (and may again go) wrong.

PANEL 2

ESTABLISHING THE NORMAL

Ideally, statistical analysis of profits and losses would form part of a bank's routine financial surveillance system. Further identification of the causes of specific losses may call for some additional qualitative analysis. The important point is that this surveillance is concerned with the identification of the "normality" of business processes.

The quantification of operational risk starts with the identification of market and credit unexpected loss thresholds obtained from VAR models. We assume that credit VAR and market VAR are known from internal risk models as a part of financial reporting. From the modelling viewpoint the reporting process must verify the assumptions of the internal market and credit models. Losses within the limits of market and credit value-at-risk can be accommodated by market and credit economic capital. The reasons for those losses may be further assessed through supervision and control.

As noted earlier, only losses of larger magnitude need be considered for operational risk capital provision. Hence, we here adopt the accepted practice of defining operational risk as everything which is not market or credit risk and *assume operational losses to be those which are larger than losses due to market or credit risks under normal market conditions.*

All forms of risk are reflected in financial reports, with market risk concentrating in the trading book and credit risk in the banking books. Current practice is for each business unit to have its own specialised risk management. Nevertheless, all business units are exposed to operational risk. Pillar 2 of the supervisory review process

> *is intended to ensure that each bank has a sound internal process in place to assess the adequacy of its capital based on a thorough evaluation of its risks.* (BIS, 2001a)

Thus, at the strategic level capital allocation for market, credit and operational risks must be assessed for an institution at least once a year. Risk management reporting is already available in the form of market or credit VARs and the corresponding profit and loss distributions supporting these calculations. Therefore, at the conceptual level, an integrated profit and loss distribution at the highest level of the organisation may be constructed with a threshold loss level obtained from market and credit risk models.[3]

❑ The level of loss due to market risk, which is exceeded with probability π is denoted by u_{VAR}.
❑ The level of loss due to both credit and market risks, which is exceeded with probability $\rho \leq \pi$ is denoted u_{CVAR}. It is assumed that $u_{CVAR} \leq u_{VAR}$.
❑ Losses beyond the u_{CVAR} level are unexpected losses and are defined as belonging to the operational risk category. Thus, operational risks are defined as excesses over normal market *and* credit unexpected losses in the P&L distribution, as shown in Figure 1.

Measures of operational risk capital may be now derived from descriptive statistics of the empirical profit and loss distribution or from the parameters of an appropriate approximating distribution. Relations between the thresholds for market and credit risk should be re-examined with respect to the overall implementation of risk management procedures and the definitions of "expected" and "unexpected" losses. For the purpose of operational risk management, the unexpected loss threshold, u, should also be consistent with statistical assumptions required for the asymptotic behaviour of extremes. From the viewpoint of *integrated* risk management, the choice of such a threshold should be such that the u_{CVAR} level approximately equals the statistically derived threshold u.

Our capital allocation for operational risks is, thus, based on results from extreme value theory. The operational risk capital will be derived from the parameters of an asymptotic distribution of extremes of profit and loss. Required theoretical results and procedures for parameter estimation are given in Medova (2000) and Medova and Kyriacou (2001).

In the case of extreme losses (ie, heavy- or long-tailed underlying P&L distributions) the modelling involves a few levels of approximation. First, one must verify that the underlying P&L distribution belongs to the class of the "max-stable" distributions – ie, the behaviour of the tail of this distribution may be explained by that of its maximum term. The generalised extreme value (GEV) distribution $H_{\xi;\mu,\sigma}$

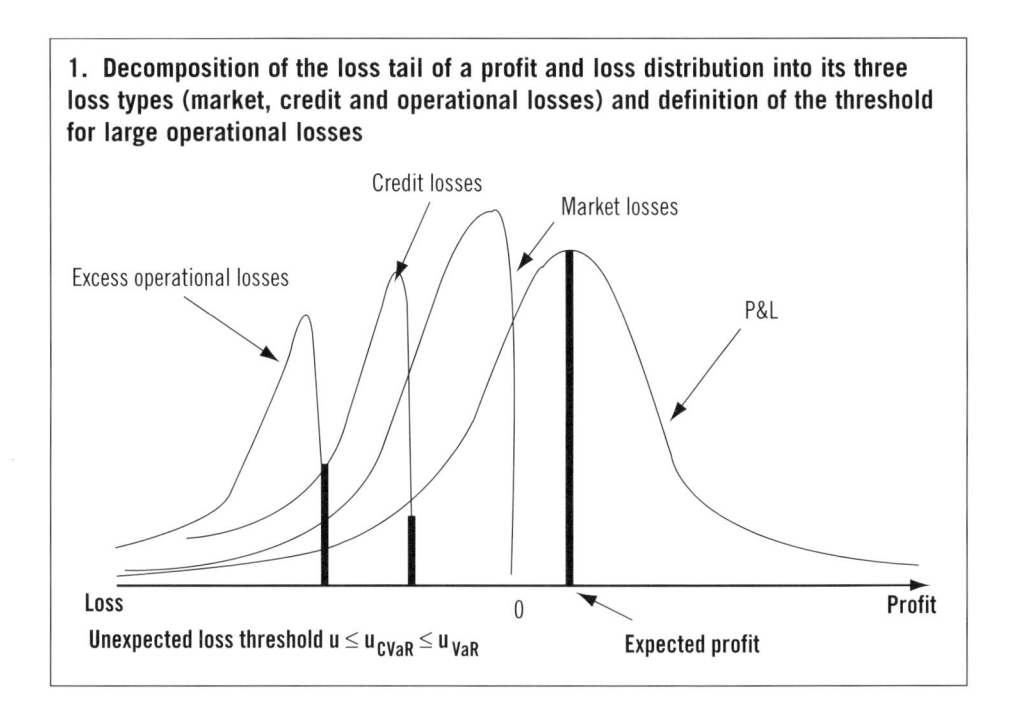

1. Decomposition of the loss tail of a profit and loss distribution into its three loss types (market, credit and operational losses) and definition of the threshold for large operational losses

provides a representation for the limiting distribution of the maximum with shape parameter ξ and normalised by the location parameter μ and the scale parameter σ. More formally, let $X_1, \ldots, X_n$ represent independent identically distributed (iid) random variables (losses, here considered as positive) with distribution function F and denote their maximum by $M_n = \max(X_1, X_2, \ldots, X_n)$. Then

$$H_{\xi;\mu,\sigma}(x) = \begin{cases} \exp\left[-\left(1 + \xi\frac{x-\mu}{\sigma}\right)^{-1/\xi}\right] & \text{if } \xi \neq 0,\ 1 + \xi\frac{x-\mu}{\sigma} > 0 \\ \exp\left[-\exp\left(-\frac{x-\mu}{\sigma}\right)\right] & \text{if } \xi = 0 \end{cases} \quad (4)$$

Second, given a high threshold level u, the distribution of excesses $Y := X - u$ is given by the *conditional distribution* function in terms of the tail of the underlying distribution F as

$$F_u(y) = P(\mathbf{X} - u \leq y \mid \mathbf{X} > u) = \frac{F(u+y) - F(u)}{1 - F(u)} \text{ for } 0 \leq y < \infty. \quad (5)$$

The limiting distribution, $G_{\xi,\beta}(y)$, of excesses as $u \to \infty$ is known as the *generalised Pareto distribution* (GPD) with *shape parameter* ξ and scale parameter $\beta = \sigma + \xi(u - \mu)$:

$$G_{\xi,\beta}(y) = \begin{cases} 1 - \left(1 + \xi\frac{y}{\beta}\right)^{-1/\xi} & \xi \neq 0 \\ 1 - \exp\left(-\frac{y}{\beta}\right) & \xi = 0 \end{cases} \text{ where } y \in \begin{cases} [0, \infty] & \xi \geq 0 \\ \left[0, -\frac{\beta}{\xi}\right] & \xi < 0 \end{cases} \quad (6)$$

The GPD is an approximation of F_u, ie, $\lim_{u \to x_F} \sup_{0 \leq y \leq y_F} |F_u(y) - G_{\xi,\beta(u)}(y)| = 0$, where x_F

(possibly infinite) is the right end-point of the support of the distribution given by F and $y_F := x_F - u$ for some positive (measurable) function of the threshold u given by $\beta(u)$, provided that the distribution F is in the max-domain of attraction of the GEV distribution. This approximation is only "good" in the asymptotic sense (ie, as the threshold $u \to \infty$). Thus the choice of threshold must satisfy the asymptotic convergence conditions, ie, be large enough for a valid approximation; but when u is too high classical parameter estimators for ξ and β_u may have too high a variance due to the small number of exceedances of such a threshold. In the literature (Embrechts, Klüppelberg and Mikosch, 1997; Smith, 1987 and 1990) various techniques have been proposed for a statistically reliable choice of threshold.

Third, we must model operational losses over time. The number of exceedances, N_u, over a threshold u and the exceedance times may be represented as a point process that converges weakly to a limiting Poisson process with intensity λ_u.[4] The resulting asymptotic model is known as the peaks over threshold (POT) model (Leadbetter, Lindgren and Rootzen, 1983; Smith, 1985) with intensity λ_u. This intensity must be measured in the same time units as the frequency (collection interval) of the underlying profit and loss data.

The threshold value u that is chosen according to the three steps described above is defined as the *unexpected loss threshold*. In Medova (2000) and Medova and Kyriacou (2001) we proposed operational risk measures and a rule for calculating an excess operational risk charge. These are summarised below.

❏ *Severity* of the losses is modelled by the GPD. The expectation of the excess loss distribution, ie, *expected severity*, is our coherent risk measure given by

$$E(\mathbf{X} - u \mid \mathbf{X} > u) = \frac{\beta_u + \xi u}{1 - \xi} \text{ with } \beta := \sigma + \xi(u - \mu) \quad (7)$$

OPERATIONAL RISK CAPITAL ALLOCATION AND INTEGRATION OF RISKS

- The number of exceedances, N_u, over the unexpected loss threshold u and the corresponding exceedance times are modelled by a Poisson point process with intensity (frequency per unit time) given by

$$\lambda_u := (1 + \xi \frac{(u-\mu)^{-1/\xi}}{\sigma}) \qquad (8)$$

- Extra capital provision for operational risk over the *unexpected loss threshold* u is estimated as the *expectation of the excess loss* distribution (expected severity) scaled by the *intensity*, λ_u, of the Poisson process:

$$\lambda_u E(X - u \mid X > u) = \lambda_u \frac{\beta_u + \xi u}{1 - \xi} \qquad (9)$$

where u, β, ξ and λ are the parameters of the POT model and time is measured in the same units as the frequency of data collection (hours, days, weeks, etc). Note that β_u and λ_u may be expressed in terms of μ and σ.

- The *total* amount of *capital* provided against extreme operational risks for a time period of length T is then calculated by

$$u_T + \lambda_u T E(X - u \mid X > u) = u_T + \lambda_u T \frac{\beta + \xi u}{1 - \xi} \qquad (10)$$

where u_T represents the total capital provision for market and credit risk, which may in the first instance be considered to be equal to u under the assumption of max-stability.

For operational risk the accuracy of economic capital allocation in Equation 10 depends, of course, on both the correct choice of threshold and accurate estimates of the GPD parameters (see Panel 3).

Integration of risk management

Success in operational risk management is dependent on the ability to handle an increasing amount of information processing related to the control and management of an institution's performance. For a large international bank involved in all types of activities the task of capital provision planning is enormous.

Various risk-adjusted performance measures have been proposed for the optimisation of capital allocation within the firm (see Punjabi, 1998, for a specification of different risk-adjusted performance measures and the regulatory capital framework's return incentives). Derived from capital asset pricing theory, the risk-adjusted return calculation is a single time period optimisation applied to the combined credit, market and operational risks of a business unit and implicitly dictates a credit risk time horizon which is much longer than that of market risk. The choice of optimisation period and the reconciliation of the time horizons in the models related to different risk types are challenging topics for research (see Panel 4).

Traditional accounting and regulatory reporting processes require banks to submit their reports to the banking supervisors once every year. The aggregation of threshold levels – and specifically adjusting with respect to a common time horizon – requires considerable co-operation between the various specialised risk management groups.

The time-dependent evolution of credit risk involves multi-year horizons. An initial one-year transition matrix used in calculations of the migration of credit ratings is usually derived from rating agency data from longer-term transition matrices, which impose the assumption of a steady state for the credit portfolio distribution.

Comparison of our threshold derived from EVT analysis with the credit VAR threshold will need the results of an internal credit model and a detailed description of the credit portfolio. Over what period such assumptions are valid and what is an

> ## PANEL 3
>
> ### OVERCOMING THE CONFLICTING REQUIREMENTS OF THRESHOLD CHOICE AND PARAMETER ESTIMATION
>
> Accurate estimation of the GPD parameters requires a sufficient amount of data. On the another hand, to obtain a valid GPD approximation the threshold must be sufficiently high – and, unfortunately, higher thresholds result in fewer data. However, hierarchical Bayesian simulation methods (Bernardo and Smith, 1994; Smith, 1998) for parameter estimation allow one to overcome the problems associated with lack of data through intensive computation.
>
> Computational procedures that take into account the dependencies of extreme events across business lines/risk types are described in Medova and Kyriacou (2001). Operational loss data are organised into a matrix according to loss type and business units, as in Table 3. In the current implementation the parameters for individual business units are estimated from business unit data pooled by risk type. The example in Medova and Kyriacou (2001) analyses the (external) operational risks caused by the Russian default of 1998 for four business units of a trading group. Alternatively, the procedure could be applied to one business unit across different loss types. Conceptually, both loss factor and business unit dimensions can be accommodated simultaneously but at the cost of increased complexity and computation.
>
> For overall capital allocation at the top level of the bank, we would hope with our methods both to reduce the overall assessed capital allocation due to portfolio diversification effects and to identify the high-risk factors for specific business units of the firm. These two aims are achieved in the limited context of the example of the Russian default (Medova and Kyriacou, 2001).

> ## PANEL 4
>
> ### TOTAL CAPITAL CHARGE RECONCILIATION
>
> Unlike credit risk, market risk management is performed daily, and the evaluation of market risk at longer time horizons becomes increasingly dependent on the assumptions made about the form of the underlying profit and loss distribution. A regulatory multiplier used in connection with internal market risk models guarantees that there are no violations of internal VAR limits.
>
> The introduction of an operational risk charge means that this market risk multiplier has to be modified. Our operational risk capital charge is proportional to the intensity of the process of exceedances of the combined market and credit risk VAR level. In the Russian default example considered by Medova and Kyriacou (2001), the 5% threshold level gives a satisfactory allocation (a 46.9% margin of safety compared with actual losses) that changes only slowly (a 2% improvement) with a nearly twofold increase (1.6) in threshold level.

appropriate procedure to identify such a time interval are questions that remain to be answered.

Conclusion
By allowing banks to use their own internal models for their trading book and with the current move towards a model-driven internal ratings-based approach for the

banking book, regulators are starting to use economic capital in lieu of regulatory capital.

Yet the operational risk regulatory charge was motivated by the worst recent financial failures and is insensitive to the quality of an institution's risk management. Should operational risk be modelled without a clearly stated relation between risks of different types?

Models for market – and to a lesser extent for credit – risk are accepted and tested. Their outputs determine capital provisions for market and credit risks. The risk capital framework proposed here allows quantification of operational risk losses based on an integrated view of risks and a high-level control chart philosophy in which extreme losses that exceed a fixed unexpected level are used annually (say) to estimate the required excess capital provision. Such a combined allocation of economic capital for market, credit and operational risks reinforces a risk-sensitive management that corresponds to the firm's mix of business, performance and level of capitalisation.

1 *For the basic theory and an extensive list of references, see Embrechts, Klüppelberg and Mikosch (1997). For a current overview of EVT applications in finance see Embrechts (2000).*
2 *The charge for operational risk is not agreed and may change from the initial 20% to 12% (see the regulatory update in* Operational Risk, *April 2003 and BIS, 2002).*
3 *Adjustment of market VAR value to include credit VAR or reconciliation of profit and loss from the relevant operations to obtain a consolidated VAR is a separate problem which depends on implementation issues that are institution-specific.*
4 *Convergence to a Poisson process requires more assumptions; see Chapter 5 of Embrechts, Klüppelberg and Mikosch (1997) for details.*

BIBLIOGRAPHY

Bank for International Settlements (BIS), 2001a, "The New Basel Capital Accord", Press Release, January.

Bank for International Settlements (BIS), 2001b, "The New Basel Capital Accord: Comments Received on the Second Consultative Package", Press Release, June.

Bank for International Settlements (BIS), 2001c, "Update on the New Basel Capital Accord", Press Release, July.

Bank for International Settlements (BIS), 2001d, "Working Paper on the Regulatory Treatment of Operational Risk", September.

Bank for International Settlements (BIS), 2002, "The Quantitative Impact Study for Operational Risk: Overview of Individual Loss Data and Lessons Learned", January.

Basel Committee on Banking Supervision (BIS), 1988, "International Convergence of Capital Measurement and Capital Standards", July.

Bernardo, J. M., and A. F. M. Smith, 1994, *Bayesian Theory* (Chichester: Wiley).

British Bankers' Association (BBA), 1997, *Operational Risk Management Survey*.

Embrechts P., C. Klüppelberg and T. Mikosch, 1997, *Modelling Extremal Events* (Berlin: Springer).

Embrechts, P. (ed.), 2000, *Extremes and Integrated Risk Management* (London: Risk Books).

Gordy, M., 2001, "A Risk-factor Model Foundation for Rating-based Bank Capital Rules", Working Paper, Federal Reserve Bank, Washington, DC.

Jameson, R., 1998, 'Playing the Same Game', *Risk*, 11, 10, pp. 38–45.

Leadbetter, M. R., G. Lindgren and H. Rootzen, 1983, *Extremes and Related Properties of Random Sequences and Processes* (Berlin: Springer).

McDonough, W., 1998, "Issues for the Basel Accord", in *Conference on Credit Risk Modeling and Regulatory Implications*, London, September 22.

Medova, E. A., 2000, "Measuring Risk by Extreme Values", *Risk*, November, pp. 20–6.

Medova, E. A., and M. N. Kyriacou, 2001, "Extremes in Operational Risk Measurement", in M. A. H. Dempster (ed.), *Risk Management: Value at Risk and Beyond* (Cambridge: University of Cambridge Press), pp. 247–74.

Ong, M. K., 1999, *Internal Credit Risk Models: Capital Allocation and Performance Measurement* (London: Risk Books).

Punjabi, S., 1998, "Many Happy Returns", *Risk*, June, pp. 71–6.

Regulatory update, 2003, "Op risk charge up for grabs again?", *OperationalRisk*, Risk Waters Group, April, p.2.

Smith, R. L., 1985, "Threshold Methods for Sample Extremes", in J. Tiago de Oliveira (ed.), *Statistical Extremes and Applications*, NATO ASI Series, pp. 623–38.

Smith, R. L., 1987, "Estimating Tails of Probability Distributions", *Annals of Statistics* 15, pp. 1174–207.

Smith, R. L., 1990, "Extreme Value Theory", in W. Ledermann (chief ed.), *Handbook of Applicable Mathematics Supplement* (Chichester: Wiley), pp. 437–72.

Smith, R. L., 1998, "Bayesian and Frequentist Approaches to Parametric Predictive Inference", in J. M. Bernardo et al. (eds), *Bayesian Statistics* Volume 6 (Oxford: Oxford University Press), pp. 589–612.

7

Developing an Operational VAR Model using EVT

Marcelo Cruz

RiskMaths

The awareness of the importance of operational risk has increased exponentially in the last few years. Even though, the definition of operational risk still varies from bank to bank. The current official definition given by the Bank for International Settlement is "the risk of loss resulting from inadequate or failed internal processes, people and systems or from external events". Today risk managers believe that about 30% of the risk a financial institution runs is due to operational losses. Despite that, very little has been done in terms of quantitative measurement of this risk.

Cruz *et al* (1998) was the first article on the subject. In that chapter, a set of statistical techniques was used to estimate the severity of operational losses and even the suggestion of an operational value-at-risk (VAR) was given. Cruz (1999) developed an operational risk derivative and demonstrated a pricing structure. Cruz (2000) designed a risk-scoring scheme based on a multivariate technique called discriminant analysis to evaluate operational risk. Cruz and Carroll (2000) also developed a fuzzy logic system to evaluate operational risk. The objective of this chapter is to provide a general guideline with an example of how the operational VAR can be derived and estimated.

The basics of operational VAR

The VAR models, whose development began in the financial industry in the early 1990s, are currently considered the standard measure for market risk and are intensively used in risk management. VAR measures the maximum estimated losses in the market value of a given portfolio that can be expected to be incurred until the position can be neutralised. In other words, in market risk, VAR calculates an eventual extreme loss resulting from holding the portfolio for a determined period, using as risk measure the volatility of the assets prices over the last n days. More precisely, extreme loss is the $100(1 - \alpha)\%$ quantile – x_p of the distribution. As a consequence, VAR estimates x_p for sufficiently low values of α.

In this chapter, I will show that a similar approach based on the same foundations of market risk management can be applied to operational risk developing an "operational VAR". This is done by using extreme value theory (EVT) applied to operational events in a financial institution and also by estimating the frequency of these events.

There are two fundamental differences between market and operational VAR models. The first one is related to the fact that the application of EVT allows us to relax the Gaussian hypothesis, on which market VAR models are based. Putting it another way, the stochastic processes underlying operational losses are by no means explained by a normal distribution, as one would expect in market risk (although this

DEVELOPING AN OPERATIONAL VAR MODEL USING EVT

assumption is questioned many times even for market risk). The second difference is that market VAR models are not concerned with the "frequency of events" as it is fairly assumed that assets prices follow a continuous stochastic process, ie, there is always a price quote available for an asset while the markets are open. Operational losses follow discrete stochastic processes, which means that they can be counted in a specific period, ie, a certain operational event happens n times per day in a certain period, which makes no sense in market risk measurement.

EVT has the mathematical capability for predicting the chances of events that have never happened. It does so by extrapolating the stochastic behaviour of past events. This is very useful for measuring operational risk in which the experience with very large losses is limited or non-existent as they are very hard to predict, even though there may always be a small possibility that they would occur.

Nevertheless, in order to estimate the operational VAR we will need more than just estimating the severity of operational losses. There is also a need to understand their periodicity. The aggregated distribution of severity and frequency of operational losses will give us a single-figure estimate of the future operational losses for a determined period in a similar way of market or credit VAR models.

In terms of this chapter organisation, I start by briefly discussing the basics of extreme value theory and then demonstrating a suggested method for operational loss database modelling. An example is provided in the following section and an application of Poisson distribution to estimate the frequency follows. I finish by estimating the operational VAR for a particular business unit.

Extreme value theory

A typical operational losses database would present a distribution that is not Gaussian. In general, an operational risk database is composed of a few very large events and several smaller ones. Nevertheless, for some businesses, eg, an investment bank back office, for example, due to the huge number of transactions processed daily, eventually a quasi-normal pattern of losses is feasible to appear. For risk management purposes, we are interested in knowing the behaviour of the tail of this curve (or the largest losses). The question for the risk manager is: how much economic capital should be allocated to a particular business to protect against an eventual operational catastrophe? The answer comes by analysing the distribution of losses that arise from extreme value distributions.

The application of EVT, as the theory that supports this type of distribution is known, is still at an embryonic stage in risk management. A good starting point is a book with applications to finance, which was edited by Embrechts (2000).

Suppose that X can denote the operational losses on the database provided by the bank. Let $X_1, X_2, ..., X_n$ be the monetary losses observed in a certain period. Extremes are defined as maxima and minima of the n ordered random variables $X_1, X_2, ..., X_n$. Let $X_{1,n}, ..., X_{n,n}$ be the order statistics of this series, with $X_{1,n}$ denoting the highest value (the maximum) observed during the period; $X_{2,n}$, the second largest, and so on. To find a non-degenerate limiting distribution, the maximum random variable $Y = X_{1,n}$ is standardised by location, scale and shape parameters, chosen to give a proper distribution of standardised extremes. We therefore focus on the asymptotic behaviour of the extremes.

Three important extreme value distributions are those defined by Frechet, Gumbel and Weibull. A convenient representation of these is given in the generalised extreme value (GEV) distribution. This three parameter distribution $F_{\mu,\xi,\psi}$ arises as the limit distribution of normalised maxima of iid (independent, identically distributed) random variables. It can be represented by (in the three parameter form): for the random variable $Y = X_{1,n}$, we let

$$Z = (Y - \mu)/\psi \text{ and } z = (y - \mu)/\psi \qquad (1)$$

where μ and ψ are location and scale parameters respectively, then

$$P(Y \leq y) = F_{\mu,\xi,\psi}(y) = F_{0,\xi,1}(z) = \exp\{-(1 + \xi z^{-1/\xi})\}, 1 + \xi z \geq 0 \quad (2)$$

where ξ is the shape parameter. Letting $\xi \to 0$ gives the Gumbel distribution; $\xi > 0$ the Frechet distribution, and $\xi < 0$ the Weibull distribution.

$F_{\mu,\xi,\psi}$ arises as the limit distribution of normalised maxima of iid random variables. Standard statistical methodology from parametric estimation theory is available if the data consist of a sample

$$X_1, X_2, \ldots, X_n \text{ iid from } F_{\mu,\xi,\psi} \quad (3)$$

The proposition (3) above assumes that X_i have an exact extreme value distribution F, which maybe is not the most realistic assumption. If a more justifiable supposition, that the X_i is approximately $F_{\mu,\xi,\psi}$ distributed is assumed, we could interpret X_i as belonging to a maximum domain of attraction (MDA). X_i would belong to a suitable domain depending on the sign of ξ, the shape parameter.

Broadly speaking, GEV amounts to full parametric assumptions, whereas MDA is essentially semi-parametric in nature, having a parametric component ξ and a non-parametric component (a slowly varying function). Because of this difference, MDA is considered a better inference for heavy-tailed distributions as opposed to inference for the GEV. For a more detailed discussion, please refer to Embrechts *et al* (1997). The estimation under MDA of GEV is of relevance for the heavy-tailed OR databases leaving us with the job of estimating and testing just one parameter, the tail index.

Another very important distribution for measuring extremes is the generalised Pareto distribution (GPD). The three-parameter df $G_{\mu,\xi,\psi}(y)$ can be defined by:

$$G_{\mu,\xi,\psi}(y) = \begin{cases} 1 - e^{-z} & \text{if } \xi = 0 \\ 1 - (1 + \xi z)^{-1/\xi} & \text{if } x \neq 0 \end{cases} \quad (4)$$

where $z \leq 0$ if $\xi \geq 0$
$0 \leq z \leq -1/\xi$ if $\xi < 0$

The GPD was introduced by Pickands (1975) and was studied by Davison (1983), Hosking and Wallis (1987) among others. It is often used in the modelling of large insurance claims and in reliability studies. The noticeable feature of the Pareto distribution is that the scale parameter is a function of a certain threshold to be determined by the analyst.

To simplify, there are basically two options when applying EVT. The first one based on the point process methods, in which we choose a threshold and work with the events above this threshold. This approach is called POT (peaks over threshold) and in general, it is compatible with GPD. The second approach considers the largest event in a certain time and, in general, will fit GEV. Figure 1 below depicts the difference between them.

For risk management purposes, perhaps the second approach might be easier to sell to the business unit managers. By choosing the largest events over a pre-determined period (and eventually discarding events that took place years ago in a different management and/or environment) it might make it easier to justify the capital figure estimated to the business units.

Modelling an operational losses database
The first challenge of the analyst is to develop an operational risk database. Such modelling has to include the losses that will affect the bank's result from an operational perspective. Table 1 provides some suggestions of loss types.

DEVELOPING AN OPERATIONAL VAR MODEL USING EVT

1. EVT: point process and block maxima

Point Process: Events are selected Based on a threshold and ignoring time

Block maxima: Events are picked Considering the largest in a certain Specified period

In general will fit a GPD and the POT (Peaks Over Threshold) method

In general will fit GEV

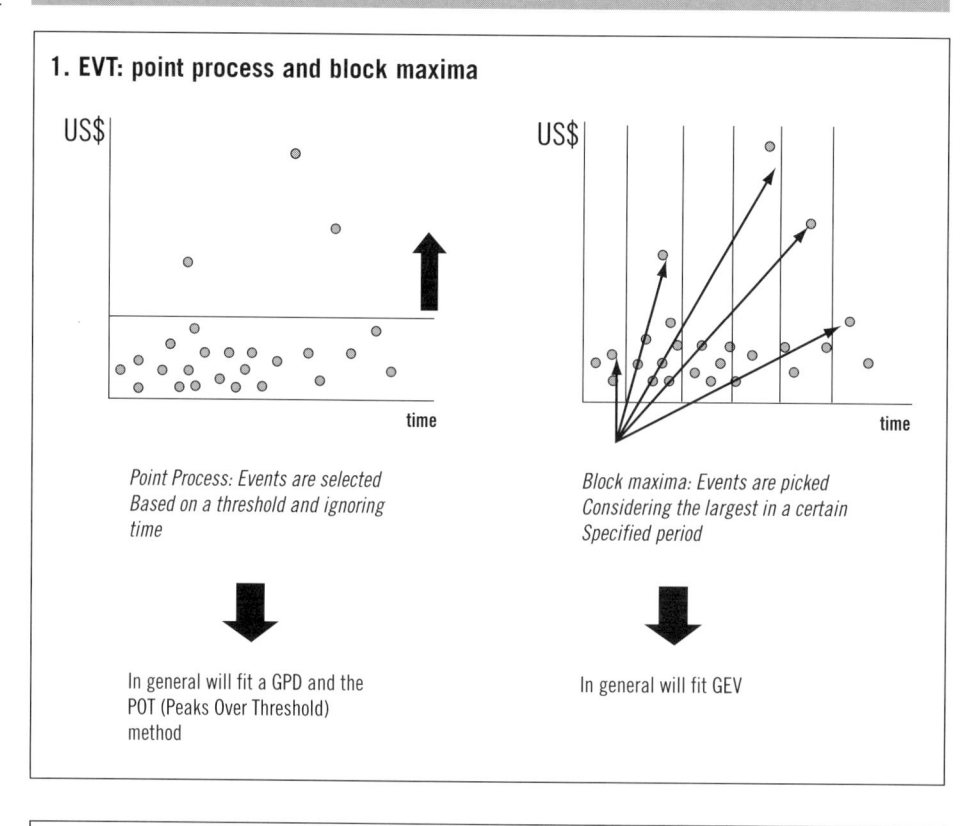

Table 1. Suggested list of operational risk loss types

Loss type	Cause	Consequence (Financial impact)
Legal and liability	Judgment, settlements, external legal and other related costs in response to an operational risk event	Lost legal suit
Regulatory, compliance and taxation penalties	Fines or the direct cost of an other penalties, such as license revocations associated costs – excludes lost/forgone revenues	Penalties paid to the regulator
Loss or damage to assets	Reduction in the value of the firm's non-financial asset and property due to some kind of accident	Neglect, accident, fire, earthquake
Restitution	Payments to third parties of principal and/or interest, or the cost of any other form of compensation paid to clients and/or third parties	Interest Claims Note: Excludes legal damages which are addressed under legal and liability costs
Loss of recourse	Inability to enforce a legal claim on a third party for the recovery of assets due to an operational error	Payments made to incorrect parties and not recovered. Includes losses arising from incomplete registration of collateral and inability to enforce position using *ultra vires*
Write downs	Direct reduction in value of financial assets as a result of operational events	Fraud, misrepresented market and/or credit risks

It is important to emphasise that all loss types above are related to direct impacts in the results, ie, there was a monetary impact caused by these events. I avoid using abstract definitions of operational risk such as "human (or people) risk", "system risk" etc. These are subjective or indirect classifications of operational risk and, as such, make it difficult to model a loss database due to the need for arbitrary judgment that it is sometimes required. This is also time consuming and, in many cases, difficult or impossible to complete. Instead, by classifying the operational losses into categories that represent direct monetary, quantitative losses like "legal" or "loss of recourse", our task is made simpler.

Applying EVT techniques to an operational risk database

An application at this point, will help to clarify the concepts discussed above. I provide operational loss data in Table 2 in which we will be testing those concepts. The database refers to legal losses and it is represented by 39 events above US$500.

Table 2. Operational loss database

Operational loss data

1,372,513.09	50,529.47	35,778.97	20,316.38	17,373.52	11,938.22	5,447.41
264,444.24	48,967.00	29,885.15	18,995.36	17,358.62	11,901.87	3,265.99
233,378.31	46,900.45	27,697.06	18,671.75	16,919.05	11,195.92	553.66
159,662.66	43,043.83	23,309.66	18,460.19	14,735.85	9,529.86	
118,229.12	42,313.46	23,294.31	17,690.14	14,524.10	8,808.65	
91,852.83	38,502.77	21,276.85	17,595.19	13,641.50	7,247.95	

To begin, it would be useful to understand how the general distribution-fitting process works. First, we need to choose a number of possible distributions (heavy-tailed or not). Then we estimate the parameters and fit the respective distributions, testing how they behave against the real data. At this stage, we choose the one that best fits the data using analytical or graphical tests. In EVT, graphical tests will be the most used as formal tests tend to overfit (ie, be too lenient). Figure 3 shows the general approach to fitting distributions.

Following the methodology above, I chose a few distributions to test the data against. Just for illustrative purposes, I picked the normal, exponential, lognormal and GEV. The parameters of the first three distributions are as in Table 3 below.[1]

The data does not exhibit Gaussian behaviour. This can be seen by the third and

Table 3. Parameters of the normal, lognormal and exponential distributions

Distribution	Parameters
Normal	$\mu = 75{,}583.34$ $\sigma = 220{,}901.88$
Lognormal	$\mu = 10.12$ $\sigma = 1.30$
Exponential	$\lambda = 1.32\text{E-}05$

fourth moments of the distribution (skewness and kurtosis) of 5.62 and 33.39. We might discard immediately the normal distribution. Operational loss databases will hardly fit a normal distribution anyway.

The parameter estimation for the GEV is a little more complicated than the distributions above. I will estimate separately the shape parameter (ξ) and the scale (ψ) and location (μ) ones.

A popular estimator of ξ was proposed by Hill (1975). This estimator is calculated by:

$$\hat{\gamma}_{k,n}^{(H)} = \left(\frac{1}{k}\sum_{i=1}^{k}\ln X_{j,n} - \ln X_{k,n}\right)^{-1} \tag{5}$$

Therefore, the estimated shape parameter becomes

$$\hat{\xi}_{k,n}^{(H)} = \gamma_{k,n}^{(H)^{-1}}$$

2. General approach to fit statistical distributions

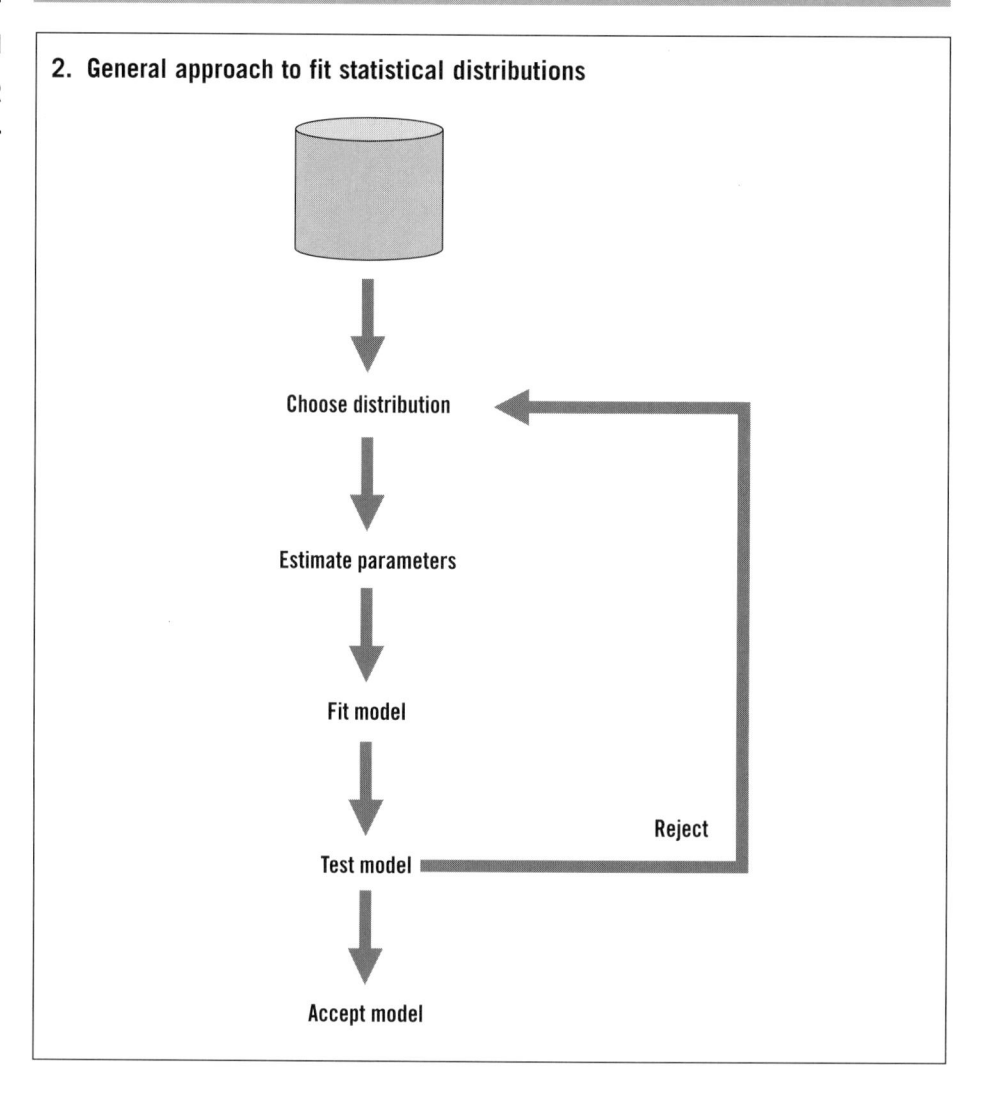

Choose distribution → Estimate parameters → Fit model → Test model → Accept model (with Reject loop back to Choose distribution)

I used the database above to plot the shape parameter using different thresholds. The result can be seen in Figure 3.

In order to choose an individual value for the shape parameter, we should avoid the higher thresholds and wait until the shape curve become more stable, thus the value of 1.1571 is suitable as the curve tended to stabilise around this value.

For estimating the scale and location parameters of GEV, the probability weighted moments (PWM) method was chosen as it has proved to be more reliable than maximum likelihood methods (for a discussion on the subject, see Cruz 2001). PWM

3. Hill (shape parameter) plot

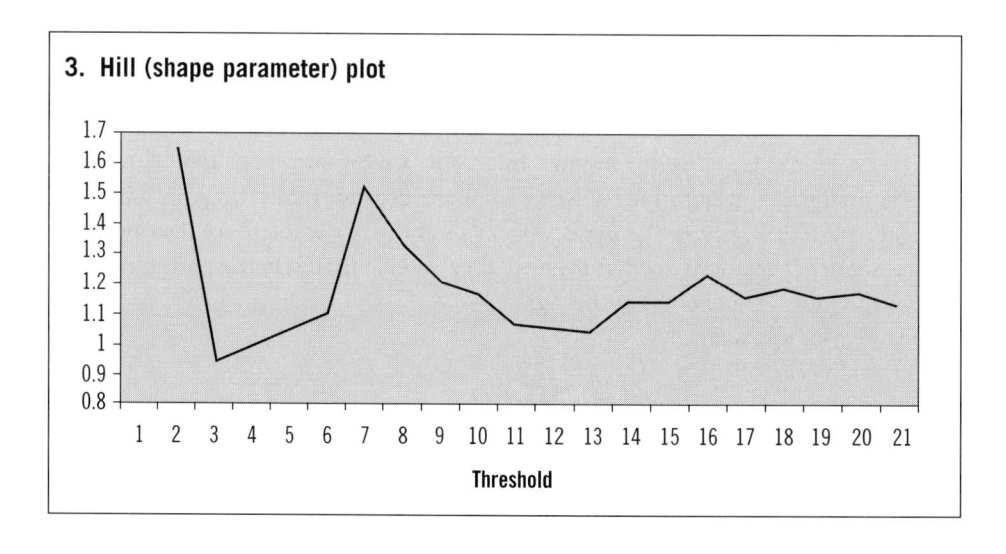

(plot of shape parameter vs Threshold from 1 to 21, y-axis 0.8 to 1.7)

consists of matching moments based on the GEV distribution ($F_{\mu,\xi,\psi}$) to the corresponding empirical moments based on the data. In order to estimate[2] μ, ξ and ψ, we must consider the rth moment m_r and its estimator $\hat{m}_r$:

$$m_r(\mu, \psi, \xi) = \hat{m}_r(\mu, \psi, \xi), r = 0, 1, 2 \quad (6)$$

We solve these three equations in these unknowns for $\hat{\xi}, \hat{\psi}, \hat{m}$. We can obtain in a straightforward way,

$$\hat{m}_r(\mu, \psi, \xi) = \frac{1}{n} \sum_{j=1}^{n} X_{j,n} P_{j,n}^r, r = 0, 1, 2 \quad (7)$$

where P is a plotting position (a distribution-free estimate of $F(X_i)$ for the sample that may be taken as $p_{j,n} = \frac{n - j + 0.5}{n}$, for example). When $r = 1$, m_r would be the sample mean. To calculate for $r = 2$ and $r = 3$ we should plot the positions using the plotting formula provided above. For the GEV, Hosking *et al* (1985) derived:

$$m_r = \frac{1}{r + 1} \left[\mu + \frac{\psi}{\xi} \left\{ 1 - \frac{\Gamma(1 + \xi)}{(1 + r)^\xi} \right\} \right], \xi > -1, \xi \neq 0 \quad (8)$$

Since the exact solution for ξ, from Equation (8), requires iterative methods, the following estimators were suggested by Hosking *et al* (1985):

$$\hat{\mu} = \frac{(2\hat{m}_2 - \hat{m}_1)\hat{\xi}}{\Gamma(1 + \hat{\xi})(1 - 2^{-\hat{\xi}})} \quad (9)$$

$$\hat{\xi} = \hat{m}_1 + \frac{\hat{\mu}}{\hat{\xi}}(1 - \hat{\xi}) \quad (10)$$

$$\hat{\xi} = 7.8590c + 2.9554c^2 \quad (11)$$

$$\text{where } c = \frac{2\hat{m}_2 - \hat{m}_1}{3\hat{m}_3 - \hat{m}_1} - \frac{\log 2}{\log 3} \quad (12)$$

Using the PWM method to estimate the scale and location parameters and the Hill method to estimate the shape, the estimate for the GEV parameters are

$$\mu = 223,681.27$$
$$\psi = 139,692.38$$
$$\xi = 1.1571$$

Having the parameters estimated, now we are ready to proceed to the next step, in which we choose the best fit for the data. We can test the exponential, the lognormal and GEV, to find which one better explains the loss behaviour.

A graphical technique that can be used to verify the goodness of fit of a model is the so-called QQ-Plot. This technique might be useful to give hints in several statistical analyses and here we use it to compare distributions. The plot will look roughly linear if the data were generated from a sample of the reference distribution. The heaviness of the tail of the distribution can also be checked in the plot. If the tail is heavy, the plot will curve up at the right.

The QQ-plot formula is:

$$\{(X_{k,n}, F(p_{k,n})) : k = 1, \ldots, n\} \quad (13)$$

where $p_{k,n}$ is a plotting position formula that can be represented again by

$$p_{j,n} = \frac{n - j + 0.5}{n} \quad (14)$$

I performed the QQ-Plot for the three remaining distributions. The result can be seen in Figure 4 below. It can be noticed that the best fit is the GEV where no huge discrepancies to the straight line happen and even the largest event is well covered. The lognormal does not fit so well and the largest event is not covered, whereas the exponential is just a very bad fit.

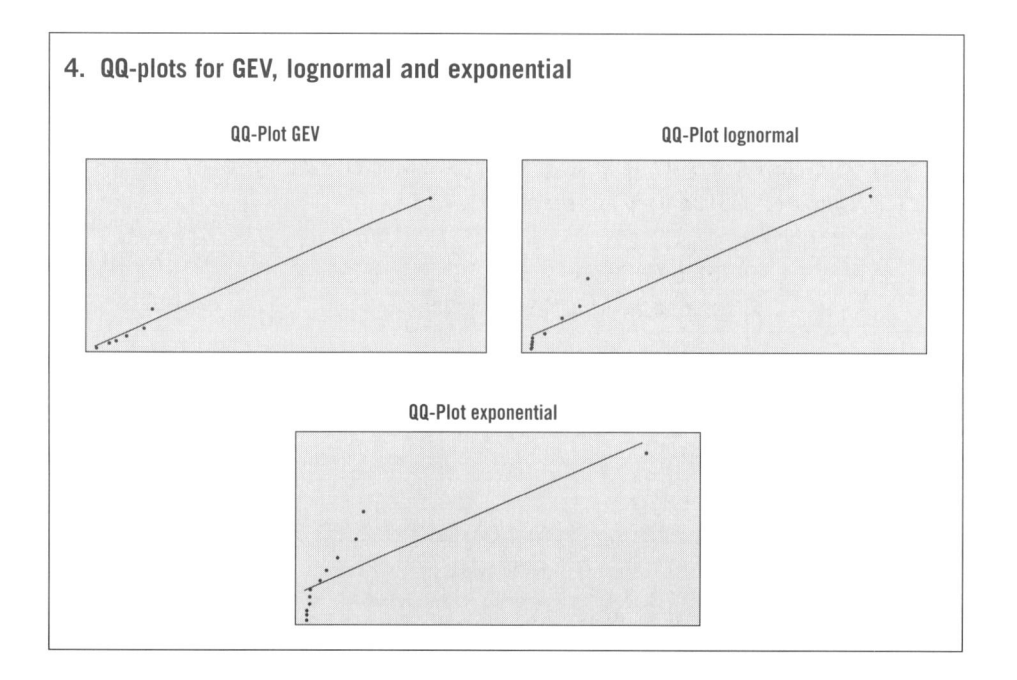

4. QQ-plots for GEV, lognormal and exponential

In practice, we would probably save processing time by not even considering distributions such as the normal for cases like that. Nevertheless, we would also like to test a higher number of suitable choices of statistical distributions, as several statistical packages offer this possibility. In the present case, I will pick the GEV for the severity distribution, as it is a very good fit indeed.

Frequency models
The same process of choosing the best fit distribution should also ideally be used for frequency. Quite a few distributions are eligible for the task, namely the negative binomial, geometric, binomial etc. Nevertheless, for simplicity, I will just work with the Poisson distribution in this chapter. The Poisson distribution (and process) is named after the French mathematician and physicist Simeon Denis Poisson and is certainly one of the most popular in operational risk frequency estimation due to its simplicity and that it fits most databases very well. As truncation of databases is frequently needed (as we are possibly working with EVT from the severity side, we may need to work with different thresholds), the Poisson distribution proves to be an interesting and simple choice as if the Poisson fits the entire database well; Poisson would also fit well a database with a different parameter. This distribution has also the interesting property of Poisson (a) + Poisson (b) = Poisson (a + b).

The Poisson distribution has probability function

$$p_k = \frac{e^{-\lambda}\lambda^k}{k!}, \quad k = 0, 1, 2, \ldots \quad (15)$$

The cumulative distribution function can be calculated by the following step function

$$F(x) = e^{-\lambda t} \sum_{i=0}^{[x]} \frac{(\lambda t)^i}{i!} \qquad (16)$$

The probability generation function is

$$P(x) = e^{\lambda(z-1)}, \lambda > 0 \qquad (17)$$

The parameter is estimated by

$$\hat{\lambda} = \frac{\sum_{k=0}^{\infty} k n_k}{\sum_{k=0}^{\infty} n_k} \qquad (18)$$

Applying to the entire losses database and to a few selected thresholds, the Poisson monthly estimated frequencies are seen in Table 4.

Table 4. Poisson parameters in different thresholds (monthly frequency)

Range	λ
Entire database	5.41
> US$500	3.25
> US$18,000	1.75
> US$38,000	1.0
> US$50,000	0.58

CALCULATING THE OPERATIONAL VAR

Having calculated separately both severity and frequency processes, we need to combine both into one aggregated loss distribution that would allow us to predict a figure for the operational losses with several degrees of confidence.

The aggregate losses at time t given by $X(t) = \sum_{i=1}^{N(t)} U_i$ has the distribution function

$$F_{X(t)}(x) = P(X(t) \leq x) = P\left(\sum_{i=1}^{N(t)} U_i \leq x\right) \qquad (19)$$

The derivation of an explicit formula for $F_{(x)t}(x)$ is, in most cases, impossible. It is usually assumed that the processes $\{N(t)\}$ and $\{U_n\}$ are stochastically independent. Deriving (19) above, we will encounter the following fundamental relation:

$$F_{X(t)}(x) = P(X(t) \leq x) = P\left(\sum_{k=0}^{\infty} p_k(t) F_U^{*k}(x)\right) \qquad (20)$$

where F_U^{*k} refers to the kth convolution of F_U with itself, ie, $F_U^{*k}(x) = P(U_1 + ... + U_k \leq x)$, the distribution function of the sum of k independent random variables with the same distribution as U. As I mentioned before, the formula above can hardly be solved analytically. We must rely on approximations, expansions, recursions or numerical algorithms.

If the frequency of operational events is very large, we must imagine that the central limit effect will be dominant. A large-scale approximation like

$$F_{X(t)}(t) \approx \Phi\left(\frac{x - EX(t)}{\sqrt{VarX(t)}}\right) \qquad (21)$$

where $\phi(x)$ denoted the standard normal distribution, might be feasible. Nevertheless, these large-scale approximations have often proven to be unreliable by actuarial researchers. Practitioners have tried to avoid this shortcoming by applying refined versions of the central limit theory. Examples are applications of Edgeworth expansions and Gram-Charlier series but they resulted in not always satisfying improvements.

However, thanks to the increasing power processing capacity of personal computers, the aggregation of severity and frequency can be undertaken satisfactorily through simulation. Nevertheless, even considering the power and speed of modern PCs, depending on the size of the simulation (given not just by the number of runs – usually 10,000 or 100,000 times – but also on the parameters of the frequency distribution), an aggregation might take hours to finish. This is not the case in our example, where the simulation performed using a VBA code took no more than a few seconds to finish.[3] More details on the processing of this aggregation can be found in Cruz (2001).

In the present example, I discarded the losses below a certain level, which can be deemed as "expected losses" and, therefore, not included in the risk calculation process and worked with losses above US$18,000. I used GEV for the severity process and Poisson for the frequency process. The results can be seen in Table 5.

Table 5. Aggregate loss distribution – extreme quantiles

Quantile	US$
99%	42,062,977.35
97.5%	23,956,764.73
95%	6,339,904.65
90%	2,998,299.88

The results in Table 5, for the extreme quantiles, seem very conservative. Indeed, the worst month had US$1,701,432.18 aggregated loss. We must be very careful when dealing with EVT, as high quantiles may well be too conservative. Nevertheless, the 90% quantile seems to work very well and can then be used as the "working quantile". This is an important consequence of not working with Gaussian distributions. In these distributions, we can always establish a certain degree of confidence as 95% or 99% as we know that the behaviour of such distributions is somehow "tamed" as their tail is not heavy. In EVT this is slightly more complicated. High quantiles for irregularly spaced ordered loss events (ie, with high shape parameters) will generally be very conservative. Put in a practical way, EVT tries to state in a robust statistical way that US$42 million of operational losses would be the worst scenario one would expect to lose in a terrible month in terms of operational losses to happen in the next 100 months based on the pattern of losses occurred so far. The aggregation with the frequency process is basically a way to perform a structured scenario analysis.

The validation of the results of the aggregate loss distribution should be made by checking against the real occurrences. This is called backtesting and it is commonly used in market VAR models. Further details of these statistical tests can be found in Cruz (2001).

Conclusion

In this chapter, I tried to prove with an example that VAR models might also measure operational risk if a few adaptations to the characteristics of its stochastic processes are made. The inclusion of EVT in the analytical framework might help to perform the analysis. Nevertheless, these models need to be validated as much as the market VAR models using backtesting statistical analysis.

1 *A reference on how to estimate the above parameters can be seen in Cruz (2001).*
2 *Instead of recalculating, we might use the shape parameter used by the Hill approach shown before.*
3 *VBA stands for Visual Basic Application – It is a Microsoft product that allows one to customise functions in MS-applications like Excel*

BIBLIOGRAPHY

Cruz, M., and J. Carroll, 2000, "Application of Fuzzy Logic to Operational Risk", *Risk* 13(11), pp. S16–S19.

Cruz, M., 2000, "Operational Risk Control Indicators and Discriminant Analysis", *Operational Risk Newsletter*, 1(1).

Cruz, M., 1999, "Taking Risk to Market", *Risk*, Operational Risk Supplement, November, pp.21–4.

Cruz, M., R. Coleman and G. Salkin, 1998, "Modeling and Measuring Operational Risk", Journal of Risk (1), pp.52–63

Cruz, M., 2001, Mathematical Models to Model and Measure Operational Risk. John Wiley & Sons. London, UK

Davison, A., 1983, "Modeling Excesses Over High Thresholds", in Tiago de Oliveira (ed.), *Statistical Extremes and Applications* (Vimeiro: NATO ASI Series).

Embrechts, P., 2000, Extremes and Integrated Risk Management. RISK Publications. London, UK

Hosking, J.R.M. and Wallis, J., 1987, "Parameter and Quantile Estimation for the Generalized Pareto Distribution", *Technometrics* 29, pp.339–49

Pickands, J., 1975, "Statistical Inference Using Extreme Order Statistics", *The Annals of Statistics* 3, pp. 119–31

8

The Use of Reliability Theory in Measuring Operational Risk

Patrick Mc Connell

Henley Management College

The Basel Committee defines operational risk as "the risk of loss resulting from inadequate or failed internal processes, people and systems or from external events". The committee estimates that such risks are not insignificant, accounting for an average of 12% of the Minimum Regulatory Capital (MRC) set aside by banks (Basel 2001a).[1] As part of the New Capital Accord the committee is proposing, for the first time, that banks set aside capital to cover losses arising from operational failures.

However, as the committee has learned in various surveys of market practices, measurement of operational risk is not yet well established in the industry, so the committee has developed approaches to capital charges that are based on gross measures of business activity (Basel, 2002a). To promote good practice the committee has stated that, as with other major risks, "increasing levels of sophistication of risk management and the precision of risk methodology should generally be rewarded with a reduction in the regulatory risk capital requirement" and that the "degree of formality and sophistication of the bank's operational risk management framework should be commensurate with the bank's risk profile".

In reaction to the extensive criticisms made by the banking industry in response to the initial proposals (mainly with regard to the new credit risk proposals), the committee has decided to delay implementation of the New Capital Accord until year-end 2006, to provide more time for banks to develop the necessary systems and processes (Basel, 2002a).

The aim in this chapter is to contribute to the debate on the methods used to measure operational risk by proposing models that have been developed in other disciplines. In particular, the chapter aims to propose methods for measuring the risks that arise during the initial phases of new business ventures. Most models of operational risk assume some degree of stability in the occurrence of operational risks, eg, the assumption of a Poisson process (Cruz, 2002). While this assumption may well be a useful approximation after operational processes stabilise, it is unlikely to hold during the development of new processes. Both the Basel committee and the Financial Services Authority, in their consultative document (CP142) warn of the problems encountered by banks during times of significant change, such as mergers, corporate restructuring, the implementation of new systems and changes in regulation (FSA, 2002).

THE USE OF RELIABILITY THEORY IN MEASURING OPERATIONAL RISK

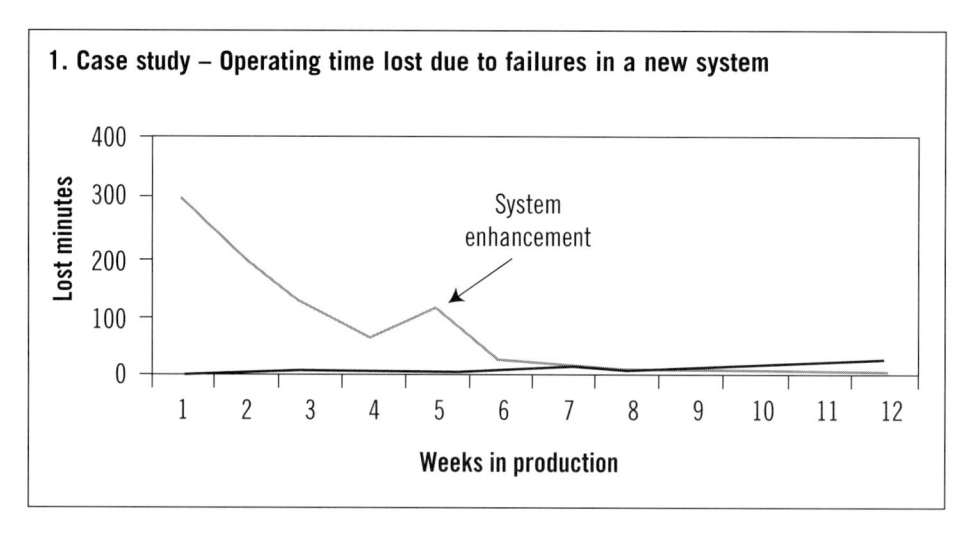

1. Case study – Operating time lost due to failures in a new system

[Figure: Line graph showing Lost minutes (y-axis, 0 to 400) versus Weeks in production (x-axis, 1 to 12). The curve starts near 300 at week 1, declines to about 60 at week 4, rises to about 120 at week 5 (labelled "System enhancement" with arrow), then drops sharply to near 0 by week 6 and remains low through week 12.]

Some examples of operational risk

In May 2001 Egg, the internet banking subsidiary of Prudential in the UK, announced that it had shut down its on-line bulletin board as a result of the large number of complaints about the performance of their systems. This cyber version of "shoot the messenger" did not address the underlying operational problems that had severely affected its customers over the previous months, but at least it reduced the bad publicity arising from their well-publicised IT problems. Egg is not alone in experiencing problems with new technology. The Basel committee has warned, "large-sale acquisitions, mergers de-mergers and consolidations test the viability of new or newly integrated systems" (Basel, 2003a).

Figure 1 shows the "time lost due to systems failures" suffered by a medium-sized regional bank during the first weeks of the implementation of a new retail banking system in 1999. Needless to say, the bank concerned would not wish these figures to be published, so its identity must remain confidential. The failures here relate to the non-availability of the bank's core banking system, which meant that customers could not withdraw money from the bank's automated teller machines (ATMs) and merchants could not accept their debit cards. It should be noted that the implementation of this major new system was not undertaken lightly by the bank's management and had been planned for well over 18 months prior to implementation of the new system.

This real-life example has some interesting characteristics:

❑ the time lost is high to begin with, then tapers off quickly to a steady state (except for a blip when a new version of the system was installed);
❑ if one assumes that the system settles down to its "normal" rate of failure (about six minutes per week), then the total lost time in the first six weeks is well over that experienced during *two years* of normal operations; and
❑ although, unfortunately, no information is available about when the problems occurred, it is reasonable to assume that long periods of unavailability would overlap with periods of heavy use – ie, more customers would be inconvenienced by more failures.

Despite the lack of precise information, it is safe to assume that the operational risk was much higher during the first six weeks than in the 100 weeks that followed. For reasons illustrated by this example, banks do not replace their core systems often and hence do not tend to estimate in advance the financial losses that could be incurred by a major failure. The Basel Committee warns specifically, "operational risk can be more pronounced where banks engage in new activities or develop new products (particularly where these activities or products are not consistent with the bank's core business strategies)". In future, under the New Capital Accord for operational risk, such losses will have to be considered when planning and implementing new systems and new products.

Nor are such situations unique. In an analysis of operational risk events, Tomski (2001) reports several instances of problems experienced with new systems since 1998:

- NatWest Bank: problems with a new computer system caused severe disruption, with 400 branches and 300 ATMs having to be closed down at one point.
- Chase and Citibank: abandonment of the Mondex pilot in New York following poor uptake.
- Bank 24: the securities accounts of 55,000 customers in Germany were overdrawn when an oversight occurred in the conversion to Euro.
- Barclays Stockbrokers: abandoned implementation of a new settlements system.
- UBS: loss of Sfr120 million incurred as a result of pricing errors in its structured equity derivatives book.[2]

Of course, problems occur during the start-up of any new venture – people are learning on the job and communication between key staff often breaks down. Risk is

---

PANEL 1

OPERATIONAL RESEARCH AND RISK

Modern risk management has lent heavily on the discipline of operational research for its theoretical and practical underpinnings.

For example, the Nobel laureate Harry Markowitz employed quadratic programming in the development of modern portfolio theory, which itself provides the basis for many other theories in modern finance (Markowitz, 1991). Binomial methods for pricing derivatives employ the techniques of dynamic programming (Hull, 1989), and Monte Carlo simulation, which is widely used in operational research, is also employed in many risk management applications (Jorion, 1997).[1]

Hiller and Lieberman (1990) have defined operations research as the practical management of organisations, which proceeds by:

observing and formulating a problem and then constructing a scientific (typically mathematical) model that attempts to abstract the essence of the problem. It is then hypothesised that this model is a sufficiently precise representation of the essential features of the situation, so that any conclusions (solutions) obtained from the model are also valid for the real problem. This hypothesis is then modified and verified by suitable experimentation.

This definition could apply equally well to the discipline of risk management, with its similar emphasis on practical outcomes, mathematical modelling and scientific methods.

Given the successful synergy of the two disciplines in the past, where better to look for models that might help in the measurement of operational risk than in the tool-box provided by operational research?

[1] It is interesting to note that Dr Markowitz, in the many years between developing modern portfolio theory and receiving overdue recognition for it, worked as an operational researcher on Monte Carlo simulation.

THE USE OF RELIABILITY THEORY IN MEASURING OPERATIONAL RISK

the constant companion of innovation; hence the high valuations put on successful new ventures.

The introduction of a new product or operational process in a large modern bank involves many staff in different departments. For example, the development of a new mortgage product would call for:

- *intellectual* effort in designing and marketing the new customer processes, involving marketing, product, legal, compliance and other specialists;
- *management* effort in creating an organisation to develop and market the new product profitably;
- *clerical* effort to manage the receipt and payment of funds (and to pursue delinquencies); and
- *IT* effort to develop and operate the information systems at each stage of the process, involving IT programming and operations specialists.

Each of the activities inherent in any new operational process can give rise to operational risk. For example, products may be marketed incorrectly; management may not develop an appropriate support organisation; mistakes may be made in processing documentation; and – unfortunately all too often – information systems may fail. Given the number of people and disciplines involved, it is little wonder that most new ventures have teething problems.

This chapter argues that the initial "learning" period required for any new product or process gives rise to a greater degree of operational risk than arises during the rest of its life. Any measurement scheme must take into account the overall operational context, in particular new processes, in which losses have occurred. Before the implications of these observations for the Basel proposals are discussed, models for the measurement of operational risk are proposed in the next section.

Measuring operational risk

Unlike market and credit risks, there are no commonly agreed measures of operational risk, which may be due to the difficulty of defining a suitable "unit" of risk and the "events" that give rise to "losses".[3] With credit risk, for example, it is relatively easy to define the unit of risk as it is the company/customer that could default on a credit and the event is the default itself.[4] Likewise, for market risk the unit of the risk is the asset (bond, equity, currency, etc) whose adverse market price movement may cause a loss. The major complexity in measuring these two risks is in estimating the potential losses in a "portfolio" of risks given that risks in the portfolio may be correlated.

However, for operational risk the unit of risk (here an "operational process") will vary not only across but also within banks.[5] Likewise the impact of a failure is difficult to evaluate as some failures are more severe than others. For example, the loss of a data centre through fire could disrupt operations for weeks, whereas a misdirected payment can be found and corrected in days.

To measure operational risk there are four factors to be considered:

1. *process*, the unit of risk to be modelled;
2. *failure*, the event that may cause losses to occur;
3. *probability*, of a failure event occurring, or PE (Probability of Event) as defined in Basel (2001a); and
4. *loss*, the size of loss that may occur "given the failure event" or LGE (Loss Given Event); Basel (2001a).

The problem is finding models that will accurately reflect the impact of failures in reality.

Reliability theory

Reliability theory is used in operational research (see Panel 1) to measure the impact of failures of components in complex mechanical and electronic systems. Research and experience have found that the likelihood of a component failure at a particular time (the instantaneous failure or "hazard" rate) follows what is called a "bathtub" shape, as shown in the example in Figure 2.

This bathtub shape has three distinct periods or phases:

1. *Learning*: (also called *burn-in* or *infant mortality*) during which failures occur relatively frequently due to inexperience or quality problems;
2. *Maturity*: (also called *useful life*) during which failures occur infrequently and randomly; and
3. *Wear out*: during which failures occur because components are reaching the end of their useful lives.

Although reliability theory is normally used to measure the performance of mechanical components, there are parallels with the occurrence of failures/errors in operational processes. In new ventures, failures occur frequently during the initial start-up, due to factors such as incomplete knowledge, inexperienced staff and the manifestation of unforeseen problems. As staff climb the learning curve, processes settle down and errors drop off, though they may still occur at a low level. After a time processes gradually diverge from industry best practice and, unless constantly renewed, become out of date and the frequency of failures begins to creep up.

RELIABILITY FUNCTION

The curve in Figure 2 can be described by the reliability function (Dhillon and Singh, 1981)

$$h(t) = k\lambda c t^{c-1} + (1 - k) b t^{b-1} \beta e^{\beta t^b} \qquad (1)$$

where $b, c, \beta, \lambda > 0$, $0 \leq k \leq 1$ and $h(t)$ is hazard rate or the likely number of failures in time $t + \Delta t$. The shape of the curve is influenced by the parameters: c and λ, which determine the shape and scale (or size) of the learning period; b and β, which determine the shape and scale of the wear-out period; and k, which determines the length of the maturity phase.

Note that Equation 1 assumes that the "time to failure" distribution is exponential, which has been shown to be reasonable in most failure situations (Hines and Montgomery, 1980). Dhillon and Singh (1981) and Kececioglu (1991), however, point out that other distributions, such as the Weibull, have also been observed in certain failure situations.[6] For a "system" with a large number of individual components, such as may exist in a complex operational process,

2. Example: reliability function – bathtub curve

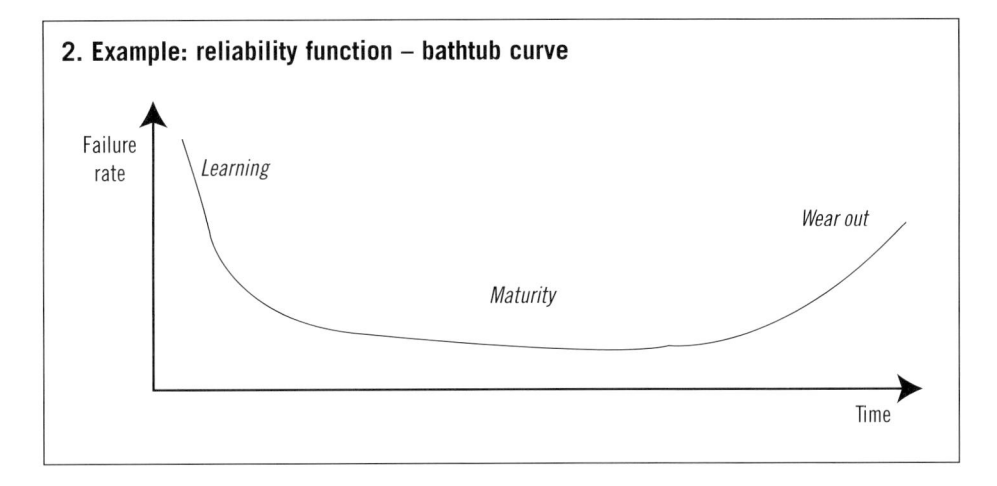

THE USE OF RELIABILITY THEORY IN MEASURING OPERATIONAL RISK

PANEL 2

COMPONENT RELIABILITY UNDER STRESS

The diagram in this panel shows examples of how excessive "stress" can dramatically change the shape of the reliability curve (Kececioglu, 1991). In operational terms, stress occurs whenever the design parameters of a new process are exceeded early in its life, causing problems to occur more frequently and shorten its useful life. This could happen for a variety of reasons, such as:

❏ greater than expected uptake of a new product or process (the "problem of success"), resulting in staff and/or system overload;
❏ uptake is different to that expected, requiring rapid and, hence, risky changes to be made to unstable processes and systems;
❏ lower than expected uptake of a new product or process, often resulting in a reduction in the number of knowledgeable staff to maintain profitability; and
❏ in too many cases, new information systems are just badly designed or full of errors.

For components that are under extreme stress, such as those used in rockets, different forms of the reliability function than that represented in Equation (1) may be more appropriate (Kececioglu, 1991). Under "normal" conditions, however, the bathtub formula is a good approximation of observed behaviour.

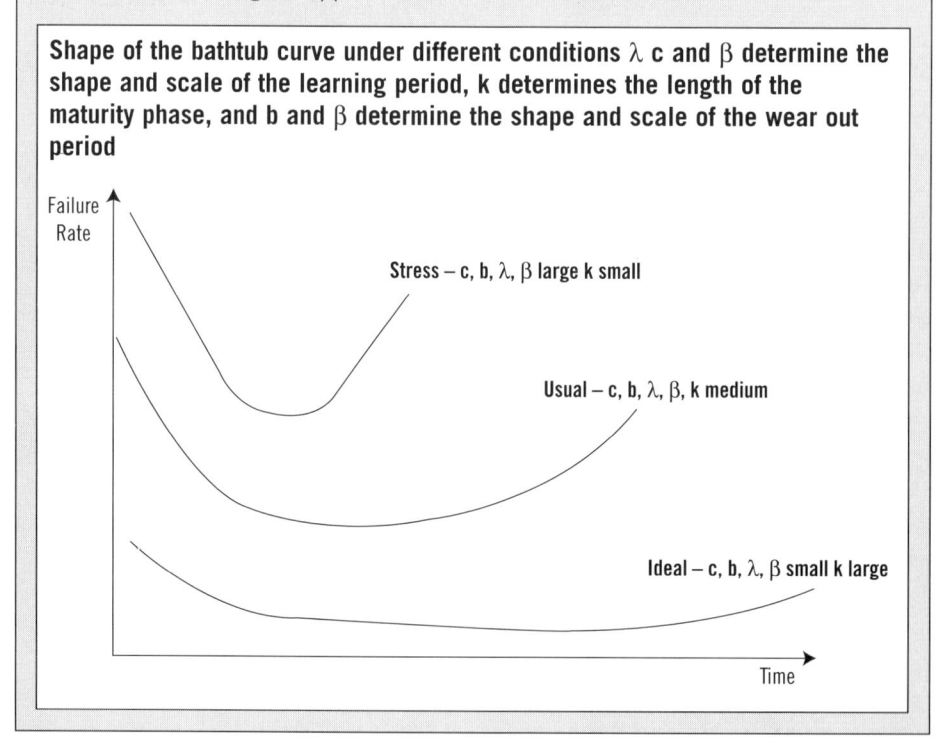

Shape of the bathtub curve under different conditions λ c and β determine the shape and scale of the learning period, k determines the length of the maturity phase, and b and β determine the shape and scale of the wear out period

Failure Rate

Stress – c, b, λ, β large k small

Usual – c, b, λ, β, k medium

Ideal – c, b, λ, β small k large

Time

Kececioglu (1991) uses Drenick's theorem to demonstrate that the overall distribution tends to exponential. Nonetheless, although the assumption of an exponential distribution simplifies the computation of hazard rates, it will be demonstrated later in the chapter how other distributions may be used to estimate losses using Monte Carlo techniques.

Ideally, to minimise failures during the life of a process, the shape and size of parameters b, c and λ in Equation (1) would be as small as possible, reducing the severity of the learning and wear-out periods. Conversely, k would be as large as possible to maximise the maturity period – ie, postpone the wear-out phase for as long as possible.

Equation (1) is the classic five-parameter function used to represent the rate of failure of typical components in many situations. It is not, however, the only model; some models use fewer parameters and some more, depending on the observed behaviour of components in real life. In particular, other models can be used to model components under stress (see Panel 2).

APPLYING THE RELIABILITY FUNCTION

If suitable parameters for a particular operational process can be determined, it should be possible using the reliability function to estimate the number of failures that are likely to occur over a particular period, for example one year. While it may be possible from historical observation to estimate failure rates for existing mature processes, it is extremely difficult to determine accurate rates for new processes (Hoffman and Johnson, 1996).

However, with reliability theory it is not strictly necessary to estimate the model's parameters accurately at the outset as it is possible to "bootstrap" the function using actual operational experience. For example, it would be possible to define an initial reliability function for a new process using information gathered from other similar processes, adopting as conservative an approach as is deemed necessary. After a time, of using actual performance data, the parameters/shape of such functions could be refined and, hence, the probability of failures (and therefore the capital set aside) could be adjusted. For a mature process, actual experience could be used for the function parameters and wear-out parameters could be bootstrapped from observations of the losses incurred in existing mature processes.

Experience can be used to determine those factors that will most impact the value of particular parameters, allowing risk managers to concentrate on the factors that will minimise operational risk. Business managers could then set hurdles for reliability function parameters that would encourage best, and penalise bad, practice.

Impact of the learning period

The duration and severity of the learning period in the reliability function will be determined by the parameters c (shape) and λ (scale), which in turn would be reduced by factors such as:

❏ use of tried and tested information systems;
❏ use of experienced staff in new ventures;
❏ market and systems testing before implementation;
❏ training given to internal staff in new procedures/systems;
❏ use of proven models and processes (controls, reconciliation, etc);
❏ identification of risks *before implementation* and actions taken to mitigate these risks;
❏ minimisation of impact on customers and external partners; and
❏ involvement of internal audit in the development process.

The cumulative impact of the learning period as a proportion of the total life of a typical component is often significant, as illustrated in Panel 3.

Translating a qualitative assessment into a quantitative value is, of course, easier said than done. Initial shape and scale parameters could be estimated in the early stages and then tracked (or revised) in the light of experience gained in observing actual failure rates. Parameters could be set conservatively high at the outset but later reduced as, for example, training programs take effect and the introduction of new control procedures is shown to be having a positive outcome. Little or no reduction in the observed values of the parameters would also bring to the attention of

PANEL 3

IMPACT OF THE LEARNING PERIOD

The figures here illustrate the impact of the learning period in two graphs of the same hypothetical, but typical, reliability curve.

Figure A is a standard reliability curve showing failure rates over a period of 36 months. Figure B plots the *cumulative* failures over the same period for the same hypothetical set of parameters. Note that, with this particular set of parameters, more than 50% of the failures occur in less than one-third of the life. This is typical for reliability functions where failures are front-loaded, ie, occur early in the life cycle.

The important lesson to draw from this illustration is that a significant part of the cumulative impact of operational failures, *and hence the capital that should be set aside to cover these failures*, will often occur during the start-up or learning period of a new venture.

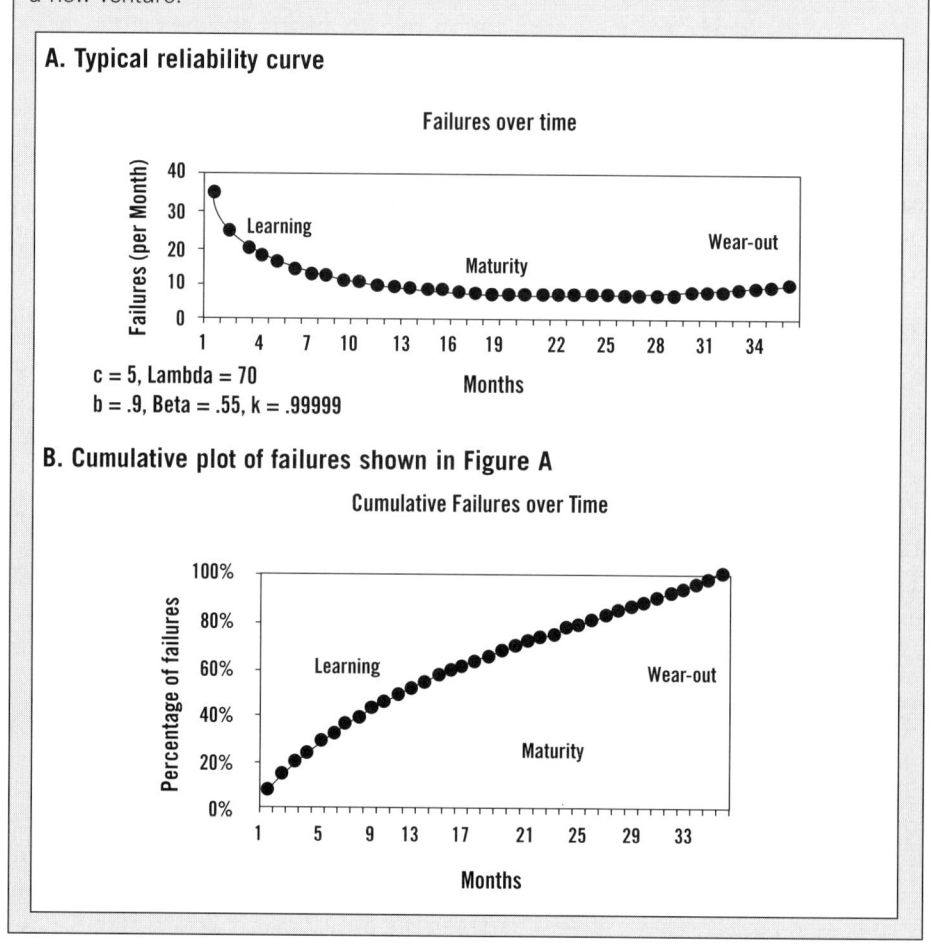

A. Typical reliability curve

Failures over time

$c = 5$, Lambda $= 70$
$b = .9$, Beta $= .55$, $k = .99999$

B. Cumulative plot of failures shown in Figure A

Cumulative Failures over Time

---

management that the introduction of the new product or process was not being managed effectively.

Although it has less of an impact overall, risk managers cannot afford to ignore the wear-out period, especially when the expected life of computer systems is now measured in decades rather than years. As the life of a process or system is extended, it should be recognised that failures will naturally increase in frequency and possibly severity (because it is being pushed beyond its design limits) and that more capital should therefore be set aside to cover losses. Since, ideally, the wear-out phase should be postponed as long as possible, management should concentrate on maximising the value of the mature life – for example, by training, minimising staff turnover and, most important, continuous improvement of processes and systems.

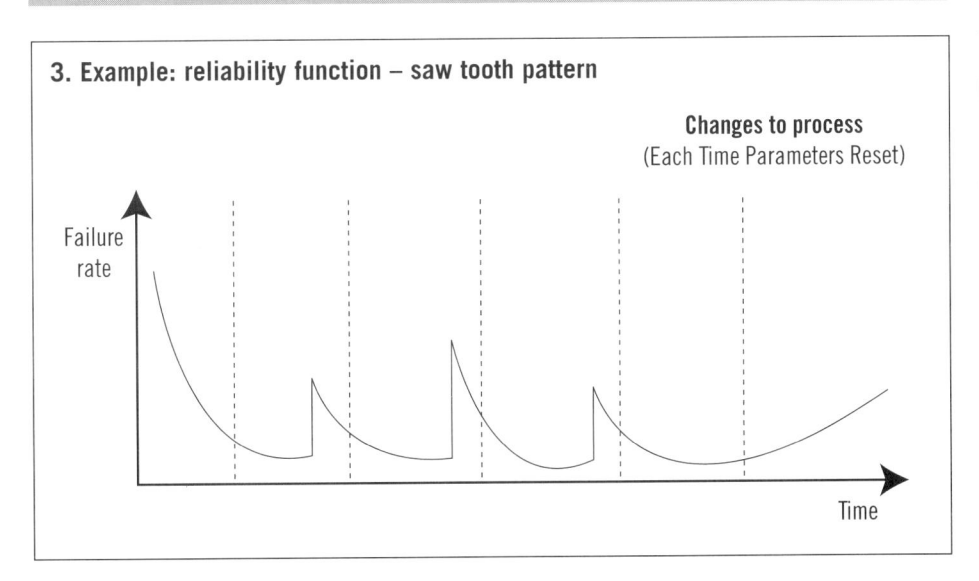

3. Example: reliability function – saw tooth pattern

[Figure 3: Graph showing Failure rate (y-axis) vs Time (x-axis) with a sawtooth pattern. Vertical dashed lines indicate "Changes to process (Each Time Parameters Reset)".]

In practice, the actual reliability function for a process measured over its life will not resemble the classic smooth bathtub shape but rather will follow a sawtooth pattern (Figure 3). As major changes to processes are introduced over time, new learning periods will cause a (hopefully) temporary upswing in the failure rate followed by reversion to a rate characteristic of a maturity phase, although different maturity phases may have different failure rates.

Defining operational processes

The discussion above ignored the definition of what constitutes an operational process. This is not an easy question to answer, and the Basel Committee has recognised that processes differ not only across banks but also across different divisions within a bank.

In practice, reliability engineers have a similar problem when identifying a mechanical "component". A computer or an aeroplane has millions of individual parts, each liable to fail at some point in time and many a potential cause of total system failure. However, engineers do not attempt to measure the reliability function for each part but look at subsystems, such as a computer disk drive or aircraft engine.[7] This is because the reliability of subsystems is not merely dependent on their individual parts but also on the quality of their assembly and maintenance, which is proved by extensive testing and actual experience.[8]

Likewise, when considering an overall business process, such as executing a foreign exchange trade, the process can be broken down ("mapped") into a number of smaller sub-processes, each sufficiently distinct to warrant measurement and management. Ideally, each sub-process would coincide with an identifiable organisational unit that can be made responsible for managing and mitigating risk; an example would be dividing a foreign exchange trade into pricing, confirmation, settlement and reconciliation processes.

However, such "process mapping" is a qualitative assessment that considers different situations on a case-by-case basis. The Basel committee notes that such "risk mapping" can "reveal areas of weakness and help prioritise subsequent management action" (Basel, 2003a). The identification of an operational process for risk management purposes should reflect the ability to manage the risks inherent in that process, and the total number of processes within an organisation should be kept to a minimum to allow effective monitoring, management and mitigation.

THE USE OF
RELIABILITY THEORY
IN MEASURING
OPERATIONAL RISK

> **PANEL 4**
>
> **HUMAN RELIABILITY UNDER STRESS**
>
> Human performance is also affected by stress, as illustrated in the diagram below. People appear to perform better when placed under a certain degree of stress (sometimes called "positive" stress), but performance drops off rapidly under high, or "negative", stress.
>
> Dhillon and Singh (1981) summarise some of the factors that have been shown to influence the rate of human errors in many working situations:
>
> ❑ poor training;
> ❑ inadequate operating procedures;
> ❑ poor working environment (eg, overcrowded, hot, noisy); and
> ❑ poor motivation.
>
> The implications are obvious: staff under too much stress will make more errors and operational risk managers may have to seek a trade-off between incurring higher capital charges to cover increased operational risks and the costs of training staff and improving morale.
>
> **Human performance under stress**
>
> *[Graph showing Performance on y-axis and Stress on x-axis, with curve rising to a plateau labeled "Positive Stress" then declining in region labeled "Negative Stress"]*

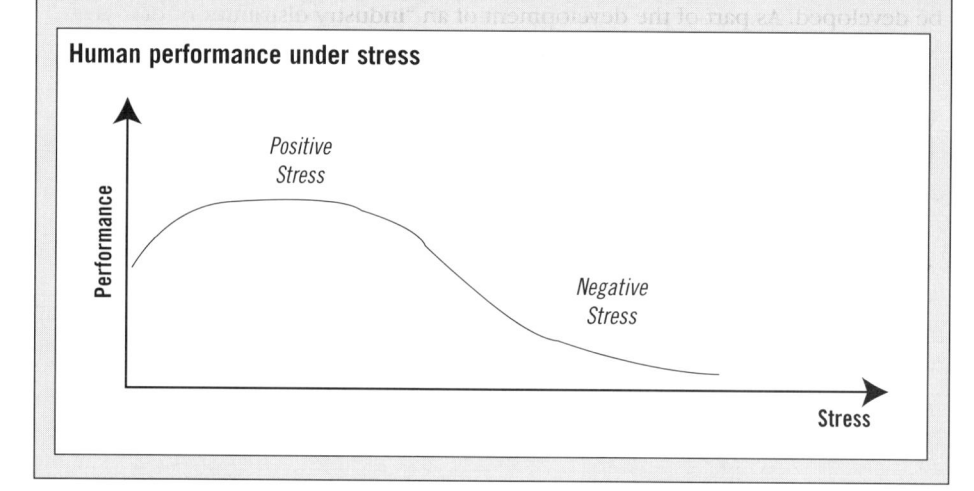

Aggregation of operational processes

Often a new banking venture will make use of capabilities already in place, such as payment systems and data centres. Once robust reliability functions for existing processes in a mature organisation have been estimated, developing an appropriate function for a new product or process would involve: breaking it down into its sub-processes; identifying those parts for which functions already exist; and estimating functions for those components that are new, always attempting to minimise the overall number of processes.

Reliability theory shows in a simple series how the failure rate of a complex combination of components may be estimated. For identical components that are configured in a simple series, the probability of failure of the total system is the sum of the probabilities of failure of each component. For identical components in parallel (ie, where there is full redundancy), the probability of failure of the total system is the product of the individual probabilities.[9] Other than operating redundant computer systems and data centres, high-level processes in banking are rarely if ever "replicated", which reduces possible combinations to simple series. However, within processes the situation is more complex in that work is often double-checked – the "four eyes" principle – reducing the frequency of error. The implications of this for the measurement of operational losses are considered below.

The reliability function discussed above considers the relatively simple case of the probability of the total failure of a single component over its life. Reliability theory extends beyond this simple case to cover the impact of replacement and preventative maintenance strategies. Beyond the simple level, however, the analogy between mechanical components and business processes breaks down. Where people are the "components" there is no parallel with preventative maintenance other than ensuring that key staff attend regular refresher courses and take their full vacation entitlements (see Panel 4). Furthermore, in a complex banking operation, failures do not have to be total to incur losses; for example, a delay in making a payment may incur charges even though the payment is made eventually.

Estimating losses

Reliability theory deals only with the probability of a failure event (PE) and does not consider the size of the financial loss that might occur given such an event (LGE). Unfortunately, as pointed out by the Basel Committee, the losses incurred are a function of the process itself and can only be estimated by observing it and the impact of failures over time.

To fix a capital charge for operational risk, it is necessary to determine a statistical distribution for losses so that meaningful parameters for estimating future losses can be developed. As part of the development of an "industry distribution" of losses, the Basel Committee circulated questionnaires (the Quantitative Impact Study QIS2 and the 2002 Loss Data Collection Exercise LDCE) . . . (Basel, 2001b, Basel, 2003b). What factors are likely to determine the loss distribution for a particular process?

Important factors that might affect the distribution of losses for a particular process within a bank would include:

❑ the probability of *no* loss;
❑ material or *de minimis* limits;
❑ internal limits;
❑ clustering of events; and
❑ market factors.

Probability of no loss

The first question that must be asked is whether there are any failure events that result in no loss (ie, LGE = 0). This is an important question because identical events may, in practice, have very different financial consequences. For example, the failure of a payments system may incur no loss if it happens early in the payment cycle. On the other hand, if the failure occurs just before "cut-off" the result could be very different, with heavy charges for delayed payments. Most banking processes have some form of pre-action check or post-action reconciliation designed to pick up errors in time to correct them before penalties are incurred. For example, banks will usually attempt to verify signatures on cheques if the amount exceeds certain limits, thus reducing the frequency of frauds that cause losses.

While the Basel Committee is interested, rightly, only in events that may affect the stability of an institution or the industry, serious events (apart from natural disasters or terrorism) rarely happen without some warning and typically arise from a pattern of neglect or errant behaviour over a period of time (McConnell, 1998). The *context* in which a significant loss occurs is important. If it is part of a pattern of smaller errors, there is probably an underlying problem in the process that requires fixing, and which, if not fixed, will undoubtedly lead to significant loss again. If, however, the failure is a genuine one-off event, a slight change to the process will minimise, but probably never eliminate, the chances of serious losses occurring again.

4. Truncation of a loss distribution

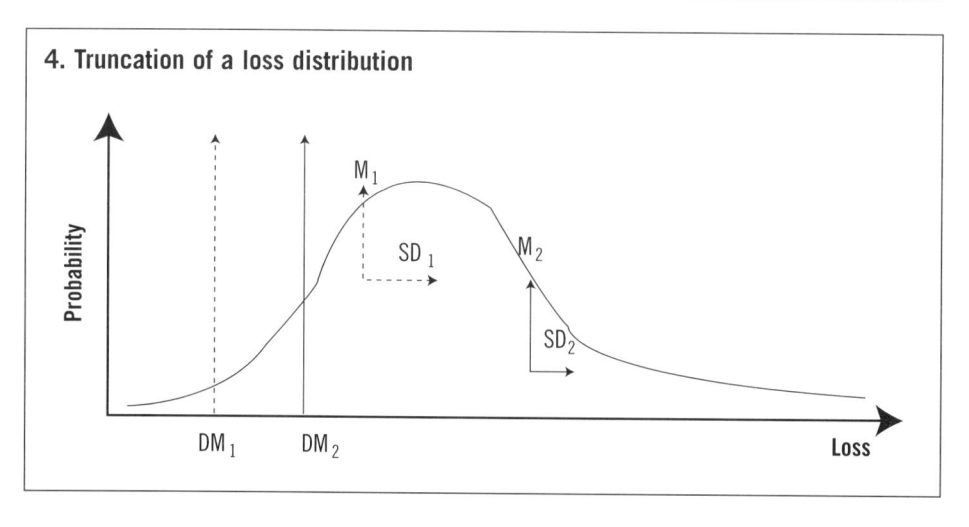

De minimis limits

As with zero losses, materiality, or the size of loss, is an important factor in constructing a meaningful distribution of losses. The Basel Committee has asked banks to report only losses above a *de minimis* level *determined by the banks themselves*. For the 2002 Loss Data Collection Exercise a *de minimis* level of €10,000 was set, but not all banks reported to that level (Basel, 2003b). The exclusion of values below this level truncates the distribution and makes it impossible to derive its moments, eg, mean and standard deviation. Figure 4 illustrates the problem. In this hypothetical case the mean, M_1, and standard deviation, SD_1, of DM_1 (the first *de minimis* level) are illustrated. With a different choice of limit, DM_2, however, the mean and standard deviation are different and cannot be compared with or derived from DM_1, nor, more importantly, can the real mean and standard deviation of the complete distribution.

Internal process limits

The next question that must be considered is the limits that have been imposed on a process from within, or even outside, its managing organisation. This is an important question when attempting to construct a distribution of losses. Credit card fraud provides a simple example: here, thieves know the limits that banks and credit card companies set on payments that do not require authorisation. Another example is that of consumer credit, where banks extend credit to a certain limit based on a lending officer's judgement and a simple scoring model; above that limit another authority must be obtained. The purpose of the second review is precisely to reduce operational risk by having a second (or third) person review the process for errors. For large transactions many levels of authority are required before commitments are extended – hopefully but not always eliminating errors. Traditionally, banks have several people check and double-check work that could result in monetary loss. From a statistical perspective the various limits within a process will affect the distribution of losses. For example, in the case of cheque or credit card fraud, one would expect the bulk of losses to occur *below* the authorisation limit, with fewer occurring above it (since fraud above that level requires a degree of criminal skill).

Clustering

Another important factor that influences the size of a loss is whether a failure event affects a single, discrete transaction or clusters of transactions. An example of a discrete transaction is a loan application, where failure to follow procedures properly will affect a single loan rather than the batch of applications in the same in-tray (always assuming that the process itself and the basic training of staff are not flawed). An example of a failure affecting clusters of transactions would be the failure of a payments system, which would affect all payments entering the queue for the duration of the failure. This is an issue that grows in importance as processes are automated, especially as the twin goals of "T + 1 settlement" and STP (straight through processing) are pursued.[10]

In clerical processing, errors can be isolated to a small number of discrete transactions, but, as the saying goes, "if you want to make a real mess, use a computer". The Basel Committee has warned that banks should be aware that increased automation could transform high-frequency, low-severity losses into low-frequency, high-severity losses (Basel, 2003a). Although automation should reduce individual errors and greatly improve controls, computer system failures have the potential to affect all transactions being processed for the duration of the problem. Unfortunately, problems may not always be detected immediately. Errors in a computer model may not be detected for months or even years, placing in doubt all transactions valued by the model until the problem has been detected and resolved.

Market factors

Market and timing factors can affect both the incidence and the size of losses. The systems failure near a payment cut-off time noted above is just one example. Others are tied to the structures of markets. Examples are the losses that arise from increased market activity and settlement errors around rate-reset dates in the swaps market and on option expiry dates in exchange-traded derivatives markets. Likewise, the increased incidence of internal fraud – undertaken to mask losses or enhance profits – near the end of the financial year is well known.

Can losses be estimated?

Because of the difficulty of developing a meaningful distribution for losses, there can be no simple formula for estimating them. However, given some heroic assumptions, it is possible to construct a loss function, (LF), which would allow operational risk managers to estimate the loss that would be incurred as the result of a particular event at some time in the future. If, for simplicity, it were assumed that the loss in the event of a failure (Cruz, 2002) in a process p is normally distributed with mean μ_p and standard deviation σ_p, the expected loss at a specified confidence level could be written as

$$LF(\alpha, t) = K_p \cdot g(\mu_p + \alpha \sigma_{p,t}) \qquad (2)$$

where K_p is a cluster factor for process p, $g(l,t)$ is some growth function that estimates loss l at time t and α is the confidence interval required.[11]

The major assumptions made in Equation (2) are that losses are *normally* distributed and that the cluster factor K_p is *fixed*. How unrealistic are these assumptions and do they underestimate or overestimate potential losses?

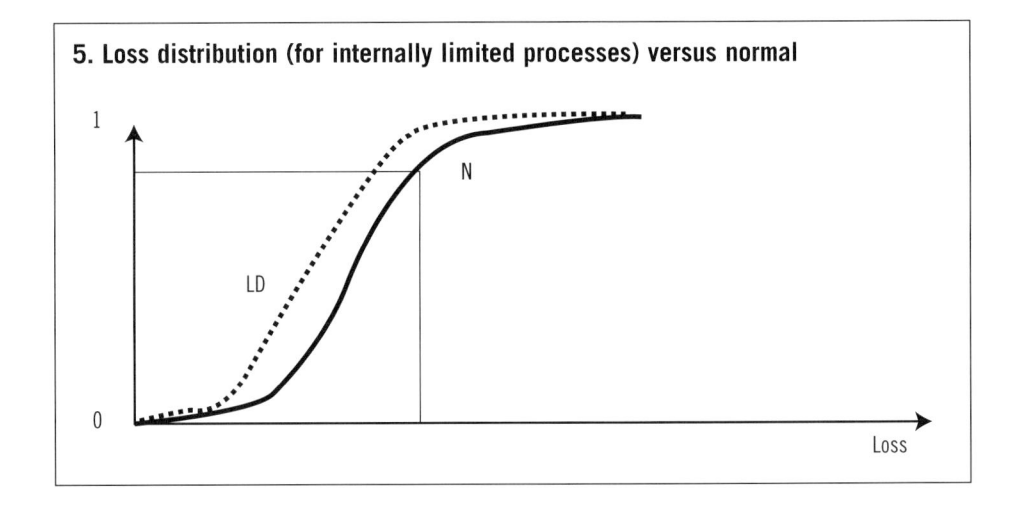

5. Loss distribution (for internally limited processes) versus normal

The assumption of normality is unrealistic, but it is hypothesised that use of the normal distribution will overestimate the loss and hence is conservative. The loss distribution for a typical banking process is likely to be skewed to the left (towards smaller losses) since problems that could lead to larger losses *would tend to be detected by internal limits*. This does not mean that large losses do not occur but that they occur much less frequently than smaller ones. Figure 5 illustrates the reasoning for this, showing two cumulative distribution functions (cdf), one for a normal distribution (N), the other for a loss distribution (LD) with the same mean. At each point the normal distribution produces a larger, more conservative loss than the loss distribution (always assuming that internal limits are in place).

The assumption of a fixed cluster factor, K_p, is more difficult to justify except in the case of a discrete process where $K = 1$. However, operational research provides tools that can help to provide some insight into the "queues" that might build up in the event of a failure. If the mean arrival rate of transactions into the process is λ_p and the mean time to repair (MTTR) a failure is μ_r, then $K_p = \mu_r/\lambda_p$ is a good approximation of the number of transactions that would be in the queue ready to be processed when the process was fully operational again.[12] A full discussion of queuing theory is outside the scope of this book but is covered sufficiently for this purpose in Hiller and Lieberman (1990).

To be conservative, estimates of the arrival rate λ_p should be taken from observations of "traffic" during a peak hour and the MTTR should be estimated from observations of the duration of failures. Using peak hour observations and a conservative estimate of MTTR will overestimate the value of K and, hence, the loss function will be conservative.[13] If the estimate is too conservative in practice, the value of the confidence interval, α, can be slackened with experience.

Although difficult to construct, the usefulness of estimating a loss function that is conservative and takes into account the number and size of transactions, as described above, will highlight those areas most likely to be subject to operational risk. For example, even with an approximate loss function the sheer volume of trading undertaken by Nick Leeson at Barings should have triggered an alert that potentially massive losses might be incurred in the event of a problem (McConnell, 1998).

Value-at-risk

Jorion (1997) defines value-at-risk (VAR) as measuring "the worst expected loss over a given time interval under normal market conditions at a given confidence level". Having developed reliability and loss functions for each operational process, it should be possible to compute a VAR for a "portfolio" of processes over a target horizon within a specified confidence level as shown in Equation (3):

$$VAR_P = \sum_{p=1}^{P} \sum_{t=T_S}^{T_E} h_p(t).LF_p(\alpha, t) \qquad (3)$$

where P is the set of operational processes, T_S is the start period, T_E is the end period, $h_p(t)$ is the hazard rate for process p at time t, $LF_p(t)$ is the loss function for process p at time t with, for example, $\alpha = 1.65$ at a 95% confidence level. Since operational processes are difficult to adjust quickly, the target horizon $(T_E - T_S)$ for any process is likely to be large, for example 12 months, and the interval small, for example one day.

Using such an estimate of VAR, it should be possible for senior management to set aside capital to cover the losses that are likely to be incurred during the target period at the confidence level required. Panel 5 illustrates how the VAR for a portfolio of processes may be estimated.

Since each operational process is described by a set of simple numerical parameters, it should be possible to stress-test the results by rerunning the VAR calculation and adjusting parameters to reflect worst-case scenarios (Jorion, 1997).

PANEL 5

CALCULATION OF VAR FOR A PORTFOLIO OF PROCESSES

The diagram below illustrates how the VAR for a "portfolio" of processes may be estimated. For each process p from P1 to PP:

1. Construct a reliability function, RF_p, and a loss distribution, LD_p, for each process p.
2. For each interval (say one day) in the period T_S to T_E, estimate the number of failures in the period and estimate the resulting losses from the corresponding loss distribution for the confidence level required.
3. Sum the losses over the period to produce a "component" VAR_p for the process p.
4. Sum all of the component VAR_p to produce VAR_{PP}, the VAR for the portfolio of processes. Note that it is assumed that the processes are not correlated, which may be unrealistic if processes are shared (as computer systems tend to be).

The advantage of such an approach is that it is forward-looking, taking into account products and processes that are being introduced (or even terminated) during the period. It would allow, for example, the VAR to be adjusted quickly if projects were delayed or encountered problems that were likely to increase operational risk (such as serious errors found during the testing of new systems).

From a management perspective, an analysis of the VAR of each component process in the portfolio would highlight which processes would benefit from closer attention.

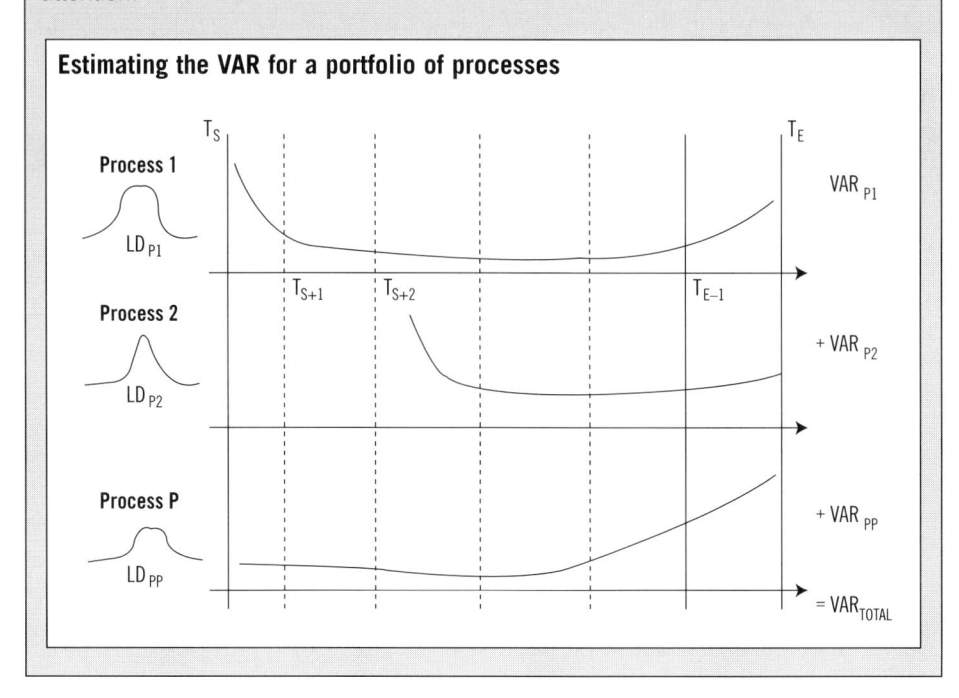

Estimating the VAR for a portfolio of processes

Likewise, back-testing of the model can be performed by comparing the actual losses incurred by process p in time t with the relevant component in the VAR computation. Ideally, predicted and actual experience would converge (as parameters are bootstrapped with actual data), but a sudden, large divergence could indicate that a particular operational process is under stress and may require attention.

Monte Carlo simulation

The estimation of VAR using Equation 3 is based on assumptions that may be overly simplistic in reality. But, as with other VAR computations, Monte Carlo methods may be used to take into account more complex situations (Jorion, 1997). For example, rather than use the assumption of an exponential failure rate in calculating the reliability function, Monte Carlo simulation could be used to draw samples from a Weibull distribution if the observed data are a better fit. Likewise, the assumption of normality of losses in the loss function will underestimate the likelihood of extreme events, however remote, and a better choice for fat-tail events may be the extreme value distribution (Dhillon and Singh, 1981). In some operational processes non-linear losses can occur, as in a failure to exercise an option, which ideally would be reflected in the loss function for that process (Dillon and Singh 1981, Cruz, 2002).

The procedures for computing VAR using structured Monte Carlo simulation, although data-intensive, are not difficult to implement (Vose, 1996). First, suitable distributions must be developed for each process and each of the parameters described above must be estimated. Then, using standard Monte Carlo random number generation techniques, the reliability and loss functions can be simulated for each process for each period up to the target horizon and a loss calculated. After iterating the computation many times, a distribution of losses is built up from which the VAR at the confidence level required can be estimated.

One major advantage of Monte Carlo simulation is that parameters and distributions can easily be changed and the simulation rerun to stress-test the model. The factors to which the model is most sensitive can then be isolated and management action taken to mitigate their impact.

Measurements of quality

This chapter does not deal with the qualitative management of operational risk, which is addressed elsewhere in the book. It is a truism, however, that "you cannot manage what you cannot measure", and some risk measures, however crude, must be in place to enable management to make rational decisions about how resources should be allocated to reduce operational risk.

Mitigating operational risk is very different to mitigating market risk (through hedging) or credit risk (through syndication or securitisation). Aside from insuring against natural disasters, such as fire and earthquake, reducing operational risk is about managing continuous processes rather than predicting extreme events. It is about the daily grind of keeping things working smoothly and gradually improving the quality of operational processes to reduce errors. Quality and reliability are two sides of the same coin.

Management theorists have long recognised that improving the quality of a process – in particular manufacturing processes – cannot be brought about by grandiose gestures but by the painstaking elimination of variations in each stage of the underlying processes (Drucker, 1992). Statistical quality control (SQC), a rigorous scientific method of identifying problems in manufacturing processes, was pioneered by Walter Shewhart in the 1930s and promoted by visionaries such as Demming and Juran to propel Japan to world leadership in manufacturing. Unfortunately, it has taken longer to apply these techniques to purely clerical processes and, especially, banking processes. But are banking processes so different that similar tools and techniques cannot be applied?

In March 2001, a number of major banks came together to discuss the creation of FS 9000 with the goal of applying tried and tested quality-management techniques to the financial services industry. FS 9000 is based on the international quality standard ISO 9000. Since 2000, a number of major banks have begun to introduce the principles of Six Sigma, an approach to improving operational processes originating in manufacturing sindustries (Kopp, 2003). Among the many claims made for FS 9000 and Six Sigma is that not only would service quality be improved and costs reduced

PANEL 6

QUALITY MANAGEMENT SYSTEMS

The proponents of quality management systems (QMS) argue that firms gain real financial benefits from attention to quality; the phrase "quality is free" has been proven in many instances where the cost of putting a QMS in place is much less than that of correcting mistakes. Hidden costs, such as the need to maintain unnecessarily high inventory levels to cover for having to re-do work, have been eliminated in some leading companies (Drucker, 1992). The economic benefits of improved quality should appeal to financial managers. Vinod and Hendricks (1998) report that, as a group, the winners of the prestigious Baldridge award for quality in the US outperform their peers – and the market in general – on many financial measures, including sales, return on assets, income and stock price.

FS 9000 is based on the ISO 9000 standard, the internationally accepted benchmark for quality management systems. In its various incarnations – the latest being ISO 9001/2000 – the standard has been applied to industries as diverse as automotive manufacturing and telecommunications. Over 300,000 firms around the world, in many different industries, have already been awarded ISO 9000 certificates. The process of winning such a certificate is not easy and firms value them highly. Undoubtedly one reason for the value placed on them is that governments have stated a preference for dealing with certified suppliers for the obvious reason that certification reduces the cost of due diligence as suppliers have already been independently assessed and certified. Anderson (2001) reports that more than 130 financial firms, mainly in the insurance sector, have already been awarded ISO 9001 certification in the US and Canada, although the number is a small proportion of the total sector. Whereas ISO 9001 is a general approach to QMS, FS 9000 would be tailored to the specific needs of the financial services sector. FSIX (or the Financial Standards International Xchange) is an association of service providers and organisations that aims to promote the acceptance of the FS 9000 standard in, and to act as a certification body for, the financial industry.

Six Sigma is an approach to management that aims at "managing, improving and reinventing business processes" across the firm (Pande *et al.*, 2000). The approach, which makes extensive use of quantitative methods, was originally developed by leading US manufacturers who were attempting to emulate (and ultimately exceed) the success of their Japanese competitors in delivering high-quality products and customer service. The goal of Six Sigma is to achieve a quality level of 99.9997% equating to a defect/error rate of less than 3.4 in a million. Leading proponents of Six Sigma, such as GE and Motorola (who own the trademark), recognised early on that achieving such a low level of defects would not be easy and that significant investments in people and money would be needed to attain the desired levels of quality and obtain the benefits that would flow from that, in terms of customer satisfaction and market share. Six Sigma methods are being adopted by some of the world's leading banks including JP Morgan Chase and Bank of America (Kopp, 2003). Operational risk and operational efficiency are two sides of the same coin and the use of Six Sigma should grow as firms attempt to streamline their operations. Hoffman (2002) argues that many of the quantitative methods and disciplines employed by practitioners of Six Sigma are also driving the development of operational risk management and that with Six Sigma "enterprise-wide operational risk management has met its soul mate".

Though in practice difficult to reconcile, the goals of FS 9000 and Six Sigma are similar – the improvement of business processes. Whereas Six Sigma has an *internal* focus, FSIX is promoting FS 9000 as a way of improving communication and

> processes across the financial industry. Regardless of their own levels of quality, banks are forced to use other firms (such as counterparties and depositories), which may not provide a similar commitment to reducing errors, thus diminishing their own customers' perception of the services provided. FSIX would argue that leading firms should embrace both FS 9000 and Six Sigma.
>
> So why should financial institutions adopt Six Sigma or become a member of FSIX? The answer is the same as for other industries – the standardisation of quality practices will improve the quality of service throughout the sector. The attraction to regulators should be apparent: those firms with a recognised certification are likely to pay more attention to the quality of their processes than those that do not and thus deserve to be required to hold less capital against operational risks.

by their deployment but also that regulatory compliance would be improved. Standardising on how quality is measured across the industry, with independent certification of firms that meet the required standards for quality, should allow meaningful comparison to be made between firms, at least on that one measure. Panel 6 gives more background on quality management systems.

Like many such proposals, a firm-wide approach to quality and formal quality management system, such as Six Sigma or FS 9000, may not wholly succeed because of the entrenched conservatism of the banking industry. However, even if it does not, participation in such initiatives – and, even better, certification to the highest standards set in other industries – should convince regulators of the commitment of a particular institution to the reduction of operational risk. In short, the achievement of an independent certification that indicates real commitment to process improvement should *automatically* attract a reduced capital charge from regulators. The British Bankers' Association (2001) argues strongly that due recognition in the form of reduced capital charges must be given in response to changes in management controls designed to reduce future operational losses. The award of an independent certificate would also indicate to the capital markets (the "third pillar" of the Basel approach) that a bank's management was committed to proactive management of operational risk.

Nor are FS 9000 and Six Sigma the only ways in which firms can demonstrate adherence to industry best practices. The US and Canadian associations of CPAs (certified public accountants) have developed the SYSTRUST and WEBTRUST schemes whereby internal processes related to systems development and operation can be benchmarked against the best practice in the industry. Again, the award of a seal of approval should convince regulators that a firm is worthy of a reduction in its capital charges.

There are many other areas where financial institutions could cooperate, without jeopardising competitive advantage, to produce industry quality benchmarks against which individual firms could be measured. These include:

❑ *human resources* creating industry measures of staff turnover, dismissals for fraud, etc;
❑ *marketing/customer service* creating industry benchmarks for customer satisfaction and complaints;[14]
❑ *settlement* using statistics such as those already provided by SWIFT, which set benchmarks for adherence to standards for settlement messages; and
❑ *IT* creating industry benchmarks for the quality of IT processes, such as the COBIT standard promoted by the IT Governance Institute.[15]

Implications for the Basel proposals

The New Capital Accord (Basel 2001a) proposes the first steps towards putting in place the quantitative and, at the outset, more important qualitative frameworks for managing operational risk. The approach, like the first Accord of 1988, are necessarily conservative owing to the lack of research that has been conducted into operational risk in real life situations. The Basel Committee received more than 250 responses to its request for comments on the New Capital Accord, some of which were highly critical – like the comment by the American Bankers Association that the "operational risk capital component is arbitrary, undeveloped and not workable" (ABA, 2001).

The three so-called Advanced Management Approaches (AMA) proposed by the Basel Committee (basic indicator, standardised measurement and internal measurement) are increasingly sophisticated in their application, but all are based on gross measures of activity (so called exposure indicators or EI), such as gross income or transaction volumes, and gross measures of loss (eg, average loss amount/ or average transaction amount). For each approach, supervisors will supply scaling factors that adjust a bank's own estimates with a buffer for unexpected losses.

The scaling factors proposed by Basel are based on assumptions about the distribution of *losses throughout the industry*. However, the committee recognised that the "risk profile of a bank's loss distribution may not always be the same as that of the industry wide distribution". After adverse industry reaction to its initial proposal to use an industry-wide risk profile index (RPI), the committee backtracked and proposed leaving the calculation of capital, for those banks that wished to use the internal measurement approach, to the banks themselves. In effect, this proposal puts the onus on banks that wish to reduce their capital charge to "prove" that their losses differ significantly from the industry distribution. Without a consistent mechanism for gathering loss data, arguing for a reduction in capital charges is a near impossible task except for those banks prepared to bend the rules.

Critical to the estimation of scaling factors for unexpected losses is the development of an industry distribution that accurately reflects the history of losses across the industry. Information to develop the first such industry distribution was collected from banks around the world as part of the QIS2 survey in mid-2001 and was repeated in the QIS3 "loss data collection exercise" of 2002 (Basel, 2003b). Pezier (2002) provides a critique of the QIS2 results in which, using the figures supplied by Basel, he demonstrates the difficulty of developing meaningful industry-wide distributions. There are several serious concerns relating to the proposed application of the information that has been collected from these surveys to the measurement of operational risk, the most important of which are discussed below.

First, and most important, the information is being collected out of context; in particular, no account is taken of the effect of the learning period. The losses reported are not being identified as being part of long-run operations or as arising as a result of new, or radically modified, processes or systems. If individual circumstances are not taken into account, banks that are adept at managing change to internal processes will be adversely affected by those banks that do not manage the change as well.

Second, the information that is being collected reflects three years of history that are highly unlikely to provide a good basis for predicting the future. There are several reasons for this:

❏ The introduction of the euro in 2002 undoubtedly increased operational risk for European banks.[16] Existing processes and systems were changed and staff retrained, giving rise to the learning period effects described above. Banks in countries that did not introduce new currencies at that time, such as the UK, were affected, though not as much, and, hence, should incur lower capital charges. Conversely, if/when countries elect to convert to the euro, the impact on their operational risk capital charges should be increased.
❏ The banking industry has undergone a period of intense consolidation, which is unlikely to abate – and may possibly accelerate – in the near term. The combined

historical losses of two (or sometimes more) institutions will neither reflect the losses of the individual banks nor those of the resulting organisation. Mergers and acquisitions bring operational risk (again through the learning period), and this should be reflected in any capital charge.

❏ Although changes in economic conditions will have a larger impact on credit and market risk measurement, operational risk measures will also be affected. For example, in a bull market volumes increase and so do operational losses. In a recession, however, margins fall and knowledgeable staff are laid off, which will also change the overall operational risk profile.

❏ Global political events affect banks in different ways. In attempting to collect information about "damage to physical assets", the Basel Committee requested information about terrorism.[17] The data collected are likely to be very varied and in some instances very large (eg, the losses arising from the September 11, 2001 attacks on New York). It is unreasonable to apply these fat-tail events to banks in countries that do not experience such disruptions. This does not mean that banks operating in countries where there are political problems should not be required to set aside capital against such events, only that such losses should not be applied across the industry as a whole.

Lastly, as the British Bankers' Association noted in its response to the committee's proposals, the surveys are collecting information that cannot meaningfully be combined across the industry and are "unlikely to be representative of the general banking population" (BBA, 2001).

❏ As shown earlier, the inclusion of only those events that have resulted in a loss above the arbitrarily selected *de minimis* level truncates the distribution such that meaningful statistics cannot be derived.[18]

❏ Different countries, and even different regions within countries, have different risk profiles. For example, usage of credit and debit cards varies from country to country, as does usage of alternative banking channels (branch, phone and the Internet).

❏ Different markets have different loss profiles. For example, markets with highly automated securities clearing and settlement systems experience losses at levels that differ from those in markets where settlement is still paper-based.

❏ Different institutions play different roles in markets. For example, a leading national clearing bank will have a distribution of losses in the payments system very different to that of even a large regional bank in the same system. In its response to the committee's proposals, the Australian Prudential Regulatory Authority (APRA), among others, questioned the assumption of a "linear relationship between [bank] size and operational risk incurred", arguing that larger institutions benefit from the greater "diversification" of their business lines, products and geographical location (APRA, 2001).

The results of the QIS3 loss data collection exercise (Basel, 2003b) also raised some very serious concerns about the feasibility of constructing industry-wide loss distributions.

❏ *Instability over time*: the LDCE showed a marked difference between the losses in different "event-type" categories between 2000 and 2001. While this was primarily due to the very large losses incurred as a result of the September 11, 2001 terrorist attacks (with a large increase in losses due to "damages to physical assets") it nevertheless illustrates the difficulty of creating a meaningful history, at last at this low level.

❏ *Differences in interpretation*: as Basel (2003b) noted it was not clear whether the LDCE survey was representative of the industry, in that there was no apparent agreement as to what constituted "comprehensive" reporting. Some banks reported a small number of loss events while claiming to be comprehensive while others reported a significantly higher number of losses yet admitted that their returns were not comprehensive.

❏ *Recovery rates*: Basel (2003b) warned that it would be inappropriate to draw conclusions about either "the frequency of recoveries or recovery rates over a longer horizon". This is because the rate of recovery appears to be a function of the size of the loss (obviously banks try harder when losses are larger) and the actual rates of insurance payouts are variable. Given that recoveries, either through insurance or "other" means, vary by individual bank policy and country there is little reason to believe therefore that a meaningful industry-wide distribution of recoveries (and hence "net" losses) can be developed.

In short, the collection of historical loss information is a useful exercise since it will identify some of the major factors that influence losses and, by looking at individual banks, highlight areas that need further research. However, if the information is collected without a proper context – in particular, how losses relate to changes taking place in individual banks – it will be difficult to apply consistent measurements of risk across the industry.

Some academics are more scathing. In a thoughtful critique of the Basel proposals after the release of the results of QIS2, Pezier (2002) concluded that "such assumptions and methods (as proposed in Basel, 2001d) are baseless and the estimation of a total operational loss distribution is as difficult as it is futile".

The results of the industry-wide QIS2 and LDCE surveys do little to support the methods of measuring operational risk proposed by Basel II. The committee must therefore consider whether it is possible to develop such methodologies in sufficient time to allow banks to build the necessary data collection and modelling systems before introduction of the new Accord by year-end 2006. If that is not possible, the committee must then develop alternative methods that attempt to achieve the same goal of calculating the capital required for operational risk. There is some time remaining but not a lot.

Conclusion

Operational risk has become a matter of concern for banks and their regulators, as most recently reflected in the Basel Committee's proposals for including operational risk in the New Capital Accord framework. Many of the responses to the committee's proposals were critical of the approach and methodologies proposed for calculating the capital required to cover these risks. Both the committee and the industry have called for further research in this area.

An attempt was made in this chapter to develop models for measuring operational risk based on reliability theory, a well-established discipline in operational research. Using simplified, but conservative, assumptions about how losses occur in operational processes, a formula was developed for calculating the value-at-risk for a "portfolio" of operational processes. The objective of the formula is to permit management to adjust the model parameters to reflect actual experience in operating processes. Recognising that some of the assumptions in the simple model may be unrealistic, the chapter described how Monte Carlo simulation may be used to estimate the VAR in more complex situations.

Unlike credit and market risk, it is difficult to "hedge" operational risk, which can only be reduced by improving the underlying processes. It was argued that operational risk, and by extension the capital needed to cover it, can be reduced by continuously improving the "quality" of individual banking processes using techniques borrowed from manufacturing industry. The development of appropriate models will highlight to management where resources should be applied to improve specific processes to minimise overall operational risk to the firm.

THE USE OF RELIABILITY THEORY IN MEASURING OPERATIONAL RISK

The collection of loss data by the Basel Committee is a useful exercise in helping regulators and banks to understand the potential sources of, especially major, operational problems. However, if the losses for which information is collected are not placed in the context of the individual institution that incurs them and the changes it is experiencing, it will not be possible to draw meaningful conclusions about the industry as a whole. It is apparent that even at this late stage, there remains much work to do to develop realistic models of operational losses that can be applied industry-wide.

By delaying the introduction of the New Accord until year-end 2006, the Basel Committee has recognised that considerable work needs to be done to achieve an industry consensus. As always, more information and research are needed into how operational risks arise, how they can be measured and what steps can be taken to mitigate them. This chapter has argued that the industry should look beyond traditional financial theories for models that may be more appropriate.

1 *The level of operational risk capital has changed during the development of the Basel proposals, from an initial 20% to 12% of MRC.*
2 *Model risk should be considered a sub-set of operational risk.*
3 *Although it should be remembered that a similar lack of models existed when the possibility of assigning capital against credit and market risks was first suggested.*
4 *The difficulty of untangling corporate structures, cross-ownership and guarantees is not underestimated here; however, it is usually possible, given complete information, to identify at least the maximum impact of any credit default.*
5 *Whereas the Basel Committee identified failures in people, (clerical) processes and systems, here the term "operational process" encompasses all of these components as the three are inextricably linked.*
6 *Note that the exponential distribution is a special case of the Weibull distribution.*
7 *Except when considering alternatives during the initial design of a particular subsystem.*
8 *There is also a cost trade-off between fixing a broken part in a subsystem and replacing the complete unit.*
9 *For non-identical components, which do not have failure rates and are exponentially distributed, the computations are more difficult but not intractable (Hines and Montgomery, 1980).*
10 *Following the events of September 11, 2001, the Securities Industry Association (SIA) delayed the implementation of the new rules for next day settlement (so-called T+1) of securities transactions in the US until mid 2005.*
11 *The growth function g could represent exponential growth (eg, $l.e^{gt}$) or a straight line (eg, $l.gt$) or some other function that would closely mirror business plans for the process over the time period being considered.*
12 *A full estimate of the number in the queue would have to include the time needed to clear the backlog after repair, which in turn requires knowledge of the mean service time of the process. However, if the MTTR includes clearing the backlog, the estimate is conservative.*
13 *This estimation makes the standard queuing assumptions of a first-in/first-out, single-server queue with a Poisson arrival process and no "leavers". In practice, multiple servers and priority processing may reduce the impact of failures (as with duplicated computer systems).*
14 *Standard measures of service quality used in other industries, such as SERVQUAL, could easily be applied to financial services.*
15 *The IT Governance Institute and COBIT are offshoots of ISACA, the worldwide accreditation body for IT auditors.*
16 *Even though the new Capital Accord will not be implemented until well after the impact of the successful euro conversion in 2002 has worked its way through the system, the loss history that is attributable to the euro event will at some stage have to be taken into account when analysing the history of losses. Likewise the losses that will inevitably arise during the*

proposed implementation of T+1 in the US securities industry in 2005 will have to be factored into the histories of losses for those firms involved.

17 *Similar issues arise with information that is being requested about organised labour activity, which will vary from country to country and from time to time.*

18 *Even though de minimis limits of $1,000 for retail operations and $10,000 otherwise are suggested, these figures cannot be compared across countries reporting in domestic currencies. For example, some countries have transactions with a higher average amounts than others.*

BIBLIOGRAPHY

American Bankers' Association (ABA), 2001, "Letter to the Basel Committee on Banking Supervision", June.

Anderson, S., 2001, "FS 9000 May Spur ISO 9001 Growth in Slow Sector", available at URL: http://www.informintl.com.

Australian Prudential Regulatory Authority (APRA), 2001, "Submission to the Basel Committee on Banking Supervision – The New Capital Accord", May.

Basel Committee on Banking Supervision, 2003a, "Sound Practices for the Management and Supervision of Operational Risk", February.

Basel Committee on Banking Supervision, 2003b, "The 2002 Loss Data Collection Exercise for Operational Risk: Summary of the Data Collected", March.

Basel Committee on Banking Supervision, 2002a, "Basel Committee Reaches Agreement on New Capital Accord Issues", July.

Basel Committee on Banking Supervision, 2001a, "Consultative Document Operational Risk, Supporting document to the New Capital Accord", May

Basel Committee on Banking Supervision, 2001b, "QIS-2 Operational Risk Loss Data", May.

Basel Committee on Banking Supervision, 2001c, "Update on the New Accord", June.

Basel Committee on Banking Supervision, 2001d, "Working Paper on the Regulatory Treatment of Operational Risk", September.

British Bankers' Association (BBA), 2001, "Response to the Basel Committee's Second Consultation on a New Basel Accord", May.

Cruz, M. G., 2002, *Modelling, Measuring and Hedging Operational Risk*, (Chichester: John Wiley & Sons).

Dhillon, B. S., and Singh C., 1981, *Engineering Reliability* (New York: John Wiley & Sons).

Drucker, P. F., 1992, *Managing for the Future* (New York: Penguin).

Financial Services Authority (FSA), 2002, "Consultative Paper 142 (CP142) – Operational Risk Systems and Controls", July.

Hiller, F. S., and G. J. Lieberman, 1990, *Introduction to Operational Research*, Fifth Edition (New York: McGraw-Hill).

Hines, W. W., and D. C. Montgomery, 1980, *Probability and Statistics in Engineering and Management Science* (New York: John Wiley & Sons).

Hoffman, D., 2003, *Managing Operational Risk: 20 Firmwide Best Practice Strategies*, (New York: John Wiley & Sons).

Hoffman, D., and M. Johnson, 1996, "Operating Procedures", *Risk* 9(10).

Hull, J., 1989, *Options, Futures and Other Derivative Securities* (Englewood Cliffs: Prentice-Hall).

Jorion, P., 1997, *Value At Risk* (Chicago: McGraw-Hill).

Kececioglu, D., 1991, *Reliability Engineering Handbook* (Englewood Cliffs: Prentice-Hall).

Kopp, G., 2003, "Six Sigma in Financial Services: Customer Focus and Institutional Performance", Banking Systems and Technology e-News, January.

Markowitz, H. M., 1991, *Portfolio Selection*, Second Edition (Oxford: Blackwell).

Mc Connell, P. J., 1998, "Barings: Development of a Disaster", *International Journal of Project and Business Risk* 1(1), pp.59-74.

Pande, P. S., R.P. Neuman and R. R. Cavanagh, 2000, *The Six Sigma Way: How GE, Motorola, and Other Top Companies are Honing Their Performance*, (New York: McGraw-Hill).

Pezier, J., 2002, "Operational Risk Management", ISMA Discussion Paper in Finance 2002-21 ISMA Centre, University of Reading.

Tomski, R., 2001, www.oprisk.freeserve.co.uk.

Vinod, R. S., and K. B. Hendricks, 1998, "The Financial Justification of TQM", *Journal of Center for Quality of Management* 8(1), pp.3.

Vose, D., 1996, *Quantitative Risk Analysis – A guide to Monte Carlo Simulation Modeling* (Chichester: John Wiley & Sons).

9

Model Selection for Operational Risk

Michel Crouhy, Dan Galai and Robert Mark

CIBC; Hebrew University; Black Diamond

Operational risk modelling has evolved rapidly over the past several years. Until recently operational risk was not a well-defined concept. In the context of trading in a financial institution it often refers to a range of possible failures in the operations of the firm that are not directly related to market or credit risk. These failures include computer breakdowns, a bug in a key piece of computer software, errors of judgement, deliberate fraud and so on.

With the New Basel Capital Accord (Basel Committee on Banking Supervision, 2003b) the financial industry is now converging on a definition of operational risk that facilitates comparison across firms. Operational risk is defined as the potential for loss due to the failure of people, processes and technology, as well as to external dependencies. An alternative broad definition is all potential losses that are not directly attributable to credit, market, business, strategic and reputational risks.

Operational risk remains a fuzzy concept because it is hard to make a clear-cut distinction between operational risk and the "normal" uncertainties faced by an organisation in its daily operations. For example, the failure of a client to pay back a loan may be due to "normal" credit risk or to human error on the part of a loan officer. Usually, all credit-related uncertainties are classified as part of "credit risk". Nevertheless, in certain situations a loan officer should not approve a loan given the information he has about the client at the time of the decision. For example, if a loan officer approves a loan contrary to the bank's guidelines (he might even have been given a bribe), this should be classified as an operational failure, not a credit loss. Typically, loans that default due to third-party fraud are classified as "loan losses", whereas loans that default due to internal fraud are classified as "operational risk losses".

A key challenge is the quantification of operational risk through the use of statistical models. For example, how can one quantify the risk of a computer breakdown? Operational risk is defined in terms of the probability of the breakdown occurring, which we will refer to as the "likelihood", and the cost of the breakdown if it does occur, which we will refer to as "severity". Both these numbers are difficult to estimate. By their nature, major operational risks occur infrequently and are discrete events. So how can one identify a historical event (or events) that can be used as part of a rational assessment? Unfortunately, a computer breakdown today is different in both probability and the extent of the damage than a similar event 10 years ago.

The difficulties in assessing operational risk do not imply that it should be ignored or neglected. On the contrary, management must give their attention to understanding operational risk and its potential sources in the organisation precisely because it is so hard to identify and quantify.

In some cases operational risk can be insured against or hedged. For example, a

MODEL SELECTION FOR OPERATIONAL RISK

> **PANEL 1**
>
> ## THE "ROGUE" TRADERS' LESSONS
>
> Failure to put in place the appropriate internal control structure and/or to identify a breakdown in internal controls, or to defuse it in a timely manner, can translate into a huge loss. In several instances, the action taken by a single trader who was able to take extremely risky positions in a market without authority and detection led to massive losses.
>
> Most recently, in 2002, Allied Irish Banks incurred losses of US$750 million through unauthorised trading due to a foreign-exchange dealer in its US unit, Allfirst, taking the wrong directional bet on the Japanese yen. From the gallery of rogue traders of the past few years, it seems that the risk management lessons of these cases has apparently to be learnt over and over again. Joseph Jett, the top government-bond trader at General Electric's KidderPeabody was accused in 1994 of generating phony profits of US$350 million. Nick Leeson, in 1995, brought the concept of "rogue trader" to new heights, bringing down Barings Bank with losses of US$1.38 billion from unauthorised trading. At Daiwa Bank, in 1995, Mr Iguchi confessed to losing US$1.1 billion over a period of 11 years through unauthorised trading in the US bond market. In 1996, Mr Hamanaka's illicit copper trades cost Sumitomo Bank US$2.6 billion in losses.
>
> In all cases, traders were able to manipulate weak controls, evade risk controls, enter numerous phony trades into the bank's system, misrepresent actual trades, systematically falsify bank records and documents, and take position beyond authorised limits without being detected. These traders were supposedly engaged in low-risk strategies. Sizeable losses were not supposed to occur and, consequently, it was much harder for traders to acknowledge them. The temptation has been for traders who have made losses to cover them up, then engage in high-risk, but potentially high-reward, trading strategies to recoup the losses before anyone notices them. Some key risk management lessons from these cases include:
>
> ❏ Proprietary trading is risky: it is not simply a question of market risk and the potential operational risks may outweigh the potential market returns.
> ❏ Risk management structure and culture, practices and oversight were flawed in all cases.
> ❏ Reporting lines and accountabilities were blurred in all cases. In the case of Allied Irish Banks, the relationship between the parent company and its overseas units was not clear and accountabilities were ambiguous.
> ❏ Strong and enforceable back office controls are essential with strict reconciliation of trade confirmations and settlement of cashflows to transactions booked. In addition, the segregation of duties between the front, middle and back offices should be enforced.
> ❏ In all cases, internal and external audit as well as compliance failed to identify fraudulent trades and activities.
>
> The Bank of England report on the Barings affair revealed four critical high level lessons about operational risk:
>
> 1. management teams have the duty to understand *fully* the businesses they manage;
> 2. responsibility for each business activity has to be *clearly* established and communicated;

MODEL SELECTION FOR OPERATIONAL RISK

> 3. relevant internal controls, including independent risk management, *must* be established for all business activities; and
> 4. top management and the audit committee must ensure that significant weaknesses are resolved *quickly*.
>
> These principles constitute the essence of "Sound Practices for the Management and Supervision of Operational Risk" published by the Basel Committee on Banking Supervision (Basel, 2003a).

bank can insure itself against losses arising from computer hardware problems, or it can hedge the risk by investing in a backup system. The price of this insurance and the cost of such a hedge immediately raise the question of the economic rationale of protecting against the risks. Inevitably, the institution will need to assess the potential loss against the certain cost of insuring against an operational risk.

Looking into the future, banks are becoming aware that technology is a double-edged sword. The increasing complexity of instruments and information systems increases the potential for operational risk. Unfamiliarity with instruments may lead to their misuse and raise the chances of mispricing and wrong hedging; errors in data feeds may also distort the bank's assessment of its risks. At the same time advanced analytical techniques combined with sophisticated computer technology create new ways to add value to operational risk management.

In this chapter we look at how a bank should construct a framework for

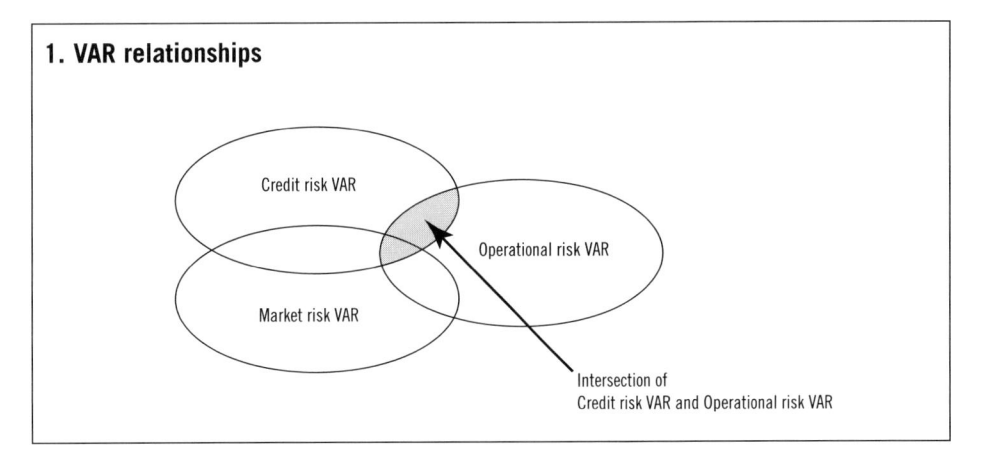

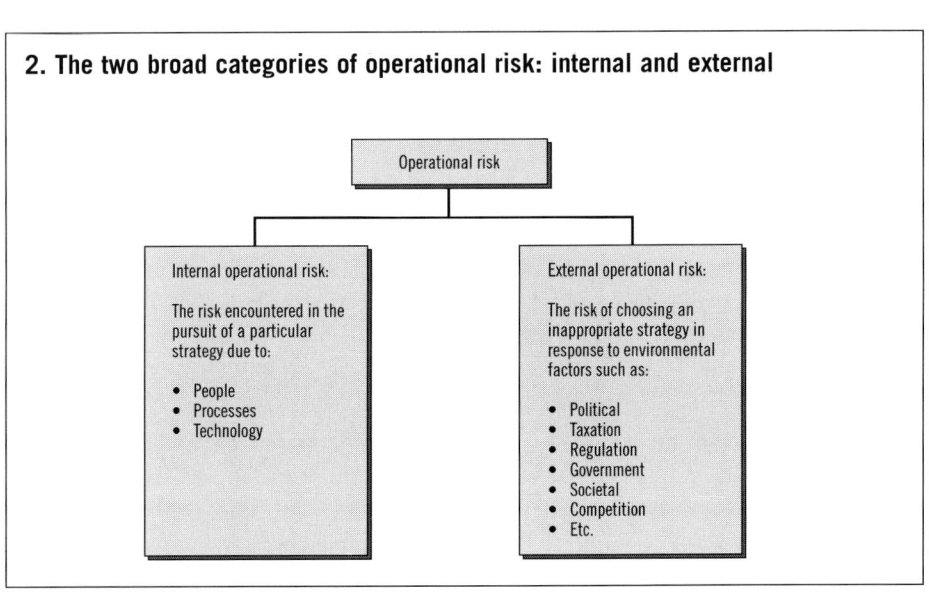

1. VAR relationships

Credit risk VAR

Operational risk VAR

Market risk VAR

Intersection of Credit risk VAR and Operational risk VAR

2. The two broad categories of operational risk: internal and external

Operational risk

Internal operational risk:

The risk encountered in the pursuit of a particular strategy due to:

- People
- Processes
- Technology

External operational risk:

The risk of choosing an inappropriate strategy in response to environmental factors such as:

- Political
- Taxation
- Regulation
- Government
- Societal
- Competition
- Etc.

MODEL SELECTION FOR OPERATIONAL RISK

measuring operational risk. After explaining the key underlying rule – that the control functions of a bank should be carefully integrated – we examine the typology of operational risks. We then review the current regulatory approaches to this class of risk. Next, we describe how one should implement operational risk models and provide an illustrative example of the application of a model. We also look at how a bank can extract value from enhanced operational risk management by improving its capital attribution methodologies.

For reasons discussed towards the end of the chapter, it is important that the financial industry develops a consistent modelling approach to operational risk – operational risk VAR or OpVAR. OpVAR should be consistent with the basic underlying principles of market risk VAR and credit risk VAR. These three VAR are often interactive and therefore overlap with one another. Thus, for example, one needs to be precise in defining situations where operational risk VAR and credit risk VAR intersect (Figure 1). We believe that our approach is in line with the findings of the working group of the Basel Committee on internal control systems in banking organisations (Basel, 1998) and the principles put forward in "Sound Practices for the Management and Supervision of Operational Risk" (Basel, 2003a) as well as with the 20 best-practice recommendations on derivative risk management put forward in the seminal Group of Thirty (G-30) report of 1993 (Group of Thirty, 1993).

Typology of operational risks
WHAT IS OPERATIONAL RISK?

Operational risk is the risk associated with operating the business. Operational risk covers such a wide area that it is useful to divide it into two components: internal and external. Figure 2 summarises the relationship between the two components.[1]

Internal operational risk arises from the potential for failure in the course of operating the business. A firm uses people, processes and technology to achieve business plans, and any one of these may experience a failure of some kind. Accordingly, as pointed out earlier, operational failure risk can be defined as the risk that there will be a failure of people, processes or technology. A certain level of failure can be anticipated and should be covered by reserves and incorporated into the price of services, such as the interest margin on Visa balances. It is the unanticipated, and therefore uncertain, failures in excess of the expected amount that give rise to the key operational risks. These failures can be expected to occur periodically, although both their impact and their frequency may be uncertain.

The impact or *severity* of a financial loss can be divided into two categories: an expected amount and an unexpected amount.[2] The latter can itself be subdivided into two classes: severe and catastrophic amounts (see Figure 4). The firm should provide for the losses that arise from the expected component of these failures by generating sufficient expected revenue to cover expected loss and a net margin that is consistent with the target return on capital. In addition, the firm should set aside enough economic capital to cover the unexpected component or resort to insurance.

External operational risk arises from "environmental" factors, such as a new competitor that changes the business paradigm, a major change in the political or regulatory regime, earthquakes and other such factors that are outside the control of the firm. It also arises from major strategic initiatives, such as developing a new line of business or re-engineering an existing business line. All businesses rely on people, processes and technology outside their business unit, and the potential for failure exists there too; this type of risk will be referred to in this chapter as *external dependency risk*.

A loss arising from an operational risk takes the form either of a direct external cost or of a write-down associated with the resolution of an operational risk event, net of recoveries (mitigation benefits are separate). The loss is recognised for measurement when it is deemed probable and estimable and is recognised as a profit and loss (P&L) event for accounting purposes. One must ensure that boundaries between separate risk types (eg, market, credit and operational) are well defined and avoid double counting.

The definition of operational losses should be as specific as possible. For example, external cost includes the gross cost of compensation and/or penalty payments made to third parties, legal liability, regulatory/tax fines or loss of resource. The *cost-to-fix* includes only the external payments that are directly linked to the incident. For example, legal costs, consultancy costs or hiring temporary staff would be included in the cost-to-fix. Internal costs associated with managing and operations are not included as they are already covered in the normal course of business. *Write-down* refers to the loss or impairment in the value of any financial or non-financial assets owned by the bank. *Resolution* refers to the act of correcting the individual event (including out-of-pocket costs and write-downs) and returning to a position (or standard) comparable to the original one (including restitution payments to third parties). Note that these definitions do not include lost or foregone revenue.

In sum, losses include payments to third parties, write-downs, resolution and cost-to-fix paid to third parties. Losses do not include the cost of controls, preventative action and quality assurance. Losses do not usually include investment in upgrades/new systems and processes.

This chapter focuses on operational failure risk – that is, on the internal factors (people, processes and technology) enumerated in Figure 2 that can and should be controlled by management. However, failure to address a strategic risk issue can easily translate into an operational failure risk. For example, a change in the tax laws poses a strategic risk, and failure to comply with tax laws is an operational failure risk. Furthermore, from a business unit perspective it might be argued that external dependencies include support groups *within* the bank, such as information technology. In other words, the two types of operational risk – internal and external – are interrelated and tend to overlap.

FROM BEGINNING TO END
Operational risk is often thought to be limited to operations or processing centres (ie, where transaction-processing errors may be made). This type of operational risk, sometimes referred to as "operations risk", is an important component but by no means covers all the operational risks facing the firm. Our definition of operational risk as the risk associated with operating the business means that significant amounts of operational risk are also generated outside processing centres. If we take the example of a derivative sales desk, one can see that operational risk arises before, during and after a transaction is processed (Figure 3). Risk begins to accumulate even before the design of the transaction gets under way. It is present during negotiations with the client (regardless of whether the negotiation is a lengthy structuring exercise or a routine electronic negotiation) and continues after negotiation as the transaction is serviced.

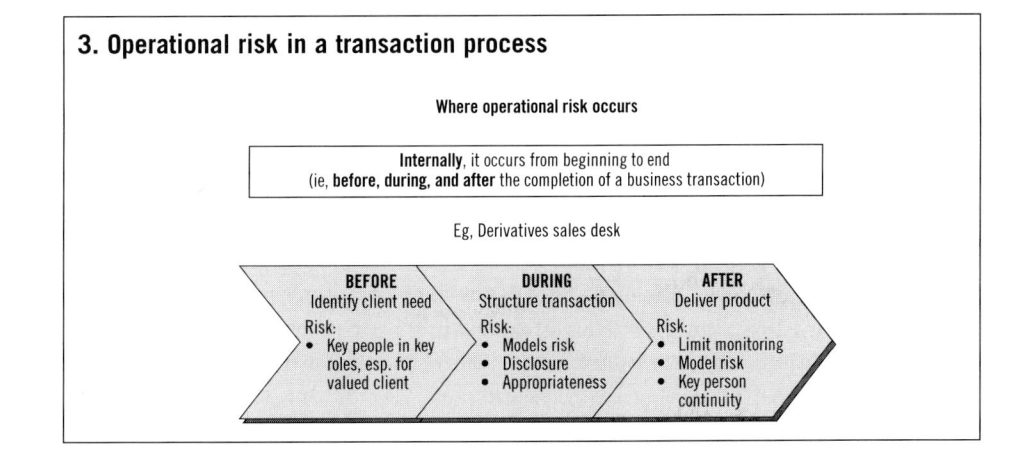

3. Operational risk in a transaction process

Where operational risk occurs

Internally, it occurs from beginning to end
(ie, **before, during, and after** the completion of a business transaction)

Eg, Derivatives sales desk

BEFORE	DURING	AFTER
Identify client need	Structure transaction	Deliver product
Risk:	Risk:	Risk:
• Key people in key roles, esp. for valued client	• Models risk • Disclosure • Appropriateness	• Limit monitoring • Model risk • Key person continuity

MODEL SELECTION FOR OPERATIONAL RISK

A complete picture of operational risk can only be obtained if the bank's activities are analysed from beginning to end. For example, at a derivatives sales desk several things have to be in place before a transaction can be negotiated, and each exposes the firm to operational risk. First, sales may be highly dependent on a valued relationship between a particular sales person and the client. Second, sales are usually dependent on the highly specialised skills of the product designer who comes up with both a structure and a price that the client finds more attractive than competing offers. This means that the institution is exposed to "people risks". For example, there may be uncertainty as to whether these key people will continue to be available. In addition, do they have the capacity to deal with any increase in the sophistication of clients, or are they dealing with too many clients to be able to handle these demands?

During the processing of the transaction, the firm is exposed to several further risks. First, the sales person may not disclose the full range of the risks of the transaction to the client. This risk might be associated with periods when staff are under intense pressure to meet bonus targets for their desk. Similarly, the sales person might persuade the client to engage in a transaction that is totally inappropriate for him or her, exposing the firm to potential lawsuits and regulatory sanctions.

People risks are not the only form of risk found early in a transaction. The sales person may rely on sophisticated financial models to price the transaction. This creates what is commonly called "model risk". Model risk can arise because the wrong parameters are input into the model, or because the model is used inappropriately (eg, outside its domain of applicability), and so on.

Once the transaction has been negotiated and a ticket is written, errors can occur as the transaction is recorded in the various systems or reports. An error here may result in delayed settlement of the transaction, which in turn can result in fines and other penalties. Further, an error in the market risk and credit risk reports might lead to the exposures generated by the deal being understated. In turn, this can lead to the execution of additional transactions that would otherwise not have been executed. These are all examples of what is often called "process risk".

This list of what can go wrong before, during and after the transaction is endless. The system that records the transaction may not be capable of handling the transaction or it may not have the capacity to handle such transactions. Or it may simply be unavailable (because the computer system is down). If any one of the steps is outsourced, external dependency risk also arises. However, each type of risk can be captured as a people, process, technology or external dependency risk, and each can be analysed in terms of capacity, capability or availability.

CLASSIFICATION BY LOSS TYPE

The latest version of the New Basel Capital Accord (Basel, 2003b) considers seven loss event types:

1. *Internal fraud* – losses due to acts of a type intended to defraud, misappropriate property or circumvent regulations, the law or company policy. For example, intentional misreporting of positions, employee theft, and insider trading on an employee's own account.
2. *External fraud* – losses due to acts of a type intended to defraud, misappropriate property or circumvent the law, by a third party. For example, robbery, forgery, cheque kiting, and damage from computer hacking.
3. *Employment practices and workplace safety* – losses arising from acts inconsistent with employment, health or safety laws or agreements, from payment of personal injury claims, or from diversity/discrimination events. For example, violation of organised labour activities.
4. *Clients, products and business practices* – losses arising from an unintentional or negligent failure to meet a professional obligation to specific clients (including

fiduciary and suitability requirements), or from the nature or design of a product. For example, misuse of confidential customer information.
5. *Damage to physical assets* – losses arising from loss or damage to physical assets from natural disaster or other events. For example, terrorism, vandalism, earthquakes, fires and floods.
6. *Business disruption and system failures* – losses arising from disruption of business or system failures. For example, hardware and software failures, telecommunication problems, and utility outages.
7. *Execution, delivery and process management* – losses from failed transaction processing or process management, from relations with trade counterparties and vendors. For example, data entry errors, collateral management failures, incomplete legal documentation, unapproved access to client accounts.

In the New Basel Capital Accord "business risk" is excluded from the regular definition of operational risk. Business risk can be defined as the uncertainty in the demand for a firm's products, in the price that can be charged for those products, and in the cost of the inputs.

Business risk is affected by such factors as the quality of the strategy and/or the reputation of the firm. Therefore it is common practice to view strategic and reputational risks as components of business risk, giving a package that is often referred to as "business/strategic/reputational risk". This risk is managed by the choice of channel, products and suppliers and how the products are marketed.[3] Although the risk should be measured and monitored, there is no industry view on how to do this and on whether it should be supported by capital.

Regulatory approach to risk models
OVERVIEW
As pointed out earlier, the definition of operational risk from the Basel Committee's perspective includes the risk of direct or indirect loss resulting from inadequate or failed internal processes, people and technology and from external dependencies. As also noted earlier, it excludes "business risk", "reputational risk" and "strategic risk".

Basel proposes a spectrum of three approaches that are increasingly risk-sensitive (Figure 4).

Basic indicator approach
The least risk-sensitive is the "basic indicator" approach, for which capital is a multiple (capital factor α) of a single indicator (base) across all businesses – Basel

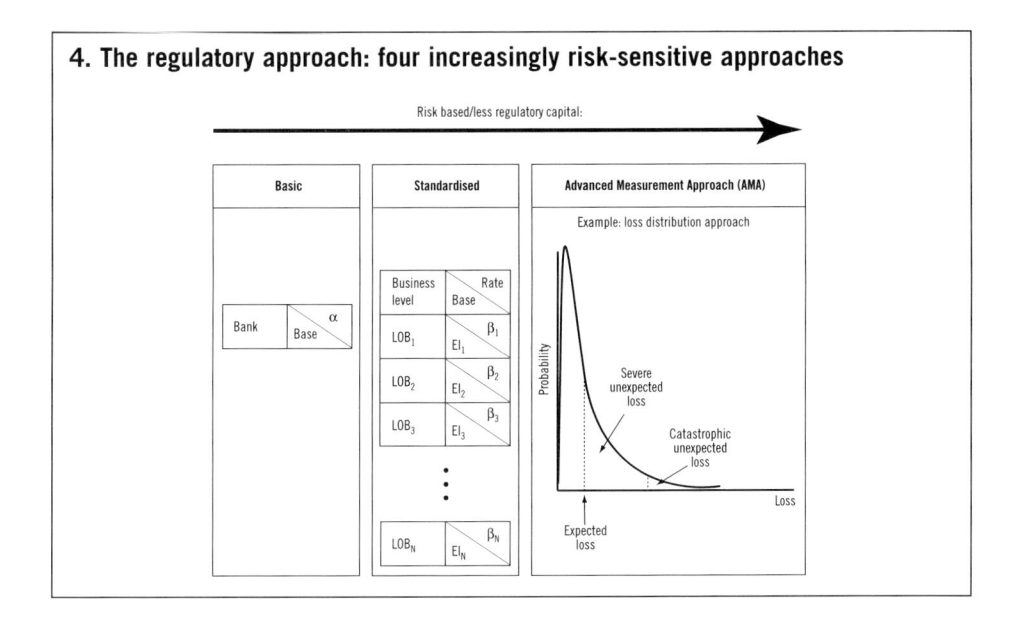

4. The regulatory approach: four increasingly risk-sensitive approaches

Risk based/less regulatory capital:

Basic | Standardised | Advanced Measurement Approach (AMA)

Example: loss distribution approach

Bank — α — Base

Business level | Rate Base
LOB$_1$ | EI$_1$ | β_1
LOB$_2$ | EI$_2$ | β_2
LOB$_3$ | EI$_3$ | β_3
⋮
LOB$_N$ | EI$_N$ | β_N

Probability vs Loss: Expected loss, Severe unexpected loss, Catastrophic unexpected loss proposes for this single indicator the average annual gross income over the previous three years. Gross income is defined as the sum of net interest and non-interest income. According to this approach

$$\text{Capital requirement (OpVAR)} = \alpha \times \text{Gross income} \qquad (1)$$

where the capital factor α will be supplied by the regulator. Currently it is tentatively set at 15%.

Standardised approach

The "standardised" approach divides banks' activities into eight lines of business, LOB_i (see below), with each business line assigned an exposure indicator, EI_i which is gross income that serves as a proxy for the scale of operational risk exposure. Each business line is also assigned a single multiplier (capital factor β_i), and the total capital requirement is defined as the sum of the products of the exposure by the capital factor for each of the N business lines:

$$\text{Capital requirement (OpVAR)} = \sum_{i=1}^{N} EL_i \times \beta_i \qquad (2)$$

The Basel Committee has set the betas to the following values:

Business line	Beta Factors (%)
Corporate finance (β_1)	18
Trading and sales (β_2)	18
Retail banking (β_3)	12
Commercial banking (β_4)	15
Payment and settlement (β_5)	18
Agency services (β_6)	15
Asset management (β_7)	12
Retaile brokerage (β_8)	12

Alternative standardised approach (ASA)

The standardised approach has been criticised because it can lead to double counting for high default rate businesses, such as sub-prime lending. For these activities, the business is hit twice: first, on the credit risk side with high regulatory capital because of the high probability of default of the borrowers, and second, on the operational risk side with high regulatory capital because of high margins to the extent that expected loss is priced in.

As an alternative to the standardised approach described above, an alternative standardised approach (ASA) is allowable at national supervisory discretion. Under the ASA, the operational risk capital framework is the same as for the standardised approach except for two lines of business: retail banking and commercial banking. For these business lines, the exposure indicator, EI, is replaced by:

$$EI = m \times LA$$

where LA is the total outstanding retail loans and advances (non-risk weighted and gross of provisions) averaged over the past three years;

$$m = 0.035$$

Advanced measurement approach (AMA)

Under the AMA, the regulatory capital requirement is the risk measure produced by the bank's internal operational risk model.

An example of internal model is the "loss distribution approach" (Figure 4).

Loss distribution approach
The "loss distribution" approach relies on the bank's internal models to derive the loss distribution. This approach has yet to be permitted by the regulators as there is still skepticism about the availability of the data required to calibrate such models.

The single indicator approach is simpler, has less granularity and is less risk-sensitive than the standardised approach. The standardised approach in turn has less granularity and is less risk-sensitive than the AMA (Figure 5).

THE EXPOSURE INDICATOR (EI), ASSOCIATED MEASURES OF PROBABILITY OF AN EVENT (PE), AND LOSS GIVING EVENT (LGE) FOR THE AMA

A measure of EI for *legal liability* related to client exposure could be the number of clients multiplied by the average balance per client. The associated PE for client exposure would then be equal to the number of lawsuits divided by the number of clients. The LGE would equal the average loss divided by the average balance per client.

A measure of EI for *employee liability* could be the number of employees multiplied by the average compensation. The PE for employee liability would then be the number of lawsuits divided by the number of employees, and the LGE would be the average loss divided by the average employee compensation.

Similarly, a measure of EI for *regulatory, compliance and taxation penalties* could be the number of accounts multiplied by the balance per account. The PE would then be the number of penalties (including cost to comply) divided by the number of accounts and the LGE would be the average penalty divided by the average balance per account.

A measure of EI for *loss of or damage to assets* could be the number of physical assets multiplied by the average value. The associated PE would be the number of damages divided by the number of physical assets and the LGE would be the average loss divided by the average value of physical assets.

A measure of EI for *client restitution* could be the number of accounts multiplied by the average balance per account. The PE would then be the number of restitutions divided by the number of accounts and the LGE would be the average restitution divided by the average balance per account.

A measure of EI for *theft, fraud and unauthorised activities* could be the number of accounts multiplied by the balance per account or the number of transactions multiplied by the average value per transaction. The corresponding measures for PE

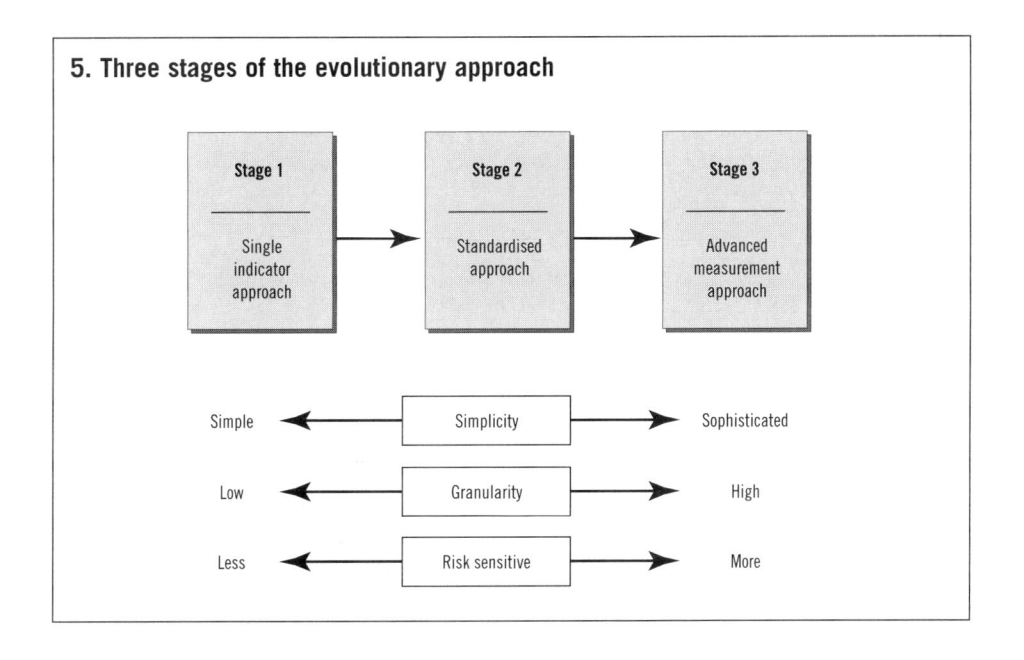

5. Three stages of the evolutionary approach

Stage 1: Single indicator approach → Stage 2: Standardised approach → Stage 3: Advanced measurement approach

Simple ←	Simplicity	→ Sophisticated
Low ←	Granularity	→ High
Less ←	Risk sensitive	→ More

MODEL SELECTION FOR OPERATIONAL RISK

> ### PANEL 2
>
> ### EXAMPLE: USE OF OPVAR TO MEASURE VISA FRAUD
>
> The exposure index, EI, chosen to measure Visa fraud can be the total dollar amount of the transactions – ie, the product of the number of transactions and the average value of a transaction. For simplicity, assume that the average value of a Visa transaction is US$100.[1]
>
> The expected probability of an operational risk event, PE, can be calculated by dividing the number of loss events due to fraud by the number of transactions. If we assume that there are 1.3 fraud loss events per 1,000 transactions, PE equals 0.13%.
>
> Assume that the average loss given an event, LGE, for Visa (conditional on the fact that a loss occurred) is US$70. Accordingly, the LGE is calculated by dividing the average loss by the average value of a transaction; in our example this comes to 70%.
>
> Assume for Visa that the statistical worst-case loss set at the appropriate loss tolerance for the industry is 52 cents (on an average transaction of US$100) and that the expected loss, or loss rate, LR, is
>
> $$LR = PE \times LGE = 0.13\% \times US\$70 = 9 \text{ cents}$$
>
> The figure summarises the components of OpVAR for Visa fraud-related losses.
>
> **Components of OpVAR for Visa fraud-related losses**
>
> [Figure: three distributions combined — Number of fraudulent transactions per 1,000 transactions (PE = 1.3 average, 9 worst case) + Loss per US$100 fraudulent transaction (LGE = US$70 average, US$100 worst case) = Loss per US$100 transaction, showing Expected loss at 9, Severe unexpected loss, and Catastrophic unexpected loss at 52]
>
> The probability distribution of operational risk events could be fitted to a Poisson distribution where the average number of events per year would be estimated from historical data.[2] The severity distribution could be calibrated to an exponential distribution. The loss distribution is itself driven by both the probability distribution and the severity distribution and could be calibrated to a lognormal distribution (see figure).
>
> [1] This is a generic example with numbers which do not reflect CIBC's experience.
> [2] The Poisson distribution assumes that the mean and variance of the probability of events distribution are the same. It also assumes that the inter-arrival time between operational risk events follows an exponential distribution and therefore that the length of time between the last event and the next is independent of the time since the last event.

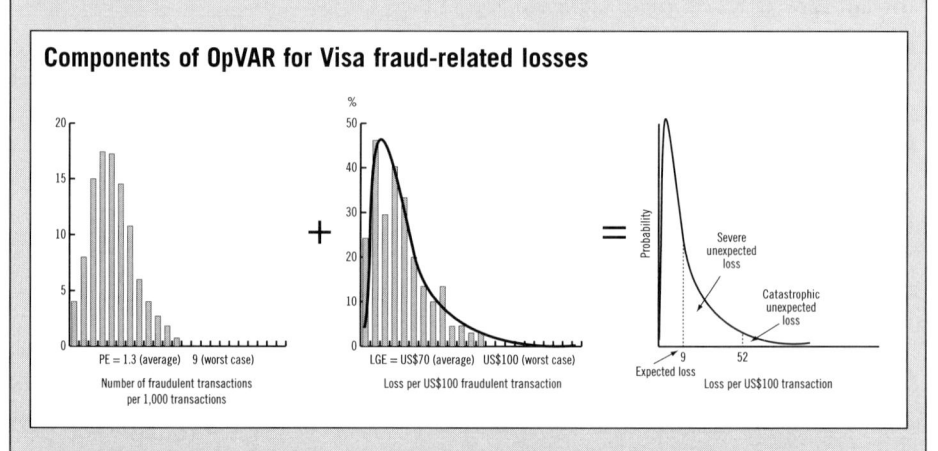

would be the number of frauds divided by the number of accounts or the number of frauds divided by the number of transactions. The respective LGEs would be the average loss divided by the average balance per account or the average loss divided by the average value per transaction.

A measure of EI for transaction-processing risk could be the number of transactions multiplied by the average value per transaction. The PE would then be the number of errors divided by the number of transactions. The LGE would be the average loss divided by the average value per transaction.

Implementing operational risk models

OVERVIEW

To qualify for and implement the AMA one has to put in place appropriate policies, methodologies and infrastructure. These include having the appropriate measures for exposure, up to date internal and industry-wide loss data, well-designed scenario analysis and key risk drivers (KRDs – discussed later in this section), as shown in Figure 6. One also needs to have the appropriate infrastructure to provide reporting to the relevant committees (eg, say an operations and administration committee as well as a capital and risk committee). One typically starts with an infrastructure that can provide the necessary key elements (eg, PEs, LGEs) to implement OpVAR. A task force would typically scope out and make recommendations to the management committee to ensure firm-wide support.

EIGHT KEY ELEMENTS IN IMPLEMENTATION OF BANK-WIDE OPERATIONAL RISK MODELS

In our experience, eight key elements are necessary to successfully implement a bank-wide operational risk management framework and the associated operational risk models (Figure 7). They involve setting policy and identifying risk on the basis of an agreed terminology, constructing business process maps, building a best-practice measurement methodology, providing exposure management, installing a timely reporting capability, performing risk analysis (inclusive of stress-testing) and allocating economic capital as a function of operational risk. Let's look at these in more detail.

The first step is to develop *well-defined operational risk policies*. This includes an explicit articulation of the desired standards for risk measurement. One also needs to establish clear guidelines for practices that may contribute to a reduction of operational risk. For example, the bank needs to establish policies on model vetting, out-of-hours trading, off-premises trading, legal document vetting, and so on.

The second step is to establish a *common language of risk identification*. For example, the term "people risk" would include a failure to deploy skilled staff. "Process risk" would include execution errors. "Technology risk" would include system failures, and so on. Risk identification would also include a qualitative self-assessment done by the business management and validated by risk management.

The third step is to develop *business process maps* for each business. For example, one should map the business process associated with the bank's dealings with a broker so that it becomes transparent to management and auditors. One should create an "operational risk catalogue", as illustrated in Table 1, which categorises and defines the various operational risks arising from each organisational unit in terms of people, process and technology risks. This includes analysing the products and services that each organisational unit offers and the action one needs to take to manage operational risk. This catalogue should be a tool to help with operational risk identification and assessment. Again, the catalogue should be based on common definitions and language.

The fourth step is to develop a *comprehensible set of operational risk metrics*. Risk measurement is carried out by operational risk management using a quantitative methodology based on loss experience and scenario analysis to derive frequency and severity distributions, which drive the loss distribution and economic capital for operational risk.

Operational risk assessment is a complex process. It needs to be performed on a firm-wide basis at regular intervals using standard metrics. In the early days, as

MODEL SELECTION FOR OPERATIONAL RISK

6. Implementing OpVAR

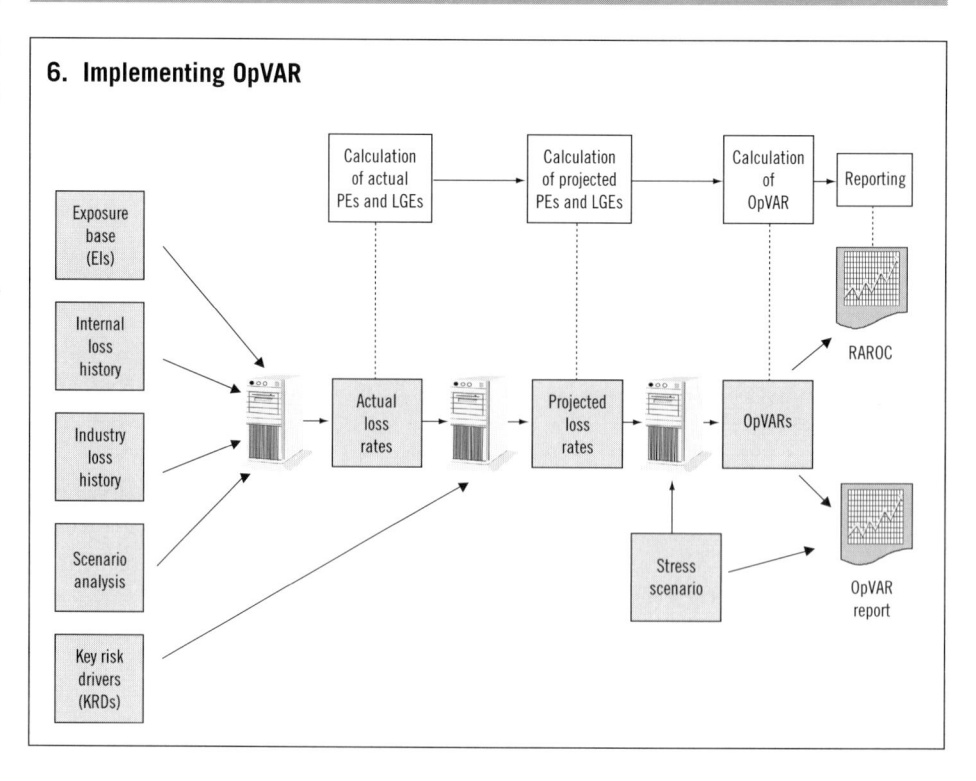

7. Eight key elements in implementation of best-practice operational risk models

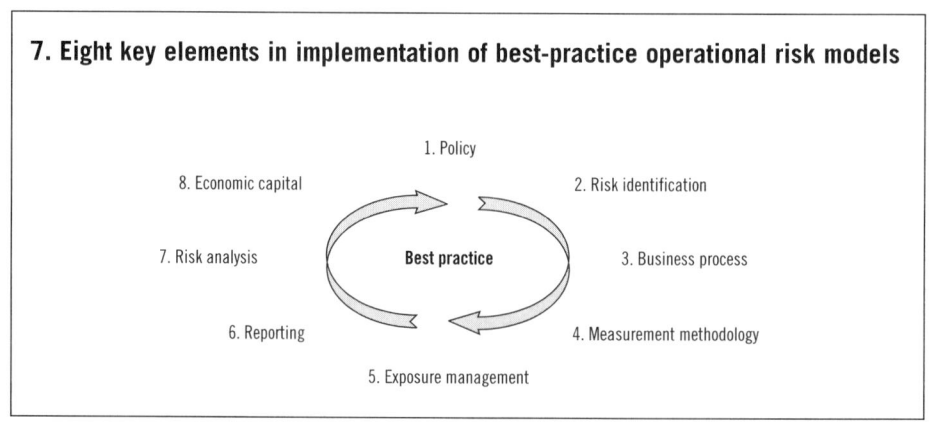

1. Policy
2. Risk identification
3. Business process
4. Measurement methodology
5. Exposure management
6. Reporting
7. Risk analysis
8. Economic capital

Best practice

illustrated in Figure 8, business and infrastructure groups performed their own self-assessment of operational risk. Today, self-assessment has been discredited – the self-assessment of operational risk at Barings Bank contributed to the build-up of market risk at that institution – and is no longer acceptable. Sophisticated financial institutions are trying to develop objective measures of operational risk that build significantly more reliability into the quantification of operational risk. We mentioned earlier that operational risk assessment must include a review of the likelihood of a particular operational risk occurring, as well as the severity or magnitude of the impact that the operational risk will have on business objectives. We examine this challenge in more detail in the next section.

The fifth step is to decide *how to manage operational risk exposure* and take appropriate action to hedge the risks. The bank should address the economic question of the cost-benefit of insuring a given risk for those operational risks that can be insured.

The sixth step is to decide *how to report exposure*. As an example a summary report for the Tokyo equity arbitrage business is shown in Table 2, from which one can see that the overall operational failure risk of the trading desk is low whereas the strategic risk is medium.

The seventh step is to develop *tools for risk analysis* and procedures for when these tools should be deployed. For example, risk analysis is typically performed as

MODEL SELECTION FOR OPERATIONAL RISK

Table 1. Types of operational failure

1. People risk
       Incompetence
       Fraud
       Etc

2. Process risk:
   A. Model risk*
       Model/methodology error
       Mark-to-model error
       Etc

   B. Transaction risk
       Execution error
       Product complexity
       Booking error
       Settlement error
       Documentation/contract risk
       Etc

   C. Operational control risk
       Exceeding limits
       Security risks
       Volume risk
       Etc

3. Technology risk
       System failure
       Programming error
       Information risk
       Telecommunication failure
       Etc

*See Crouhy, Galai and Mark (2000, Chapter 15).

Table 2. Operational risk reporting worksheet for Tokyo equity arbitrage trading desk

Category	Risk profile
1. People risk	
Incompetence	Low
Fraud	Low
2. Process risk	
A. Model risk	
Model/methodology error	Low
Mark-to-market error	Low
B. Transaction risk	
Execution error	Low
Product complexity	Medium
Booking error	Low
Settlement error	Low
Documentation/contract risk	Medium
C. Operational control risk	
Exceeding limits	Low
Security risk	Low
Volume risk	Low/medium
3. Technology risk	
System failure	Low
Programming error	Low
Information risk	Low
Telecommunication failure	Low
Total operational failure risk	**Low**
Strategic risk	
Political risk	Low
Taxation risk	Low
Regulatory risk	Medium/high
Total strategic risk measurement	**Medium**

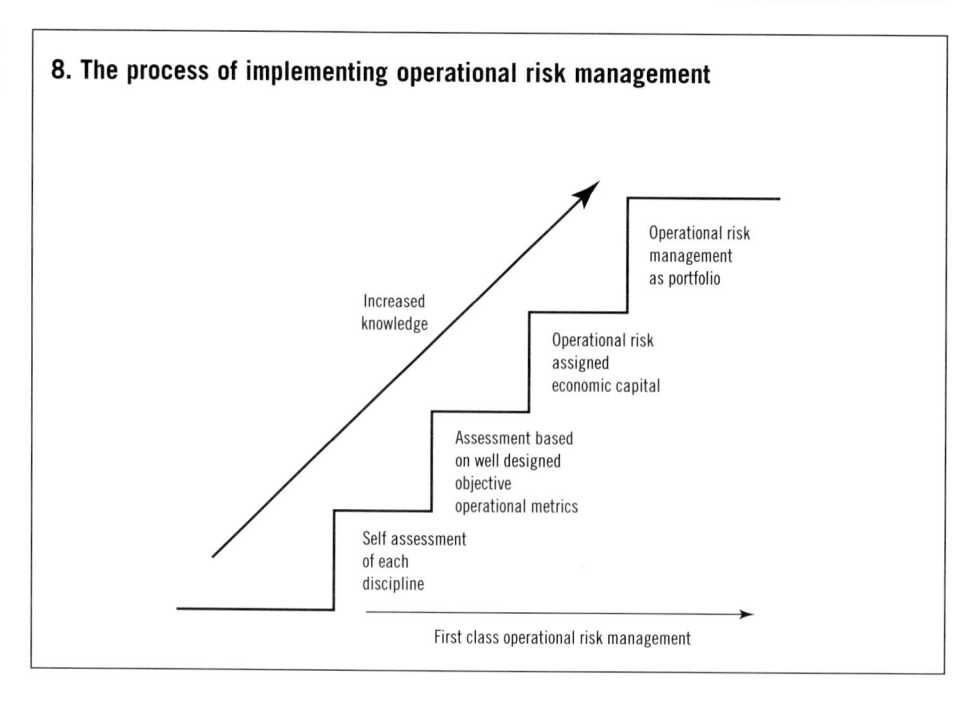

8. The process of implementing operational risk management

Steps (ascending): Self assessment of each discipline → Assessment based on well designed objective operational metrics → Operational risk assigned economic capital → Operational risk management as portfolio. Arrow labeled "Increased knowledge". Horizontal axis: "First class operational risk management".

part of a new product process, periodic business reviews, and so on. Stress-testing should be a standard part of the risk analysis process. The frequency of risk assessment should be a function of the degree to which operational risks are expected to change over time as businesses undertake new initiatives or as business circumstances evolve. This frequency might be reviewed as operational risk measurement is rolled out across the bank. A bank should update its risk assessments more frequently (say semi-annually) following the initial assessment of operational risk within a business unit. Further, one should reassess whenever the operational risk profile changes significantly – for example, after the implementation of a new system or entering a new service.

The eighth step is to ensure *appropriate attribution of operational risk capital* (RAROC), where operational risk capital is attributed to every business.

ASPECTS OF IMPLEMENTATION
Short-term aspects
The OpVAR implementation process usually requires the development of both short-term and long-term approaches to its execution. The short-term approach, as illustrated in the unshaded portions of Figure 9, calls for efforts to be prioritised to ensure that the OpVAR is kept current. Accordingly one needs to ensure that data on changes in the level of activities are kept current and, therefore, are incorporated into the OpVAR calculation on a timely basis. For example, one would need to ensure that exposure bases (the EIs) are feeding into the OpVAR calculation on, say, a monthly basis. One might also ensure in the short term that the internal loss history is complete, but this typically takes a significant effort in the form of building a comprehensive database of loss factors.

Longer-term aspects
The intermediate-term implementation priorities, shown in the unshaded space of Figure 10, focus on adjusting the OpVAR measures to reflect changes in the risk parameters. This would include developing a robust internal and industry loss history database for appropriate calculation of the PEs and LGEs. One would also want to ensure that key risk drivers (KRDs) are properly formulated. Further, one would want to ensure that robust scenario analysis is included in the determination of OpVAR.

MODEL SELECTION FOR OPERATIONAL RISK

9. OpVAR process – short-term

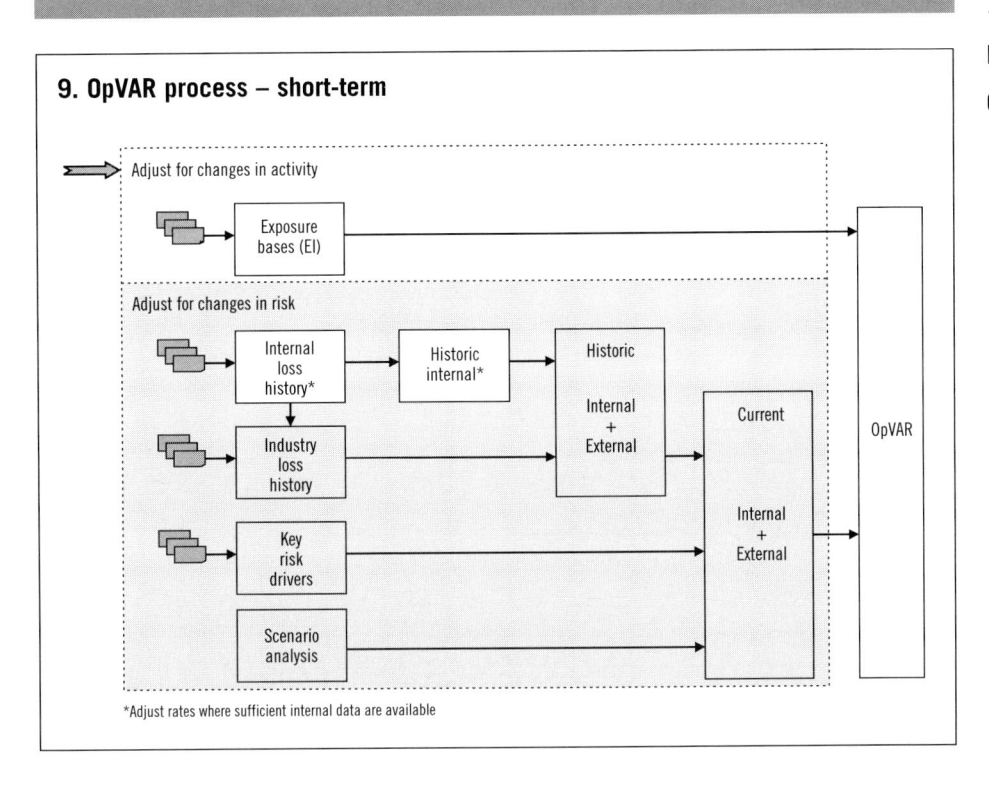

*Adjust rates where sufficient internal data are available

In the long term insufficient internal loss data need to be supplemented with industry loss data, as illustrated in Figure 11. For example, as shown in Figure 12, each business (say Visa) would have an appropriate matrix of statistics for each loss type that would be developed over the relevant time period.

One would need to factor in the degree to which one would weight industry data versus internal data to arrive at the appropriate calculation. For example, in our hypothetical Visa example OpVAR is given by

$$\text{Dollar value of transactions (say, US\$100)} \times (Z \times \text{Internal loss rate} + (1-Z) \times \text{Industry loss rate}) \times \gamma$$

10. OpVAR process – intermediate term

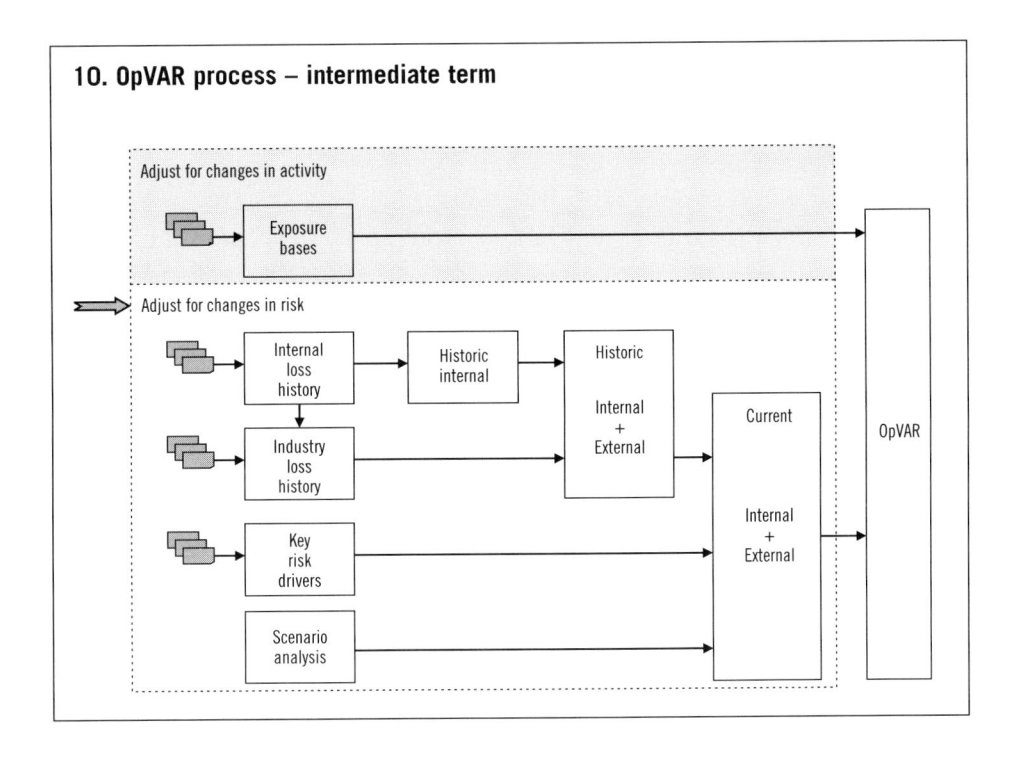

where Z is the proportional weight applied to internal data. Using Z = 0.5 and substituting the illustrative numbers given in Table 3, we obtain:[4]

$$\text{OpVAR} = \text{US\$100} \times (Z \times 0.09\% + (1 - Z) \times 0.14\%) \times 8 = \text{US\$0.92}$$

Table 3. Visa general industry loss rate due to theft/fraud

Derived from industry data	0.14%
Derived from internal data (see Panel 2 figure)	0.09%

Similarly, if analysing theft/fraud in trading and sales where the value of transactions is US$2 billion, where industry data indicate a 0.08% chance of fraud and company-specific internal data indicate a 0.05% chance, then (with Z = 0.5) capital equals

$$\text{US\$2 billion} \ (0.05 \times 0.50 + 0.08 \times 0.50) \times 8 = \text{US\$10 million}$$

Key risk drivers like that shown in Figure 13 need to be developed and used to monitor changes in operational risk for each business and for each loss type before

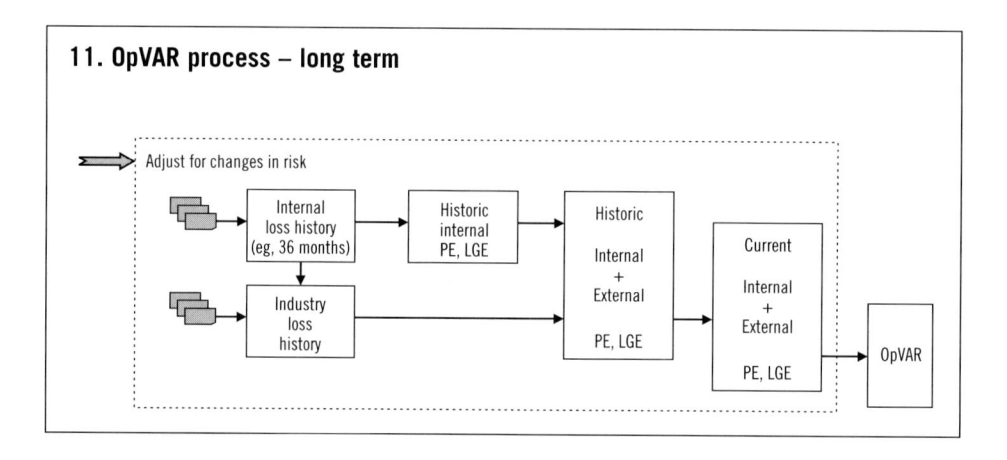

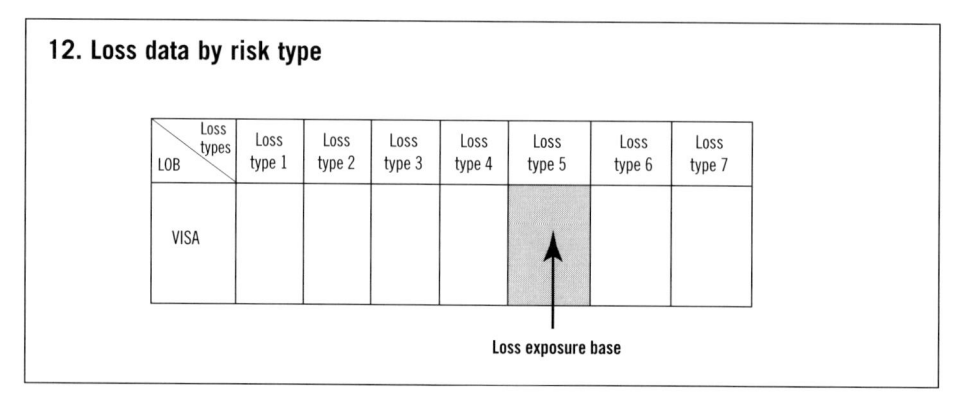

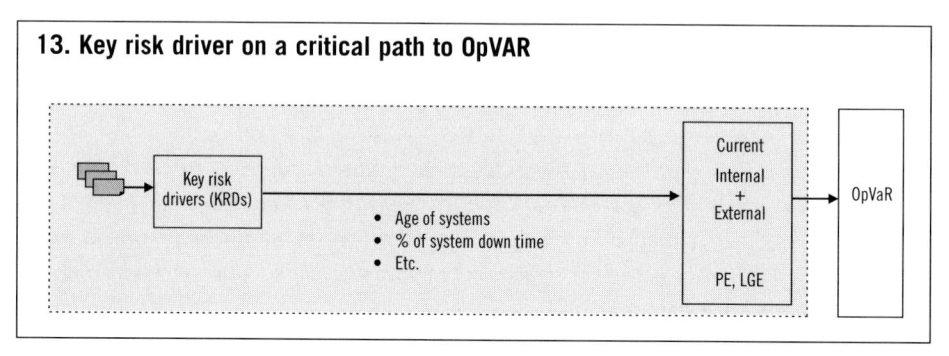

11. OpVAR process – long term

12. Loss data by risk type

13. Key risk driver on a critical path to OpVAR

the change in loss experience can be observed due to the inherent lag in low-frequency events. KRDs can be incorporated into OpVAR by modifying the risk determined by the loss history and then used to reward or punish for positive or negative changes in the risk profile as detected by the drivers. For KRDs there need to be objective standard measures ranging from a simple system that relies on audit scores to systems based on more elaborate metrics, such as the age of systems or the percentage of system downtime.

Table 4. Example linkage of a key risk driver to OpVAR

	Δ KRD %	Δ OpVAR %
	+20	−15
	+10	−10
Base	0	0
	−10	+15
	−20	+25

Once the KRDs have been established we need to map changes in a driver into the corresponding changes in OpVAR. For example, as shown in Table 4, if the KRD score rises by 20%, OpVAR is reduced by 15%.

QUALIFYING FOR AMA

To achieve the measurement and validation eligibility criteria for AMA, the bank needs a well-defined management plan for each infrastructure and business unit (Figure 14).

One of risk management's main responsibilities is then to draw up and disseminate operational risk reports (Figure 15) to key stakeholders (Figure 16). Standard reporting and tracking needs to be in place to produce, for example,

❑ Top 10 operational risks: what are my biggest operational risks?
❑ OpVAR expected losses: what hits can the P&L expect to take from my biggest operational risk?
❑ OpVAR worst-case losses: how bad can those hits get?
❑ Stress analysis: how bad can those hits really get?
❑ Key risk drivers: how will changes to my business strategy or control environment affect those hits?
❑ Industry and internal benchmark loss rates: how do my potential hits compare internally or externally?

The key to a successful implementation of the AMA approach is to bring together all the pieces shown in Figures 14–16 so that accountabilities, policies, methodologies and infrastructure are fully aligned, as shown in Figure 17.

Implementation sequence

Implementation of the AMA OpVAR approach should be carefully planned and sequenced. An important part of planning is to determine the scope and associated costs of the project (Figure 18).

The typical first step (at time t_0 in Figure 18) after obtaining approval from the management committee is to create a *project structure*. This calls for the appointment of a steering committee chaired by risk management. The steering committee would be composed of business representatives as well as representatives from the chief administrative office, technology and operations, audit and compliance, etc. One would also appoint working groups chaired by operational risk group representatives from business infrastructure.

The second step (at time t_1) is to *scope and cost* the effort of following through on the eight key elements outlined earlier (Figure 7). One needs to inventory existing processes and infrastructure and review what it takes to calculate the EIs, PEs, LGEs and KRDs. The gaps in the current reporting of operational risk and the cost of closing those gaps then have to be identified. Available industry tools have to be inventoried, such as loss rate database infrastructures, so that decisions can be made on buying the best and building the rest.

Operational risk policies, including roles and responsibilities, should be

MODEL SELECTION FOR OPERATIONAL RISK

14. Infrastructure units and business units

(a) Infrastructure/business unit

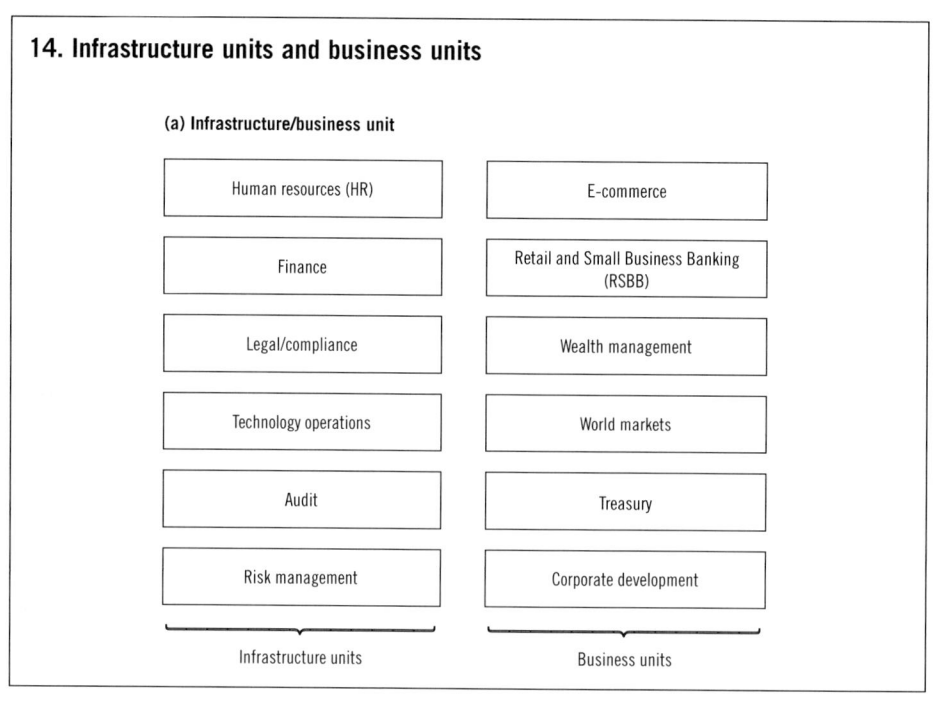

Infrastructure units:
- Human resources (HR)
- Finance
- Legal/compliance
- Technology operations
- Audit
- Risk management

Business units:
- E-commerce
- Retail and Small Business Banking (RSBB)
- Wealth management
- World markets
- Treasury
- Corporate development

15. Key reports
- Top ten loss experience report
- Op VAR report
- KRDs trend report
- Event analysis report
- Stress analysis report
- Industry benchmark report
- Risk identification report

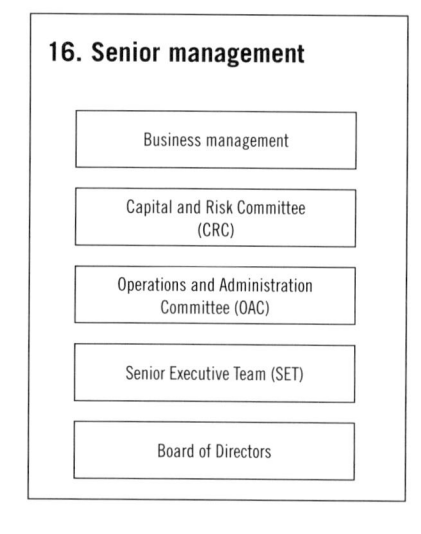

16. Senior management
- Business management
- Capital and Risk Committee (CRC)
- Operations and Administration Committee (OAC)
- Senior Executive Team (SET)
- Board of Directors

formulated. Typically, as pointed out earlier, a methodology has to be developed for calculating OpVAR on the basis of standard definitions of the EI, PE and LGE associated with each of the loss types. The business units should review each of the operational processes and associated operational risks. A common understanding of OpVAR has to be developed, and definitions of the components of operational risk need to be uniformly applied to ensure consistency and transparency. Typically, a patchwork informal network to gather EI and loss experience has to be set up. Also, one needs to develop KRDs as well as foster an enterprise-wide view of operational processes and associated operational risk.

The AMA approach is then *implemented* (at time t_2) after obtaining management committee approval. This includes decisions to build or buy systems and databases. One should leverage internal processes, such as a new initiative and approval process (NIAP), and provide monthly progress reviews to the relevant supervisory committee. The approach, including a risk reporting and review structure, can be piloted in several businesses. The last step is to go live bank-wide.

CAPITAL ATTRIBUTION FOR OPERATIONAL RISKS

A few guiding principles for regulatory capital are that they should be risk-based, transparent, scalable and fair. Specifically from a risk-based perspective, capital

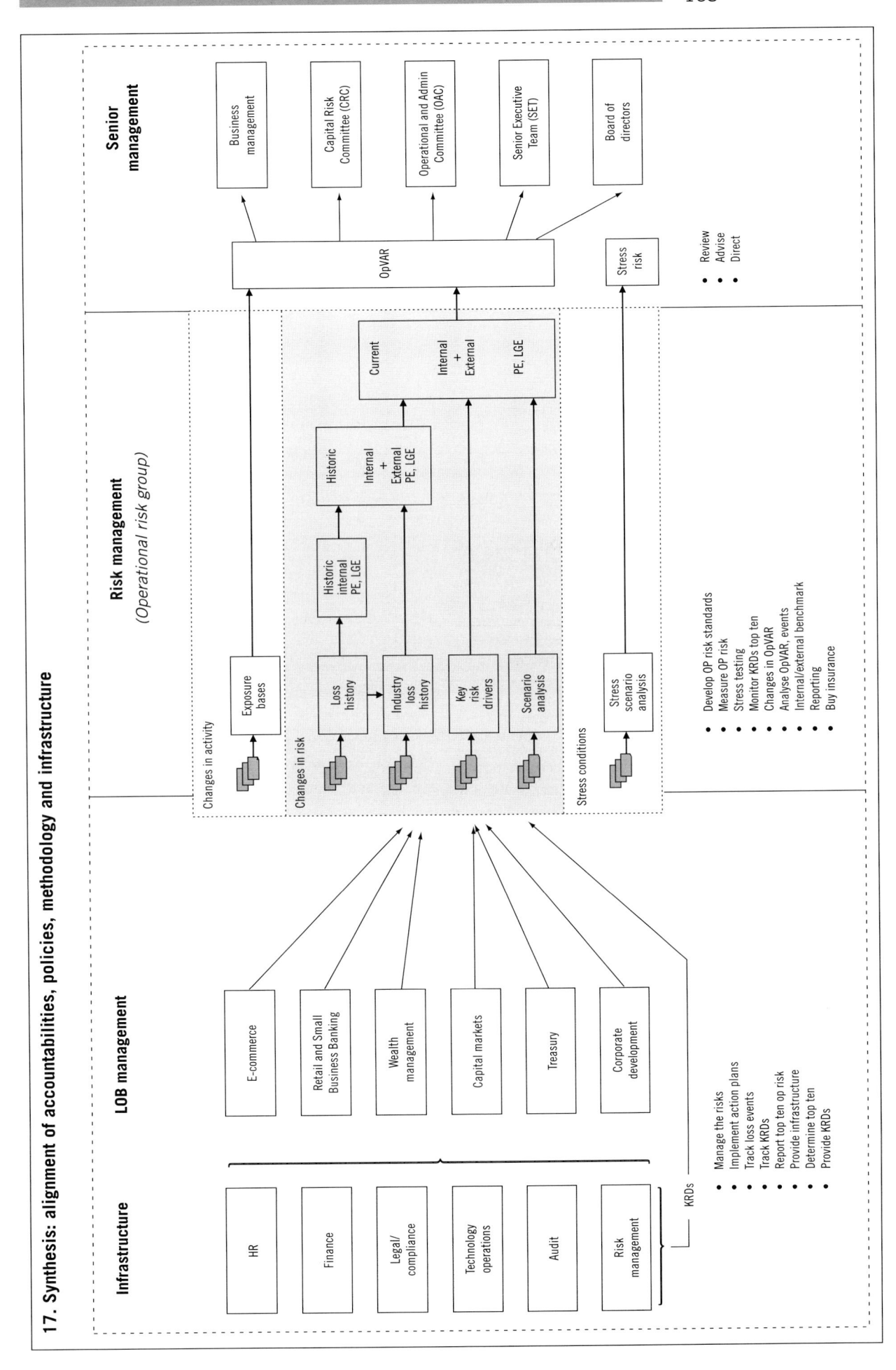

17. Synthesis: alignment of accountabilities, policies, methodology and infrastructure

Infrastructure
- HR
- Finance
- Legal/compliance
- Technology operations
- Audit
- Risk management

} KRDs

LOB management
- E-commerce
- Retail and Small Business Banking
- Wealth management
- Capital markets
- Treasury
- Corporate development

- Manage the risks
- Implement action plans
- Track loss events
- Track KRDs
- Report top ten op risk
- Provide infrastructure
- Determine top ten
- Provide KRDs

Risk management *(Operational risk group)*

Changes in activity: Exposure bases

Changes in risk:
- Loss history → Historic internal PE, LGE → Historic Internal + External PE, LGE → Current Internal + External PE, LGE → OpVAR
- Industry loss history
- Key risk drivers
- Scenario analysis

Stress conditions: Stress scenario analysis → Stress risk

- Develop OP risk standards
- Measure OP risk
- Stress testing
- Monitor KRDs top ten
- Changes in OpVAR
- Analyse OpVAR, events
- Internal/external benchmark
- Reporting
- Buy insurance

Senior management
- Business management
- Capital Risk Committee (CRC)
- Operational and Admin Committee (OAC)
- Senior Executive Team (SET)
- Board of directors

- Review
- Advise
- Direct

ADVANCES IN OPERATIONAL RISK

requirements should vary directly with levels of verifiable risk and provide incentives to institutions to manage operational risk so as to increase the risk-adjusted return on capital. The calibration of operational risk should reflect current circumstances. Operational risk should not be used as a "top-up" or "plug" mechanism. *Transparent* implies that the computation of any regulatory capital should be readily understood and verifiable. *Scalable* implies that the capital framework should be modifiable to suit the characteristics and capabilities of all institutions. The framework should provide incentives that encourage institutions to apply increasingly sophisticated methods. *Fair* implies that the framework should enable capital to be assessed even-handedly, without prejudice to sector differences within financial services companies and/or across jurisdictions. To the extent possible, the framework should not disadvantage regulated institutions.

We can make sure that businesses which take more operational risk are allocated more operational risk capital by attributing economic capital to operational risks using the most rational approach. We want each strategic business unit to incur a transparent capital charge. This in turn will allow whole firms and individual businesses to use risk/reward analysis to improve their operational decisions. In most banks the methodology for translating operational risk into capital is developed by the RAROC group in partnership with the operational risk management group.

Note that for the purpose of capital allocation we need to take special account of the kind of worst-case scenarios of operational losses illustrated in Figure 19. To understand this diagram, remember that operational risks can be divided into those losses that are expected and those that are unexpected. Management knows that in the ordinary course of business certain operational activities will fail. There will be a "normal" amount of operational loss (due to error corrections, fraud and so on) that the business is willing to absorb as a cost of doing business. These failures are explicitly or implicitly budgeted for in the annual business plan and are covered by the pricing of the product or service. We assume that a business unit's management is already assessing and pricing expected failures.

By contrast, the focus of this chapter is on the unexpected failures shown in Figure 19 and the amount of economic capital that should be attributed to business units to absorb such losses. However, as the figure suggests, unexpected failures can themselves be further subdivided as shown below.

❑ *Severe but not catastrophic losses* Unexpected severe operational failures should be covered by an appropriate allocation of operational risk capital (Table 5). These losses are covered by the measurement processes described in the sections above.
❑ *Catastrophic losses* These are the most extreme but also the rarest forms of operational risk events – the kind that can destroy the bank entirely. VAR and

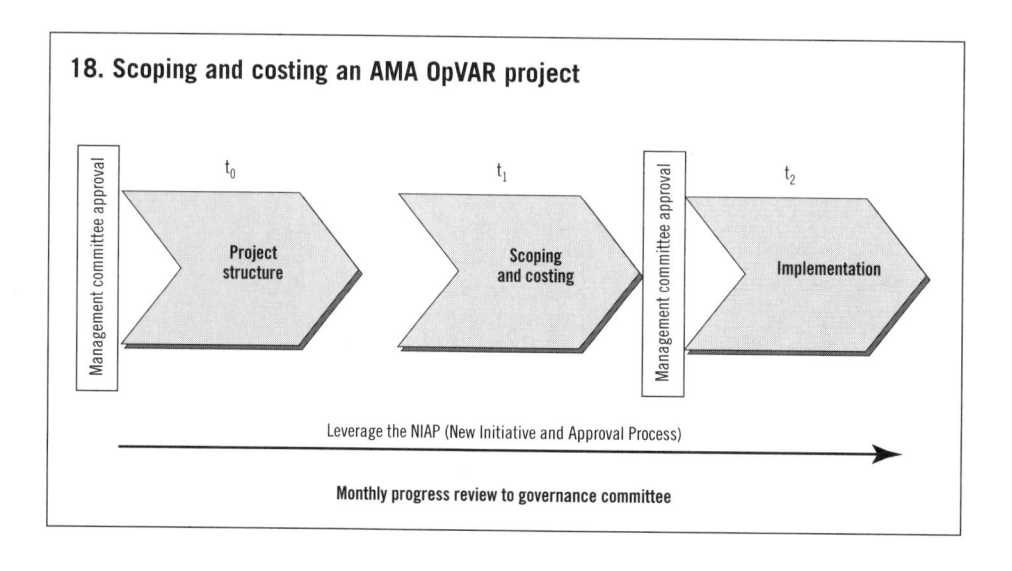

18. Scoping and costing an AMA OpVAR project

Management committee approval | t_0 Project structure | t_1 Scoping and costing | Management committee approval | t_2 Implementation

Leverage the NIAP (New Initiative and Approval Process)

Monthly progress review to governance committee

RAROC models are not meant to capture catastrophic risk since they consider potential losses only up to a certain confidence level and catastrophic risks are by their very nature extremely rare. Banks may use insurance to hedge catastrophic risk because capital will not protect a bank against these risks.

OPERATIONAL RISK MITIGATION

There is a major factor that distinguishes operational risk from both market risk and credit risk. By assuming more market or credit risk, a bank expects to yield a higher rate of return on its capital. There is a trade-off between risk and expected return. By assuming more operational risk, a bank does not expect to yield more on average. Operational risk usually destroys value for all claimholders.

At the same time, trying to reduce the exposure to operational risk is costly. A bank, for example, can install a better IT system with more security devices, and also a back-up system. By doing so, the risk due to system failure is reduced, but there is a cost involved in taking these measures. While there is no economic incentive to increase operational risk, the question arises of whether the bank should invest in operational risk mitigation. Should it spend resources to reduce the exposure?

There is an inherent conflict of interest in the bank between the shareholders and depositors, and between them and the regulators (and especially, the deposit insurance authorities). When a bank buys an insurance against, say, the failure of its computer system, the question arises of who is hurt by the payment of the insurance premium, and who benefits from such a protection. The alternative to insurance is self-insurance, thus saving the payment of the premium, at a cost of potential failure with small probability. The issue is even more complicated when the cost of insurance is taken into consideration, compared to its actuarial benefit.

The major question is under what conditions and terms should a bank buy insurance against the operation risk exposure? Insurance is not always necessarily good for the bank, since it may destroy value, if it is too costly. There is a trade-off between the cost of insurance and the capital allocation against such risk.

The issue of insurance against operational risk events is more complex in a bank

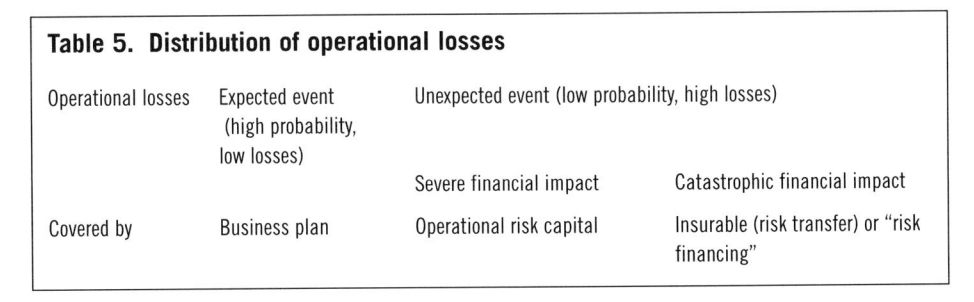

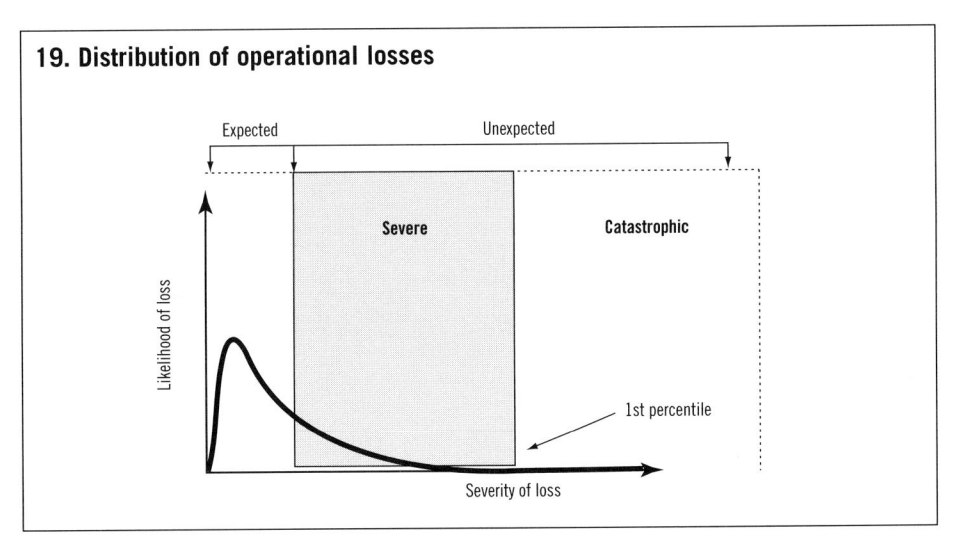

Table 5. Distribution of operational losses

Operational losses	Expected event (high probability, low losses)	Unexpected event (low probability, high losses)	
		Severe financial impact	Catastrophic financial impact
Covered by	Business plan	Operational risk capital	Insurable (risk transfer) or "risk financing"

19. Distribution of operational losses

than in an industrial company. Obviously, depositors benefit the most from the bank buying insurance when deposits are uninsured, but are they willing, ex-ante, to bear the cost? Do shareholders have the incentive to buy insurance against an exposure to operational risk whose cost cannot be passed through to the depositors?

Both depositors and shareholders are hurt by a realisation of an operational risk event. But if the avoidance of an operational risk event is costly, a conflict of interest can emerge between shareholders and depositors, since the depositors benefit the most from insurance. Depositors are mainly interested in the liquidity and immediacy of the service provided by the bank. They are willing to sacrifice some return but expect to benefit from immediacy so that they can settle transactions immediately at low cost. Crouhy, Galai and Mark (2003) elaborate in greater details on these issues.

Insurance against catastrophic losses
The AMA will recognise the risk mitigation impact of insurance in the measures of operational risk used for minimum regulatory capital requirements. But the benefit will be limited to 20% of the total operational capital charge. Also, the bank's methodology needs to capture, through discounts and haircuts in the amount of insurance recognition, the following residual risks: residual term of the insurance policy is less than one year, policy's cancellation and non-renewal terms, and uncertainty of payment as well as mismatches in coverage of insurance policies.

It is common for a bank to purchase insurance to protect itself from large single losses arising from acts of employee dishonesty (eg, fictitious loans, unauthorised activities), robbery and theft, loans made against counterfeit securities and various forms of computer crime. Insurance protection for low-probability but highly severe losses such as these is available through contractually written insuring agreements included in an insurance vehicle known as the "financial institution bond and computer crime policy". Policies are also available from the insurance marketplace for catastrophic exposures associated with lawsuits (eg, liability exposures arising from allegations of misrepresentation, breach of trust and fiduciary duty, negligence, etc.) and for property damage resulting from major disaster such as a fire or earthquake. Limits of up to US$500/600 million per loss occurrence for large financial institutions are common.

It should be understood that, in essence, insurance is a mechanism for pooling and transferring common loss exposures within an industry or across economies. The availability of insurance for specific risks depends on the ability of an insurer or group of insurers to generate sufficient premium volume and an adequate spread of risk to "make a market" and enable them to take on the risks of others.

Reinsurance and securitisation
Insurance companies protect themselves against catastrophic loss through reinsurance agreements, as well as through the use of securitisation vehicles to transfer the risk of catastrophic loss to the capital markets.

Reinsurance is an arrangement whereby a reinsurer agrees to indemnify another insurance or reinsurance company (known as the ceding company or "cedant") against all or a portion of the insurance or reinsurance risks underwritten by the ceding company under one or more policies. While there are no standard reinsurance contracts as such, two basic types of reinsurance known as "treaty" and "facultative" reinsurance generally describe the reinsurance agreements that are available.

Treaty reinsurance extends cover to all risks written by an insured or ceding company unless under the terms of the "treaty" specific exposures are excluded. Historically, treaties remain in force for long periods of time and are renewed on a fairly automatic basis unless either party wishes to negotiate a change in terms.

Excess of loss reinsurance is a term that describes the arrangement under which the ceding company is indemnified against all or a specified portion of losses on underlying insurance policies in excess of a specified amount, which is known as a "retention". Excess of loss reinsurance is written in layers and normally involves the participation of a number of insurers/reinsurers. Any liability exceeding the upper level of the layers reverts to the ceding company, which also bears the credit risks associated with the reinsurers utilised under the agreement.

A *facultative reinsurance* agreement covers a specific risk of the ceding insurer. Facultative reinsurance agreements are therefore used to cover catastrophic or unusual risk exposures. Terms and conditions are covered in individual contracts, and these agreements generally require a significant commitment of underwriting and technical expertise. Facultative reinsurance contracts are often used to supplement treaty arrangements.

Finally, reinsurers also purchase their own reinsurance protection, known as "retrocessions", in the same form and for the same reasons as ceding insurers. By protecting reinsurers from catastrophic losses as well as an accumulation of smaller losses, retrocessions stabilise reinsurer results, thus serving the same risk-spreading objective as the initial reinsurance transaction.

Although VAR/RAROC models do not capture catastrophic loss, banks can use these frameworks to assist their thinking about how insurance policies can be used to protect against operational risk. For example, it might be argued that one should retain a risk if the cost of capital to support the asset is less than the cost of insuring it. This sort of risk/reward approach can bring discipline to an insurance programme that has evolved over time into a rather ad hoc set of policies – eg, where one type of risk is insured while another is not, with very little underlying rationale.

Banks have begun to develop databases of historical operational risk events in an effort to quantify unexpected risks of various sorts. They are hoping to use these databases to develop statistically defined "worst-case" estimates that may be applicable to a select subset of a bank's businesses – in the same way that many banks already use historical loss data to drive credit risk measurement. Firms such as OpVantage are also building databases of operational risk.[5]

It should be admitted that this is a new and evolving area of risk measurement. A

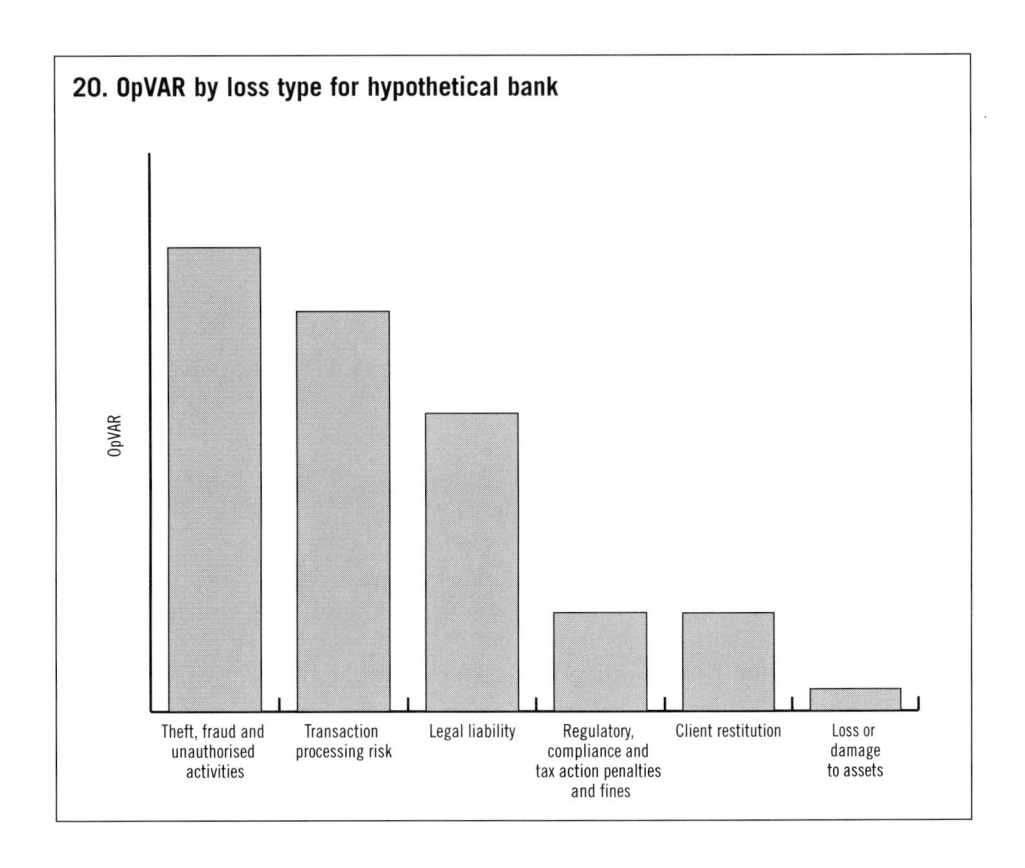

20. OpVAR by loss type for hypothetical bank

[Bar chart showing OpVAR values for: Theft, fraud and unauthorised activities; Transaction processing risk; Legal liability; Regulatory, compliance and tax action penalties and fines; Client restitution; Loss or damage to assets]

MODEL SELECTION FOR OPERATIONAL RISK

bank's internal loss database will most likely be relatively small, and it is unlikely to reflect the major losses suffered occasionally by its peers. Hence, to be useful, the database should reflect the experience of others. Blending internal and external data requires a heavy dose of management judgement.

Some banks are moving to an integrated or concentric approach to the "financing" of operational risks. This financing can be achieved through a combination of external insurance programmes (eg, with floors and caps), capital market tools and self-insurance. Where risks are self-insured, the risk should be allocated economic capital.

Regulators require sufficient capital to be set against the market risk (ie, BIS 98) and the credit risk (ie, modified BIS 88) of a banking book, but there are no formal requirements to set capital against operational risk. At this stage it remains an open issue whether the Bank for International Settlements could reasonably ask banks to set capital aside to cover operational risk at, say, the 1% level of confidence. If regulators move in this direction, the focus will quickly shift to determining the criteria that will allow an appropriate allocation of capital to operational risk.

Illustration of the impact of implementing operational risk models

COMPARISON OF OPVAR BY LOSS TYPE

A typical distribution of OpVAR by loss type for a hypothetical bank is shown in Figure 20. The highest OpVAR is for theft, fraud and unauthorised activities, while the lowest is for losses or damage to assets. The total OpVAR across the six loss types is US$2.5 billion. In our example this total OpVAR would benefit from diversification. Specifically, the diversification effect across loss types results in an overall OpVAR of US$1.2 billion (ie, a US$1.3 billion portfolio effect).

Indeed, if we assume the six types of operational risk to be independent of one another, we can calculate the overall OpVAR for the firm as

$$\text{OpVAR} = \sqrt{\sum_{i=1}^{6} \text{OpVAR}_i^2} = \text{US\$1.2 billion}$$

where OpVAR_i denotes the OpVAR for loss type i.

COMPARISON OF OPVAR BY BUSINESS

A typical distribution of OpVAR by business is shown in Figure 21, and we will take this to apply to our bank. Here the OpVAR for Electronic Commerce, Technology and Operations is the highest, while that for Corporate Development is the lowest. Electronic Commerce in our bank includes the credit card, mortgage and electronic banking businesses. The total OpVAR is the sum of the OpVARs for the individual businesses. Recall that the Basel guidelines allow one to calculate portfolio effects across loss types within a strategic business unit but do not allow one to calculate portfolio effects across businesses.

COMPARISON OF OPVAR BY REGULATORY APPROACH: INCENTIVE ISSUE

A key comment of the New Basel Capital Accord relating to incentives for banks to move towards more sophisticated approaches is that "The Committee intends to calibrate the spectrum of approaches so that the capital charge for a typical bank would be less at each progressive step on the spectrum". For example, typical relationships between the operational risk capital for our hypothetical bank calculated under the three approaches are shown in Figure 22. Observe that the benefit in terms of regulatory capital saved under the AMA approach compared to the standardised approach is US$1 billion, or US$173 million per annum.[6] If the bank had a capital base of US$10 billion, the operational risk capital based on the AMA approach would be 12% of the total regulatory capital – ie, (US$1.2 billion/US$10 billion).

Moving up the three evolutionary stages should result in a progressive lowering of the bank's overall operational risk capital as a percentage of total regulatory capital. However, from the preliminary results of the third Quantitative Impact Study (QIS3) conducted by the Basel Committee under the direction of the local supervisors of the various countries that participated in the study, it is not clear that the proposed calibration of both the basic indicator approach and the standardised approach will produce higher capital charges than the AMA.

One of the goals of the Basel Capital Accord is to give the incentive to banks to move over time from the less to the more risk-sensitive risk measurement framework. This can only be achieved if the capital charge of the AMA is significantly less than the other less sophisticated approaches. Since banks adopting the AMA will be required to calculate their capital requirement using this approach as well as the existing Accord for a year prior to implementation of the New Accord at year-end 2006, the Basel Committee should take this opportunity to reconsider the proposed calibration based on the differences in the capital requirements across the various approaches reported by the banks having adopted the AMA.

EXAMPLE: CALCULATING TRANSACTION-PROCESSING RISK FOR DISCOUNT BROKERAGE

The first step in this example is to calculate the exposure on the basis of an analysis of trade volume for discount brokerage (Figure 24). Assume that the transaction-processing volume, as measured in terms of total frequency of trades, EI_f, is 1.52 million trades per annum based on the last 36 monthly totals (Figure 25). The average trade size, EI_s, is US$13,100 (Figure 26).

If we multiply the total frequency of trades, EI_f, across the relevant time period by the average trade size, EI_s, we get the appropriate EI for that time period – ie, EI = $EI_f \times EI_s$. Specifically, 1.52 million trades × US$13,100 average trade size is rounded up to an EI of US$20 billion.

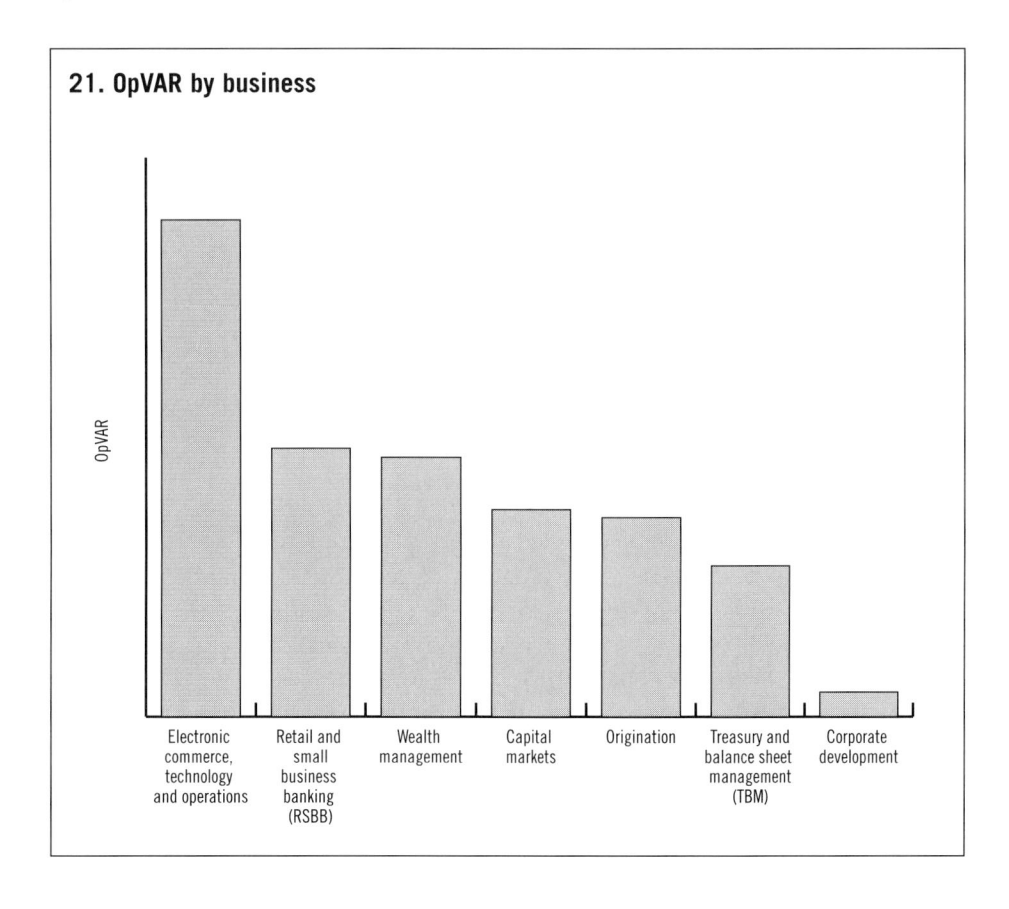

21. OpVAR by business

MODEL SELECTION FOR OPERATIONAL RISK

22. OpVAR by regulatory approach – absolute savings

Standardised approach provides regulatory capital savings as compared to the basic indicator approach

AMA approach provides regulatory capital savings as compared to standardised approach

AMA approach provides regulatory capital savings as compared to standard approach

OpVAR

Basic indicator 15% of gross income | Standardised approach | AMA OpVAR

24. Adjustment for changes in activity

Exposure bases (EI) for transaction processing risk → OpVAR

- EI_f
- EI_s
- $EI = EI_f \times IE_s$

25. Total frequency of trades, EI_f

Total number of trades

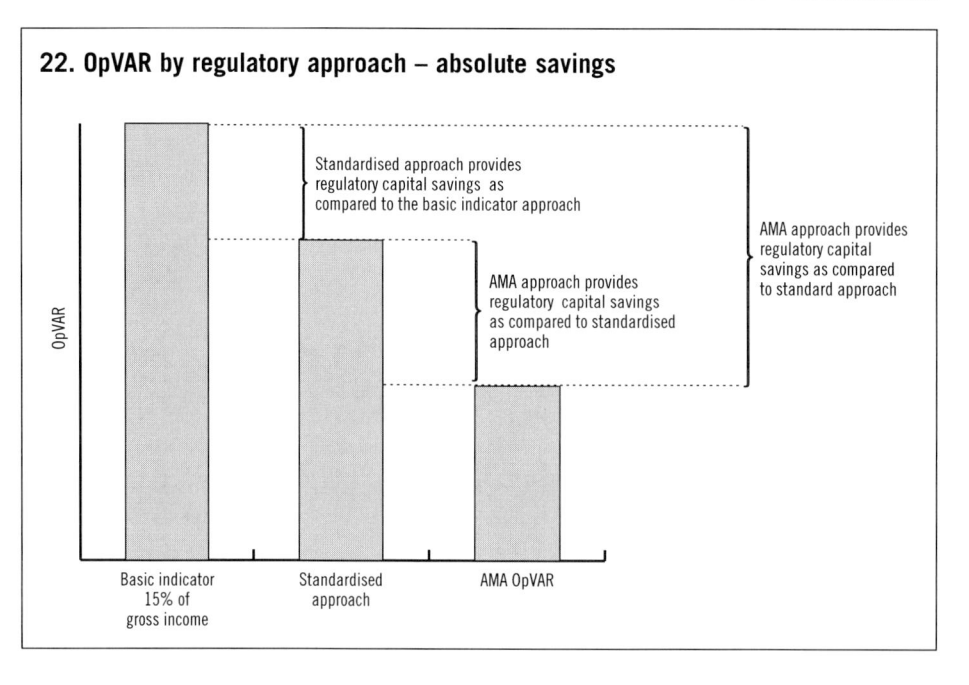

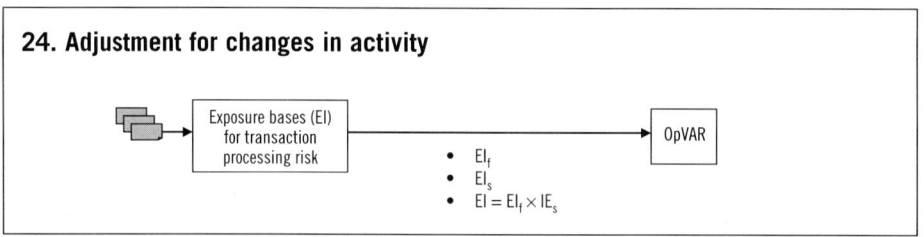

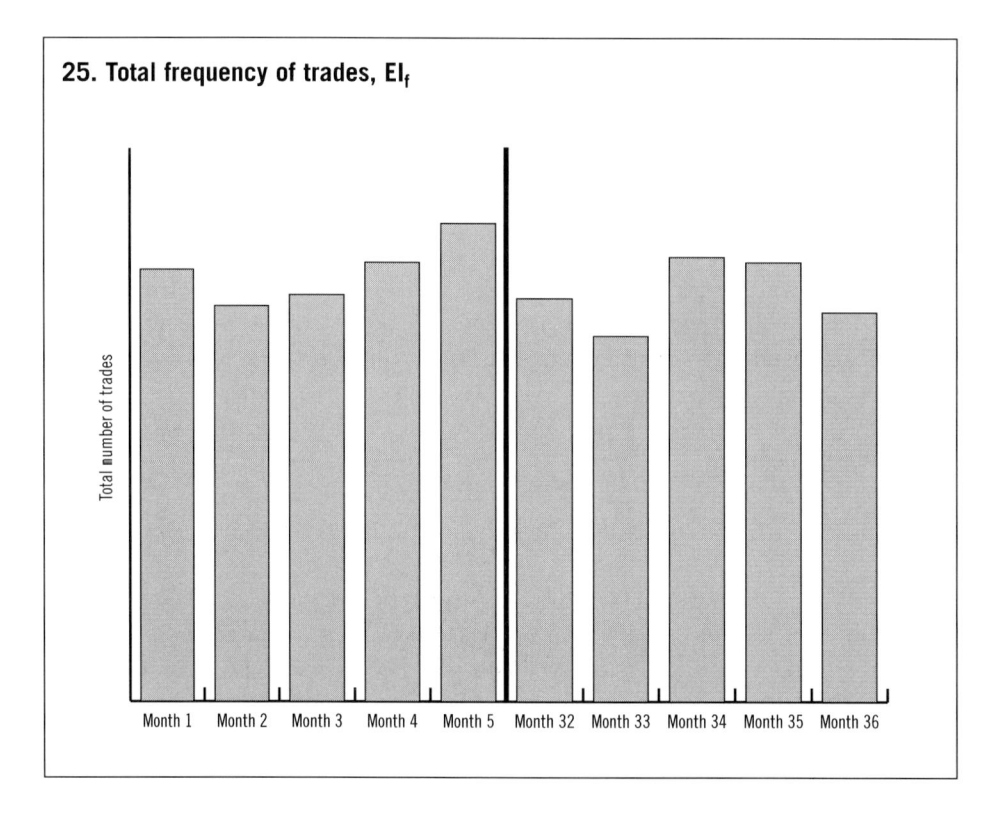

Month 1, Month 2, Month 3, Month 4, Month 5, Month 32, Month 33, Month 34, Month 35, Month 36

Next, as illustrated in Figure 27, we calculate the frequency and severity of losses by looking at the loss history. Transaction-processing risk for discount brokerage is defined in terms of error rate. The error rate, PE, is the number of losses divided by the number of trades, as shown in Figure 28. For example, the error rate in month 36 is 13 per 10,000 trades, with an average of 11 per 10,000 over a one-year period.[7]

RISK BOOKS

26. Average trade size, EI_s

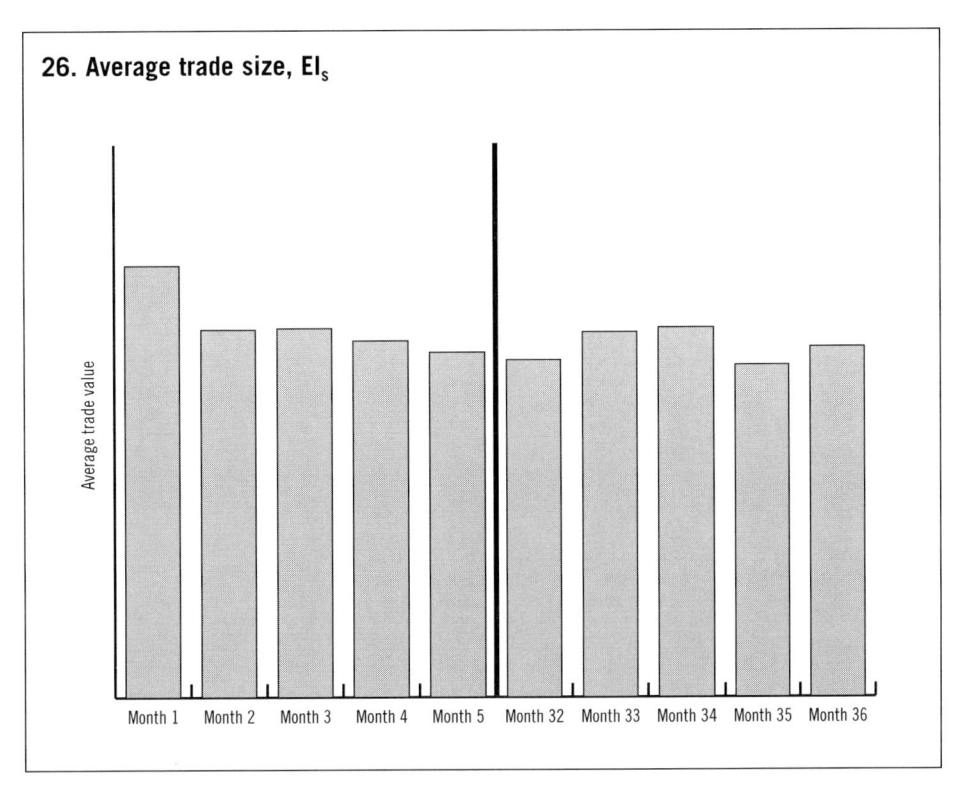

[Bar chart showing average trade value across Month 1, Month 2, Month 3, Month 4, Month 5, Month 32, Month 33, Month 34, Month 35, Month 36]

In practice, the PE information can be decomposed into different types of trades or trade-processing systems. Observe that in Figure 28 the line graph for error rate per 10,000 trades is superimposed on the rectangular bars from Figure 25, which shows EI_f.

The LGE or severity is defined as the average loss divided by the average trade value. This is shown on the right-hand axis of Figure 29, where the exposure base (EI_s, grey bars) from Figure 26 is also shown. For example, LGE equals 4% of average trade value. As seen on the right-hand side of Figure 29, the error rate has been declining over the past several months and is well below the peak that occurred in month 4.

Next we need to tie the PE and LGE information into a loss distribution. For example, as shown in Figure 30a, on average 11 trades per 10,000 have errors (PE).[8] The statistically defined worst case is 41 trades per 10,000. Then, as we can see in Figure 30b, on average 4% of the value of the trade has to be written off (LGE). The statistically defined worst case is 190%. Accordingly, on average US$0.43 per US$10,000 traded is lost, as shown in Figure 30c. The worst-case loss, WCL, is US$1.72 per 10,000.

OpVAR = EI × WCL = US$24,300 million trades × 0.0172% = US$4.2 million

The OpVAR can be lowered by taking action to reduce either PE (the rate of loss) or LGE (the cost per loss). In our example business management achieved success by acting to reduce both PE and LGE. This can be illustrated by examining the response of OpVAR (on a relative basis) to changes in PE and LGE in Figure 31 for

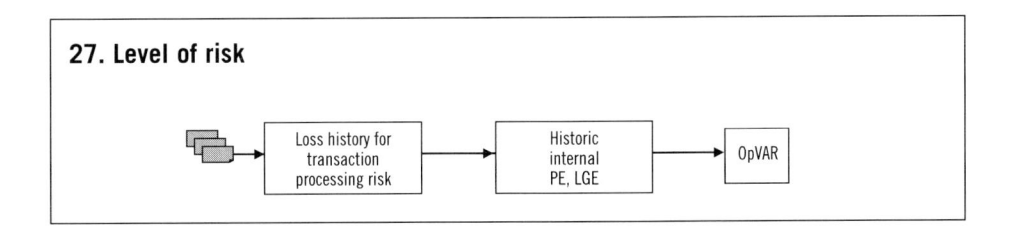

27. Level of risk

[Flow diagram: Loss history for transaction processing risk → Historic internal PE, LGE → OpVAR]

MODEL SELECTION FOR OPERATIONAL RISK

MODEL SELECTION FOR OPERATIONAL RISK

our discount brokerage example. One would also need to analyse OpVAR for each loss type and component business of the overall wealth management business.

The process of operational risk assessment should include a review of the likelihood, or frequency, of a particular operational risk, as well as a review of its possible magnitude or severity. For example, risk managers can publish graphs displaying the potential severity of a risk set against its frequency, as shown in Figure 34. This diagram allows managers to visualise the trade-off between severity and

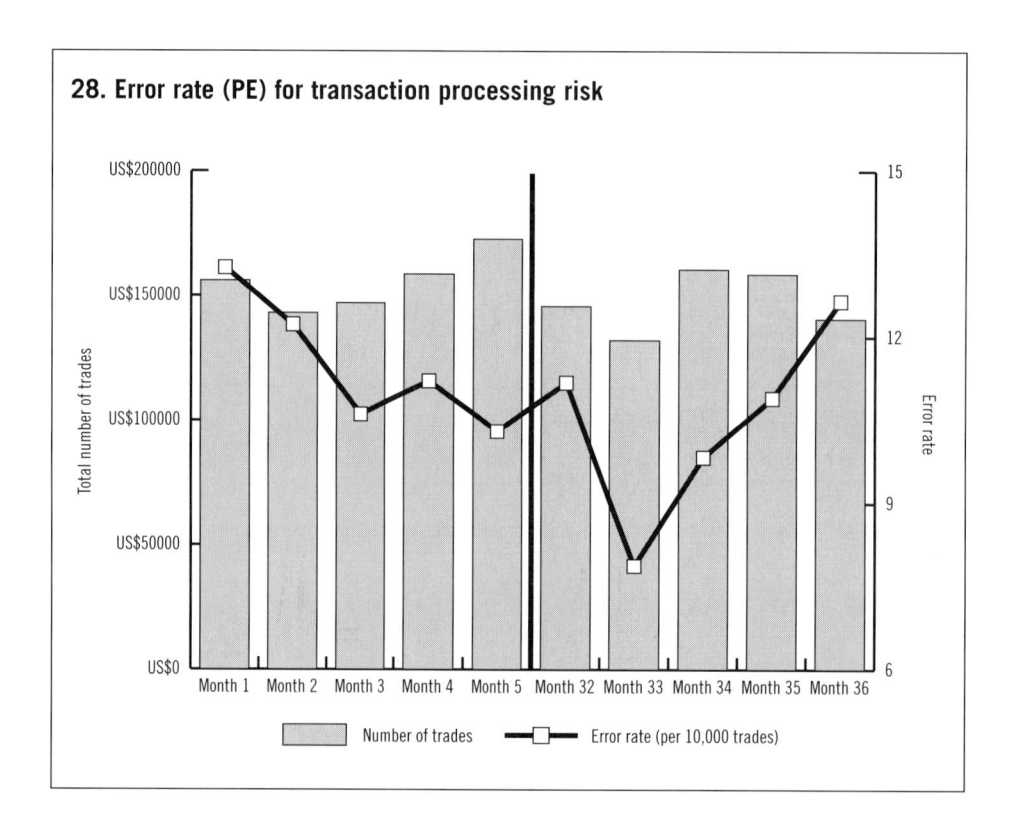

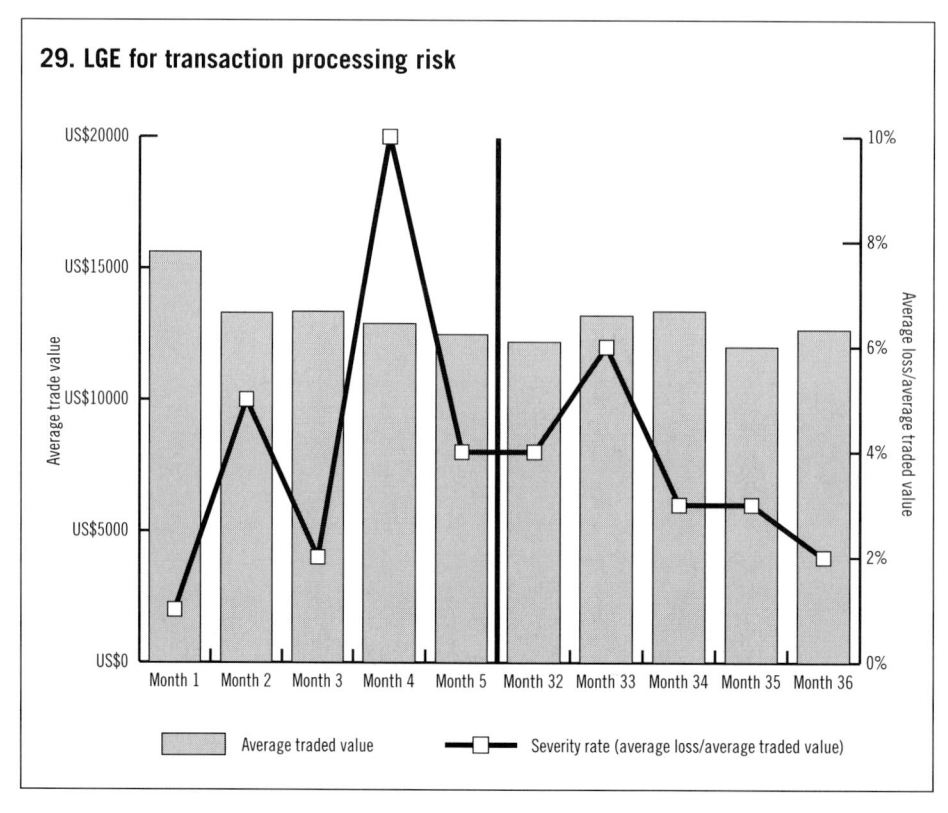

28. Error rate (PE) for transaction processing risk

29. LGE for transaction processing risk

likelihood. Point A5, for example, represents a low likelihood and a medium level of severity. All risks along the curve exhibit the same expected loss, ie, likelihood multiplied by severity. Given an acceptable level of expected loss, management should take appropriate action to mitigate risks located above the curve – here A7 and A8. A7 has a medium likelihood and medium severity, while A8 has a medium severity but a high likelihood. For both of these risks the expected level of loss is above the acceptable level.

Conclusion

The developments discussed in this chapter are helping institutions to select the appropriate operational risk model and manage their portfolios of operational risk more effectively. Increasingly, an institution will be able to gain a competitive advantage by monitoring and managing its operational risks on a global basis – although to achieve this it is likely to have to confront some fundamental infrastructure issues.

Infrastructure aside, an integrated goal-congruent risk management process that puts all the elements together, as illustrated in Figure 35, will open the door to

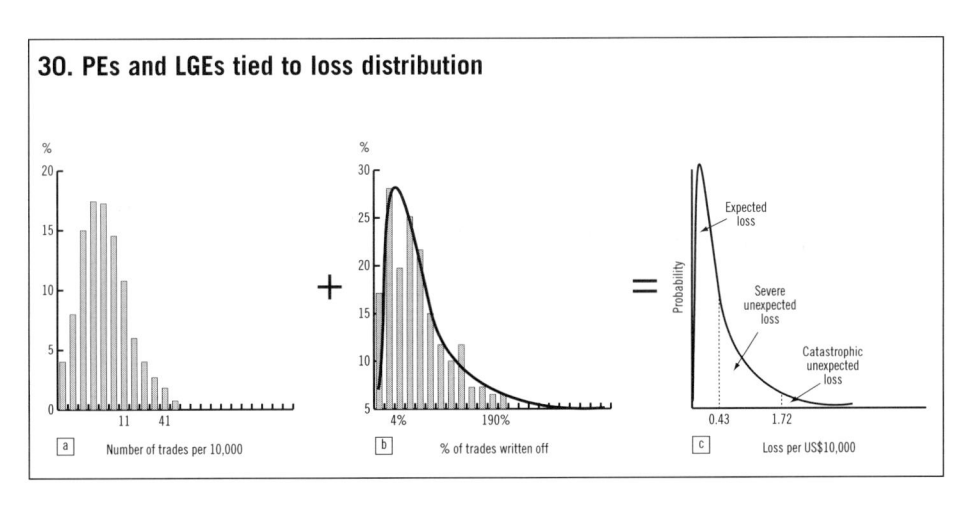

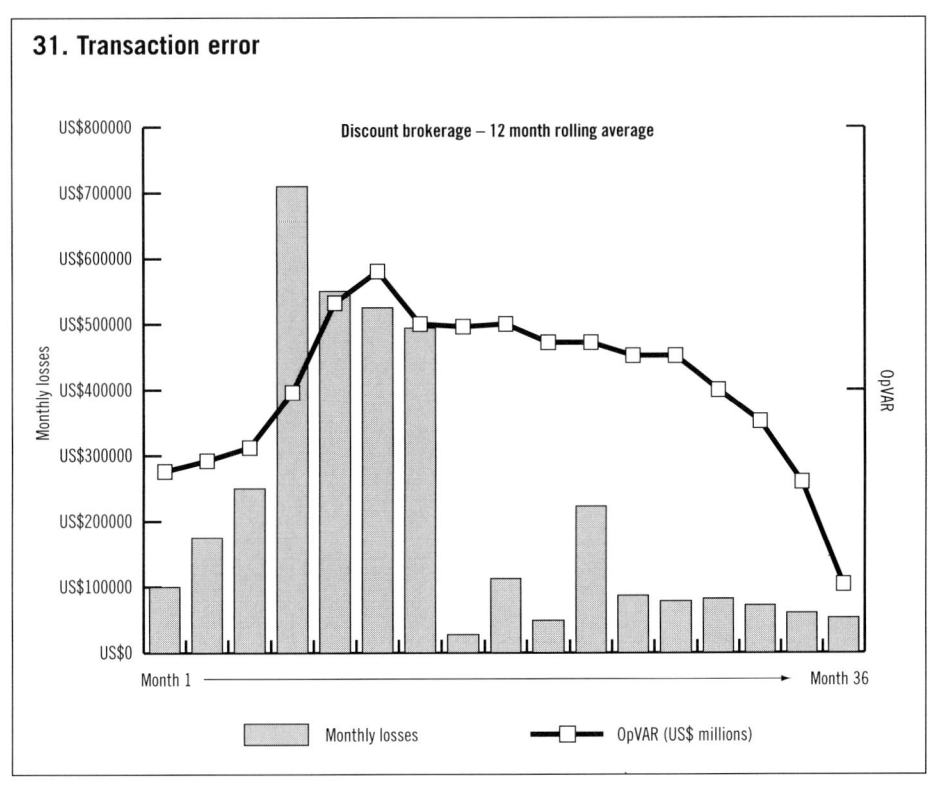

30. PEs and LGEs tied to loss distribution

31. Transaction error

MODEL SELECTION FOR OPERATIONAL RISK

optimal firm-wide management of risk. "Integrated" refers to the need to avoid a fragmented approach to risk management – which is only as strong as its weakest link. "Goal-congruent" refers to the need to ensure that policies and methodologies are consistent with each other and the aims of the institution. For example, one goal is to have an "apple-to-apple" measurement scheme so that one can compare risk across all products and aggregate risk at any level.

The measurement of operational risk is based on analytical techniques that are widely used in the insurance industry to measure the financial impact of an operational failure. The foundation for this is the historical experience of operational losses. Where there are no loss data, inputs have to be based on judgement and scenario analysis. OpVAR is used to determine the expected loss from operational failures, the worst-case loss at a desired confidence level, the required economic capital for operational risk and the concentration of operational risk.[9]

A list of the sources that give rise to the main categories of operational risk exposure should be developed so that a common taxonomy of the drivers of risks can be established. The end product is a best-practice management of risk that takes a "one firm, one view" approach but at the same time recognises the complexity of each business in the firm.

Management objectives include making operational risk "transparent". For example, key questions that need to be answered clearly and explicitly include: what is the largest risk; how large is the risk; what drives the risk; how is the risk changing; what risks are on the horizon; how does our risk level compare to others, etc. Another obvious objective is to provide better management of operational risk. This is achieved by activating specific action plans and implementation schedules. Risk management should also ensure that risks are appropriately capitalised – ie, that enough capital is allocated to absorb unexpected losses.

An important aim is to achieve the lowest regulatory capital given the level of risk. Here there are three options under the coming Basel regulations. Most sophisticated banks will start off with the standardised approach or the alternative measurement approach (AMA). The standardised approach would, typically, require minor changes to existing processes. One would collect exposures for each business line and then apply the regulatory capital beta factors. Annual self-assessment and existing review

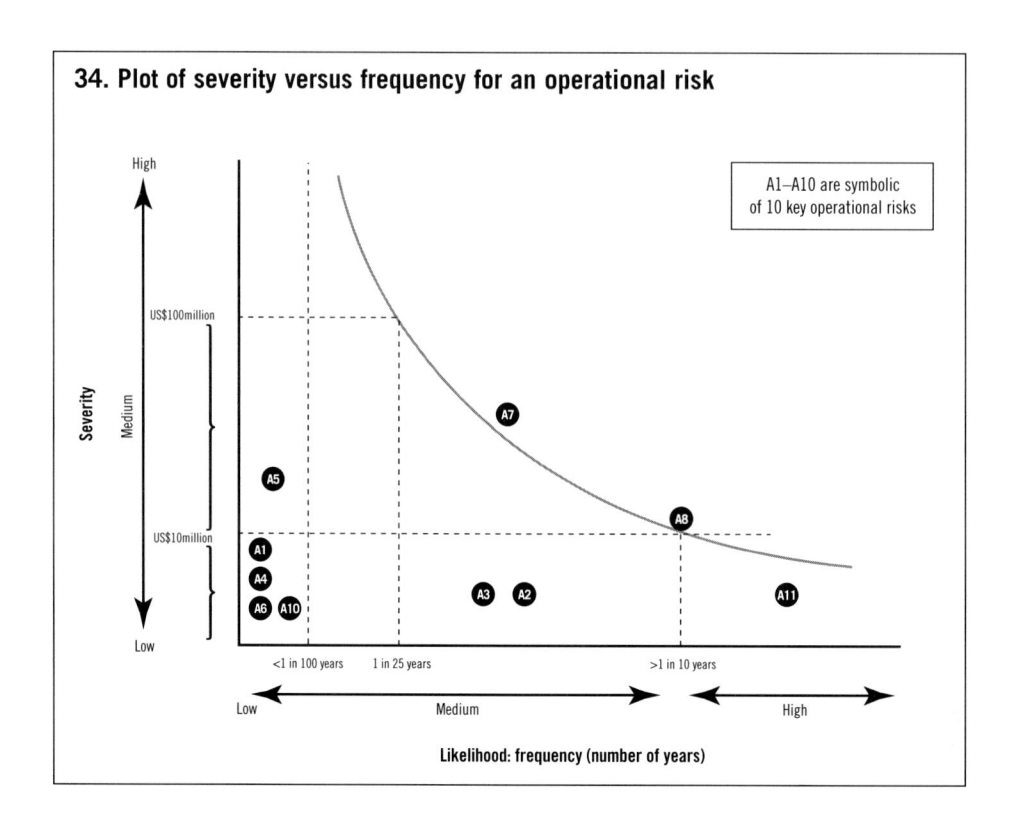

34. Plot of severity versus frequency for an operational risk

A1–A10 are symbolic of 10 key operational risks

processes would be continued. The standardised OpVAR approach is basically a tax-based approach (ie, a fixed percentage of some indicator).

Exposure bases are a measure of the size of the exposure (eg, total dollar value of transactions). Failure rates (frequency) measure the likelihood of an operational failure (eg, number of failed transactions as percentage of total transactions included in the exposure). There would be a separate rate for each loss type and line of business. Severity measures the total financial impact of a failure (eg, the percentage of the value of the failed transaction that is lost). Failure rates and severity are collected over an appropriate time horizon, the term "time horizon" referring to an observation period (usually 36 months) as well as a period of application (one year).

The AMA approach typically requires significant changes to existing processes. For example, for each loss type and business line one needs to collect loss type-dependent exposures, loss data and key risk drivers. These are used to calculate expected losses (EL) and to apply regulatory capital factors to EL. This would require monthly self-assessments (of say, the top ten) as well as an integrated review process. One would need to invest in businesses/infrastructure at a pace that reflected the risk.

To obtain approval to use the AMA approach for operational risk one must satisfy reporting and reviewing requirements. This includes having sound internal loss and event reporting practices supported by a loss database. One would also need to have an appropriate risk reporting system to generate aggregate data used for use in capital calculation and to report results to management.

In this chapter we have stressed that operational risk should be managed as a

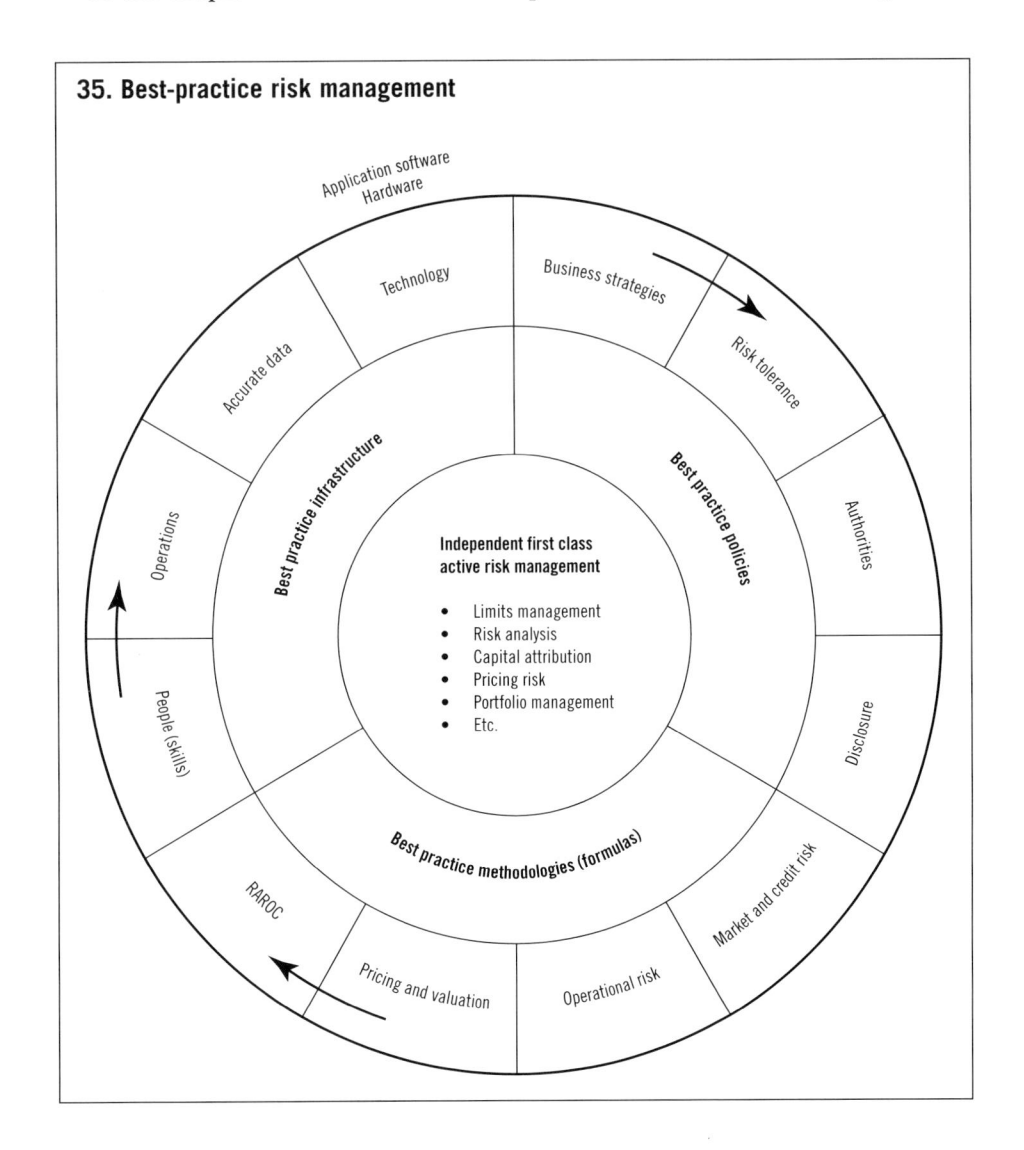

35. Best-practice risk management

partnership between business units, business infrastructure groups and corporate governance units such as internal audit and risk management. We have also mentioned the importance of fostering a risk-aware business culture. Senior managers play a critical role in establishing a corporate environment in which best-practice operational risk management can flourish. Personnel ultimately behave in a manner that is dependent on how senior management train and reward them.

Indeed, arguably the greatest single challenge for senior management is to harmonise the behaviour patterns of business units, infrastructure units, corporate governance units, internal audit and risk management. Senior management must create an environment in which all sides "sink or swim" together in terms of managing operational risk.

1 Operational risk, as pointed out at the beginning of this chapter, is not a well-defined concept. The academic literature dealing with the risk faced by financial institutions tends to ignore operational risk, or, more precisely, relates operational risk to operational leverage, ie, to the shape of the production cost functions and in particular to the relationship between fixed and variable costs.

2 The New Basel Capital Accord (Basel, 2003a) has proposed that the regulatory capital for operational risk should be based on expected and unexpected losses. Losses are uncertain or stochastic in nature, and are defined in terms of a probability distribution, such as a lognormal distribution. The mean of the distribution is what is referred to as the "expected loss", and the distance from the mean of the percentile of the distribution at a given confidence level (say 99%) is referred to as the "unexpected loss". Given these definitions there is a probability of, say, 1%, that the actual loss will be higher than the expected loss (See Figure 4). It is common practice to cover the expected loss, which is viewed as the cost of doing business, with reserves; it is also incorporated in the price of the service – for example, the interest margin charged on Visa balances. Unexpected losses are covered by economic capital, which acts as a cushion to absorb losses in excess of the average level of losses that is expected to occur during the normal course of doing business.

3 For example, should one measure the business risk associated with potential project cost overruns (eg, building branches)? Further should one include loss of clients due to branch restructuring, etc?

4 Opvantage results from the strategic alliance between NetRisk and the consulting firm PriceWaterhouse Coopers. Fitch ultimately acquired NetRisk.

5 Per annum savings = Capital saved × before tax cost of capital or US$1 billion 17.25% = US$172.5 million.

6 For regulatory purposes and statistical significance a 36-monthly average should be used.

7 See also Figure 28.

8 The same confidence level as market and credit risk capital.

BIBLIOGRAPHY

Basel Committee on Banking Supervision, 2003a, *Sound Practices for the Management and Supervision of Operational Risk* (Basel: Bank for International Settlements), February.

Basel Committee on Banking Supervision, 2003b, *The New Basel Capital Accord* (Basel: Bank for International Settlements), April.

Basel Committee on Banking Supervision, 1998, *Framework for International Control Systems in Banking Organisations* (Basel: Bank For International Settlements), September.

Crouhy M., D. Galai and R. Mark, 2003, "Insuring vs Self-Insuring Operational Risk: The Viewpoint of Depositors and Shareholders", Working Paper.

Crouhy, M., D. Galai and R. Mark, 2000, *Risk Management*, (Columbus: McGraw-Hill).

Crouhy, M., D. Galai and R. Mark, 1998, "Key Steps in Building Consistent Operational Risk Measurement and Management", Chapter 3 in R. Jameson (ed.) *Operational Risk and Financial Institutions* (London: Risk Books).

Group of Thirty, Global Derivatives Study Group, 1993, *Derivatives: Practices and Principles* (Washington, DC: Group of Thirty).

10

Model Error in Enterprise-wide Risk Management: Insurance Policies with Guarantees

Andrea Consiglio and Stavros A. Zenios

University of Cyprus and University of Palermo;
University of Cyprus and The Wharton School

Enterprise-wide risk management is the new arena for risk modelling. Its purpose is to deal with the manifold aspects of risk in an integrated fashion so that natural hedges are identified and explored, risk transparency is achieved and efficient capital allocation is attained. Enterprise-wide risk management ensures that the firm-wide risk exposure is less than the sum of individual exposures. A task this challenging can be accomplished by a detailed analysis of the disparate sources of risk to which the company is exposed. The use of quantitative methods by banks dates from the time of the Medici family in the 13th century. But today we are witnessing an unprecedented ability to aggregate disparate sources of risk in a global market place, to cope with the increasing pace of innovation of financial products and to integrate complex liability structures.

In striving for enterprise-wide risk management, however, the lines between financial risks and model risks become blurred. Did Long-Term Capital Management (LTCM) drive the world's financial markets to the brink of a global meltdown due to divergent spreads and liquidity risk, or due to inappropriate operational use of models? Was Barings' demise due to the tail below its value-at-risk (VAR) exposure, due to the lack of controls between front and back office risk measures or was it brought about by a rogue trader? Was Nissan Mutual driven into bankruptcy by the declining interest rates in Japan or by inadequate models for pricing the options embedded in its policies?

The operational risks of using inappropriate or inadequate models can be measured in these examples by the standard norms of financial risks, such as VAR. However, the analysis must made of the models and not the market data. For instance, the events that destroyed LTCM had a likelihood of occurrence that could not have happened during the life of the known universe – according to market data volatility that is. An analysis of the model with changing volatility, however, reveals a likelihood of such an event once every seven years or so and this we know now is what happened within the life span of LTCM.

In this chapter, we focus on enterprise-wide risk management for a popular but complex insurance produce: a life policy with a minimum guaranteed rate of return. We will illustrate the workings of an integrative model for insurance policies with guarantees and then describe the source of model errors arising for this type of model and show how model mis-specification can affect the final results.

MODEL ERROR IN ENTERPRISE-WIDE RISK MANAGEMENT: INSURANCE POLICIES WITH GUARANTEES

Enterprise-wide risk management for such products is characterised by a coordinated estimate of the optimal asset allocation and pricing of the embedded minimum guarantee option. The complex liability is non-linearly dependent on the asset return and must be properly accounted for. Disparate sources of risk on the asset side must be integrated and the effects of any risk factors otherwise neglected or approximated must be assessed. An integrative asset and liability management model for these products was suggested recently by Consiglio, Cocco and Zenios (2001a) and it was shown to possess some significant advantages over the traditional mean variance surplus optimisation models in Consiglio, Cocco and Zenios (2001b). However, the model errors inherent in this powerful tool remained unexplored – much as the model errors in index arbitrage were left unexplored by Long-Term Capital Management. In this chapter we study the effects of these errors, showing that model error is a significant source of risk. Careful analysis of the model – *not* of the market data – is the way to eliminate this source of operational risk.

Policies with guarantees

The popularity of mutual funds and asset management creates competitive pressures on the insurance industry to deliver policies that combine traditional insurance against actuarial risks, with attractive returns. Products with minimum guarantee combine the attractive returns of equities with the stability of fixed income. Such products are common investment tools for households. They provide a shield from market turmoil that makes them particularly attractive to the investors who are planning their retirement income.

The most notable characteristic of policies with guarantees is that they promise a guaranteed return upon maturity. If the asset portfolio performance is below this guarantee, the company must compensate for the shortfall with its own capital. When the asset portfolio performs better than the guarantee, then a fraction – say 80% – of the asset return is given as bonus to the policyholders, with the remaining part contributing to the firm's revenues. In the policies issued by Italian insurers, the minimum guaranteed return applies to the bonus as well. What is given cannot be taken away – the liability is lifted every time a bonus is paid. Figure 1 illustrates the growth of a typical liability. Because of this provision, the dynamics of the liability depend in a complex way on the dynamics of the assets. This dependency precludes the use of mean variance analysis for surplus optimisation. Instead, an integrative scenario-based optimisation model is developed.

MODELLING GUARANTEES
Usually, the minimum guarantee feature is modelled like an option. Since the 1970s, the pricing of these embedded options was addressed either as a portfolio (Brennan and Schwartz, 1976; Boyle and Schwartz, 1977) or as distinct derivatives (Grosen and Jorgensen, 2000). These advances have been gaining increasing attention from industry (Giraldi *et al*, 2000).

Consiglio, Cocco and Zenios (2001a) have developed a scenario-based optimisation model for asset and liability management of participating insurance policies with minimum guarantees. Extensions and refinements of this model can be found in Consiglio, Cocco and Zenios (2001b) and Consiglio, Saunders and Zenios (2003). The model allows the analysis of the trade-offs facing an insurance firm in structuring its policies as well as the choices in covering their cost.

Two sources of error are liable to affect this model both in terms of assets and liabilities:

❑ scenarios of asset returns are not uniquely determined so the optimal solution thus depends on the set of scenarios assumed by the model; and
❑ individual policy holders exhibit a tendency to surrender their policy due to changing attitudes or economic conditions. This "lapse behaviour" is not easy to

1. Typical returns of the asset portfolio and the participating policy with a minimum guarantee 3% and participation rate 80%. The minimum guarantee applies to a liability that is lifted every time a bonus is paid as illustrated at period seven. The asset portfolio experienced substantial losses at period seven while the liability grew at the 3% guaranteed rate. Subsequent superior returns of the assets allowed the firm to recover its losses by the 10th period and achieve a positive net return at maturity.

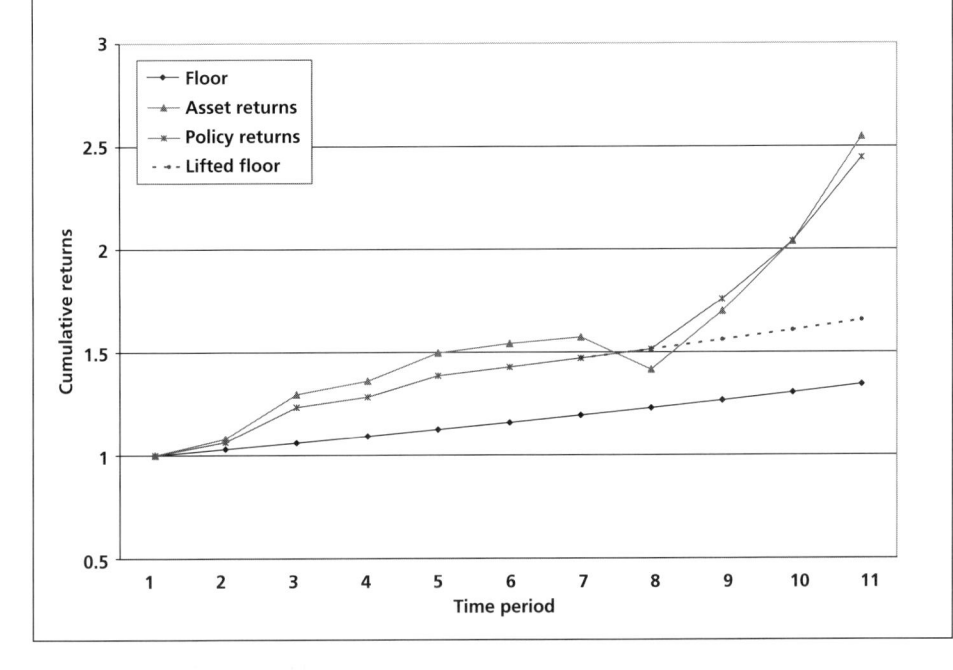

capture empirically because of the unavailability of historical data though it can be analysed through sensitivity analysis.

The effects of both sources of error are addressed in the next section and are illustrated with some numerical examples.

Integrative asset and liability modelling

The dynamics of the value of the liability are denoted by the random variable $\tilde{L}_t$, where t ranges from 0 (today) to T (maturity). Similarly the dynamics of the assets are denoted by $\tilde{A}_t$, and the dynamics of the firm's capital by $\tilde{E}_t$. The firm collects a premium L_0 by issuing a policy, invests its own capital according to a regulatory ratio, $E_0 = \rho L_0$, and purchases assets $A_0 = L_0(1 + \rho)$. Upon maturity of the policy the shareholder value can be measured by the excess return on equity.

$$\text{exROE} = \frac{\tilde{A}_T - \tilde{L}_T}{\tilde{E}_T}$$

This measure of shareholder value is also a random variable and in order to compare alternative policies we will compute their certainty equivalent excess return on equity and incorporate a suitable utility function $U(.)$ to capture preferences. In particular, we define the *certainty equivalent excess return on equity* (CEexROE) by the expression:

$$U(CEexROE) = \varepsilon\left[U\left(\frac{\tilde{A}_T - \tilde{L}_T}{\tilde{E}_T}\right)\right] \quad (1)$$

where $\varepsilon[\cdot]$ denotes expectations of the random variable. CEexROE is a measure of the reward of the firm for assuming the cost of the guarantee.

The cost of the guarantee is the downside risk for the firm, namely, the cost of the firm's own capital when a shortfall is realised, such as the one that occurred at period seven in Figure 1. The variable $\tilde{E}_t$ tracks precisely the differential $\tilde{A}_T - \tilde{L}_T$ when a shortfall is realised, which is the total amount of funds required up to time t; see Equation 15 in the Appendix.

The dynamics of the liability are given by:

$$\tilde{L}_t = (1 - \tilde{\Lambda}_t) \tilde{L}_{t-1} (1 + \max[\alpha \tilde{R}_{Pt}, \bar{g}]), \text{ for } t = 1, 2, \ldots T \qquad (2)$$

where $\tilde{R}_{Pt}$ is the random variable portfolio return, α denotes the contractual percentage of the portfolio return that is passed on to the policyholders, $\bar{g}$ is the minimum guaranteed return, and Λ_t^I denotes probabilities of actuarial events or policy surrender.

The dynamics of the asset are driven by the random portfolio return $\tilde{R}_{Pt}\lambda$, by any shortfalls created when the portfolio return is below the minimum guarantee, and the surplus accumulated by the fraction $1 - \alpha$ that is not returned to policyholders when the portfolio return exceeds the guarantee. The asset dynamics are given in the Appendix; see Equation 16.

The equity variable $\tilde{E}_t$ also embeds the initial amount of equity required by the regulators. This is not a cost and it must be deducted from $\tilde{E}_t$. The cost of the minimum guarantee, assuming that shortfalls can be funded at the risk-free rate, is then given as the expected present value of the final equity $\tilde{E}_T$ adjusted by the regulatory equity, that is,

$$\bar{O}_G = \varepsilon\left[\left(e^{-\int_0^T r_u du} \tilde{E}_T\right) - \rho L_0\right] \qquad (3)$$

The random variables can be approximated using a finite and discrete scenario set. It is then possible to derive a scenario optimisation model that trades off the policy's upside (cf. 1) against the portfolio's downside (cf. 3). This model was developed by Consiglio, Cocco and Zenios (2001a) and is outlined in the Appendix. Note that the non-linear dependence of the liability on the asset portfolio (Equation 2) is complicated by the presence of the max operator. This precludes the use of classic mean-variance analysis. Indeed, in Consiglio, Cocco and Zenios (2001b) it was shown that there is nothing efficient about efficient portfolios generated by a mean-variance model when the complex non-linearities of the liability are properly accounted for.

Figure 2 shows the broad asset allocation among asset classes from the Italian markets: 23 stock indices listed on the Milan Stock Exchange and three indices of government bonds of different maturities.

Figure 3 illustrates the trade off between the cost of the minimum guarantee and net of the annualised CEexROE. At a value of $\bar{g}$ less than 7%, the option embedded in the liability is out-of-the-money and any excess return is passed to the shareholders thus improving CEexROE. As the minimum guarantee increases above 7%, the option goes deeper into-the-money, the cost of the guarantee increases significantly and the CEexROE erodes. Note from Figure 2 however that higher values of minimum guarantee must be backed by aggressive portfolios with high equity content. Alas, in this case, the portfolio volatility is not translated into high CEexROE but into higher guaranteed returns for the policyholders.

These two figures provide valuable managerial information for designing and managing policies with a minimum guarantee. Figure 3 illustrates the trade-off between profitability and cost for different products, thus illustrating the policies that can be sold for a profit to shareholders. Figure 2 provides guidelines for the best asset allocation in the case of each product.

2. Broad asset allocation for different levels of the minimum guarantee

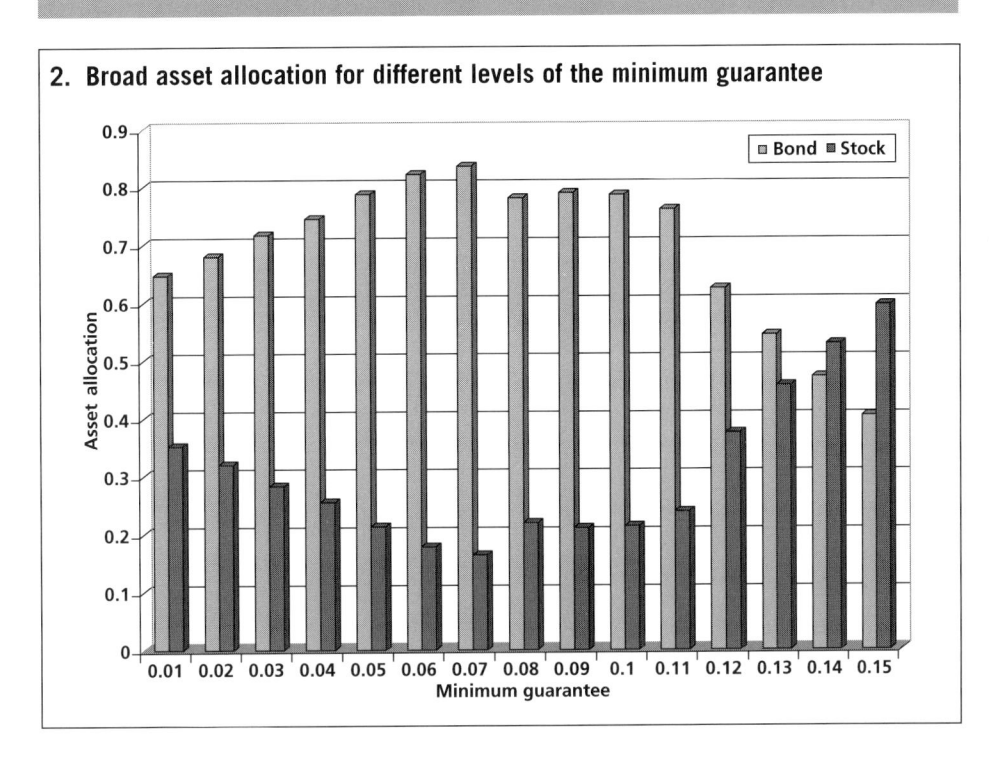

3. Cost of the minimum guarantee vs net CEexROE

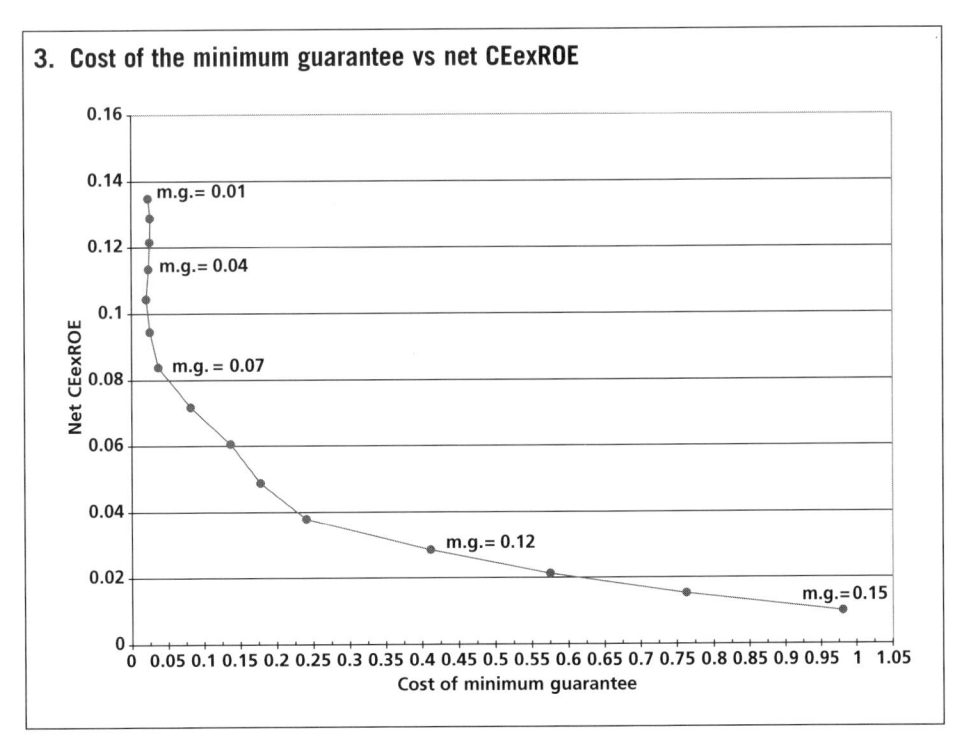

Sources of model error

Are the results of the two figures above to be trusted? Are there any hidden, catastrophic, events to which the managers are oblivious when making decisions guided by the optimal trade-offs in these figures? The scenario optimisation model – integrated and sophisticated as it may be – is vulnerable to two sources of model error: first, in estimating asset returns; second, in modelling the liabilities. The former affects the asset side of the model through Equation 16, while the latter is directly connected to the liability dynamics of Equation 2 through the lapse behaviour which is embodied in parameters $\tilde{\Lambda}_t$.

Asset returns mis-specification is tightly bound to the identification of the functional form and the parameters of the return distribution of asset classes. For instance, Figure 4 shows how the distribution of future prices of a corporate bond

4. Distribution of future prices of a corporate bond with and without modelling of credit events (ie, rating migration and defaults) – substantially different price distributions are obtained assuming two different functional forms of the underlying stochastic process, with and without credit events

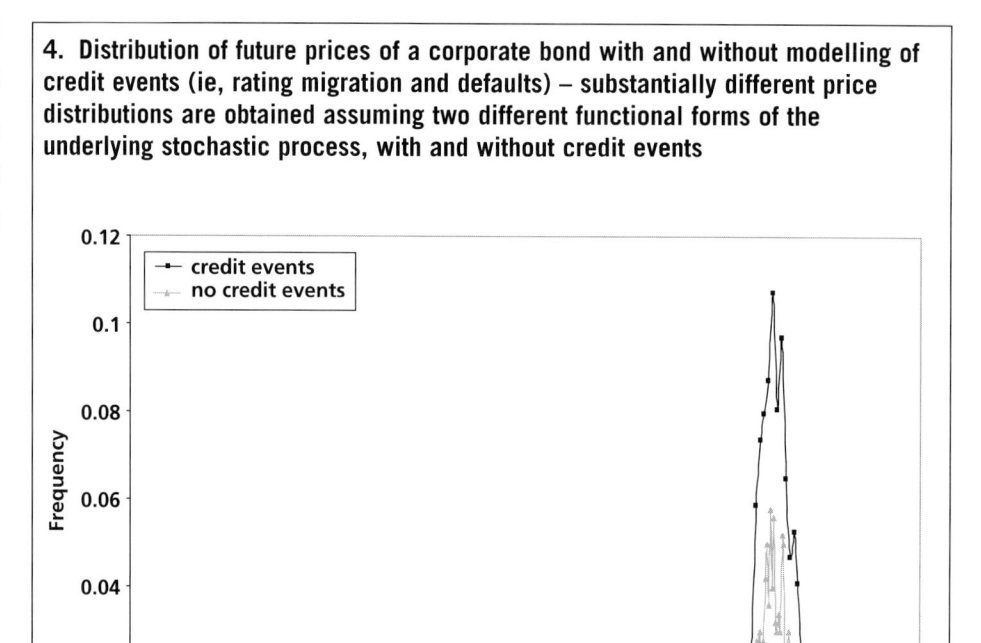

[Figure: Frequency vs Bond value, showing two distributions — "credit events" and "no credit events" — peaking around bond value 100–110.]

can be substantially altered when different functional forms of the underlying stochastic process are assumed, see Jobst and Zenios (2001). Moreover, for large-scale applications, such distributions are sampled and the scenarios obtained are used to calibrate the model under analysis. Sampling error can, of course, be substantially reduced by drawing a relatively large number of scenarios. In enterprise-wide risk management applications, however, the number of scenarios is quite relevant since it determines the size of the optimisation model. There is a trade-off between the computational tractability of the model and the sampling error introduced by limiting the size of the scenario set.

Liability mis-specification can be addressed with the significant advances of actuarial methods of the last decade and the accuracy of statistical estimation procedures for actuarial risks. However, in the type of policies we address in this chapter there exists a hidden interaction between the two sources of model error. The liability value depends on the asset's performance (as shown in Equation 2) and thus, indirectly, asset scenario modelling error will influence the liability levels. Such interactions can be explicitly captured via a lapse model as described, for instance, in Asay *et al* (1993). The probability of abandoning a policy can be expressed as function – a sigmoid function – of the observed mismatch between the credit rate offered by the policy and the average yield provided by the market. We show here that the parameterisations of the lapse function affects the performances of a minimum guarantee liability. Model mis-specification is another source of error in the liability value that goes beyond the usual need for accurate, actuarial analysis.

SCENARIO MODELLING OF ASSET RETURNS
The model developed in the Appendix deals with optimal decision making in the face of uncertainty. Uncertainty is treated with discrete probability spaces and assumes that all random quantities take values drawn from a finite set of scenarios. Each random variable – asset return, value of a liability, timing of an event such as default etc – may take one from a finite number of values. A scenario is defined as a particular realisation of uncertain data, indexed by l from a set Ω. Each scenario has a

probability p^j associated with it so that $\sum_{j \in \Omega} p^j = 1$. Three desirable properties of a scenario are discussed in Panel 1.

A general recipe for calculating asset returns is not possible. Different asset classes have different characteristics that necessitate the development of different models. We discuss some examples of scenario generation methods to illustrate the issues below.

One approach is to sample historical data through *bootstrapping* to develop scenarios of the random variable of interest. A second approach develops statistical models to fit the observed data and then sample the fitted probability distributions. A third approach develops continuous time theoretical models, with estimated

---

PANEL 1

SCENARIO PROPERTIES FOR FINANCIAL PLANNING

To be useful for financial planning, scenarios should possess certain properties.

Correctness
Scenarios should conform to the prevalent theories that model the variable described by these scenarios. For instance, term structures should exhibit mean reversion: intertemporal volatility of the random variables should be persistent; disturbances of exchange rates should follow a lognormal distribution. Scenarios should be derived from a "correct" theoretical model of the random variable – to the extent that prevalent theoretical models are considered correct. Scenarios that satisfy this property will cover all relevant history. It is plausible that any events observed in the past may also occur in the future. Furthermore, scenarios should also account for events that were not observed in the past but are plausible under current market conditions. Scenarios derived from correct theoretical models should not only be able to account for all past observations but also foresee possible events that were not observed in the past.

Accuracy
Scenarios should approximate the theoretical model from which they are derived. As scenarios are discretisations of some probability distribution function, it is unavoidable that some errors will be introduced in the discretisation process. Accuracy is ensured when, for instance, the first and higher moments of the scenarios match those of the underlying theoretical distribution. A large number of scenarios may be necessary using a fine discretisation grid to achieve sufficient accuracy.

Consistency
Scenarios that model more than one variable should ensure that the values of these variables are internally consistent. The generation of event trees with multiple bonds or derivatives requires special attention. The prices of bonds with different maturities are often driven by a small number of underlying factors such as the short-term interest rate, a long-term yield and the credit spread. Because of the close relationship between bond prices and interest rates, the price movements of bonds of a similar type but with different maturities, should be consistent with each other. For instance, arbitrage opportunities between the short and long rates should be avoided in term structure models. Similarly, arbitrage opportunities should not be present in scenarios of multiple exchange rates.

parameters to fit the historical data. These models are then discretised and their performance is simulated in order to generate scenarios. Sampling is a data-driven method for scenario generation, while statistical analysis and discretisations of continuous time models are model-based methods.

Bootstrapping methods are correct in describing historical data but are not able to generate scenarios that have not been observed in the past, even if they are plausible given current conditions. As these scenarios have been observed in practice they also satisfy consistency requirements and, given large enough samples, they are also accurate.

Statistical modelling is correct to the extent that the fitted probability distributions satisfy the necessary theoretical properties. For instance, a normal distribution for modelling exchange rates is incorrect because exchange rates cannot become negative. A lognormal distribution has better theoretical properties for modelling exchange rates, while normality may be a reasonable approximation for stock returns. However, both distributional assumptions are unrealistic for those assets whose empirical distribution exhibit fat tails.

Continuous time models can be developed that are both theoretically correct and consistent. Accuracy may be sacrificed in the discretisation step: coarse discretisations introduce errors, while finer discretisations create a very large scenario universe. Sampling from this scenario universe introduces additional inaccuracies.

The simplest approach for generating scenarios using only the available data without any mathematical modelling is to bootstrap a set of historical records. Each scenario is a sample of returns of the assets obtained by sampling returns that were observed in the previous sample. Dates from the available historical returns are selected randomly and for each datum in the sample we read the returns of all asset classes or risk factors during the month prior to that date. These are scenarios of *monthly* returns. If we want to generate scenarios of returns for a long horizon – say one year – we sample 12 monthly returns from different points in time. The compounded return of the sampled series is the one-year return. Note that with this approach the correlations among asset classes are preserved.

THE EFFECTS OF ERRORS IN MODELLING ASSET RETURNS
To illustrate the effect of sampling error we bootstrap a set of monthly records for the 10-year period from January 1990 to February 2000. For each asset class we generate two sets of 500 scenarios of returns for a 10-year planning horizon. Multiple samples are generated by initialising the random generator with seeds S_1 and S_2. We denote by CEexROE $(X_{S_1}|S_1)$ and $\bar{O}_G(X_{S_1}|S_1)$ the quantities computed on out-of-sample scenarios S_2, having first optimised the model with respect to S_1. The same procedure is then applied to X_{S_2} so that the out-of-sample performance of X_{S_2} is assessed with respect of S_1.

To reduce the model risk arising from sampling we can either increase the number of scenarios or accurately choose the most representative scenarios for the economic factors driving the assets' returns. The first solution can be adopted only if a valid alternative is available for solving large-scale programming models. Model decomposition and parallel computing could provide the technological support in this case. The second solution can be implemented by picking those scenarios which look more significant. Identifying the most significant scenarios is itself a major task, which is particularly cumbersome when many assets are considered. An alternative is to develop a "quasi-Monte Carlo" algorithm, which reduces the discrepancy between scenarios (see, eg, Birge, 1995). A simple example of quasi-Monte Carlo sampling consists in choosing a scenario and including its antithetic version in the set of scenarios (see Boyle *et al.*, 1997).

In Figures 5 and 6 we show the two curves: the in-sample optimisation denoted by S_1 (resp. S_2) and the out-of-sample analysis denoted by $S_2|S_1$ (resp. $S_1|S_2$). In each figure, we also show the performance of the model when merging the two sets of

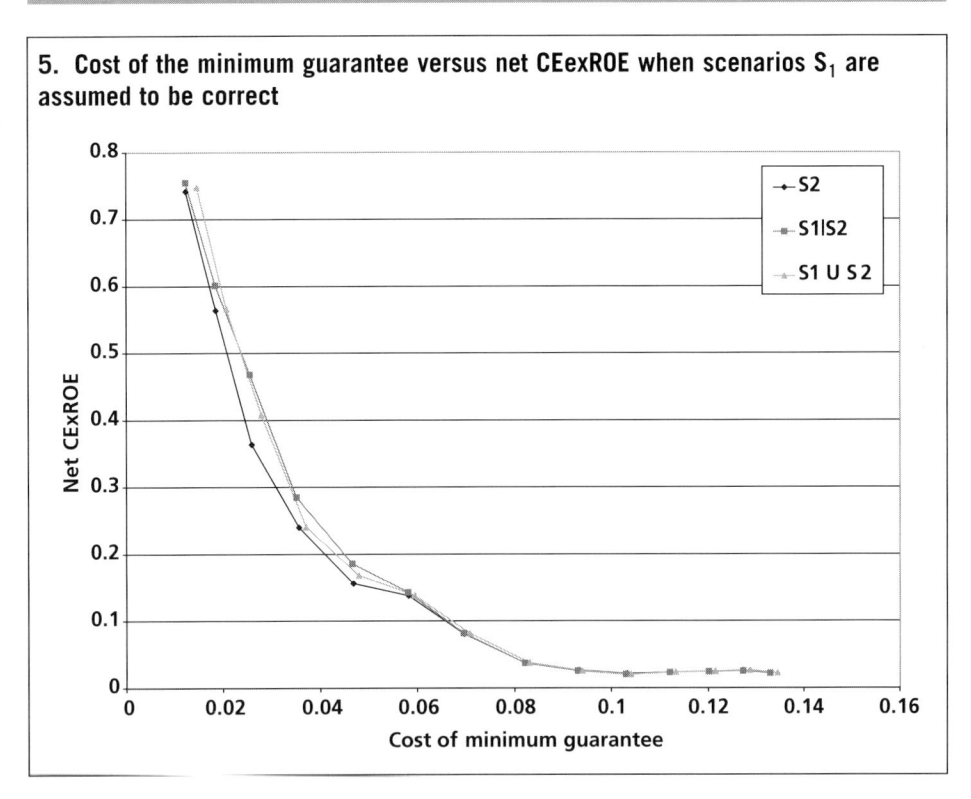

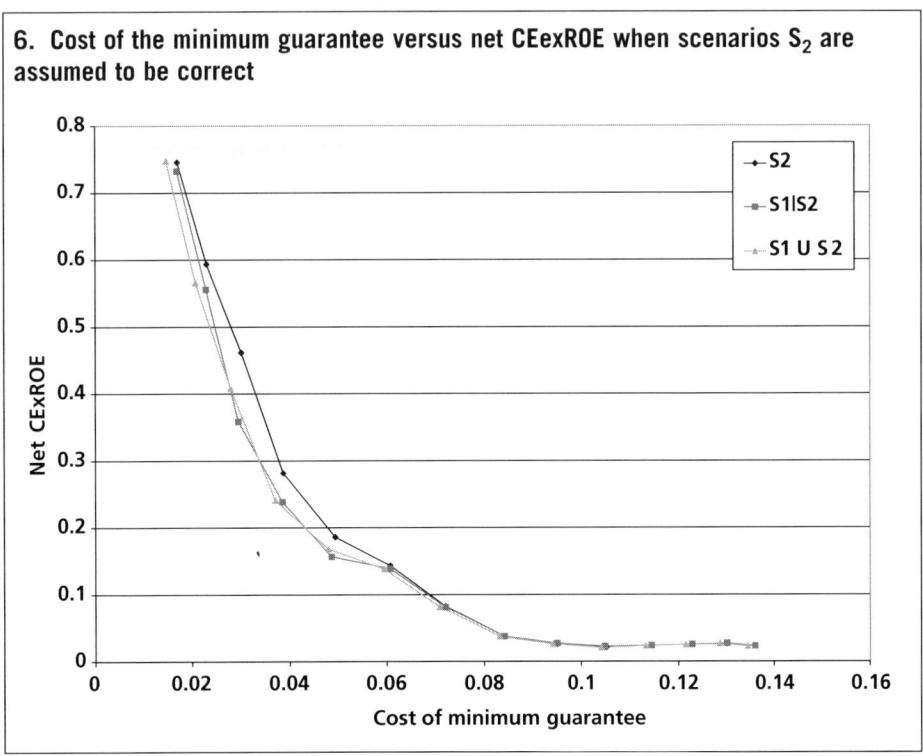

5. Cost of the minimum guarantee versus net CEexROE when scenarios S_1 are assumed to be correct

6. Cost of the minimum guarantee versus net CEexROE when scenarios S_2 are assumed to be correct

scenarios ($S_1 \cup S_2$). As it can be observed, the curves obtained from the union of S_1 and S_2 are closer to the curves that are obtained on the sample of scenarios assumed to be the correct one in each case. There is no out-of-sample error in this case, as it is assumed that the union $S_1 \cup S_2$ exhausts the set of plausible scenarios. Therefore, increasing the number of scenarios, when possible, does reduce model error. There is still the issue of how many scenarios should be used to eliminate model error? This is not an easy question to answer and it requires techniques from probability theory and contamination analysis. However, the simple analysis conducted here shows that both S_1 and S_2 are inadequate for small levels of minimum guarantee, while they may be adequate for guarantees above 6%. (Typical products offered today come with guarantees around 3% to 4%.)

Liability modelling

We now turn to the modelling of the future values of liability streams in an enterprise-wide risk management model. The liabilities typically represent future obligatory payments by the financial institution or firm. Examples include liabilities resulting from bank deposits, pension funds or social security liabilities owed to future benefit payments as well as liabilities resulting from the sale of insurance contracts, such as the minimum guaranteed product considered in this chapter. Hence we cannot provide a general recipe for calculating the value of the liabilities. For pension funds and insurance companies, actuarial methods can be very important, while other financial institutions might require financial/economic valuation models.

The liabilities of pension funds and insurance companies usually consist of a large number of individual contracts and the development of the total liability value is influenced by multiple sources of uncertainty. As this setting frustrates mathematical analysis, simulation is an important approach for risk management applications with a complex liability structure. A simulation model must be able to capture the complex interactions between the state of the economy, the financial markets, security prices and the value of the liabilities. For instance, the liabilities of defined benefits pension funds are driven by inflation. The liabilities created by insurance investment products may depend, through a surrender option, on the yield curve: high, long-term yields encourage policyholders to surrender their policies before maturity and turn to other investments.

LIABILITY RISK
We consider now the effects of lapse behaviour on the model for optimising the minimum guarantee products. In our formulation, we have so far taken into account only the actuarial risk – the probability of abandoning a policy due to death. Actuarial risk can be compared to the stochastic phenomena encountered in physics. The shape of the distribution and the parameters which govern the phenomena do not change over time, or at least over relatively short periods of time.

In recent years, however, many actuaries have pointed out that the aging of the population has introduced a modelling risk in the actuarial framework. The "longevity risk" accounts for the probability of death by increasing the probability of survival for that sector of the population who are in their retirement years. Pension fund managers then are faced with the risk of higher liabilities than those planned for. However, life insurance products can also benefit from an aging population because any payments made due to death are reduced. Any kind of model error arising from actuarial model inaccuracies however, must also be analysed with respect to the financial risks that affect liabilities. Actuarial events are not affected – at least significantly – from the changes in the financial markets but complex products that combine insurance with investment are.

We consider here one such example, and in particular, the role played by lapse modelling on products with minimum guarantees. We formulate two hypotheses about lapses that can be embedded into our scenario optimisation model.

❏ Fixed lapse: the probability of surrender the policy, Λ_t, is considered constant throughout the life of the contract. This hypothesis is not unrealistic. For example, a study carried over a panel of British households shows that the percentage of lapse is constant over the period 1994–97 and it averages to 1.4% (see the Personal Investment Authority report, 1999). We assumed, in our experiments, annual lapse rates of 2%, 4% and 6%.

❏ Variable lapse: economic factors can affect the policyholder withdrawal from an insurance policy. As with mortgage backed securities (see Kang and Zenios, 1997) where prepayment models assume specific patterns in order to describe households attitude towards market (prevailing interest rates) and social (age of the household) factors, we can link the dynamics of Λ_t^l to the economic outlook. In particular, in the case of lapse driven by the minimum guarantee level, the lapse probability is a function of the spread between $\bar{g}$ and the rate on other investments offered in the capital market.

$$\Lambda_t^l = f(r_t^l - \bar{g}) \qquad (4)$$

Note that the surrender probability is now indexed by scenarios as it depends on the competitors' rates r_t^l. We expect policyholders to sell back their policies when alternative investments provide a return higher than the amount guaranteed $\bar{g}$.

Another key factor in lapse modelling is the crediting rate strategy of the company. If the insurance company's crediting rate is significantly lower than that of the competition, substantial lapses will occur. Observe that in the scenario optimisation model for guaranteed products the credit rate depends on the performance of the portfolio, therefore the model error of the asset side is linked with the model error of the liability side. Assuming that the competitors offer rates equal to the relevant market benchmark we can write lapses in the form:

$$\Lambda_t^l = f(r_t^l - (\bar{g} + \epsilon_t^{+l})) \qquad (5)$$

This formula embodies the complex gaming situations facing the insurer: large minimum guarantees subdue the effects of the competition but come at a large cost or low CEexROE, as illustrated in the previous figures.

A convenient general form for function $f(\cdot)$ governing the surrender behaviour has been studied by Asay *et al* (1993). In this chapter the lapse probability is given by

$$\Lambda_t^l = a + b \tan^{-1}[m(r_t^l - i_t^l - y) - n] \qquad (6)$$

where a, b, m, n are parameters chosen to give a minimum lapse rate of 0.01, a maximum lapse rate of 0.40 and a lapse rate of 0.03 when $r_t^l = i_t^l$. The variable r_t^l is the competitor's rate of return. (In the numerical result, we use the annual return on the 10-year Italian bond index as the competitor rate.) The variable r_t^l is the company's credit rate that can be modelled as a constant (Equation 4) or as a market-driven variable (Equation 5).

In Figure 7, we present different lapse curves when changing the parameter m and n using the rule described in Equation 5. In this case we set $a = 0.219$, $b = 0.140$, $m = 78.932$, $n = 4.298$. The curves are very different especially when the spread is positive, namely, when the company is offering a credit rate which is less than the competitor rate. Recall that a positive spread occurs when assets perform poorly with respect to the rest of the industry. Thus, we need a careful modelling of lapse in these cases in order to avoid igniting a vicious circle which could lead to bankruptcy.

In Figure 8 we show the effect of the error in modelling lapse on the option cost for different levels of the minimum guarantee. It is worth noting that the difference between no lapse at all and fixed lapse is quite relevant for the high level of the minimum guarantee ($\bar{g} \geq 7\%$). This difference is less evident when the lapse is modelled as in Equation 6.

Finally, in Figure 9 we display the effect of the error in modelling lapse on the net CEexROE. Again, error is more evident when we switch from no lapse to fixed lapse.

It is interesting to highlight how the modelling error affects the option cost and the net CEexROE for low minimum guarantees, say $\bar{g} \geq 6\%$. On the contrary, modelling uncertainty yields substantially different minimum guarantee cost when $\bar{g}$

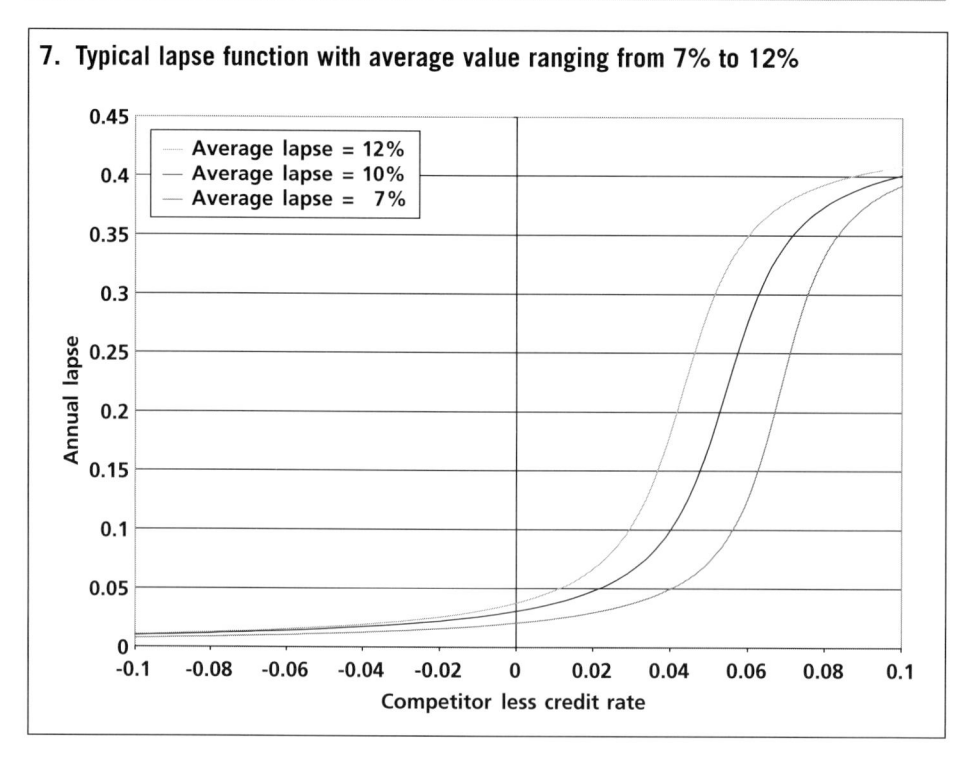

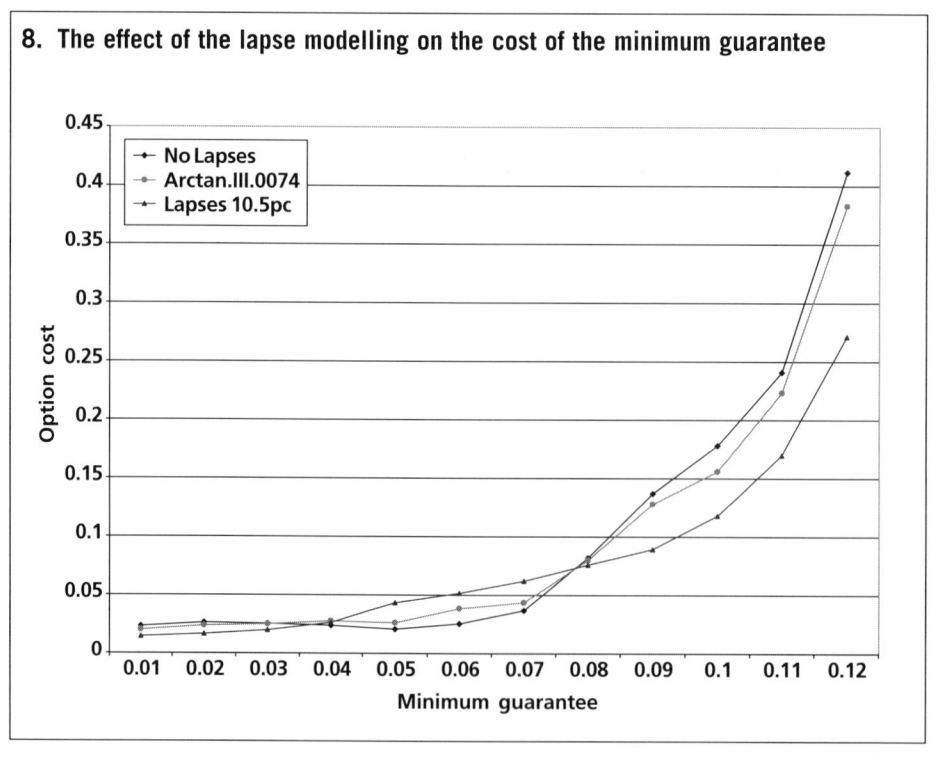

7. Typical lapse function with average value ranging from 7% to 12%

[Figure: Annual lapse vs. Competitor less credit rate, showing three S-curves for average lapse = 12%, 10%, and 7%]

8. The effect of the lapse modelling on the cost of the minimum guarantee

[Figure: Option cost vs. Minimum guarantee, with three curves: No Lapses, Arctan.III.0074, Lapses 10.5pc]

is greater than the 6%. This effect can be explained in the light of the option embedded in the policy (see Grosen and Jorgensen, 2000). For a low level of the minimum guarantee, the option is almost always out-of-the-money and fixed lapse will depress the net CEexROE through a constant outflow due to actuarial events (see Equation 13). For a high level of the minimum guarantee, the insurance company will benefit from lapses since shortfalls are more likely, thus exceeding the cost for actuarial expenses.

Conclusion

In this chapter we have dealt with an analysis of the modelling risks arising in an asset and liability model for minimum guarantee products. It is hard to separate market

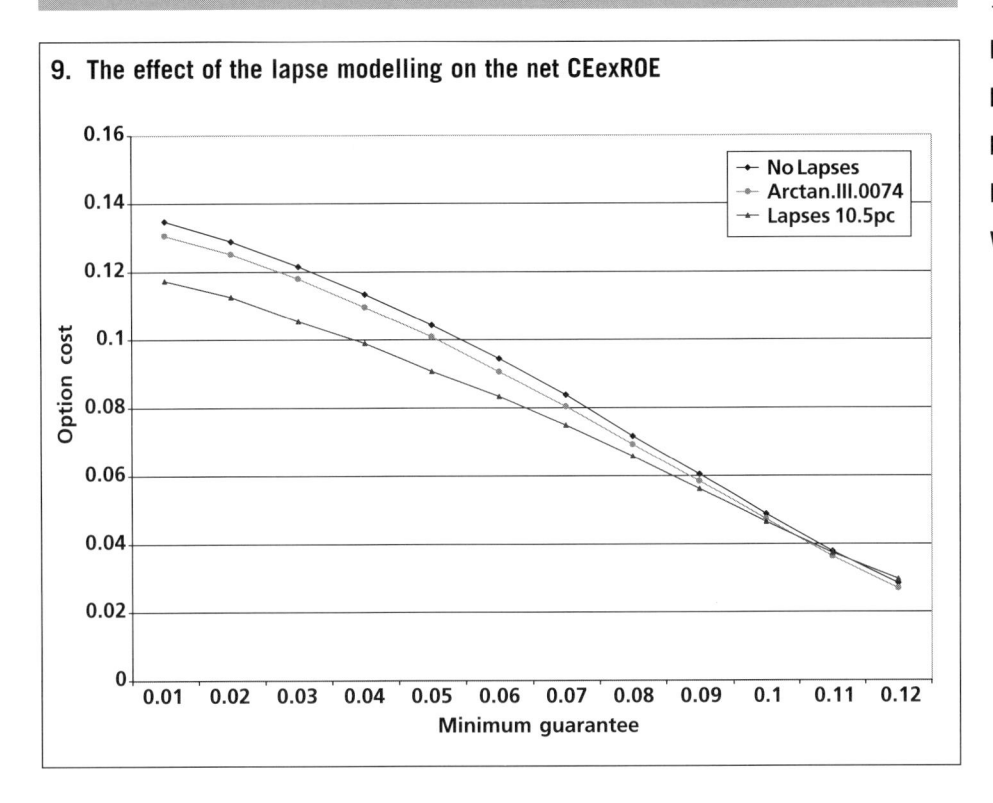

9. The effect of the lapse modelling on the net CEexROE

[Graph: Option cost vs Minimum guarantee, with three curves: No Lapses, Arctan.III.0074, Lapses 10.5pc. X-axis from 0.01 to 0.12, Y-axis from 0 to 0.16.]

risks from operational risks arising when calibrating an asset and liability management model. Given the prevalence of models for risk management, the risks arising from model mis-specification or inaccurate calibration deserve attention.

We have highlighted the sources of error modelling in the asset side and in the liability side and how the interactions between the two affect the model outputs. This chapter has shown that by a careful analysis of the pitfalls that characterise the distribution of the returns and the lapse behaviour, the decision maker is able to assess the impact of model errors and gain confidence in the strategic outcomes recommended by the model.

Appendix
THE SCENARIO OPTIMISATION MODEL

In this Appendix we supply the integrative model for insurance products with minimum guarantees as suggested in Consiglio, Cocco and Zenios (2001a); additional details and extensive analysis are given in this reference. We let Ω denote the set of scenarios, A the universe of available asset instruments, and $t = 1, 2, ..., T$ discrete points in time from today ($t = 0$) until maturity T. We use index l to denote scenarios from Ω, and i to denote assets from A. The data of the problem are as follows:

- r_{it}^l, rate of return of asset i during the period $t-1$ to t in scenario l;
- r_{ft}^l, risk-free rate during the period $t-1$ to t in scenario l;
- $\bar{g}$, minimum guaranteed rate of return;
- α, participation rate indicating the percentage of portfolio return paid back to the policyholders;
- ρ, regulatory equity to debt ratio; and
- Λ_t^l, probability of abandon of the short rate during the period from t to T in scenario l.

The variables of the model are defined as follows:

- x_i, percentage of initial capital invested in the ith asset;

- y^l_{At}, expenses due to lapse or death at time t in scenario l;
- z^l_t, shortfall below the minimum guarantee at time t in scenario l;
- A^l_t, asset value at time t in scenario l;
- E^l_t, total equity at time t in scenario l;
- L^l_t, liability value at time t in scenario l;
- R^l_{pt}, portfolio rate of return at time t under scenario l;
- y^{+l}_t, excess return over $\bar{g}$ at time t in scenario l; and
- y^{-l}_t, shortfall return under $\bar{g}$ at time t in scenario l.

With this notation we can now define the model. All variables are constrained to be non-negative except R^l_{pt}, thus short sales are not allowed. We invest the premium collected (L_0) and the equity required by the regulators ($E_0 = (L_0)$ in the asset portfolio. Out initial endowment $A_0 = L_0(1 + \rho)$ is allocated to assets in proportion x_i such that

$$\sum_{i \in A} x_i = 1 \qquad (7)$$

The dynamics of the portfolio value are given by

$$R^l_{pt} = \sum_{i \in A} x_i r^l_{it}, \text{ for } t = 1, 2, \ldots T, \text{ and for all } l \in \Omega \qquad (8)$$

The dynamics of the liability are given by

$$L^l_t = (1 - \Lambda^l_t) L^l_{t-1} (1 + \max[\alpha R^l_{Pt}, \bar{g}]), \text{ for } t = 1, 2, \ldots T, \text{ and for all } l \in \Omega \qquad (9)$$

Λ^l_t denotes probabilities of actuarial events or policy surrender. To circumvent the discontinuity introduced by the max operator we introduce variables y^{+l}_t and y^{-l}_t to measure the portfolio excess return over the minimum guarantee and the shortfall below the minimum guarantee, respectively. They satisfy:

$$\alpha R^l_{Pt} - \bar{g} = y^{+l}_t - y^{-l}_t, \text{ for } t = 1, 2, \ldots T, \text{ and for all } l \in \Omega \qquad (10)$$

$$y^{+l}_t \geq 0, y^{-l}_t \geq 0, \text{ for } t = 1, 2, \ldots T, \text{ and for all } l \in \Omega \qquad (11)$$

The dynamics for the value of the liability can be written as:

$$L^l_t = (1 - \Lambda^l_t) L^l_{t-1} (1 + \bar{g} + y^{+l}_t), \text{ for } t = 1, 2, \ldots T, \text{ and for all } l \in \Omega \qquad (12)$$

Note that liabilities grow at least at the rate of $\bar{g}$. Any excess return is added to the liabilities and the minimum guarantee applies to the lifted liabilities in subsequent time periods.

At each period, the insurance company will face a cash outflow due to policyholders abandoning their policies either because of death or lapse. The amount to be reimbursed is given by the liability value times the probability of abandon:

$$y^l_{At} = \Lambda^l_t L^l_{t-1} (1 + \bar{g} + y^{+l}_t), \text{ for } t = 1, 2, \ldots T, \text{ and for all } l \in \Omega \qquad (13)$$

Whenever the portfolio experiences a shortfall below the minimum guarantee, we need to infuse cash into the asset portfolio in order to meet the final liabilities. Shortfalls are modelled by the dynamics:

$$z^l_t = y^{-l}_t L^l_{t-1}, \text{ for } t = 1, 2, \ldots T, \text{ and for all } l \in \Omega \qquad (14)$$

We consider first the case where shortfalls are funded through equity. With the modelling construct Equations 10–14, it is assumed that equity is reinvested at the risk-free rate and is returned to the shareholders at the end of the planning horizon. (This is not all the shareholders get; they also receive dividends.) The dynamics of the equity are given by:

$$E_t^l = E_{t-1}^l(1 + R_{pt}^l) + z_t^l - y_{At}^l, \text{ for } t = 1, 2, \ldots T, \text{ and for all } l \in \Omega \quad (15)$$

We now have all the components needed to model the asset dynamics. The equation describing the asset dynamics has to take into account the equity infusion that funds the shortfall, z_t^l, and the outflow due to actuarial events, y_{At}^l. Thus, we have:

$$A_t^l = A_{t-1}^l(1 + R_{Pt}^l) + z_t^l - y_{At}^l, \text{ for } t = 1, 2, \ldots T, \text{ and for all } l \in \Omega \quad (16)$$

In order to satisfy the regulatory constraint the ratio between the equity value and liabilities must exceed ρ, that is,

$$\frac{V_{ET}^l}{L_T^l} \geq \rho, \text{ for all } l \in \Omega \quad (17)$$

where V_{ET}^l is the value of equity at the end of the planning horizon T. If the company sells only a single policy, the value of its equity (V_{ET}^l) will be equal to the final asset return – which includes the equity needed to fund shortfall – minus the final liability due to the policyholders, so we have

$$V_{ET}^l = A_t^l - L_T^l \quad (18)$$

Finally, we define an appropriate objective function. We model the goal of a for-profit institution to maximise shareholder value. We use return on equity, after liabilities are paid, as a proxy for this. Because return on equity is scenario dependent, we maximise the expected value of the utility of excess return, where the utility function reflects the decision maker's risk aversion. This expected value is converted into a certainty equivalent value for easy reference. The objective function of the model is to compute the maximal Certainty Equivalent Excess Return on Equity (CEexROE) given by:

$$U(CEexROE) = \text{Maximize}_X \sum_l p^l U\left[\frac{A_T - L_T}{E_T^l}\right] \quad (19)$$

where $U\{\cdot\}$ denotes the decision maker's utility function and p^l are the statistical probabilities of the scenarios. Our numerical results were obtained using a logarithmic utility function.

How much does a given level of minimum guarantee cost? (This is the question addressed through an options pricing approach in the literature, Brennan–Schwartz, Boyle–Schwartz and Grosen–Jorgensen.) The cost of the minimum guarantee is the total amount of reserves required to fund shortfall due to portfolio performance below the minimum guarantee. Variable E_T^l is able to model precisely, the total funds required up to time t, valued at the risk-free rate. However, E_T^l also embeds the initial amount of equity required by the regulators. This is not a cost and it must be deducted from E_T^l. Thus, the cost of the minimum guarantee is given as the expected present value of the final equity E_T^l as adjusted by the regulatory equity, which gives

$$\bar{O}_G = \sum_l p^l \left(\frac{E_T^l}{\Pi_{t=1}^T(1 + r_{ft}^l)} - \rho L_0\right) \quad (20)$$

The mathematical programming model defined by Equations 7–19 is a non-linearly constrained optimisation model, which is computationally intractable for large-scale applications. However, the non-linear constraints in Equations 12–16 are definitional constraints that determine the value of the respective variables at the end of the horizon. These dynamic equations can be solved analytically and the model is reformulated to a linearly-constrained model, which is solved with standard optimisation packages. Details of the reformulation and an analysis of the model are given in Consiglio, Cocco and Zenios (2001a). The same reference discusses alternative reserving methods for funding shortfalls – equity, short-term or long-term debt – and tradeoffs between shareholder value and policy holder cost. The effects of leverage on shareholder value are also analysed.

BIBLIOGRAPHY

Asay, M. R., P. J. Bouyoucos and A. M. Marciano, 1992, "An Economic Approach to Valuation of Single Premium Deferred Annuities", in S. A. Zenios (ed), *Financial Optimization*, pp. 100–35 (Cambridge University Press).

Birge, J. R., 1995, "Quasi-Monte Carlo Methods Approaches to Option Pricing", Technical report 94-19, Department of Industrial and Operations Engineering, The University of Michigan.

Boyle, P. P., M. Broadie and P. Glasserman, 1997, "Monte Carlo Methods for Security Pricing", *Journal of Economic Dynamics and Control* 21(8–9), pp. 1267–321.

Boyle, P. P., and E. S. Schwartz, 1977, "Equilibrium Prices of Guarantees under Equity-Linked Contracts", *The Journal of Risk and Insurance* 44, pp.639–60.

Brennan M. J., and E. S. Schwartz, 1976, "The Pricing of Equity-Linked Life Insurance Policies with an Asset Value Guarantee", *Journal of Financial Economics* 3, pp.195–213.

Consiglio, A., F. Cocco and S. A. Zenios, 2001a, "Asset and Liability Modelling for Participating Policies with Guarantee", Working paper 00-41-c, *The Wharton Financial Institutions Center*. University of Pennsylvania.

Consiglio, A., F. Cocco and S. A. Zenios, 2001b, "The Value of Integrative Risk Management for Insurance products with Minimum Guarantees", *Journal of Risk Finance*, Spring, pp. 1–11.

Consiglio, A., D. Saunders and S. A. Zenios, 2003, "Insurance League: Italy vs UK", *Journal of Risk Finance*, forthcoming.

Giraldi, C., et al, 2000, "Insurance Optional", *Risk* 13(4), pp. 87–90.

Grosen, A., and P. L. Jorgensen, 2000, "Fair Valuation of Life Insurance Liabilities: the Impact of Interest Rate Guarantees, Surrender Options, and Bonus Policies", *Insurance: Mathematics and Economics* 26, pp. 37–57.

Jobst, N. J., and S. A. Zenios, 2001, "Extending Credit Risk (Pricing) Models for Simulation and Valuation of Portfolios of Interest Rate and Credit Risk Sensitive Securities", Working Paper 01-03, HERMES Center of Computational Finance & Economics, University of Cyprus.

Kang, P., and S. A. Zenios, 1992, "Complete Prepayment Models for Mortgage-Backed Securities", *Management Science* 38(11), pp.1665–85.

Personal Investment Authority, 1999, Fifth Survey of the Persistency of Life and Pension Policies, *PIA editions*, London.

PRACTICAL IMPLEMENTATION

11

Building and Running an Operational Loss Database

John Thirlwell
ORRF; BBA Global Operational Loss Database

Despite the effort and attention which has been given to it, operational risk management as a central discipline in banks is still at a relatively early stage in its evolution. The industry's mind had been concentrated by the various high-profile cases involving Barings, Daiwa, NatWest and Sumitomo. However, when the British Bankers' Association (BBA) conducted a survey of its 300 members in 1997, it became obvious from the 40 replies that many banks had not thought through a definition of operational risk, few had anybody responsible for the risk throughout the firm and there were few who were reporting operational risk losses in any systematic way. A very different picture from that applying to credit risk, where even relatively small losses were reported up through the hierarchy and there were significant management structures in place and a whole raft of management information to provide a basis for analysis.

When the BBA, together with the International Swaps and Derivatives Association (ISDA) and Robert Morris Associates, commissioned a more extensive survey in 1999, it was clear from the 55 responses from internationally active banks that much work had been done in the interim. However, while much had been achieved in a short time by leading banks, there was still an enormous amount to do, especially among the many thousands of banks that were outside the top few dozen.

It is probably true that the biggest catalyst for those banks to wake up to the need to understand and manage operational risk better was the decision by banking regulators to allocate capital to this type of risk, just as had been done for credit and market risk.

Drivers for industry to develop a database

It was against this background of its members becoming more preoccupied with the management of operational risk that the BBA established in June 2000, the means for them to pool their operational loss data. The initiative is known as the BBA's Global Operational Loss Database (GOLD).

BENCHMARKING AND IMPROVING THE QUALITY OF OPERATIONAL RISK MANAGEMENT

A fundamental driver for banks was the ability to benchmark their performance against their peers. This raises two issues. The first is the use to which risk managers can put the loss data they receive. For most banks, the happy truth is that they experience relatively few significant operational losses. As a result it is difficult to create a history that identifies where these losses are likely to occur in future. The benefit of a database is that it provides information on where other banks have lost money or incurred extraordinary costs. It can therefore enable a risk manager to question why the bank's performance differs from the evidence provided by the database, whether better or worse. If the bank has not recognised losses in a particular area, is this because its controls are exceptionally good or because its reporting systems are exceptionally poor?

A database can also inform the various risk matrices that banks use to identify where they should be paying more attention to risk management – whether at the business line level, by central risk management or through internal audit. It can therefore contribute a relatively qualitative basis for assessments of risk, in terms of both impact and probability, which banks often use for these purposes.

VALIDATING ASSUMPTIONS IN RISK SELF-ASSESSMENT
Risk self-assessment, in which firms assess the probability and likely maximum impact of operational risks, is one of the many methodologies used by banks in assessing their risk exposure. However, they have little hard information to substantiate these assessments. An external database provides additional information against which risk assessments, and the assumptions underpinning them, can be validated.

DATA FOR QUANTITATIVE ANALYSIS AND MODELLING
Patently, where banks – through their own lack of experience – have few data on material operational risk losses, pooled data can provide more information on both frequency and severity of loss. This has considerable value for their ability to model these risks. Although this can help to refine models, a number of issues make it difficult to use this information in a precise way; these are discussed under 'Limitations' later.

ALLOCATION OF CAPITAL
Similarly, the data give banks better information on the basis by which they allocate economic capital within the firm. Again, though, care must be exercised in the use of this external data. See 'Limitations' below.

General issues
CONFIDENTIALITY
A, perhaps *the*, key factor in developing a database is that of confidentiality between the providers and the holder of the data. What safeguards are in place to protect the data and prevent their being offered to or used by unauthorised persons?

It is a commercial decision of participants as to who they will accept as a data holder and manager. Does the data holder have as much reputation to lose as the database participants? Does it have sufficient experience of running similar projects satisfactorily? Does it have any commercial interest in the data that may lead to information leaking out despite whatever 'Chinese walls' are erected within the firm? What precautions or contractual terms are in place to prevent the data being offered to regulators or others, should they ask?

The last issue is one which has exercised many potential participants. It is probably generally accepted that a data holder will ensure that data remain anonymous. But, despite that, there are concerns as to whether even aggregated data should be given to supervisors without the agreement of participants. The answer probably lies in the extent to which participants believe that supervisors will be responsible in what they seek and how they understand and use the data provided. However, some banks may well consider that they would only contribute to an 'offshore' database, such as one domiciled in Switzerland, for instance, where secrecy laws are relatively robust. This is a serious concern and will affect the extent and speed with which industry databases develop.

ANONYMITY
It is essential that data are anonymous. This does not just mean that there is no obvious identifier in the data themselves but also that there are no clues in the nature of a loss reported that could trace it back to a particular participant unless, of course, the event is so public that its owner is readily known.

One precaution is to ensure that the various data fields themselves are such that participants cannot be identified. Clearly, the more participants there are, the less is the risk to anonymity. An example might be the need for geographical information. In the case of GOLD, participants were interested in having this information but, given the membership of the database, it would have been too granular to go down to country level as many losses would have been easily attributable to one participant or another. We therefore decided on a geographical classification by region and/or continent. However, it would be possible to add a country code and provide separate reports for countries where there were sufficient data to create critical mass.

TRUST BETWEEN PARTICIPANTS
Trust is fundamental if the participants are to contribute their data. Clearly, the database will grow in usefulness the more data are provided. In the end, trust will be a better driver than some form of audit. The BBA experience has been that the group of banks around the table got to know each other, were all involved in setting up the database and therefore felt a commitment both to it and to their colleagues. This resulted in a relatively high level of reporting from the outset and a product that was perceived to be successful. From that start, the database can grow.

CONSISTENCY
As well as completeness of reporting, which is effectively what 'trust' is all about, there is the question of consistency. GOLD has over 100 categories of loss. Will different banks place similar losses in the same categories? And will losses be reported consistently within an individual bank?

This is a difficult area since, without considerable detail in the reports, it is difficult to validate the accuracy of reporting. The GOLD management committee has had an interesting experience as an 'appeals' tribunal, ruling on where certain losses should be allocated. It is key, therefore, to any database, that the loss categories are readily understandable and that sufficient detail is given in loss reports to enable them to be correctly allocated and validated.

FLEXIBILITY/EVOLUTION
At the beginning of the chapter, I emphasised that operational risk management is at an early stage of its evolution in banks. Operational loss databases are at an even earlier stage. It is inevitable that the original categorisations, and possibly the original data fields, will not fully match the needs of participants as they become more experienced in identifying and managing operational risk. New types of risk, such as the SARS epidemic in the Far East in 2003, may emerge, which will need to be added to the list. The database must therefore be structured in such a way that it can easily be modified as users' needs change.

Specific issues
OPERATIONAL LOSS VERSUS OPERATIONS LOSS
Operational risk covers a far broader category of risk than simply operations risk and losses, which are effectively those encountered in the back office. Four broad categories of risk were identified in the BBA/ISDA/Robert Morris Associates report (1999). The report provided a definition of operational risk that has been adopted by international bank regulators:

The risk of loss caused by inadequate or failed people, processes or systems, or from external events.

The definition therefore covers aspects such as documentation and legal risks.

Although it is probably true that the biggest operational risk which a bank faces is to its reputation (ie, a loss of market confidence in it), this is specifically excluded from the definition used by regulators for capital assessment – as are the broader operational risks, which might be described as business and strategic risks. These effectively cover management decisions, affecting the direction and policy of the business which, by their nature, are difficult to quantify if they generate additional costs and do not produce anticipated benefits.

AGREEING THE CLASSIFICATION/CATEGORISATION OF LOSSES

A number of approaches can be adopted in deciding on an appropriate taxonomy of loss. One is to analyse processes in individual business lines, activities or products and work from there, basing the taxonomy very much on business activity. A disadvantage of this approach is that it can be extremely time-consuming, and of course it has to be repeated for every business line or product.

It is probably now accepted that, for the purposes of a database, it is best to identify generic causes of loss, or loss events, since they can often apply to a number of business activities. Good examples of this would be breakdowns in settlement processes, non-adherence to health and safety regulations, embezzlement, input errors, modelling errors, fire, flood, etc.

In the case of GOLD, we approached the problem from the point of view of the four major categories of operational loss identified above and then sought to identify the detailed loss events that fell in each category. Gradually, sub-categories emerged into which the loss events could logically be grouped. The categories and sub-categories are set out in Panel 1. Partly because they were determined earlier, but

PANEL 1

LOSS CATEGORIES IN THE GOLD DATABASE

Category	Sub-category
People	Employee fraud (malice – criminal)
	Unauthorised activity/rogue trading/employee misdeed
	Breach of employment law
	Disruption by workforce
	Loss or lack of key personnel
Process	Payment/settlement/delivery risk
	Documentation or contract risk
	Valuation/pricing errors
	Failures in internal/external reporting
	Compliance failures
	Failures in project change management
	Selling risks
Systems	Technology investment risk
	Systems development and implementation
	Systems – lack of capacity
	Systems failures
	Systems security breaches
External	Legal/public liability
	Criminal activities
	Outsourcing/supplier risk
	Insourcing risk
	Disasters and infrastructure (utilities) failures
	Political/government risk
	Regulatory risk

partly because participants wanted the greater granularity provided, the categories obviously exceed the seven major categories identified by the Basel Committee of the BIS, or even the number of sub-categories provided by the Committee. GOLD has decided to retain its own categorisation but has mapped its classification into the major Basel groupings.

HARD LOSSES, SOFT LOSSES AND NEAR MISSES

The other categories of risk that are excluded are what might be called 'soft' losses, contingent losses and near misses. The main reason for excluding these risks is, quite simply, that they are extremely difficult, if not impossible, to quantify, let alone in any objective way. To achieve an acceptable degree of objectivity and consistency, it is important that the losses or costs being captured are identifiable. Effectively, this means that they are represented by debits to the profit and loss account. This view also led regulators to decide that only 'hard' losses should be used as a basis for calibrating regulatory capital.

There has been much debate about whether, for instance, the 'costs to fix' should be reported in the case of a systems failure. The problem with this is that the assessment of these costs, where it involves the bank's employees, will be assessed subjectively and the costs themselves based on cost allocations that could vary considerably between institutions. Even if it were possible to identify these direct internal costs, there has to be an opportunity cost in that the employees will be diverted from their paid job to resolving the problem. The total cost should therefore reflect the fact that they are not doing the job for which they are paid, which presumably is one that will affect the bank's income or costs if it is not done. If, of course, the 'fixing' is undertaken by outside contractors, the cost will appear as a specific incremental debit to the profit and loss account, which will correctly fall to be reported in the database.

Internal costs to fix should undoubtedly form part of a bank's reporting of its operational costs or losses, but it was decided that they were too imprecise and open to subjective assessment to make them suitable for inclusion in an industry database. For the same reasons, opportunity costs arising, for example, from poor project management are excluded. They would, however, be included where a project failed and led to a specific debit to the profit and loss account.

Finally, we decided against including 'near misses'. These are the occasions when a loss would have occurred but for good internal controls. There is a value in capturing such data – if only to enable a firm to scale potential exposure to loss and also to evaluate the cost-benefit of a particular control. Internally, this undoubtedly has value, and it helps in risk modelling. Again, however, assessment of the size of a near miss is open to subjectivity, and of course one bank's near miss may be another's hit depending on the level and quality of controls that each applies.

CAUSE/EVENT VERSUS IMPACT/EFFECT

Another key question is whether the database is intended to reflect the causes of operational risks or their impact as reflected in a bank's accounts. From a management point of view, the important thing is to identify the causes of a loss or cost. First, you need to identify the number or size of the events that give rise to a loss. This is where the loss database comes in. Then you need to identify the causes underlying the most numerous or most significant categories of events. This is provided, within GOLD, by a narrative field. Finally, it is useful to identify where a loss has a particular impact or effect. The impacts or effects identified in the BBA's GOLD database are given in Panel 2.

Identifying the impact categories of a loss may not be particularly interesting from a management point of view where there is a direct link between cause/event and impact/effect. What is often true, however, is that a single cause can involve more than one impact, or even a multitude of impacts. So, although the information has

PANEL 2

IMPACT/EFFECT CATEGORIES IN THE GOLD DATABASE

Accounting adjustment
Assets stolen
Customer compensation
Damages awarded against participant
Damage to physical assets
Irrecoverable erroneous funds or asset transfer

Professional costs/fees
Loss on transaction or contract
Lost income
Other charge to profit and loss account
Penalties
Regulatory fines
Unbudgeted staff costs

some value and we record it in the database, it is not particularly useful in helping to improve the quality of risk management.

It is worth touching on the approach of the insurance industry, which tends to allocate data between hazards, perils and losses. The process there is inevitably much more geared to the loss end of the spectrum. Hazards and perils relate more closely to causes and events and probably help insurers in their risk assessments. However, as with events and impacts, a particular hazard can result in a variety of perils, and individual hazards and perils can result in a multiplicity of losses. The chains of cause and effect are complex.

REPORTING THRESHOLD
Another fundamental issue in building a database is to establish a threshold for reporting. This will be influenced by two main factors: the purpose of the database and the perceived cost/benefits in gathering data.

Participants in the GOLD database agreed at the outset that its main purpose was to provide them with data on larger, less expected losses. There were two reasons for this. First, they had a multitude of data about smaller, so-called "expected", losses. Second, they were aware that the regulators were considering allocating capital against a bank's operational losses, as they had done for credit and market risks. Since the primary purpose of capital is to protect markets and consumers from the effect of a bank suffering a major unexpected, loss, it seemed sensible to concentrate on these losses, of which individual banks would have little experience or data. It was initially agreed, therefore, that the threshold for reporting should be US$50,000 equivalent for losses incurred in retail business and US$100,000 for losses incurred in wholesale business. These figures are not rigid and banks are welcome to contribute data below these levels if they think it would be useful. In practice, there is now a general threshold of US$50,000 equivalent.

These levels also reflect the fact that most participants would face considerable costs in gathering data to a lower level from all their constituent parts and submitting them to the database, and that such costs would not be compensated by any improvement in assessing risk exposure that might be gained from the greater volumes of data available.

The agreed levels provide banks with more data than if they used their own data. It is questionable, though, whether at this level there are sufficient data to enable some reasonable modelling of operational risk exposure. For this, greater volumes are needed, which inevitably means a much lower threshold. This is the trade-off.

SCALING
Of course, one bank's minor hit is another bank's catastrophe. This makes a strong argument for introducing some form of scaling into the data. The main problems are

that it is difficult to identify appropriate scaling factors (assets, transaction volumes, turnover, income, expenses can all be used), and to agree whether these should apply to the whole organisation or only that part affected by the loss. It would seem preferable to apply a scaling factor to each business line, comparing like with like, or at least attempting to do so. However, as there are few audited data to facilitate this, banks would have to release internal management information, which they may be reluctant to do. It is also arguable whether there is any direct correlation between size, however measured, and operational risk. A smaller issue, but highly relevant, is that banks allocate different activities or products to different business lines, which means that it is difficult to compare like with like.

Another question is whether, having scaled the data, you report a loss as being the true amount or the scaled amount. Overall, the participants in GOLD decided that they would rather see the actual amounts and avoid the lack of precision of scaling.

But there may still be ways in which losses can be related to the broad size of a bank or of a particular business activity and so provide helpful additional information for users of the database.

Data fields

Participants in GOLD report losses within the following data fields.

DATE

Given the nature of material operational losses, their frequency and the relative lack of importance of timing in respect of when a loss takes place, this field does not have the relevance it would have for, say, market risk. Losses may emerge some time after the event, they can be recovered at some later date, or they may increase, so time recording is not critical. However, the date of the loss, or when the loss was recognised, is useful because the risk environment changes over time and it is helpful to know when a loss, or clutch of losses, occurred.

LOSS CLASSIFICATION AND CATEGORISATION

This field relates to the 110 or so event categories that were referred to above and is the core of the report.

LOSS DESCRIPTION

As explained in the section 'Consistency', it is important – both from the point of view of improving risk management and in assisting consistency and report validation – that some description is given of the circumstances of the loss beyond those contained in the bare loss classification. This information points to the underlying cause of a loss event. It also indicates that however many loss categories are used, they will not provide this essential management information. On the other hand, the narrative field provides a major benefit of database membership.

GROSS LOSS

As explained in the sections on hard and soft losses and near misses, a database should only record quantifiable losses. However, it is acknowledged that an originally reported figure may change over time. This can be dealt with by a report of revisions to previously reported losses (see 'Revisions' later). But it is also important to see the gross loss, as opposed to one that has already been reduced by, for instance, insurance receipts. In practice, the timing of these adjustments means that this is not a problem, but it is nevertheless important that the gross loss is reported as well as the net.

PRIMARY CATEGORISATION OF IMPACT/EFFECT

This field has already been explained in some detail above (see Panel 2).

BUILDING AND RUNNING AN OPERATIONAL LOSS DATABASE

SOFT LOSS

Having explained why reports should consist only of 'hard' losses and why it is not possible to record reputation loss, it might seem strange to include this data field heading. If anything, it is more closely related to scaling.

It was accepted that it was difficult, and not particularly valuable, to attempt a relatively accurate scaling model. Nevertheless, it was recognised that some losses have a greater impact on one bank than another. This would probably reflect their size, but it might be that reputational loss was some form of proxy. It was therefore decided to introduce a simple scale of 0 to 5 to reflect reputational damage. The grades in the scale, with their defining characteristics, are given in Panel 3.

BUSINESS ACTIVITY

A key element in assessing operational risk exposure is to know what business lines are involved. For some banks it may be more helpful to view losses by product; for others, distribution channels may be the appropriate criterion. For most, though, business lines seem to be the most accepted, and core, element of operational loss data. Again there is a difficulty of consistency. GOLD divides banking activities into the 14 lines shown in Panel 4.

This differs from regulatory proposals, which have only eight lines. It has not been easy for banks to fit their business activities easily, or consistently, into the regulatory lines, although GOLD has mapped its lines to those of the regulators. From a risk management point of view it is important to introduce sufficient granularity into the process. This may well increase the number of lines reported beyond those suggested in Panel 4.

One area of decision-making that can have a material impact on operational loss is something, which can loosely be described as central functions or support, ie, cost, as opposed to income, centres. This would cover decisions from, perhaps, legal or personnel divisions, which can affect the profit and loss account across all business lines, or at least many of them. On occasions a failure within a service division, such as IT or foreign exchange dealing, may affect all business activities. It is, of course, possible to allocate these losses, but it would be perfectly reasonable to regard them as not allocatable or as part of some central overhead. In constructing a database, banks should consider whether they wish to include this as a separate business line. If they do, they must also ensure that it does not become a dumping ground for losses that are merely difficult, rather than impossible, to allocate accurately.

PANEL 3

SOFT LOSS

Grade	Some defining factors
0	No external effects
1	No media coverage; increased customer complaints
2	Limited media coverage; possible account closures; no negative effect on share price
3	Limited national media coverage; large-scale customer complaints; informal regulatory enquiry
4	Sustained national media coverage; serious customer loss; formal regulatory enquiry; negative impact on share price
5	Sustained negative national and international media coverage; large-scale customer loss; formal regulatory intervention; significant effect on share price

> ### PANEL 4
>
> ## BUSINESS LINES IN THE GOLD DATABASE
>
> | Business line | Detail |
> |---|---|
> | Retail banking | Retail lending/deposit-taking; cheque clearing |
> | Plastic cards | Debit, credit, Mondex |
> | Mortgage lending | |
> | Private banking | |
> | Trade finance | |
> | Corporate banking | Lending/deposit-taking; leasing; project finance |
> | Investment banking – trading/markets | Securities (bonds and equities); money market and forex, derivatives and commodities |
> | Investment banking – advisory | Corporate finance; mergers and acquisitions; structured finance; project finance |
> | Insurance | Life assurance; health and critical illness insurance; associated reinsurance; marine; aviation; motor; household; other associated reinsurance |
> | Asset management | Unit trusts; OEICs; mutual funds; pension funds; venture capital and private equity |
> | Banking support – custody activities | |
> | Banking support – trust activities | |
> | Banking support – settlement and clearing services | |
> | Broking | Securities broking; money broking; retail broking; insurance broking |

GEOGRAPHICAL REGION OF LOSS

It is almost certainly a fact of operational risk that national differences play their part, so national identifiers of the country or region where a risk occurs are an important part of analysis. This is therefore one of the database data fields.

REVISIONS

It is the nature of many – particularly larger – operational losses, that they change over time. This may be because losses are recovered – through counterparties paying, settlements being negotiated, litigation achieving recovery or insurers paying claims lodged. Or it may be that original estimates of losses prove to be seriously short of the mark. A database needs, therefore, to have the means to report these adjustments as they have a material impact on perceptions of loss severity and of the time it takes to arrive at accurate estimates of loss.

Limitations of an operational risk database

There is no doubt that industry databases of operational risk losses are a useful risk management tool and provide additional data for more quantified approaches to analysing risk exposure. Fundamentally, they provide a wealth of information with which to assess cause, frequency and severity of loss events and increase the range of information that would be available to a firm if it drew solely on its own experience. There are, however, limitations, or health warnings to the extent to which they can provide an accurate profile of the risks faced by the industry as a whole or even of individual institutions within the industry.

AUDITABILITY
The first problem is that the data provided are not independently and externally audited. To the extent that the data represent debits to the profit and loss account, they will have been audited, or are at least are capable of being audited, once reported. The great majority of events, however, require manual reporting. They do not flow direct from transaction reports or the General Ledger. A database, almost by definition, will be incomplete. If the database is seeking to attempt a high level of predictive capability, it is then an issue whether to accept data that have not been independently audited. Much comes back to the cost-benefit equation and therefore the extent to which participants are prepared to rely on trust.

LEVELS OF CONTROL AND CONSISTENT REPORTING
The next significant point is that, in bringing together data from across the industry, like is not being compared with like. Banks do not have common levels of control and monitoring. Nor do they have similar quality of control. Some may have decided to reduce the level of control for certain risks, either because of their perception of the cost-benefit involved or for competitive motives. Whatever the reason, the database can only indicate where certain banks have lost money rather than providing an overall picture of exposure to certain types of loss.

THRESHOLD LEVELS
The choice of the reporting threshold will also affect the quantity of data being reported and, in any case, will not provide an accurate impression of materiality. A threshold has to be chosen that has some relevance to all users of the database, but the level will vary with the nature of the contributors and of the losses being reported. Some data will be readily available, particularly where they relate to transactions. Data on non-transaction-related losses will, however, be less readily available and their reporting will be more affected by the cost-benefit arguments mentioned above.

COMPLETENESS OF REPORTING
Whole firm
However committed the central operational risk management function may be, its data will only be as good as the commitment of the providers of data and the level of risk awareness throughout the firm. Since, historically, operational losses have not formed part of the risk reporting within banks, this can represent a fair gap, either because of a reluctance to report or due to lack of understanding of what constitutes an operational risk loss. In the case of documentation losses, for instance, their reporting may demand a significant change in the approach to loss reporting and recognition right through the organisation. There must also be a question mark over the completeness of reporting where a group is particularly diversified, whether by product or by geography.

Double counting of operational risk, credit risk and market risk
The general lack of understanding of what constitutes operational risk raises an interesting issue. Although many of the categories mentioned earlier (in 'Agreeing the classification/categorisation of losses') would be recognised as operational risk, and not as either market or credit risk, documentation risk in particular is one that has to date been largely subsumed under market and credit risk. When there is a bad debt

it is recognised as such, including any deficiencies in documentation that may have exacerbated the loss. Leading bankers argue that this is correct since the loss itself is triggered by a credit default. From an operational risk management point of view, the effect of this deficiency should be disaggregated and the actual credit loss reported at a lower figure.

The difficulties of this approach are that it overturns years, if not centuries, of bank practice. It would also destroy banks' historical credit loss data, which are invaluable in modelling risk and supporting loan gradings and ratings. Similarly, it is probably true that fraud – a classic operational risk – accounts for a large element of the credit losses incurred by credit card companies, as well as those which can arise with Internet banking. However, again, to disaggregate this risk and report it elsewhere would require a total rewrite of banks' credit management systems in these two businesses.

The Basel Committee has suggested that banks that wish to be on the advanced measurement approach must undertake this disaggregation. It will be interesting to see whether this proposal is adopted and implemented.

Legal and other reasons preventing reporting
There are often very good legal or similar reasons which prevent the reporting of losses, generally as a result of the terms of settlements. This can often apply to insurance settlements. A lesser problem is that, to avoid legal discovery, provisions for potential losses may not be reported until litigation has been concluded, even though the rules of the database demand that losses are reported as soon as they are recognised internally. This is reality, but unfortunately it will often involve the more serious losses. There may also be a reluctance to report large losses because this information is market-sensitive and would not otherwise be publicly available.

Purpose of the database
Finally, and importantly, the purpose itself of the database will materially affect the data that are provided and the priorities that apply to its development. This will be especially true of the database fields and the detail of the loss classification that is agreed. It is important to recognise that the different constituencies of potential users – whether banks, insurers or regulators – have different needs.

To be successful, databases need a cohesive group of users who have a clear idea of their needs and of the limitations highlighted above. In such circumstances a database can greatly improve the quality of risk management by adding greatly to the information available for assessing exposure to operational risk. Ignoring this simple fact will only lead to confusion. Successful databases represent the art of the possible. This may be disappointing for some, but it is a helpful truth to bear in mind when considering their future use and development.

BIBLIOGRAPHY

BBA, ISDA and Robert Morris Associates, 1999, "Operational Risk: The Next Frontier".

12

Reputational Risk

Peter Schofield

American Express Corporate Audit

The intent of this chapter is to use a simple and clear approach to outline some proactive attitudes to the management of reputational risk. It has not been prepared from the perspective of a mathematical quant or public relations executive and should, hopefully, engage the reader who might not be from these backgrounds.

When this chapter was first written, Enron was a high flying energy company, Arthur Andersen was one of the leading accountancy companies, WorldCom was known for its boldness in telecommunications and HealthSouth was a growing health provision services organisation. Enron and Andersen are now gone, WorldCom represents the largest accounting fraud ever (to date) and HealthSouth stretches incredulity more each day as to the number of senior officers actively participating in fraud (including four former CFOs to date). The common theme behind these tales of corporate deceit was personal greed coupled with a weak or completely absent sense of moral compass in the leaders in these organisations. The lesson to be learned from these cases is NOT primarily that financial disclosure and controls need tightening, nor that auditor independence needs to be made explicit and enforced, nor necessarily that any of the other processes put in place to strengthen controls were required. All of these are important but as buttresses to the real ultimate control. The critical lesson to be learnt from these self-inflicted corporate scandals is that the personal integrity and values of corporate leaders is the driving force behind company reputation.

Having said that, there are lessons to be learned from Enron et al, and I have made some additions to the chapter in the section on areas of generic risk for financial services institutions. They include accounting practices, disclosure and reporting as well as governance. There is one other lesson to be learned from Enron and that is not only the degree of corporate mistrust and scrutiny that it brought about, but also the range of institutions that have had to examine their own roles.

Enron – In a class of its own?

The multi-layered system of safeguards that was put in place over the years to protect investors and employees from a catastrophic corporate implosion largely failed to detect or address the problems that felled Enron. . . . The breakdown in checks and balances encompassed the company's auditors, lawyers and directors and extended to groups monitoring Enron from the outside, including regulators, financial analysts, credit rating agencies and Congress. . . .

Minneapolis Star Tribune, January 20, 2002

What is reputational risk, and does it really matter? Reputations or lack of them have been the subject of discussion since time immemorial. They have been applied equally to individuals and to divergent groups – how many jokes are there about different nationalities and their respective skills? The development of organisations and their brands as measures of reputation is a more recent development, growing

REPUTATIONAL RISK

in tandem with the growth of organisations themselves. Their increasing visibility in a globally integrated environment where both consumer advocacy and what I will term "environmental awareness" has brought the subject to the forefront of senior management attention. I will return to both these themes of the globally integrated environment and environmental awareness later in the chapter. Does reputational risk have anything to do with operational risk? It is safe to assume that all outcomes of operational risk, whether positive or negative, have the potential to affect reputational risk? This may range from the apparently mundane (eg, in higher penalty fees this month), to the more serious such as an inability to process transactions – either within given timeframes or at all.

This chapter will cover the following topics:

❑ a definition of reputational risk;
❑ whether reputational risk matters;
❑ the visibility of outcomes;
❑ how reputational risk events manifest themselves;
❑ steps to anticipate reputational risk areas;
❑ weighting these risks;
❑ assessing and monitoring control and detection mechanisms;
❑ the importance of a crisis management plan; and
❑ some guiding principles.

What is reputational risk?

A DEFINITION

Rather than debate everything that may make up reputational risk, it might be easier to use this succinct definition provided by Brotzen (2000), with one small addition.

> *Reputation risk can be defined as the set of threats that affect the long-term trust placed in the organization by its stakeholders, which includes its suppliers, customers, staff and shareholders. It covers risks to products, the company or the whole industry.*

I would add the words "and services" after the word products, in the second sentence, but this definition nonetheless encompasses the key factors to be considered, which are:

❑ set of threats;
❑ long-term trust;
❑ suppliers, customers, staff and shareholders;
❑ the individual company; and
❑ the entire industry.

OTHER FACTORS TO CONSIDER

As a practical matter, there are other factors that will need to be considered in both judging corporate reputations from an external perspective and in internally weighting and prioritising the risk.

❑ The degree of impact – is the particular scenario one that is a severe threat? Examples could arise in numerous industries: pharmaceuticals (product failure), or airplane and automobile manufacturers (equipment failure); these are obvious cases when an impact is potentially life threatening to someone. There is however, the chance – particularly in countries with a higher likelihood of lawsuits – that financial services could also fall in this category. Anything that severely damages an individual's financial well-being – eg, that arises out of the perceived actions or products of a financial services company and results in that individual taking some extreme action – could provide the basis for a lawsuit. Accordingly, this has the potential to ignite negative publicity.

Other stages of the degree of impact scale could range from major inconvenience to minor irritant.

❏ The number of occurrences of an incident, combined with the size of group affected. For example – you have at one extreme – utility bills being sent to all clients of a particular company were in error for three consecutive periods. At the other end of the scale you might have one individual being overcharged on only one occasion.

❏ The intent behind the event. Is the billing "error" a deliberate attempt to raise prices by stealth, or, perhaps more likely, did an error occur as a result of deliberate cost-cutting (cheaper and less-tested components or a quality control procedure dropped)? Alternatively is the event caused by purely "accidental" circumstances – for example, a computer operator runs a program out of sequence, causing interest to be calculated on incorrect balances.

❏ The existing level of controls that are in place, which should prevent the incident. This is particularly important as to how those controls compare to those of competitors or industry standards. The example that comes to mind most readily is that of Barings, where – among many other control lapses – the lack of segregation of duties in a trading environment literally caused the demise of an institution. More recently, the events of Allfirst clearly display a lack of industry standard controls and oversight.

❏ How is the event handled after it hits the public domain? I mentioned above that I did not intend to pursue this subject from the viewpoint of a public relations executive, but I do consider this point to be important. How often has one seen news of "incidents" being drip-fed to the public as opposed to a one-off and open *mea culpa* from the organisation's CEO? The reality is that Boards and management should assume that company dirty laundry is going to be made public at some point and therefore take the responsibility themselves for discussing such information.

If all of these factors are considered then one can possibly assess the impact of an unintentional, one-off and non-material incident. Is the incident quickly and openly admitted to, and are additional controls – exceeding industry standards put in place? The potential result of any of those factors being changed could also be assessed.

Does reputational risk matter?
BAD PRESS

Media headlines do play a role. Panel 1 gives a few chosen from a few months in 2003.

Does all this media attention matter, apart from causing red faces and heightened blood pressure in corporate headquarters? Reputational risk and risk events can have an impact on all parts of a company and can be categorised as falling under the following broad and overlapping headings.

❏ Financial:
  ● sales;
  ● profit margins;
  ● share price; and
  ● ability to raise capital/borrow funds.
❏ Non-financial:
  ● litigation;
  ● employee retention and attraction;
  ● customer retention and attraction;
  ● defects/recalls/inquiries/complaints;
  ● regulatory scrutiny;

REPUTATIONAL RISK

PANEL 1

MEDIA DAMAGE

❏ "Scandal – Filled Year Takes Toll on Companies' Good Names" – *Wall Street Journal*, February 12, 2003.
❏ "Ahold and other European scandals" – *The Economist*, February 27, 2003.
❏ "NYSE Probe Reaches 5 of 7 Specialist Firms" – *Wall Street Journal*, April 18, 2003.
❏ "Culture of Loopholes Bred Corporate Abuse" – *Washington Post*, April 18, 2003, referring to the bookkeeping abuses of the 1990's involving "stretching or breaking rules and ethics guidelines that have been in place for decades."
❏ "Another Ex-HealthSouth Executive Charged with Fraud" – *The New York Times*, April 8, 2003 referring to the (at that point) third HealthSouth CFO to be charged with a fraud that had apparently occurred over more than a 15-year period.
❏ "Analysts' Repute as Stock Pickers under Challenge" – *The New York Times*, November 13, 2002, referring to New York State Attorney General Elliot Spitzer's assertion that analysts competencies and how firms promoted them, bore little reality to their actual stock picking results.
❏ "Wall Street's Bid for Credibility" – *The Christian Science Monitor*, November 12, 2002, referring to the inherent and actual conflict of interest between investment banking groups and research groups housed under the same corporate umbrella.

- management focus;
- your job; and
- the company's existence.

I refer back to the opening of the chapter and the lesson that the personal integrity of corporate leaders is probably the ultimate control in managing reputational risk. It also has an impact, as stated above, on employee attraction and retention, which I feel most companies would agree represents their engine of growth for the future. I quote from the book *Organizing Genius: The Secrets of Creative Collaboration* (Ward Biederman and Bennis, 1998)

> *But most talented people have little incentive to defer to an individual without a strong moral core. Genius, even simple excellence, multiplies personal options. Why follow someone you can't trust or who makes you feel soiled?*

There may be a need for more research across a broad spectrum of businesses to definitively prove the correlation between reputational strength and positives in the factors mentioned above. The corresponding correlation between reputational weakness and negative outcomes in the same factors should also be researched further. There is, however, some existing evidence to prove these correlations.

ANALYSTS' ASSESSMENTS
The reverse of this situation is when, eg, *Fortune* and other magazines run annual surveys on such things as the "Most Admired Companies", the "Best Places to Work", and so on. Other than a desire to fill advertising space, sell their publications and give out bouquets and criticism, the impression is given that business analysts and their magazines' readers consider the awards to be a likely pointer to corporate success.

One such survey is that of the Financial Services Reputation Quotient, a study published as a joint venture between *American Banker*, the Internet-based research company Harris Interactive and the Reputation Institute, a research and advisory firm based in New York. Harris and its executive director, Charles J. Fombrun, developed the Reputation Quotient in 1998 as a means of qualitatively measuring reputational strength. They jointly produced the Financial Services Reputation Quotient, and the results of their first survey were presented in the *American Banker* in May 2001. In an accompanying article in the same issue, Professor Fombrun referred to a study by professors at the University of Kansas who studied the relationship between market value, book value, profitability and reputation for all the firms rated in *Fortune*'s "Most Admired Companies" survey between 1983 and 1997. Their finding was that a one-point change in reputation was associated with an average of US$500 million in market value. I quote Professor Fombrun verbatim from the *American Banker* article of May 2001:

> *More recently, the Reputation Institute examined some 35 companies whose Reputation Quotient (RQ) scores we had measured with Harris Interactive in both 1999 and 2000. Specifically, a positive one-point increase in the RQ was associated with higher average market values of some US$147 million, while a one-point decrease was associated with market values that were lower by about US$5 billion. These results suggest that a "value spiral" operates through which better-regarded companies attract more investors who bid up their market value and further improve their reputations. The good news is that research confirms that reputations are valuable intangible assets. The bad news is that the size of the effect is still in question.*

It is a safe assumption that most, if not all, company CEOs and outside directors are very concerned with reputational risk – they do not want their businesses to be known as the ones that produce faulty products or deliver shoddy service and, then, ultimately lose clients and relevance.

VISIBILITY OF OUTCOMES

I leave it to the reader to decide where the highest degree of visibility is in all the industries mentioned in Figure 1 and whether some industries are simply more susceptible to reputational risk events. For example, as the CEO of a tobacco company, you know that there will be continual reporting of litigation and new anti-smoking legislation will be proposed; what action, if any, could be taken to lower the tobacco profile to the public? Will this be mirrored in actions taken regarding your revenue dependence on tobacco or perhaps rebranding the business itself?

In another example, would the approach to reputation of the editor of a quality newspaper be different from that of a tabloid editor? The latter might consider it a

1. Is anybody safe?

Degree of visibility	Industry	
• **Extreme**	• Accountants	• Health care providers
	• Airlines	• Insurance
	• Architects	• Lawyers
	• Automobile manufacturers	• Mining companies
	• Computer equipment manufacturers	• Petroleum companies
		• Pharmaceuticals
• **Moderate**	• Construction	• Plane manufacturers
	• Doctors/dentists	• Publishing
	• "Dotcom" companies	• Regulators
	• Event organisers	• Software companies
	• Fast food outlets	• Tyre makers
• **Low**	• Financial services	• Tobacco
	• Food and beverages	• Toy makers
	• Gun manufacturers	• Utilities

"failure" if their staff's reporting did not produce the threat of lawsuits – or actual lawsuits – on a regular basis! Libel is part of their cost of doing business.

The final point of Figure 1 is not to show a yellow pages of industries but to emphasise that there is almost certainly no industry or profession that does not have reputational risk.

How reputational risk events manifest themselves
I would suggest that the following channels are most likely to be the harbingers of reputational risk events:

❑ the media;
❑ pressure groups;
❑ customer complaints/dissatisfaction;
❑ litigation; or
❑ employee issues.

There is no particular order in which these events occur – it could be an article in the *Wall Street Journal*, a mention in an Internet chat room or a call for a consumer boycott initiated by some action group against a company.

A reputational risk checklist
Figure 2 is neither intended to be an all-inclusive list of generic reputational risk areas for financial services institutions, nor is there any prioritisation, and it is up to the reader to decide whether the risk is high, medium or low for an institution.

In looking at the generic risks shown in Figure 2, there are some specific points to be made on the examples:

Accounting practices – are your policies understood, appropriately approved and followed? Wherever judgements are made, is there an independent review? As with many of the areas raised here, do you have any policies you would feel uncomfortable about, if disseminated in the media?

PANEL 2

TRUTH WILL OUT

The beginning of the chapter mentioned the two themes of a globally integrated environment and consumer advocacy combined with "environmental awareness". Twenty or thirty years ago, if a consumer purchased a product from a company that was paying below market wages to raw material producers or assemblers in other parts of the world, the likelihood was that the consumer would never have known.

In recent years, however, there has been a growing awareness of the impact of actions such as these (or other impacts viewed, for example, as being ecologically not friendly), and that impact has come not only from the growth of pressure groups but, more importantly, from the greater global availability of information due particularly to the rise of the Internet.

The Internet has been a global force for change – any issue that arises, no matter how it first comes up, has a much, much higher probability of being picked up than in the past due to the immediacy and the global availability of information that the Internet provides.

Disclosure and reporting – do you really disclose to investors sufficient and comprehensible information for them to understand your business? Do you provide non-financial data – what are your controls as to the accuracy of that data? Do you provide any data used for public indices/benchmarks – could you benefit from manipulation of such data – are there any controls?

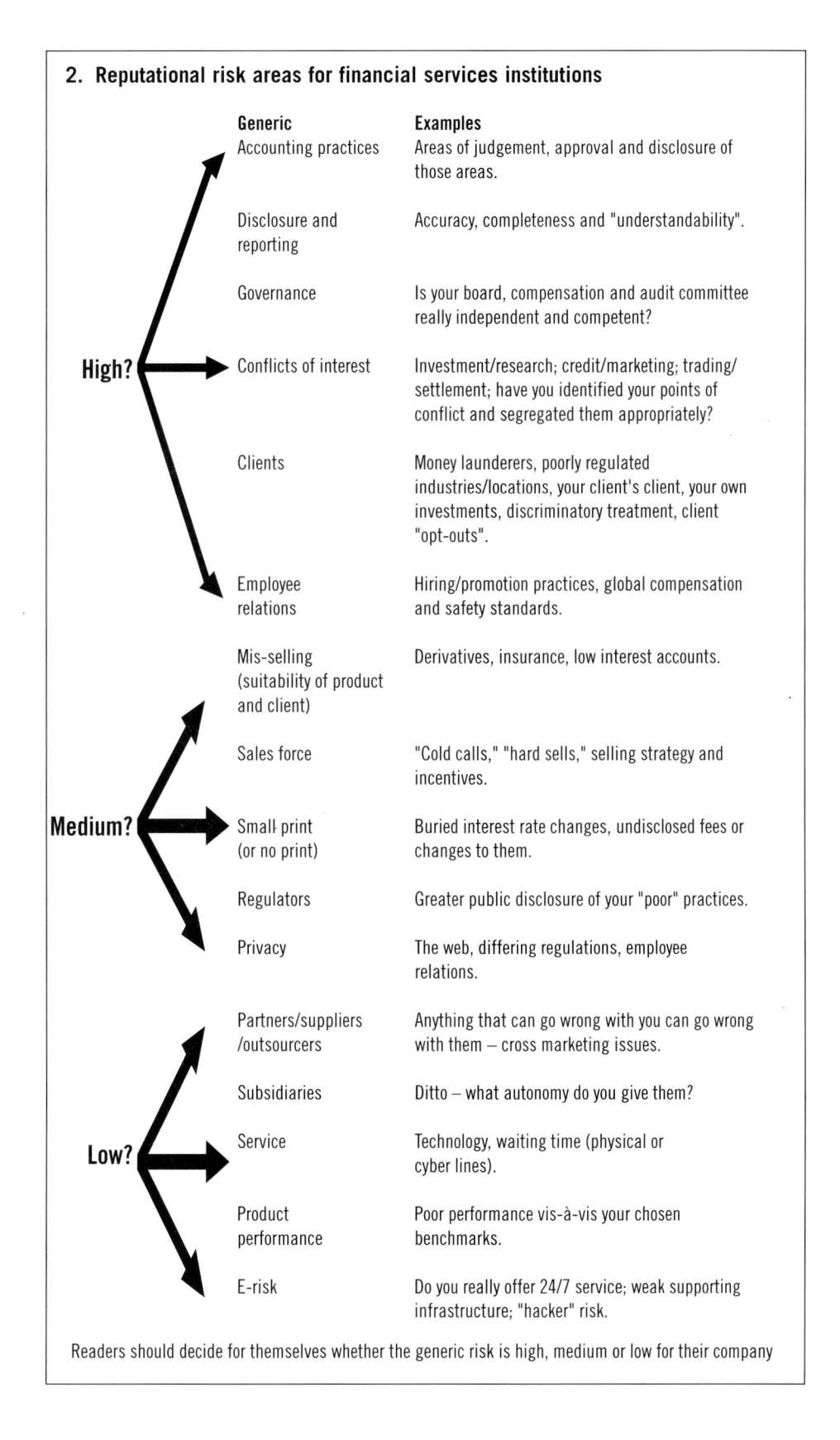

REPUTATIONAL RISK

2. Reputational risk areas for financial services institutions

	Generic	Examples
High?	Accounting practices	Areas of judgement, approval and disclosure of those areas.
	Disclosure and reporting	Accuracy, completeness and "understandability".
	Governance	Is your board, compensation and audit committee really independent and competent?
	Conflicts of interest	Investment/research; credit/marketing; trading/settlement; have you identified your points of conflict and segregated them appropriately?
	Clients	Money launderers, poorly regulated industries/locations, your client's client, your own investments, discriminatory treatment, client "opt-outs".
	Employee relations	Hiring/promotion practices, global compensation and safety standards.
Medium?	Mis-selling (suitability of product and client)	Derivatives, insurance, low interest accounts.
	Sales force	"Cold calls," "hard sells," selling strategy and incentives.
	Small print (or no print)	Buried interest rate changes, undisclosed fees or changes to them.
	Regulators	Greater public disclosure of your "poor" practices.
	Privacy	The web, differing regulations, employee relations.
Low?	Partners/suppliers /outsourcers	Anything that can go wrong with you can go wrong with them – cross marketing issues.
	Subsidiaries	Ditto – what autonomy do you give them?
	Service	Technology, waiting time (physical or cyber lines).
	Product performance	Poor performance vis-à-vis your chosen benchmarks.
	E-risk	Do you really offer 24/7 service; weak supporting infrastructure; "hacker" risk.

Readers should decide for themselves whether the generic risk is high, medium or low for their company

Governance – is your board and various board committees really independent, as well as competent? Are there any cross-serving directors? What is your proxy voting process for your own and other managed investments?

Conflicts of interest – have you identified the points of conflict of interest within your organisation and are there controls in place to avoid/mitigate such conflicts? The investment/research conflict is not a new one – did it simply not occur before; was it effectively monitored before; did the changing economic environment make it "economically tempting" in the 1990s – what was different, and what lessons are there to be learnt?

Clients: money launderers – hopefully the risk is self-evident, but clearly the focus needs to be on poorly regulated locations, on businesses known to be cash generators and, last but not least, on a company's employee training and pattern/transactional analysis programs.

The client's client – particularly for institutions that have other financial institutions as clients. What do you know about your primary clients' "know your client" policies and their effectiveness in implementing them? Essentially, has the homework been done and would detection systems pick up potential red-flag patterns or transactions?

A company's own investments – be they as investor or lender. Hopefully no company will encounter clear situations where they should not invest (eg, Child Labour Inc), but there may be "grey" areas. Should a company invest or lend to a tobacco company, to a company experimenting in cutting-edge cloning techniques? Do you limit your investment "opportunities" to certain (senior) staff? An interesting development was highlighted in the *Wall Street Journal* (2002), which read "JP Morgan to review deals for risks to banks' reputation" – does anyone in your organisation look at such things?

Discriminatory treatment – discrimination against particular groups or geographic areas, however defined. Does the company engage in what could be considered "predatory lending"?

Mis-selling – this relates to the suitability of products and clients for each other. There are plenty of examples of what has come up in this area in the last few years, ranging from derivative investments sold to corporations, "tax-advantaged" investments to tax-sheltered plans or sales of high-risk, high-return products to individuals looking for secure income. Is there a possibility that suitability will become a requirement for selling or providing credit products?

Sales force – consider how comfortable it would be if any sales training material, a company's sales policies, sales incentive programmes and sales force hiring/review programmes and policies were to be published in the *New York Times* or *Wall Street Journal*. If there are any doubts about any of the language or underlying intent, it means something needs changing.

Privacy – clearly the Gramm–Leach–Bliley legislation in the USA has brought this to the forefront of everyone's mind.[1] A company has completed all of its required mailings to clients, setting out their rights to privacy and its policies, but would it know who inside the company has access to client data, how such access is controlled, what audit trails exist, etc?

Many of the generic risks mentioned here overlap with one another, and privacy combined with "outsourcing", "partnering", or whatever one calls it, is a prime example. A company provides client data to another institution for the purpose of, for example, statement production; something goes wrong. No doubt the contract with the "outsourcer/partner" has all the necessary contractual legalese in it, but when the client complains to you, the media or the regulators, who will they look at to protect your client's rights to privacy?

The focus on privacy is further complicated by such factors as differing regulations in different jurisdictions (eg, US versus EU); the complexities introduced by "account aggregation" as well as not forgetting that rights to privacy extend to employees and vendors as well as to clients.

The area of privacy is – and will continue for the foreseeable future to be – a hot issue, not necessarily just for the sake of fraud/identity theft prevention, for example, but also because of the feeling of "violation" and emotion that privacy misuse or theft leaves in victims.

Partners/suppliers/outsourcers – one of the most acute lessons to be learned from the Firestone affair is from the perspective of Ford. Apart from the obvious negative recall and publicity issues and the relationship issues, do not think only about the contractual relationship you have with a partner/supplier or outsourcer, think about what the public perception will be if that part or product fails to perform with a range of severity of consequences.

The situation is related to your client's client and knowing what its "know your client" policies, procedures and effectiveness of implementation are. In this case your company is potentially putting its reputation on the line, based on the performance of your partners/suppliers/outsourcers.

As Figure 2 says, anything that can go wrong with you can go wrong with them.

Subsidiaries/affiliates – the same range of issues as for partners/suppliers/outsourcers applies to subsidiaries and affiliates. What degrees of autonomy do they really have – do their clients understand that you are merely a minority/majority shareholder? "We bought Company X with the intention that existing management stay in place, and that they continue to run the company as an independent entity." Will that reasoning wash when something goes wrong with X?

Service – everyone has their own horror tale of appalling service, whether it is wasted time (in person, on the telephone or online), the number of hand-offs, the knowledge of front-line staff and their attitude, and, last but not least, did you, as a consumer, feel that you received excellent or even good customer service? How does your company measure service – proactively by seeking out customer comments, reactively by measuring customer inquiry/complaint levels or market share, or through some combination of the two allied with other measures?

Employee relations – ask yourself a question similar to that in the "mis-selling" risk area – would your hiring, training and promotion policies and procedures and actual practice stand scrutiny, if made public? In today's economic environment in particular, what is your treatment of displaced employees? Other than being non-discriminatory and equitable, was sufficient sensitivity shown to those employees – and if you wanted them back later, would they come?

Small print – don't bury important disclosures, avoid "teaser rates" or similar offers and negotiate with your legal department to make contractual language as clear as possible for an average consumer.

Regulators – as the public and issue/pressure groups demand greater information and disclosure, anticipate that regulators may be required to make much greater disclosure of industry standards and individual companies' performance against these standards. Disclosure could potentially be used by regulators as a public

REPUTATIONAL RISK

> **PANEL 3**
>
> **HIT IT BEFORE IT HITS YOU**
>
> For some readers the assessment of control and detection mechanisms together with their ongoing monitoring will be a regular part of their business routine and little value might be added for them if time is spent on this area.
>
> It might be relevant however, to refer to the February 7, 2001, edition of the *Wall Street Journal* and an article on company reputations. One section of the article refers to Bridgestone's handling of the Firestone tyre situation with Ford and its subsequent efforts to regain the public's trust. It quoted a Bridgestone spokesperson: "we are committed to regaining the public's trust in Firestone...We are enhancing our quality assurance programs to provide early warning systems and are reviewing our production operations to find areas for further improvement".
>
> It is difficult to comment without knowing the full context of the statement, but it appears likely that both Bridgestone and Ford would have preferred their new systems to have been put in place some years earlier.

defence mechanism, or as an offensive tactic. Regulators also have to prove their value.

Product performance – what will be the impact of your individual products or family of products' poor performance *vis-à-vis* benchmarks – or your competitors' – in the short, medium or long term?

E-risk – this risk is probably worth identifying in its own right, even though some of it overlaps with other generic risks mentioned. To quote the executive summary of the Bank for International Settlements (BIS) Risk Management Principles for Electronic Banking published in May 2001: "Continuing technological innovation and competition ... have allowed for a much wider array of banking products and services to become accessible ... and delivered, through an electronic distribution channel, collectively referred to as e-banking."

To summarise the BIS Committee's conclusions, they felt that e-banking – although not creating inherently new risks – did increase the risks associated with technological speed of change, the "ubiquitous and global nature of open electronic networks", integration of e-banking with legacy systems and an increasing dependence on third parties to provide the necessary information technology.

Clearly, e-banking needs to be delivered not only on a 24-hour, seven-day-a-week basis but the infrastructure supporting it should be capable of handling expected peak loads and have "hacker-attack" mechanisms in place. There should also be in existence sufficient and available back-up capacity as well as tested business continuation and disaster recovery plans.

Something that needs to be remembered is that all risk areas – credit, market, operational and others – can and do give rise to reputational risk. For example, continued poor credit decisions will ultimately affect shareholder value, share price and the ability to attract desirable new clients.

Steps to anticipate reputational risk areas

Anticipating reputational risk is not often enough considered in its own right as being necessary to plan for. Market, credit, and increasingly operational risk are considered, and risk avoidance and mitigation measures put in place as well as the acceptance of "understood" risk in these areas. As mentioned previously, all of these risks – both alone and combined – can lead to the loss of reputation, yet an analysis of the reputational risks facing an organisation is less frequently performed.

It is essential therefore to take the following steps in order to assess an organisation's potential for handling a multitude of reputational risk occurrences.

❑ List.
  Each organisation should be able to draw up a list of its own pertinent risks.
❑ Assess.
  Policies, controls, fault detection mechanisms, complaint monitoring systems, etc, that exist should be evaluated to prevent and – in the case of failure – detect reputational risk events.
❑ Measure.
  Metrics should be developed to monitor those risks where early detection is considered vital.
❑ Contingency planning.
  Should the worst-case scenario occur (or even something not quite as earth-shattering), a current crisis management plan must be available.
❑ Weighting.
  (This is discussed in detail below.) Consideration also needs to be given to the related:
  ❑ Impact.
  ❑ Likelihood of occurrence.

WEIGHTING THE RISK

Some risks may be regarded as "acts of God" – such as being located in an earthquake zone; does this mean that they are excluded from the weighting? The answer should be no. Other events may be similar to all organisations within a specific industry – for example, the tobacco industry – the decision has to be made whether or not to stay within that sector and accordingly accept that certain risks are inevitable but "economically justified".

Basically, weighting the risk has to be done on an individual, company by company basis, and below some simple directional examples are provided.

❑ An asset management company that has financial institutional clients only from OECD countries probably has less client risk than a bank that deals with anyone anywhere via numerous channels, including online.
❑ An insurance company that runs all first-year premiums – above a certain amount – through a second-level review process will be less at risk than a firm that undertakes no screening.
❑ Any company with a written code of conduct and appropriate training in existence – both for new employees and refresher training – will be less exposed in a number of generic risk areas than a company without any such code. In the same vein, if two companies both have similar codes of conduct but one has an office of the ombudsperson, that company will be at a lower risk than the one without such a facility.
❑ Any company with geographically dispersed – including international – operations has higher potential for reputational risk than one operating in a single location or country.

There is no magic formula for weighting the risks, but clearly the weighting decisions need to consider the potential impact and likelihood of occurrence of each risk. Given that lack of data may be a factor to companies that embark upon this exercise, getting a group of senior managers from different functional/geographic areas together in one room might prove helpful to the process. This would then enable them to start the process by setting up a list, then prioritising each entry on the list.

REPUTATIONAL RISK

This may be just as efficient a way of beginning the process as any lengthy data collection and analysis process.

ASSESS THE CONTROL/DETECTION MECHANISMS AND MONITOR THEM
As assessments of monitoring of control and detection mechanisms are addressed, it might be useful to suggest a few basic questions that need to be asked of business unit managers. Accordingly satisfactory replies need to be gained from them:

❑ Do the risks that are weighted and prioritised actually have appropriate controls in place, and how do they compare to industry/peer standards, if they are known or available?
❑ Do the organisation's existing key performance/control indicators include the most critical of these controls? Who monitors the indicators, and what is the procedure if the indicators do not meet appropriate standards?
  ● If major changes occur in products, processes, technology, partners/ outsourcing arrangements, regulatory functions or key people, is there an automatic review/ update of the control/detection mechanism?
  ● How does the organisation – and more to the point the appropriate decision-makers in the organisation – become aware of any increased levels of customer inquiries/complaints or sales contract cancellations during the relevant cooling-off period?
❑ Is there a unit in the company that monitors media activity on the company's peer group/competition? It is always better to learn from somebody else's mistakes than your own!

HAVE A CRISIS MANAGEMENT PLAN READY

Imagine that one of your employees takes part in an Internet chat room where someone mentions that there's a whole list of the company's own personal client data in existence on a new website!

Which of the following might describe the organisation's reaction under such circumstances?

❑ What do we do now?
❑ Don't worry, I'm in charge. Help!
❑ How did those systems people let this happen?
❑ Who wants to take this call from CNN?

Companies need a crisis management plan for undesirable moments like these. This should be an integral part of a good business continuation plan. It will not be possible to address all the possible incidents that could severely damage the company's reputation, but if the example of client data theft is identified as one of the company's top-weighted and prioritised concerns, there should be clear notification processes and alternative courses of action laid out in preparation. This should identify clearly accountability for decision-making and decision implementation.

In this example such steps could include calling an emergency meeting of the formal crisis management team; informing the police; taking the necessary action to get the Internet Service Provider to shut the offending website down immediately; – if possible – starting your own internal investigation into how the data has been stolen; making a decision on when, where and how to communicate the theft of such data both to your clients and to the media; and deciding what steps your company can take to protect the interests of clients – this could include recommending that they take certain actions that the company will pay for.

Planning for such events can – and often is – be carried out on an ad hoc basis, but advance planning is far more likely to result in a recovery of the situation than making it up as you go along.

As a minimum, the company needs:

- a formal crisis management team;
- clear and delineated delegation of authority to the crisis management team, allowing them appropriate discretion under specific circumstances;
- well-documented and understood policies on the notification of senior executives;
- key contact information kept with the policies by senior executives;
- media and internal communication responsibilities laid out; and
- alternative action steps to be taken in the event that one of the prioritised reputational risk events occurs.

GUIDING PRINCIPLES

Reputations are an extremely precious commodity and every facet of risk has a potential impact on a company's reputation. Once a reputation is lost it is extremely difficult to regain, so the maintenance and enhancement of a good reputation has to be a key corporate goal. Within many corporations positions exist for any combination of the following: a chief financial officer, chief credit/risk officer, chief information officer, chief investment officer, chief operating officer and so on. Who should fulfill the role of the chief reputational risk officer? The only individual who can meaningfully fill this role is the chief executive officer. This leads on to some guiding principles as closing comments:

- reputation awareness and attitude must start at the top of the organisation;
- there must be an organisational culture of protecting and enhancing the company's reputation and establishing and maintaining a risk-conscious environment;
- ongoing training is required to reinforce the company leaders' message;
- actions should be geared toward what is right for the customer; and
- there should be transparency in a company's dealings with its customers.

A parting thought (or was it a premonition?)

"There may still be two good reasons for companies to worry about their ethical reputation. One is anticipation: bad behaviour, once it stirs up a public fuss, may provoke legislation that companies will find more irksome than self restraint.

The other, more crucial, is trust. A company that is not trusted by its employees, partners and customers, will suffer. In an electronic world where businesses are geographically far from their customers, a reputation for trust may become even more important.

The Economist April 22, 2000

1 See http://www.senate.gov/~banking/conf.

BIBLIOGRAPHY

BIS, 2001, *Risk Management Principles for Electronic Banking*, May [http://www.bis.org/publ/bib582.pdf].

Brotzen, D., 2000, "Mastering Risk", *Financial Times*, 13 June.

Fombrun, C., 2001, "Reputations: Measurable, Valuable and Manageable", *American Banker*, 23 May.

Ward Biederman, P., and W. G. Bennis, 1998, *Organizing Genius: The Secrets of Creative Collaboration*, (Perseus Publishing).

13

Corporate Reputation: Not Worth Risking

Knowledge@Wharton in association with Aon Corporation*

It was a story that would be repeated decades later to young accounting recruits at Arthur Andersen: A railroad executive burst into Arthur Andersen's office one day in 1914, demanding that the firm's founder approve the railroad's books. Accountants had discovered that the railroad was inflating its profits by failing to properly record expenses. Andersen refused, saying that there wasn't enough money in the city of Chicago to make him approve the fraudulent accounting.

Andersen's independence cost him the client, but it gained him something far more valuable – a reputation for integrity that gave investors confidence in Arthur Andersen audits, a reputation that helped the firm become one of the top five accounting firms in the US.

After nearly 90 years in business, Andersen imploded in 2002 after acknowledging that its auditors had shredded documents relating to its audits of Houston energy trader Enron. The ensuing scandal highlighted how crucial an organisation's intangible assets can be and the damage that reputational risk can cause.

Indeed, in a survey of 2,000 top private and public sector organisations by Aon, reputation was cited as the biggest business risk. A survey of 100 leading European firms by the European Strategic Account Management Group last year reported similar results, with reputational risk and product liability/tampering and brand protection ranking behind business interruption as the top risks.

The Arthur Anderson scandal and the Sarbanes–Oxley Act enacted in response to it have once again raised awareness of reputational risk at the CEO and Board levels, according to Randy Nornes, managing director of the Strategic Risk Management Group at Aon Risk Services. But many companies mistakenly believe that they have addressed the issue with crisis planning exercises, media training, and purchase of product recall insurance.

"Risk transfer [through insurance] is not the end of the line," Nornes said. "Most companies shoot right to the solution and say, 'We'll buy a product like recall insurance or business interruption that solves our problem.'"

What companies need is a more comprehensive program that identifies and mitigates the major sources of risk in the first place, says Nornes. Risk assessment, measurement, mitigation, planning and transfer all have a role to play in a complete reputational risk management strategy.

"The fundamental truth, which you only discover when you have gone through the fires of hell, is that your reputation will always mirror the absolute reality of who you are," says Steve Marshall, who became chief executive of Railtrack, the United Kingdom's rail system operator, three weeks after the Hatfield rail crash that killed four passengers in October 2000. "Anyone who thinks that they can change their reputation without changing the company is mistaken."

* *This chapter is reprinted with the kind permission of Aon Corporation.*

CORPORATE REPUTATION: NOT WORTH RISKING

Robert E. Mittelstaedt, Jr, vice dean and director of Wharton's Aresty Institute of Executive Education, also argues for a holistic approach. After studying Three Mile Island, Watergate, aviation accidents and numerous corporate public relations meltdowns, Mittelstaedt concluded that the incidents resulted not from a single mistake, but from a series of mistakes over weeks or years.

"The investigation into the crash of Korean Airlines flight 801 in Guam in 1997 showed that about a dozen separate mistakes led up to that crash," Mittelstaedt said. "What you begin to realize – especially in light of such other incidents as the Tylenol tampering scare in 1982 and the Union Carbide chemical leak in Bhopal, India in 1984 – is that the same types of compounded errors can occur within corporate systems, organizational structures and processes, with equally dire consequences. If any one of those mistakes had been caught, especially during the early stages of the problem, the accident could have been averted".

Catastrophes begin with an initial mistake, often minor, that goes uncorrected, Mittelstaedt says. A subsequent problem compounds the effect of the initial problem. Attempts to correct the problem are often half-hearted and ineffective because there is no recognition of the increasing seriousness of the situation. When the problem eventually becomes too big to ignore, attempts are often made to hide the truth while efforts at remediation get under way. Finally, there is a recognition that the situation is out of control.

Nonetheless, the behavior of the CEO and other senior executives can minimise damage to the company. The CEO must play a central role in managing the crisis, particularly in communication with employees, the media and the public.

New York's chief executive, then-Mayor Rudolph W. Giuliani, saw his popularity soar because of the sober, steadfast visibility he displayed after the terrorist attacks on the World Trade Center. After leaving office, the former mayor started a consulting firm with his former police commissioner, fire commissioner and director of emergency management. The firm, Giuliani Group LLC, formed an alliance with Aon in October 2002 to provide corporate crisis management services, including continuity planning, development of crisis operations protocols, and advice on emergency communications procedures.

John Bugalla, a managing director of Aon Risk Services says that during a crisis, the CEO cannot defer to a spokesperson. "The CEO must be intimately involved and be highly credible". The CEO also must balance conflicting interests within the company, he adds. At a large company, as many as 20 people may control functions that must respond in a crisis, including marketing, public relations, continuity planning and quality control.

The CEO also may find disagreement with the company's general counsel. "The general counsel wants to limit public statements to protect against lawsuits. The CEO is trying to save the business and needs to communicate," said Nornes. "When a crisis happens, it's essential that employees know who's in charge and who's driving the process".

The CEO also must overcome institutional resistance to admitting a problem. "Disbelief is a very big issue," says Bugalla. "You're a company that's been around for 50–100 years, and you've made a very reliable, safe product. You've built in safety, you've done due diligence. It's very difficult to believe that your product is going to be tampered with or it's going to be found to have problems".

Developing a risk management plan

Organisations that have attempted to design their own reputational risk management strategies are often too close to the issues or don't take the necessary actions because of political sensitivities within the company, Bugalla adds.

Nornes notes that when Aon helps a client develop a reputational risk management plan, it starts by determining what factors drive the company's reputation and what events could affect it. "The kings of the world today are the

[debt] rating agencies and stock analysts. They are most likely going to ask questions like: 'What are the risks that drive the business? How much of the firm's value is derived from a good reputation? How effectively is management reacting to a difficult situation?'"

Reputational risk can be caused by accounting scandals, product recalls, consumer safety issues, even environmental issues. Protests in 2000 by the group Rainforest Action forced Home Depot to promise to stop selling wood from environmentally sensitive forests.

One frequently unrecognised risk is that of collateral damage or the so-called knock-on effect. "Say a large fast food chain is hit with a beef recall," said Bugalla. "Do you honestly think that the other fast food chains are not going to be at least initially affected?"

Moody's Investor Service warned last December that investors may abandon Japan's consumer finance industry, which is facing pressure to take on riskier borrowers to maintain growth levels. A negative event at a single company "could trigger a sharp change in market perceptions toward the entire industry," Moody's said.

The risk management plan should eliminate causes of potential crises and minimise the impact if a crisis arises anyway, Nornes says. The plan should include development of standards and controls to provide early warning of problems as well as training, education, and communication to obtain employee commitment. Media training, crisis planning and crisis simulations also are essential.

Impact of reputational impairment

Damage to the perception of a brand or product's quality can mean a sharp and perhaps irreversible loss of market share. Accounting questions can prompt credit downgrades, whereas a crisis event can create a liquidity problem as lenders refuse to provide additional cash to a company just when it needs it most. Aon is developing integrated financial solutions, including "contingent capital" products that would insure a company's liquidity if an event occurred that caused its lenders to invoke the "material adverse change" provisions that might be a part of a company's loan or revolving credit agreements.

Less widely acknowledged is the impact that reputational damage can have on the ability to recruit top talent or maintain political influence – as Enron's Ken Lay found out when his calls to Washington stopped getting returned. Depending on the damage suffered, it can also result in negligence claims that seek damages from directors and officers.

All of this is reflected in a company's stock price. Once investor confidence is lost, says Nornes, it is virtually impossible to win it back without changing top management and rebuilding trust.

A company's stock market capitalisation is the sum of its book value (tangible assets such as plants and equipment) brand value and additional reputation assets. And reputation equity is becoming increasingly important, says Dr Deborah J. Pretty and Dr Rory E Knight, whose UK-based Oxford Metrica helps senior executives develop policies and procedures on reputation risk and corporate governance.

Pretty and Knight have developed the ValueReaction model to analyse the impact of reputation crises on company stock prices. The ValueReaction strips out market-wide factors to ensure the price movements are not due to interest rates or other macroeconomic factors. It also risk-adjusts the returns to avoid distortions for companies that are more sensitive to market movements.

Pretty says their research shows that investors make up their minds within a couple of weeks of an event whether a company is going to recover well from a loss. Thus the actions of senior management immediately after an incident are crucial.

"If the crisis is handled badly, investors may decide that management isn't very good at dealing with the unexpected, so their estimates of future cash flow go down, as does the price", Pretty said in an interview with ERisk magazine.

After the July 2000 crash of the Concorde, for example, British Airways chose not to ground its Concorde fleet until it learned that British air safety regulators were going to force it to do so. British Airways' stock fell within three weeks after the crash and did not recover until about 81 trading days afterward, according to Pretty's analysis.

In contrast, Air France grounded its remaining Concordes immediately. Chief executive Jean-Cyril Spinetta took personal responsibility, attending the victims' memorial services providing free transportation for their families and offering them an interim payment before agreement on any compensation deal. Air France's stock fell only briefly.

Pretty said Spinetta and Air France demonstrated the traits of a "recoverer": immediacy of response, honesty and compassion, personal involvement by the CEO, transparency of management, and timely, relevant communication.

Pretty also looked at the comparative fortunes of Ford and Bridgestone – Firestone after news reports in August 2000 describing an investigation by US regulators into the safety of Firestone tyres. Most of the 175 deaths and 1,400 accidents linked to the tyres involved Ford Explorers.

After initially presenting a unified response, Ford and Firestone quickly began blaming each other. Firestone blamed Ford for telling owners to inflate the tyres to pressures below those recommended by Firestone an attempt to counter the risk of rollover for the Explorer. Ford insisted it was the tyres, not the Explorers design, that was at fault.

But Nornes says the court of financial opinion – the stock market – went with Ford. Ford stock rebounded after 110 days. Bridgestone's value reaction was still 40% below expectations 250 trading days later. The company reported an 80% drop in profits for 2000.

Reputation risk is not just about numbers; it's about people's emotional response. While no company wants a crisis, it can actually enhance its reputation by making the right management decision. Johnson and Johnson (J&J) is often cited for its actions after seven people died in 1982 from ingesting cyanide-laced Tylenol capsules in the Chicago area.

J&J immediately recalled 31 million bottles of the pain reliever and warned the nation not to consume any type of Tylenol product. Then it offered consumers coupons for future purchases, free replacement of capsules with caplets, and reintroduced the product in a new triple-seal tamper-resistant package.

It took only a few months before J&J regained its 35% market share in the pain reliever market, and the company continues to benefit from that goodwill today.

Johnson and Johnson ranked number one for the fourth consecutive year in Harris Interactive's annual National Corporate Reputation Survey. J&J is the only company that has scored 80 or higher each year on the 100-point scale.

Bridgestone, which had spent the two previous years in last place moved up to number 55 this year, above only five companies involved in corporate scandals in 2002: Enron, Global Crossing, WorldCom, Adelphia and Andersen Worldwide.

14

Moody's Analytical Framework for Operational Risk Management of Banks

Brendon Young
Moody's Investors Service Limited

Moody's believes that the assessment of operational risk is becoming increasingly central to the fundamental analysis of a rated bank. Put simply, operational risk management improves the quality and stability of earnings (see Figure 1), thereby enhancing the competitive position of the bank and facilitating its long-term survival. Risk has always been present in banking and, indeed, the *raison-d'être* of the financial services sector is the commercial transfer of risk to those better able to accept it. However, the increasing rate of change and the level of sophistication have resulted in the need for more responsive approaches to risk management.

The financial services sector has seen considerable advances in the field of risk management, with operational risk now receiving greater prominence and being recognised as a separate, although impinging, category in its own right. Over a comparatively short period of time, a significant number of high-impact losses, some of which have resulted in institutional failure, have clearly demonstrated the significance of operational risk. Predictably, this has influenced practices in the business environment and has necessitated a corresponding change in the regulatory agencies.

As part of the revision of the Basel Capital Accord, the regulators are intending to introduce a risk-based capital requirement specifically for operational risk. While this has been of great importance in driving understanding and development in the banking industry, it is the commercial impact of operational risk that is of greatest significance.

While capital is important, it is merely one defence against risk and is unlikely to be the preferred solution. An increase in capital will not in itself reduce risk; only management action can achieve that. Indeed, risk will vary continuously.

Consequently, there is no simple, direct relationship between the credit rating awarded by Moody's and the level of capital held by a bank. Moody's considers that true economic capital must be available (without any management, operating, market-driven, or regulatory restrictions) to bear the full brunt of massive losses before general creditors are affected in any way. However, holding excessive levels of capital will impair the financial performance of a bank and thereby impact upon its competitiveness.

The control of operational risk is fundamentally concerned with good management, which involves a tenacious process of vigilance and continuous improvement. This is a value-adding activity that either directly or indirectly affects bottom-line performance. It must, therefore, be a key consideration for any business.

MOODY'S ANALYTICAL FRAMEWORK FOR OPERATIONAL RISK MANAGEMENT OF BANKS

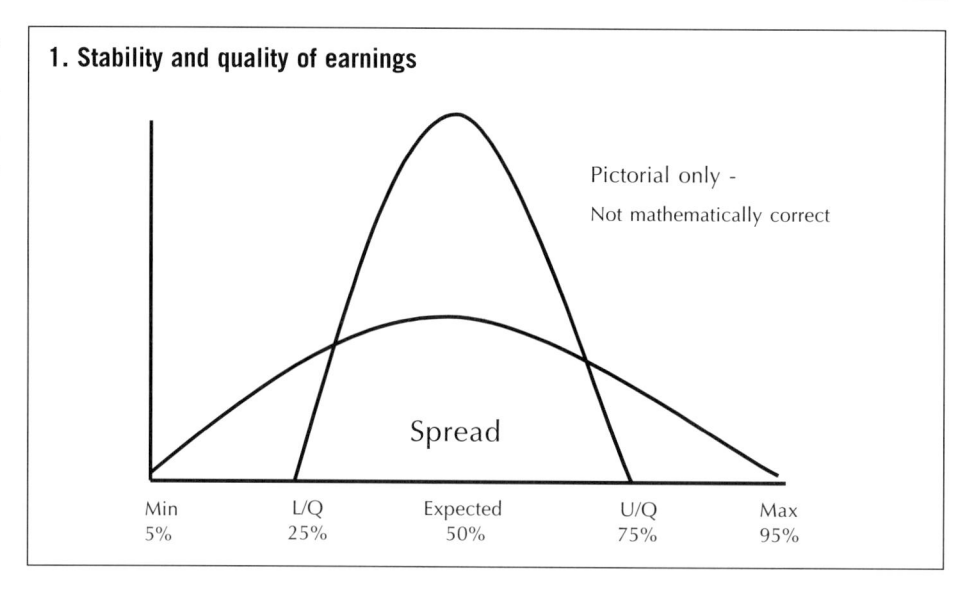

1. Stability and quality of earnings

Pictorial only - Not mathematically correct

Spread

| Min | L/Q | Expected | U/Q | Max |
| 5% | 25% | 50% | 75% | 95% |

Since operational risk will affect credit ratings, share prices, and organisational reputation, analysts will increasingly include it in their assessment of the management, their strategy and the expected long-term performance of the business.

Key considerations in the field of operational risk, which both analysts and bank management will need to take into account, are:

1. determination of the overall risk profile of the bank;
2. identification of main risks, showing how they affect profitability and the quality and stability of earnings;
3. optimisation of the risk–reward relationship; and
4. verification and validation of underlying factors.

The efficient and effective use of resources requires the continuous and diligent identification, assessment, monitoring and control of operational risks. Furthermore, the collection and analysis of in-house historical data enhances knowledge and understanding, thus facilitating the development and stress testing of new or improved systems and models. Consideration also needs to be given to possible future scenarios, although it should be recognised that it is not possible to pre-determine all risks and their interactions.

Transparency, promoted through the third pillar of the new Basel Capital Accord (Basel II), is deliberately intended to lead to greater control through market forces. It will inevitably lead to a further transfer of power to the customer and a consequent tightening of margins, thus fuelling competition. It is Moody's belief that given the increasing sophistication and complexity of the world's global financial services industry, operational risk management will be seen as a potential differentiator and a source of competitive advantage.

Emphasis will be placed on quality of management and their ability to correctly assess and manage risk, thereby improving the bank's overall credit strength.

This chapter seeks to provide an overview of the analytical framework used by Moody's in assessing a bank's approach to, and management of, operational risk.[1] The framework seeks to raise issues of a fundamental nature. As such, a simple box-ticking approach is considered inappropriate. Contingency and complexity paradigms indicate that there is no single "right" solution in a dynamic, constantly changing business milieu, although pattern theory and benchmarking enable identification of the more successful solutions.

Moody's methodology

Moody's considers the assessment of operational risk within a bank to be an ongoing process. Our assessment is based upon an in-depth analysis, structured around a series of discussions with the bank's management. The outline framework for this thorough review is provided below. A holistic approach is adopted and is based on consideration of four inter-related areas.

The framework, outlined in Figure 2, recognises that, when assessing any business, a primary consideration is the quality of management and its leadership capability. Ultimately, the success of management can be determined from the results achieved, which are a function of how efficiently and effectively the various resources have been applied, together with how effectively external threats have been mitigated.

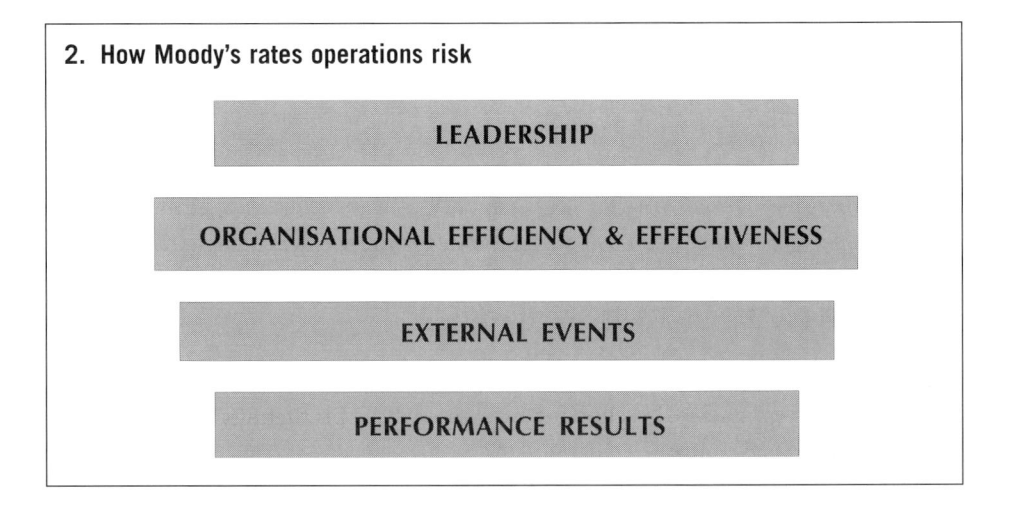

2. How Moody's rates operations risk

- LEADERSHIP
- ORGANISATIONAL EFFICIENCY & EFFECTIVENESS
- EXTERNAL EVENTS
- PERFORMANCE RESULTS

General background

Moody's would like to know the key operational risks faced by the bank and to understand how these may impact upon the quality and stability of its earnings.

As a principle, Moody's does not adopt a checklist approach to the determination of ratings. This framework provides background information to support future risk assessment meetings and is not meant to be comprehensive.

DEFINITION AND BOUNDARIES OF OPRISK
1. What is the bank's definition of operational risk?
2. How was the definition determined?
3. Does it have any restrictions (ie, exclusions such as business risk and reputational risk; inclusions such as legal risk)?
4. Are risks put into categories (eg, credit, market and operational)?
   - ❑ What are they?
   - ❑ How are they determined?
   - ❑ How is double-counting dealt with?

THE DRIVING FORCES AND LIMITATIONS (REGULATORY AND COMMERCIAL)
1. Has the board of directors formally expressed its full support for operational risk management – and if so, how has this support been demonstrated?
2. What are the main driving forces with regard to operational risk?
3. Which of the following benefits are expected to result from operational risk management?
   - ❑ A lower regulatory capital requirement.
   - ❑ Reduced losses (due to speed of response, actions and oversight, incentives, training, etc).
   - ❑ Lower operating costs.

- ❏ Improved prioritisation and targeting of resources (possibly through knowledge capture and leverage).
- ❏ Pricing improvements (ability to price risk more accurately).
- ❏ Lower insurance premiums (from improved risk environment).
- ❏ Lower cost of finance.
- ❏ Improved share price.
- ❏ Improved quality and stability of earnings.
- ❏ Enhanced competitive position.
- ❏ Improved probability of survival.
- ❏ Others.

4. Currently, does the bank assess these benefits and, if so, how?
5. What are the main limitations to progress? Prioritise and assess the significance of each of the following:
   - ❏ Lack of senior management buy-in.
   - ❏ Limited budget.
   - ❏ Difficulty in demonstrating cost-benefit analysis.
   - ❏ Current economic climate, resulting in a concentration on cost-cutting.
   - ❏ Lack of skilled or professionally qualified people.
   - ❏ Bureaucratic organisation structure.
   - ❏ Inappropriate approach by group risk.
   - ❏ Business-unit fiefdoms.
   - ❏ Technology and infrastructure problems.
   - ❏ Lack of common definitions and categories.
   - ❏ No clear group-wide approach.
   - ❏ Others.
6. What are the bank's main operational risk management weaknesses?
7. Who are the main competitors – how does the bank rate itself against these with regard to operational risk management?

MANAGEMENT[2]

1. Moody's considers the quality of management to be a key determinant in the credit rating of a bank – how does the bank assess the quality of its management and guard against perfunctory management problems?
2. Are managers set clear and measurable objectives and are these linked to the overall strategy? To what extent do managers have the opportunity to influence these objectives?
3. How are managers motivated – are both short-term and long-term considerations taken into account?
4. Do all managers receive regular ongoing training to maintain and further develop their competence levels (continuous professional development) – is the attained level of competence assessed and approved?
5. Does the bank operate an upward assessment system?
6. Is a whistle-blowing system in place – if so, how is internal political subversion prevented?
7. As rigid approaches based upon command and control, using specialisation and division of labour may prove too inflexible in a dynamic business environment, how does the bank address this issue and which management styles are encouraged within the bank?
8. Poor management and leadership can lead to a "blame culture", resulting in weaknesses and losses being hidden – how is this avoided?

STAGES OF DEVELOPMENT AND ORGANISATIONAL STRUCTURE

1. Has the bank developed an operational risk framework – if so, how long has it been in place and does it cover the whole organisation? Moreover, what difficulties did the bank experience in establishing the framework?

2. Does the bank have a chief risk officer – if so, how senior is this position?
3. Does the bank have an operational risk committee – and if so, is there a non-executive director on the committee?
4. With regard to Pillar 1 of Basel II:
   - Which method will the bank opt for and why (basic/standard/advanced measurement approach (AMA))?
   - Will the bank employ different methods for different business units and different countries?
5. What level of progress has been made with regard to the following stages?
   - Identification.
   - Data collection and analysis.
   - Management.
   - Mitigation.
   - Quantification and modelling (including stress testing and scenario analysis).
   - Re-engineering/change management.
   - Risk transfer.
6. Is there a gap between capability and need (ie, organisationally, what stage of development has the bank reached and how does this relate to its strategic aim)?

KEY RISKS – THEIR SIGNIFICANCE AND IMPACT
1. What are the key operational risks faced by the bank?
2. What are the relative priorities of these and what will cause the priorities to change?
3. What actions are being taken and what level of resources has been assigned to each risk? What benefits are expected and when?
4. What impact do these risks have on the quality and stability of earnings (both individually and collectively)?
5. What other impacts may result and have these been fully assessed?

OPRISK PROFILE DOCUMENT, REPORTS AND INDICATORS
OpRisk profile document
1. Does the bank have an operational risk profile document and, if so, how long has it been in existence?
2. Has this document been signed off and approved by the board of directors?
3. How is it updated and who has responsibility for approving changes?
4. Is access to this document restricted in any way?
5. If the bank does not have an operational risk profile document, does it intend to create one?

Reports and indicators – existing and planned
1. Is the chief executive officer provided with a regular operational risk briefing paper and, if so, how frequently?
2. Is the report made available to all members of the board, including the non-executive directors?
3. What other reports are produced, how frequently, and how long have they been in existence? Examples may include:
   - Corporate governance report.
   - Chief risk officer's report to the board.
   - Key performance indicators and key risk indicators.
   - Internal audit report.
   - Contingency report.
   - Insurance report.
   - IT report.
   - Human resources report (key employees, etc).
   - Customer complaints report.

- Intangible assets report (reputational risk, branding, etc).
- Strategic business units reports.
- Error and escalation reports.
- Key indicators.
- Others.

4. Are reports regularly reviewed for importance and relevance? How many have been upgraded and how many deleted over the past 12 months?
5. Has the burden of reporting increased or decreased over each of the last three years – and by how much?
6. What tools and techniques does the bank use in relationship to operational risk and how long has it been using them? Examples may include the following:
   - Control risk self-assessment.
   - Score cards.
   - Key performance indicators and key risk indicators.
   - Loss data collection and analysis.
   - Extreme value theory.
   - Value-at-risk.
   - Risk-adjusted return on capital.
   - Event-cause-effect analysis.
   - Stress testing and scenario analysis.
   - Bayesian belief networks.
   - Quality and stability of earnings.
   - Cost/income analysis.
   - Competitive positioning.
   - Others.

Organisation structure for risk management

Organisation structures will vary from bank to bank depending upon the strategy being pursued, the size and complexity of the bank, its activities, and possibly the countries in which it operates, together with local cultures. The framework and underlying questions given below represent an idealised structure.

BOARD OF DIRECTORS
1. Is there a main board director with specific responsibility for risk?
2. Is there at least one non-executive director with expertise in the area of risk management (including operational risk) to provide independent oversight?
3. Is there an organisational structure for risk that links the board to the individual employee (and vice versa) – does the board ensure validation and verification of risk at all levels before issuing risk statements?

RISK COMMITTEE
1. Is there a high-level risk committee in existence? Is it a sub-committee of the board of directors? Does it report directly to the board?
2. What are its terms of reference?
3. Is it chaired by a main board director?
4. Are there any independent non-executive directors on the committee?
5. Which departments/functions are represented on the risk committee?
6. What other committees exist that may affect the risk profile of the bank (eg, audit, remuneration, nomination, etc)?

GROUP RISK FUNCTION (AND OTHER SUPPORT FUNCTIONS)
1. What is the organisation structure for the group risk function – is it simply market, credit and operational risk – or are there other forms of risk specifically identified and managed (eg, liquidity, compliance, reputational, legal, etc)?

2. What skill sets are represented in the group risk function (eg, auditing, IT, legal, quants, etc)?
3. Does the group risk function have any direct authority and control – or is it simply a reporting activity – or does it act in a facilitating and mentoring role?
4. Is the group risk function responsible for risk policies and procedures and are these approved at board level?
5. What is the relationship between group risk and internal audit? Is there a clear demarcation or is there any overlap?
6. What is the relationship between the group risk function and insurance? Is the insurance department seen as a completely separate function – or is it integrated into the risk management activity – and if so, how?

BUSINESS UNITS
1. Does each business unit have its own risk management team?
2. Do these teams have dotted responsibility to the group risk function?
3. Where does responsibility for data aggregation lie?

INDIVIDUALS
1. With regard to risk, who is responsible for training, competence and continuous professional development (CPD) throughout the organisation?
2. Are all individuals aware of their responsibilities and are they competent to perform their duties? Are verification and validation records available?

Systems and procedures, including information technology and contingency planning

This section seeks to address the following three fundamental questions:

1. Does the bank have adequate and appropriate systems?
2. Are they regularly and independently reviewed?
3. In the event of failure, what would be the impact on the bank, its earnings and its reputation?

This particular subject area is very broad and can be technically complex. Therefore, the following elements are merely presented to give an overview of the subject.[3]

ADEQUACY AND APPROPRIATENESS
1. Is there a comprehensive set of policies and procedures, including systems – are these fully documented and readily available to all users (ie, are they available on the company Intranet)?
2. Which departments are responsible for sign-off (ie, creating and approving policies and procedures) – eg, external auditors, internal auditors, group operational risk function, compliance, IT, security, legal, etc?
3. Which departments are responsible for ensuring that policies and procedures remain adequate and appropriate – how is adequacy and appropriateness determined?
4. Does the bank have a fully integrated reporting system? Or are reports proprietary to individual business units, departments and employees? Are there automatic escalation triggers and reports?
5. Are IT systems sufficiently flexible or do they contain ossifying legacy systems that place limitations on reporting capability?
6. Does the bank maintain its own IT department or does it outsource any of its activities, and if so, to whom? Does the outsourced company represent a weak link?

FREQUENCY AND INDEPENDENCE OF REVIEWS

1. Who is responsible for ensuring that systems and procedures are regularly reviewed, independently validated and verified? How often are independent reviews undertaken and by whom?
2. With which codes and guidelines does the bank comply (eg, Systems and Security – ISO 17799; Data Protection Act; etc)?
3. Are there adequate audit trails? How is data integrity (legality and accuracy) ensured and how frequently are security violation reports produced and investigated?

IMPACT OF FAILURE

1. What continuity and contingency plans are in place – does this involve geogrphic dispersion and "hot running" of all key facilities?[4]
2. In the aftermath of a major disaster, how quickly could the bank be up and running?
3. Have the potential costs of such events been thoroughly determined?
4. Could any key data or information be lost due to the failure of outside external links – if so, what action has been taken to minimise this possibility? What could be the potential loss?
5. Could a failure event result in the loss of a key customer or supplier, which could seriously jeopardise the bank?
6. Have key employees been identified and the loss of these people been thoroughly determined? What contingency plans are in place?

Fraud, corruption and financial crime

Financial crime, in its various guises, is considered to represent a serious risk to all businesses. In the UK, for example, the National Criminal Intelligence Service has identified fraud as one of the most serious risks that companies face and has said it may represent between 2% to 5% of turnover for most organisations. The Basel Committee recently identified seven key risks faced by banks, two of which were internal and external fraud. Unfortunately, fraud is notoriously difficult to detect and around 75% of fraudulent acts are only discovered by chance. The primary defences against financial crime are considered to be an ethical culture and a vigilant management.

The following elements provide an overview of some of the key areas to be considered when addressing the issues of fraud, corruption and financial crime.

CULTURE AND ETHICS

1. How does the bank ensure a high ethical culture in which openness and transparency are encouraged and mistakes not hidden?
2. Is there an ethics policy that sets out expected standards of business conduct (including guidance on matters such as gifts, hospitality, bribes, conflicts of interest and conduct of private life)? Are customers and suppliers made fully aware of the policy?

DIRECTORS AND SENIOR MANAGERS

1. Who has overall responsibility for prevention of fraud, corruption and financial crime, including money laundering? Is there a specific person with clear responsibility and authority? How senior is this person?
2. Are directors and senior managers rewarded with short-term share options and bonuses? If so, could this lead to distortion and prevent a balanced view from being taken?
3. Do the directors or senior managers have any relationships with suppliers or customers of the bank?

POLICIES, PROCEDURES AND SYSTEMS
1. Are there appropriate policies and procedures in place, including a financial crime response plan?
2. Are staff encouraged and incentivised to report crime – if so, how would any whistle-blower be adequately protected?
3. Does the bank maintain a financial crime register, and, if so, what levels of fraud and other criminal activity does this show? Does the bank always take legal action – what levels of recovery have been achieved?
4. How does the bank ensure that it does not fall foul of legislative requirements (eg, Data Protection Act, Regulation and Investigatory Powers Act, Public Interest Disclosure Act, The European Convention of Human Rights) that may make detection of crime more difficult?

MANAGEMENT OVERSIGHT
1. Does the bank have a sound management control environment (ie, active management oversight and reporting, authorisation controls, segregation of duties, physical security, transaction controls, etc)?
2. Have the potential crime hot spots been identified – if so, are they continuously monitored and managed?
3. Is there a rotation policy for moving staff to different jobs? How frequently is this done? Are there any people who have been in the same position for five years or more?
4. Are employees required to take a complete break from work – if so, are there any departments or individuals excluded from this requirement?
5. Are there any people with computer facilities that enable them to work away from the office – if so, are there any checks to detect possible fraud or other financial crime?

Business activities
1. What methods of detecting unusual or suspicious patterns of behaviour does the bank have, with regard to trading activities?
2. How does the bank cope with the threat of E-fraud? If there have been any instances of this, have these been verified and validated by external experts?
3. What measures has the bank taken to combat money laundering? Have these been verified and validated by external experts?

OUTSOURCING
1. Does the bank use outsourced services and contractors – if so, does this pose a risk from financial crime?

Data, quantification and modelling
Data collection and analysis is necessary in order for a bank to gain a proper understanding of the losses being incurred.

Where appropriate, quantification can represent a significant step forward, although it should be recognised that not all risks can be quantified. An enhancement of knowledge and understanding can be more important than the derivation of any absolute figure itself. Quantification exposes underlying tacit assumptions and tests empirical views concerning the size and importance of losses, and, as such, can lead to greater accuracy and control with respect to resource allocation.

With regard to modelling, in theory there are a number of powerful mathematical tools and techniques available. However, given data limitations and a high level of uncertainty in the results, they have yet to be proved of practical value for operational risk management. This situation may change in the future as further research and development is undertaken. Moody's believes that quantification

MOODY'S ANALYTICAL FRAMEWORK FOR OPERATIONAL RISK MANAGEMENT OF BANKS

clearly has its place. However, truly effective operational risk management will continue to remain primarily underpinned by qualitatively stronger elements such as solid corporate governance, a healthy risk culture throughout the organisation, effective operational risk management at all levels, tight procedures and controls, performing technology, and not least, well qualified and honest people.

In assessing data, qualification and modelling consideration is given by Moody's to various factors including the following.

1. Does the bank collect loss data? If so, what is the attachment point (ie, at what value does the bank start to collect losses) and how was this determined?
2. Does the bank actively seek to detect near misses and, if so, how are these reported? Is senior management made aware of all significant near misses – and who decides what is significant?
3. How are unexpected gains, resulting from operational events, shown in the management reports and published accounts?
4. Data that is incorrectly categorised or apportioned can cause distortion – how does the bank avoid this problem?
5. If data is not analysed in sufficient detail initially, it may be practically impossible to analyse it further at a later date – what efforts does the bank make to avoid this problem?
6. Does the bank use external loss data to compensate for the paucity of internal (low-frequency high impact) events – if so, how is this data adjusted to take account of the following limitations?
   - *Time*: Over time, an organisation will change and adapt, consequently within that organisation, the same causal factor may not give rise to exactly the same event and have precisely the same effect.
   - *Place*: All organisations are, to some extent, different. They will have different franchises and different business activities. Their people, culture and ethics will be different and they will employ different systems and procedures.
   - *Size and scalability*: Banks of different sizes are likely to use different systems, procedures and technology. Indeed, even within the same bank, systems and procedures will change as the different business units grow, develop and decline. Consequently, there may be a lack of direct scalability of data.
   - *True value*: Ensuring that all costs and compensations are properly recorded is challenging. Clearly, this is more likely to represent a problem when trying to use data from other organisations, particularly if it is merely taken from non-validated and non-verified sources, such as published newspaper articles. The final outcome may not be known for some considerable time after the event and details of subsequent compensation or penalties may not be published or recorded.
   - *Current values*: In considering historical data, it is necessary to take into account such factors as inflation and currency variations over time.
7. Does the bank use extreme value theory (EVT) and/or OpVAR as possible methods for determining the level of capital required for protection against extreme loss events? If so, what problems are perceived with these methods and how are they overcome?
8. Does the data-set include any extreme events? If so, how are these dealt with and how is distortion avoided?
9. Does the bank determine loss distribution curves for all losses – if not, why not?
10. How is correlation taken into account?
11. Has the bank considered the use of Bayesian Belief Networks – if so, what conclusions were reached and why?
12. Value-at-risk is defined as the value of the expected loss, at a chosen confidence level, for a particular time period. The Basel Committee has indicated that, under the advanced measurement approach (AMA), it will require a one-year holding

period and a 99.9% confidence level. As stated previously, high confidence levels are difficult to establish given relatively few extreme data points. How will the bank address this issue?
13. Statistical theory states that it is not possible to predict losses beyond the range for which data is available. Does the bank use op-risk models for predictive purposes and, if so, how does it take into account this theoretical limitation?
14. Models are a simplification of the real world; therefore, their applicability needs to be constantly evaluated, given the changing financial environment. How often are models thoroughly evaluated – and do external experts with appropriate qualifications and experience carry out this validation?

Reports and results

With regard to reports, typically, these exist at three levels: strategic, management and operational. It is important to know all the links between these and the degree to which reports (and supporting databases) are integrated, thus facilitating escalation and rapid response.

Particularly important areas for consideration are the chief executive officer's summary report, the risk profile document and transparency disclosures.

Also relevant are any special reports, produced at the request of the regulators, the board of directors, or the risk committee, as well as any initiated or undertaken by the internal auditors.

Other elements for consideration are identified in the earlier section of this report entitled "General background".

CEO'S SUMMARY REPORT
1. Does the chief executive officer currently receive a high-level operational risk report?
2. If so, when was the report introduced?
3. How frequently is this report produced?
4. Does the report show the following details:
   ❏ Earnings diagram (showing probability and distortion).
   ❏ Risk-weighted capital.
   ❏ Economic capital.
   ❏ Regulatory capital.
   ❏ Main risk elements (identifying their size and current priority rating):
      ● Internal fraud.
      ● External fraud.
      ● Employment practices and workplace safety.
      ● Clients, products and business practices.
      ● Damage to physical assets.
      ● Business disruption and systems failure.
      ● Execution, delivery and process management.
      ● Others.

RISK PROFILE DOCUMENT
1. Does the bank have a risk profile document, similar to an auditor's standing file, covering such matters as:
   ❏ Corporate governance, culture and ethics
   ❏ Strategy, flexibility and earnings stability
   ❏ Organisation structure for risk management
   ❏ Systems and procedures (including existing and planned IT facilities)
   ❏ Contingency plans
   ❏ Fraud, corruption and financial crime
   ❏ Audit and compliance
   ❏ Competency and key skills development

❏ Outsourcing (including insurance)
❏ Any other key issues impacting upon the risk profile of the bank

TRANSPARENCY
1. What efforts are being made by the bank with regard to transparency (ie, as required under Pillar 3 of Basel II)?
2. What other public disclosures is the bank required to make (eg, as specified by the Combined Code for UK-listed companies or the Sarbanes-Oxley Act)?
3. Does the bank make any further public disclosures, and if so, why?
4. Does the bank assess the cost and impact of disclosures, and if so, how?
5. What does the bank say about operational risk in its financial reports? Are these statements more than just platitudes relating to perceived best practice?

1 *A strategic overview of Moody's approach to operational risk is given in Moody's special report entitled "Bank Operational Risk Management: More Than An Exercise in Capital Allocation and Loss Data Gathering", published June 2002.*
2 *Given the importance of management and the related fields of corporate governance and leadership, Moody's will be issuing a special report covering these topics.*
3 *For further details, please refer to URSIT (Uniform Rating System for Information Technology) used by United States federal and state regulators. It is also recommended that reference be made to the following papers issued by the Basel Committee on Banking Supervision: "Risk Management Principles for Electronic Banking", issued May 2001; and "Electronic Commerce Systems Form (Annex 1)", issued August 2001.*
4 *"Hot running" refers to an alternative facility that is already active and therefore available for immediate use in case of emergency.*

15

From Operational Risk to Operational Excellence

Barbara Döbeli, Markus Leippold and Paolo Vanini

Swiss National Bank,[1] University of Zurich, University of
Southern Switzerland and Zurich Cantonal Bank[2]

Introduction

In June 1999 the Basel Committee on Banking Supervision (the Committee) released its consultative document "The New Basel Capital Accord" in which a regulatory capital charge to cover *other risks* was proposed. Operational risk is one such *other risk*. Since the release of this document the financial industry and the regulatory authorities have been engaged in vigorous and recurring discussions. In the meantime, the Committee released two further documents (BIS (2001, 2003)). Even with the third consultative document, however, the "Philosopher's Stone" concerning operational risk has not yet been found. For example, three out of the four approaches are not risk sensitive and, therefore, the figures derived are of no use to manage operational risk. Further, the only risk sensitive methodology, the so-called Advanced Measurement approaches, is not specified within the Basel documents but largely left to the financial industry to be defined. By and large, no risk sensitive instruments have been offered by the Committee to the financial industry to calculate their operational risk exposures. This stands in contrast to credit and market risk, where the Committee has provided such instruments in the past.

Indeed, the momentum in the development of operational risk methodologies has shifted more and more to the financial industry. Recently, some US regulatory authorities even clearly stated that the lead in research and implementation of operational risk should be on the banking industry's side. Why has the Committee failed in the last years to develop a risk sensitive operational risk approach?

Possibly the Committee underestimated the difficulties to develop a meaningful quantitative approach based on their definition and formulated sound practices. We will show below that indeed operational risk is not a simple copy-and-paste exercise of successful approaches used for credit and market risk. Besides, we will address a question often raised by practitioners and so far unanswered by the Committee. This question is "*Why* does it pay to care about operational risk differently than in the past?" A possible reason for such a methodological change could be that the risks increased in the last years due to the surge of highly integrated systems and the emergence of banks as very large-volume service providers and the former instruments failed to cope with this fact appropriately. From our point of view, however, there is no predominant evidence supporting this explanation.[3] We argue that independent of any increase in operational risk exposure and irrespective of a regulatory framework, there are economic reasons to consider operational risk in a

Markus Leippold and Paolo Vanini gratefully acknowledge financial support from the National Centre of Competence in Research "Financial Valuation and Risk Management" (FINRSIK).

FROM OPERATIONAL RISK TO OPERATIONAL EXCELLENCE

different way in the future. Our contribution leaves the regulator's point of view on operational risk and starts looking at the issue from a purely business-oriented perspective. The discussion will therefore be about profitability and not about regulation.

The economics of operational risk

A possible rationale for the existence of banks is their ability to meet the demands of the society for risk transformation. By offering risk transformation services banks earn money. Products within the classic risk categories like market and credit risk provide these risk transformation services and generate the banks' income. But what makes the management of operational risk profitable? To precisely specify this question, we loosely define operational risk at this point as the risk a bank faces in producing goods and services for its clients. According to this definition, the bank itself is demanding for risk transformation. This means that operational risk is mostly a risk factor arising in intra-institutional activities. Exceptions are heavy operational risk losses, where the bank's reputation will be affected. In such a case, the operational risk event exhibits externalities. Figure 1 illustrates the operational, market and credit risk for a value chain.[4] It also shows that there is an internal market for operational risk whereas the market for credit and market risk is external.

The reason that the bank itself asks for risk transformation lies in the role that operational risk as a major risk factor plays in the profitability of banks. This means nothing else other that redundant, inefficient, faulty or belated production of goods and services decrease the bank's profitability. However, why should a financial institution suddenly care about these issues in a different way than it has before?

To address this point, we have to consider a second factor enhancing profitability, which is product innovation. Since profitability depends on earnings, costs and risks, we next consider these three components. The earnings are gained with products and they carry innovation risk. Costs, however, occur in the process and are characterised by operational risk. The reason why a bank should consider operational risk differently now as opposed to in the past is because of the convergence of banks in innovation, and hence in the products they sell to their clients today. As an example, fixed mortgages offered by banks are all similar today. Furthermore, the margin and fees of many products are under stress. Therefore, an increase in profitability or the ability to compete will not be made with products (the end of the value chain) but with the process (the "how-side" of the value chain).

Is there potential on the bank's operational side, which can be significantly

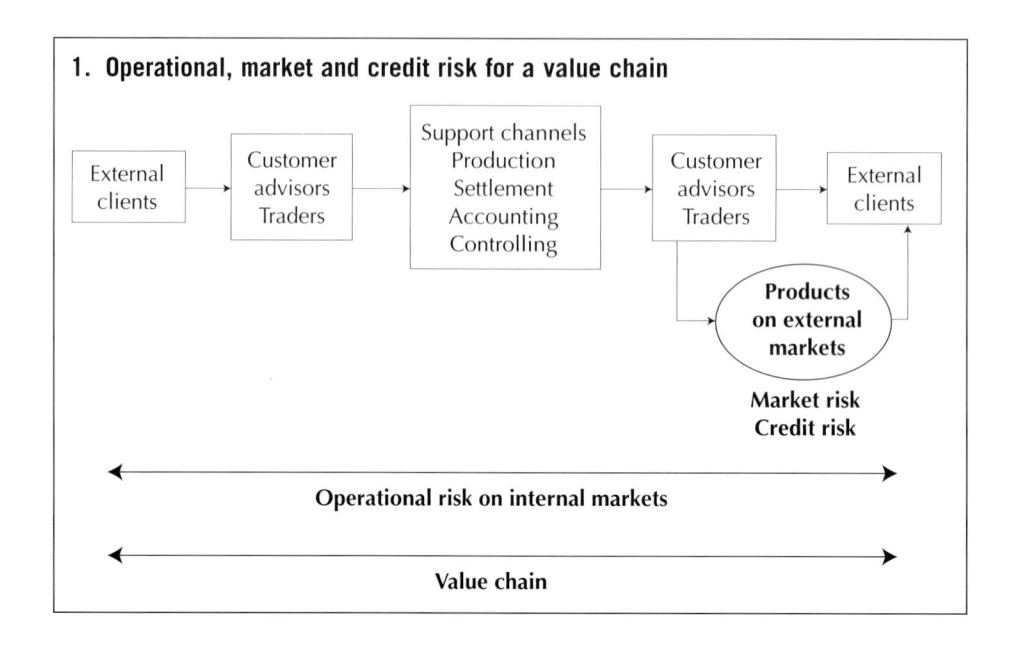

1. Operational, market and credit risk for a value chain

External clients → Customer advisors / Traders → Support channels / Production / Settlement / Accounting / Controlling → Customer advisors / Traders → External clients

Products on external markets

Market risk
Credit risk

Operational risk on internal markets

Value chain

transformed into an operational excellence? Although banks have continuously improved their process efficiency, they have not yet reached the level of efficiency of, for example, the automobile industry. Can banks reach this level or is banking simply different than producing cars? From our point of view, no fundamental difference is given in producing and administrating the goods and services in both industries. The crucial difference, however, arises in customer relationships, where a completely different information structure is in existence.

Modelling operational risk
By modelling operational risk from a business point of view, the first questions we address are:

❑ What is the scope?
❑ What will be the best methodology to meet the scope?

The scope is defined by ranking the different value chains, whereby the most important value chains should be prioritised. To value, two other characteristics, the all-in costs and the operational risks are attributed. The methodology for attributing the risk figure, ie operational risk, is then analysed. There, the methodologies vary from quantitative to qualitative approaches or even verbal descriptions of the risks.

In this chapter, we concentrate on quantifiable operational risk only. For value chains where quantitative risk figures can be assessed, we end up with a risk-adjusted return on investment (RAROI) measure of profitability. To set up such a quantitative operational risk model, the following different steps are discussed in the sequel:

❑ Definition of operational risk assets
❑ Model frameworks
❑ Calibration and data issues

In our subsequent exposition we will be sketchy in the formalism and, instead, stress the intuition. The reader interested in the formal approach is referred to Ebnöther, Leippold and Vanini (2003) (ELV).

OPERATIONAL RISK ASSETS
An indispensable requirement for quantitative risk assessment to be carried out is that well-defined operational risk assets exist. Else risk can possibly be measured approximately but certainly cannot be efficiently managed. Therefore, business activities or processes generating the value chain need to be modelled in a quantifiable manner. A mathematical toolkit serving this purpose is provided by graph theory. In all its abstraction, a graph G is a pair of sets, Z and V, where every element of V is a two-member set whose members are elements of Z, for example

$$Z = \{a, b, c\}, V = \{\{a, b\}, \{a, c\}\}.$$

More intuitively, a graph is a collection of nodes and of edges connecting the nodes (see Figure 2). Sometimes, we also use the term "states" for nodes. Preferably, processes and value chains are modelled as a collection of *directed graphs*, where each edge can be traversed in only one direction. In the context of IT networks, we henceforth call the set of all graphs $G_1, G_2, \ldots, G_n$ a *network*.

The nodes, which represent a machine or a person, are the carriers of the actions or decisions in the business activities. The effect of the actions, which defines the performance, is then attributed to the outgoing edges of the respective node. In our graphs, we allow for self-loops and multiple edges. Self-loops represent, for example, control processes. Since information flows in just one direction, the edges of the graph are directed.

FROM OPERATIONAL RISK TO OPERATIONAL EXCELLENCE

Given this skeleton, we next attach risk information to the graphs. As the nodes represent either a machine or an individual performing an action, we assume that they are in one of the three possible states: in a running, down or in an intermediate state. We therefore model the *operational risk nodes* $n_{i,j}(t)$ as stochastic processes, where $n_{i,j}(t)$ is a random variable with values in $[0,1]$ at time t which can either be continuous or discrete. The variable $n_{i,j}(t)$ represents the functioning or malfunctioning status of the node j in the graph i. The randomness of the nodes is due to the risk factors X affecting them.

Examples of risk factors are system failure, theft, fraud and human error. Figure 3 shows the relationship between the directed graphs and the risk factors. It follows that the operational risk assets can be considered as a two-layer object. The first layer represents the graph for the business activities. The second layer collects the risk factors affecting the nodes. As it follows from Figure 3, a single risk factor can simultaneously influence several nodes, yielding non-trivial dependence structure. From a business point of view, the two layers possess qualitatively different characteristics. While the risk profile will be measured on the graph level, risk management typically touches the risk factor level since eventually the causes, not the symptoms, have to be managed. This is a different situation compared to market or credit risk models, where the sources of risk are taken as given and are not affected by the management of risk.

Three important issues regarding assets will not be considered in the subsequent analysis. Firstly, we do not take into account the fact that more than one input generally is needed to produce an output. To consider this fact would mean to go

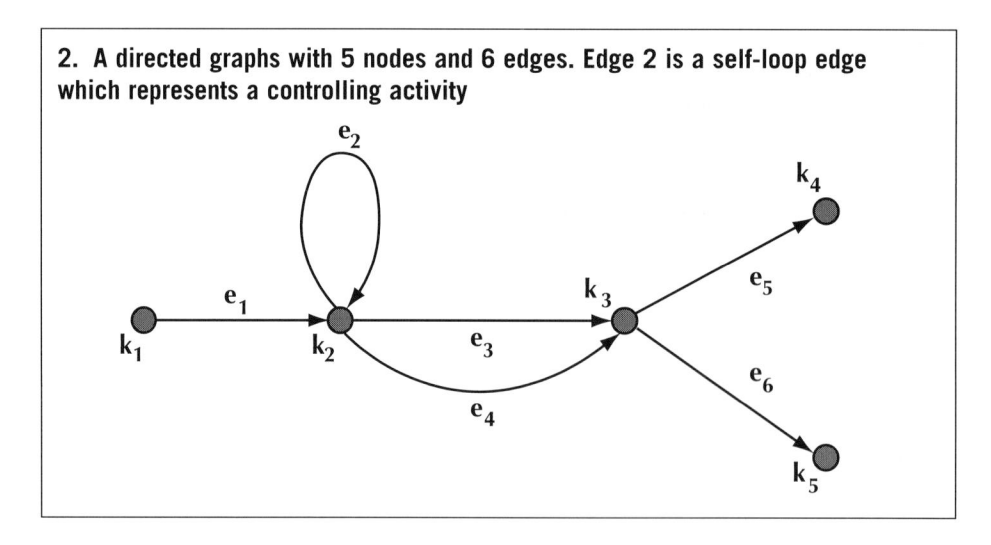

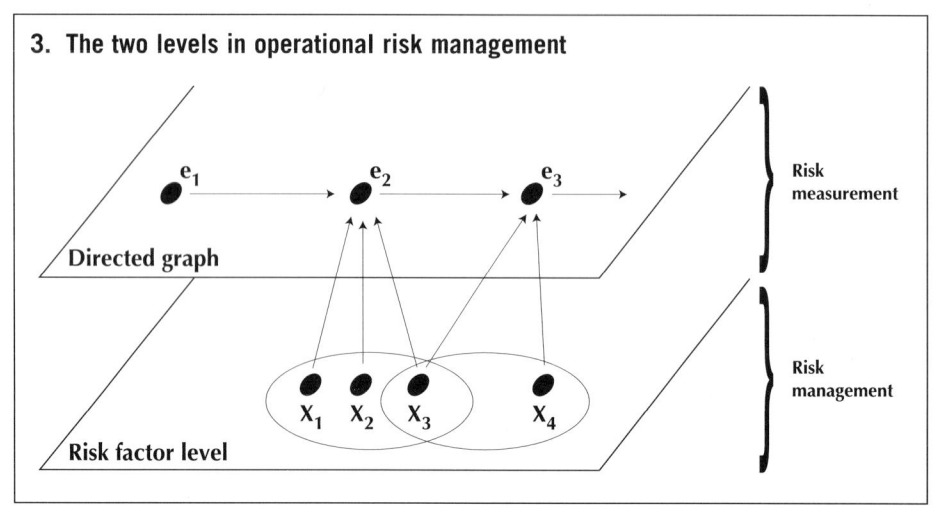

2. A directed graphs with 5 nodes and 6 edges. Edge 2 is a self-loop edge which represents a controlling activity

3. The two levels in operational risk management

deeper into the graph theory. Secondly, we leave nodes unspecified apart from their risk factor dependence. The appropriate level of modelling the nodes, ie the attribution of costs for example or the splitting of nodes into different software packages is important for practical implementation but is not essential to understand the logic of our approach. Finally, the edges are perfect. This means that we do not discuss capacity problems of the links for example.

MODEL FRAMEWORKS

There are many different approaches to quantitative operational risk. Since we strongly believe that operational risk adds value only if it is related to the important processes of a bank, not only pure statistical dependence among the risk factors but also workflow or topological dependence matters. Following Kühn and Neu (2002), we call such models functional dependence models. More precisely, functional dependence models make explicit the asset structure whereas a pure statistical model, in our definition, reduces the operational risk assets to point objects. For pure statistical models, we refer the reader to eg Embrechts *et al.* (2002).

Within the class of functional models, different approaches can be imagined and some of them have been worked out. The approach we sketch below is from ELV. Their setup, based on a stochastic dynamical system approach, is very flexible and general. In particular, the functional model of Kühn and Neu (2002) can be obtained as a special case. The dynamics of the node j in graph i, ie $n_{i,j}(t)$, is assumed to follow the stochastic differential equation:

$$dn_{j,i}(t) = a(n_{j,i}(t))(b(n_{j,i}(t)) - T_{j,i}(n(t))\,dt + \sigma(n_{j,i}(t))dZ_{j,i}$$

with initial value $n_{i,j}(0) = 0$, ie the system is running perfectly at time zero. The network dynamics is a coupled system of mean-return type stochastic equations. The terms are defined as follows and capture the following intuitions:

❑ The term models the dependence of the node j on the surrounding nodes that affect the functioning of j. The simplest dependence structure used in Kühn and Neu (2002) is of the form

$$T_{j,i}(n(t)) = \sum_{k \in A_j} \omega_{j,k} n_{k,m}(t)$$

with Aj the neighbourhood of nodes of j which affect the performance of j and $\grave{u}_{j,k}$, the coupling or infection strength between the nodes j and k. It follows that if all neighbourhood systems are running, ie all n's are equal to zero, the state of the system under consideration is not affected by its neighbourhood. However, it is common in IT networks to mirror sensitive systems. Such a mirroring reflects in a quadratic T-expression such that the system is affected only if both surrounding systems are down.

❑ The difference between the functions b and T measures the discrepancy of the state of the node under consideration to the status of its neighbourhood. The intuition is that, in the long-run average, a system breaks down if the depending neighbourhood systems are all malfunctioning.

❑ The term reflects the speed of convergence towards the long-term equilibrium (if there is any).

❑ Apart from the drift term, the noise term can exhibit various different forms. The stochastic component can be a combination of correlated Brownian motions or of jump processes. A simple approach as in Kühn and Neu (2002) is to set

$$Z_{j,i}(t) = \sqrt{\rho}Y(t) + \sqrt{1 - \rho}X_{j,i}(t)$$

with Y a common risk factor affecting all nodes and graphs and $X_{j,i}$ a node specific risk factor. For example, Y could be an external event such as an earthquake, while the specific risk factors $X_{j,i}$ capture eg people error, system failure, and fraud. The similarity to the Merton-type credit risk models is apparent in such a simple setup, with the only difference lying in the drift term accounting for the topological dependence structure.

Given the node dynamics as outlined above, the next step is to define the loss dynamics. This will then lead to the risk figures. In ELV we choose the dynamics

$$dL_{j,i}(t) = a_L(n_{j,i}(t))(L_{j,i}(t) - \lambda_{j,i}(t))\,dt + \sigma_L(n_{j,i}(t))dZ_{L_{j,i}}$$

with the following definitions:

- The difference $L_{j,i}(t) - \lambda_{j,i}(t)$ measures the actual loss level to the contracted or acceptable level λ. This captures the fact that operational risk is a support risk for business and therefore, the business representatives define and pay for levels of excellence. If the node represents an IT system, the level is typically defined by a service level agreement (SLA). In the case of a human decision node, the level is more difficult to define and in fact, it might turn out that it cannot be done in a meaningful way. At this point, the best approach is to replace the node dynamics by a static random variable, which captures the risk profile of the employee in the process.
- The term $a_L(n_{j,i}(t))$ is again the speed measure toward the value λ. In operational risk, this term is of particular importance since the counter-measures and hence the costs of operational risk management have to be captured in this term. Such counter-measures are both state-dependent and, as in ELV, path-dependent. The latter means that the longer a node is not functioning or malfunctioning, the more efforts have to be undertaken to remove the loss source for business. So far, most endeavours to quantify operational risk neglect the fact that operational risk measurement becomes meaningless if counter-measures are not simultaneously considered.
- The random variable $Z_{L_{j,i}}$ models the severity of a given malfunctioning on the nodes.

Using this model setup, we can finally define quantitative operational risk and the concept of the operational risk acceptance set.

Definition
For a process j the quantifiable operational risk is the probability distribution of the loss function at a given specified time horizon. The operational risk acceptance set α_j for the process j is the probability that the losses do not exceed the contract of acceptance loss level λ_j, ie

$$\alpha_j = \text{Prob}\left(\sum_{i \in \text{Graph } j} L_{j,i} \geq \sum_{i \in \text{Graph } j} \lambda_{j,i}\right)$$

From the above definition it follows that many different meaningful refinements of operational risk management can be made. For example, the acceptance level could be defined for the single nodes and not for the whole graph (see ELV for details). Further, different risk measures could be defined, again for single nodes or for the whole graph. Besides the process risk measures, it is also important to know the riskiness of the neighbourhood of the process under consideration. This defines what we call the background risk measures. Finally, from a planning point of view, incremental risk measures could be considered. They provide an answer to questions as "how does a change in the network architecture affect the risk figures of the actual network?"

After having selected a model for the specific nodes and for the loss dynamics, the next task is then the calibration of the model. Before turning to this issue, we comment on the profitability issue. Once we have defined the stochastic processes for the nodes and the losses we indeed have fixed risks and costs of the business activity. The risks are clear and the costs follow from the calibration of the loss dynamics to the self-assessment of the costs variables. Therefore, we end up with the costs and risks of those processes being selected in the past to be important because of their value added to business.

We end this section with an example. Thereby, we consider two nodes in the node dynamics and to simplify the notation we omit the process indices. We assume the model specification to be

$$dn_1(t) = a(n_1(t) - \omega_{1,2} n_2) \, dt + \sigma_1 dZ_1$$
$$dn_2(t) = a(n_2(t) - \omega_{2,1} n_1 - \omega_{2,3} n_3) \, dt + \sigma_2 dZ_2$$
$$dn_3(t) = a(n_3(t) - \omega_{2,3} n_2) \, dt + \sigma_3 dZ_3$$

with Z_1, Z_2, Z_3 one-dimensional Brownian motions which may be dependent or independent. Although the model is over-simplistic for practical application its analytical tractability allows us to discuss some relevant features. From Figure 4 follows that the three states or nodes define an information or control part of a process.

The system of stochastic equations can be solved using Itô's Lemma, the stochastic integration by parts formula and the Jordan Decomposition of linear algebra to partially decouple the system. For the system under consideration the singular value decomposition of the interaction matrix between the nodes, ie, the drift matrix of the system, leads to a Jordan-type matrix with the eigenvalues on the diagonal and one's directly above the diagonal. The eigenvalues can be both, real or complex numbers. This implies that the expected values and the variances of the nodes are exponential functions or, in case of complex eigenvalues, oscillatory functions. Which one of the two cases holds depends on the relative magnitude of the coupling and infection parameters ω and on the speed parameter a. Therefore, a coupling and infection parameter of node 3 acting on node 2 can possibly lead to an unstable or oscillatory node performance of node 1. The strength of ω is calibrated to data and therefore it reflects the quality of operational risk management. Hence, an unsatisfactory management of operational risk in one system can trigger through the topological dependence a malfunctioning of other systems. The importance of the network topology is also emphasised by changing the topology in the example as follows:

if we remove the control $\omega_{3,2}$ flow and maintain the rest of the network unchanged, the eigenvalues are always real and no oscillatory behaviour at all is possible.

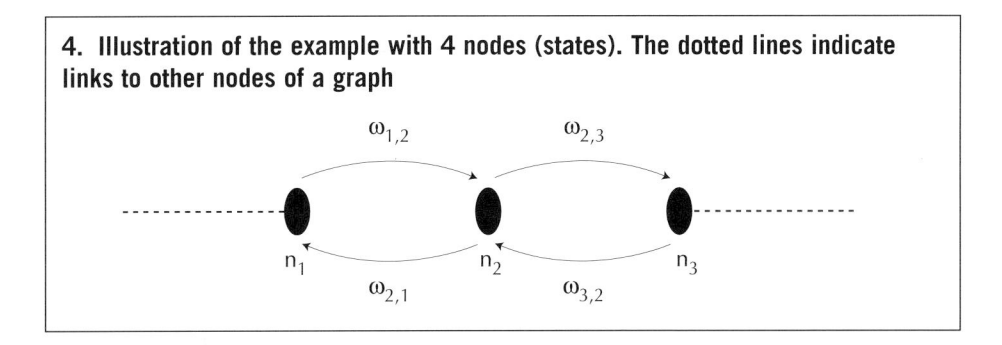

4. Illustration of the example with 4 nodes (states). The dotted lines indicate links to other nodes of a graph

CALIBRATION AND DATA ISSUES

The calibration of the different models mentioned above depends on their specifications and therefore ranges from straightforward to very complicated. We discuss the calibration in the discrete time approach of Kühn and Neu (2002), which can be done explicitly. Since they assume Gaussian risk factors, it is possible to obtain the conditional probability for a failure of a node i at time $t + \Delta t$, given a configuration[5] at time t and a realisation of the common risk factor Y. The result of the integration can be expressed by the cumulative normal distribution and the unknown parameters ω and Y. In a next step, a specific configuration is chosen. Then, simple formulas for the unknown parameter ω are derived within the model. In a final step, the model consistency condition for ω can unambiguously be related to self-assessment data. These data consist of answers to the two following questions concerning the frequency of events:

❏ What is the expected period, until node i fails for the first time in a fully operative environment, and
❏ Given that only node j has failed, what is the expected period for node i to fail also?

An important issue in operational risk is the availability of data. We suggest the use of both self-assessment and historical data. The former are based on *expert knowledge*. More precisely, the respective process owner values the risk of the process. To achieve this goal, standardised forms are used where all questions are properly defined. The experts have to assess the following two random events among other non-random events such as questions about costs:

1. The frequency of the random time of loss and in the severity self-assessment.
2. The estimated maximum and minimum possible losses in their respective processes.

By using expert data, we usually possess data to fully specify the risk information. The disadvantage of such data, however, is not only their confidentiality but also their reliability and possible biases. As Rabin (1998) lucidly demonstrates in his review article, people typically fail to apply the mathematical laws of probability correctly but instead create own "laws" such as the so-called "law of small numbers".

The behavioural literature provides dozens of example about humans failing in applying the laws of probability correctly. One example is in the research on the *representativeness heuristic* (see Kahnemann and Tversky (1974)). Thereby, it is demonstrated that people tend to over-use "representativeness" in assessing probabilities. The Bayes' Law tells us that our assessment of likelihood should combine representativeness with base rates. People, however, under-use base-rate information in forming their judgements. As an example, a test person ("the estimator") is asked to assess a conditional probability that another individual is either a lawyer or an engineer given an *a priori* distribution in the sample. If an individual looks more like a lawyer from the estimator's point of view, the conditional probability estimate will be biased towards their belief independent of the *a priori* distribution. Such behavioural observations are usually tested in laboratory experiments.

The insights of the behavioural literature show that an expert-based database needs to be designed in a way that the most important and prominent biases are circumvented and a sensitivity analysis has do be done finally to test for robustness. Another implication is to replace direct probabilistic judgements by related real life situations. For collecting the data the following three principles were therefore formulated and discussed in Ebnöther *et al* (2003):

1. *Principle I*: Avoid direct probabilistic judgements;

2. *Principle II*: Choose an optimal interplay between experts "know-how" and modelling; and
3. *Principle III*: Implement the right incentives.

After the generation of self-assessment data, we can use historical data for different purposes. First, they are very important for plausibility analysis of the self-assessment data. Second, historical data are needed for calibration whenever self-assessment data cannot be generated.

A case study for an IT network

We apply the model framework to a pure IT network. We assume that there are three business activities (graphs) which produce three goods or services with values V_i, $i = 1, 2, 3$. To produce these outputs, six inputs are assumed to be necessary. The different inputs are connected to the different outputs in several so-called walks (see Figure 5).

We further assume that there are two risk factors. The first factors affect all nodes or systems in the same way. Hence, it can be considered as an external event. The second risk factor is system-specific and these risk factors are independent for different nodes.

The model dynamics for the nodes and loss distribution is discretised for the simulation, where one unit time step Δt is equal to one day. The different equations for the nodes are specified as follows:

A system can be either in a running or a down state. Which state is realised depends on the support a system gets at each point in time. The support function at each time is a sum of three terms:

❏ the average support;
❏ the support due to the counter-measure weighted topological dependence; and
❏ the support reduction due to the risk factors.

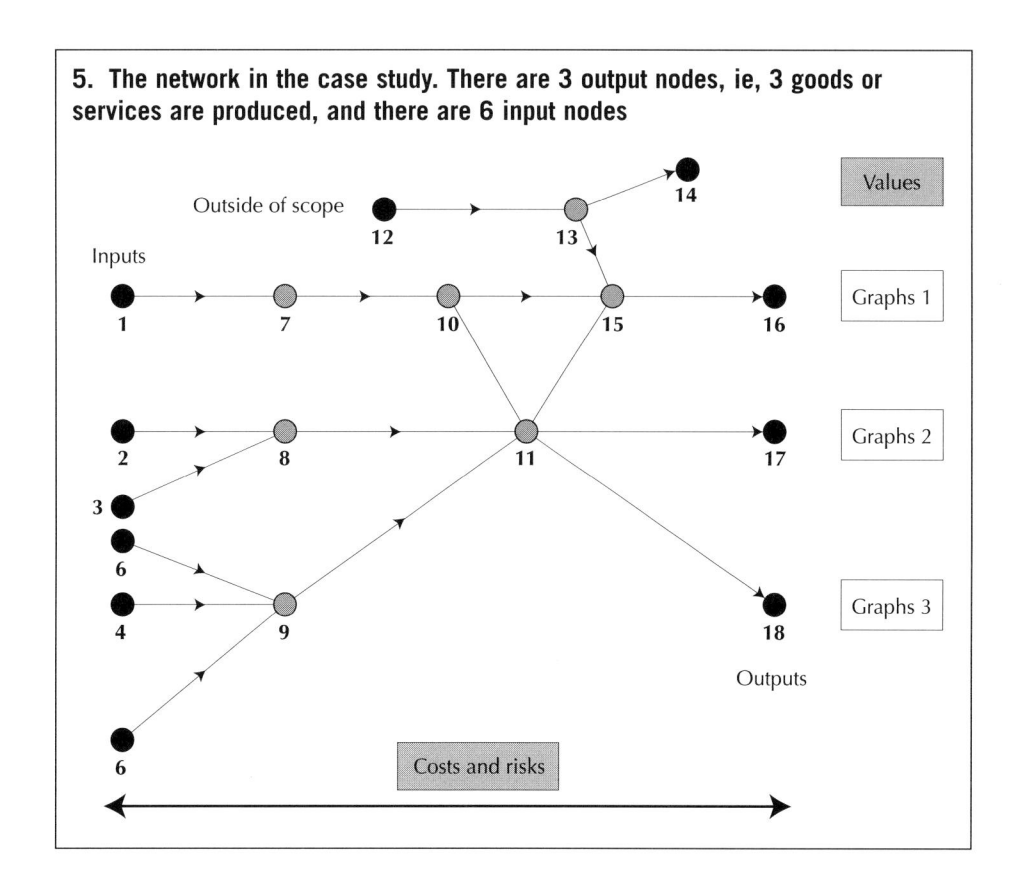

5. The network in the case study. There are 3 output nodes, ie, 3 goods or services are produced, and there are 6 input nodes

The state dynamics for all systems is then defined as: a state at time $t + \Delta t$ is down if the support of the system is below a threshold and is running if the support is above the threshold.

Therefore, the state dynamics of the nodes is given by an indicator function acting on the support function. The counter-measure function is a path-dependent function, which increases in value the more periods a system has been down in the past. The efficiency of the counter-measures is measured by a constant value. Therefore, counter-measures serve as an index for the costs needed in maintaining a network performing.[6]

We use 10,000 simulation runs and a time horizon of 30 days. This time horizon can be appropriate for some value chains whereas for other ones, such as a network supporting the trading floor, a much more shorter time horizon should be chosen. For more details about the model, see ELV.

What does the simulation of the model produce? First, it gives us a loss distribution over the following three graphical objects: the network, the different walks and the individual nodes. Second, for each of the objects, the value of the counter-measures can be calculated. Since counter-measures are costs, we are able to link potential losses (risks) with the associated costs caused by the counter-measures provided for a node in down state. Together with the three values generated by the network, we have all ingredients for managing operations in an integrated way.

Comparing different specifications of operations management shows the value of such an integrated analysis for decision-making. We consider the following cases:

Specification 1
A bank taking into account all key variables defines sophisticated operational risk management:

the dependencies within the network and the counter-measures, together with their efficiency, are fully modelled.

Specification 2
In this specification, the management is able to incorporate all dependencies in the network, but there are no counter-measures, apart from the average support for the systems. Therefore, independent of the status of the network, the costs of intervention are kept constant.

Specification 3
This specification defines the naïve view of operational risk management: the operational risk manager neglects any dependency within the network and is basing the loss simulation according to this view. Since the counter-measures act on the dependence terms, they are irrelevant.

We first compare the loss distributions for the specifications 1 to 3, where additionally, 1* is a management operating under the same conditions as the sophisticated management, but with less effective counter-measures. The upper panel in Figure 6 plots the distributions of losses under the different specifications. The curves are generated using kernel density estimation with Epanechnikov kernel function. Note that once the distribution is obtained, the calculation of risk figures, such as Value-at-Risk (VAR) or Expected Shortfall, is a straightforward task.

Comparing operational risk management under Specification 1 and Specification 2, we observe that when there are no state- or path-dependent counter-measures there will be much higher potential losses. These losses are even larger than for the less effective counter-measures given in Specification 1*. As expected the naïve management largely underestimates risk compared to the sophisticated management. This highlights a most striking feature of operational risk: considering dependencies in a network increases risk contrary to the case of financial assets,

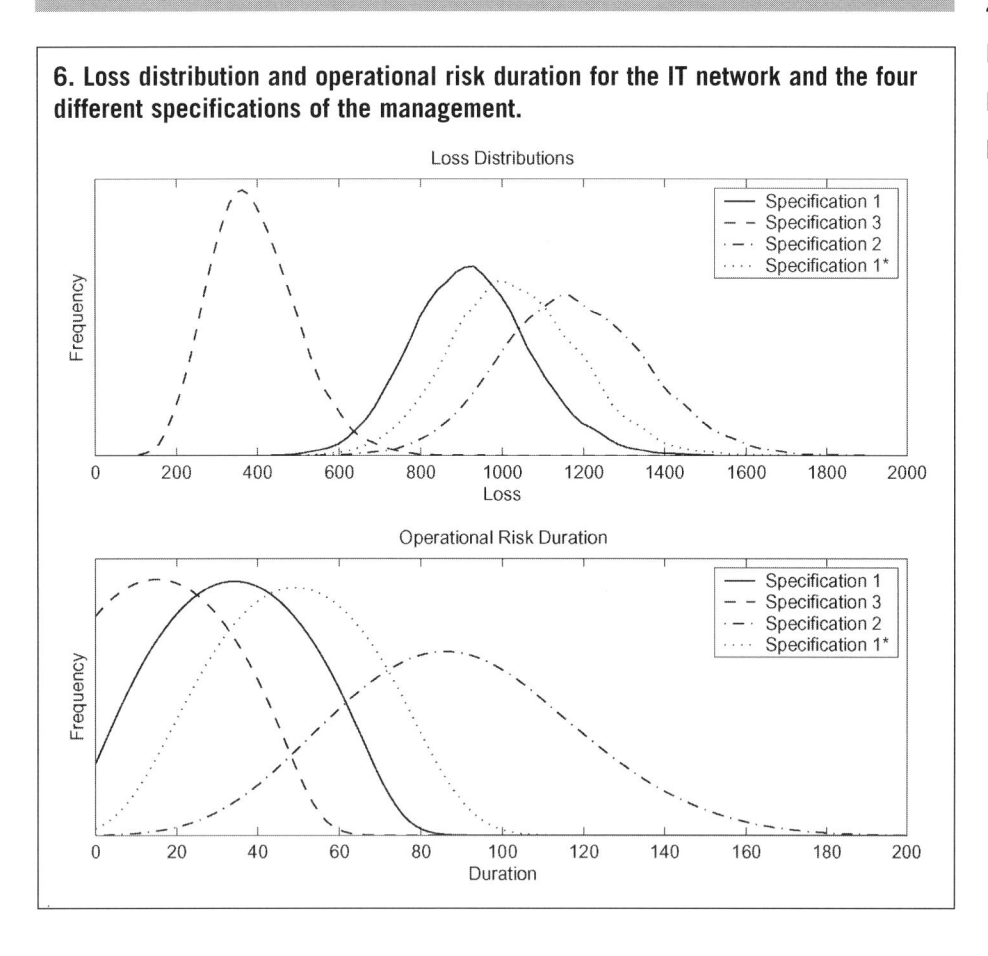

6. Loss distribution and operational risk duration for the IT network and the four different specifications of the management.

where a portfolio view on the dependence structure should lead to a lower risk. In other words, for operational risk *anti-diversification* holds.

In the lower panel of Figure 6 we plot the duration of operational risk for the four specifications. By our definition, the duration in each run is the sum over all nodes in the network of the maximum connected time length where the nodes are in the down state. Intuitively, if duration increases, the recovery time for broken down systems also increases. From such a duration point of view, the naïve management is closer to the sophisticated one's duration distribution compared to Specification 2 (no counter-measures). In the loss distribution panel, the conclusion is different: Specification 2 is closer to Specification 1 than Specification 3 is. Figure 7 shows these different findings using scatter plots.

In panel (A), neglection of counter-measures leads both to higher potential loss assumptions and higher recovery assumptions. Therefore, a management operating on a basis of Specification 2 has to consider in its planning larger operational risk losses and more time to recover the systems in a down state. This final point will affect the SLA – the operations department will charge a SLA-price to the buyer of the IT support activities, which are lower than the same department could charge using Specification 1.

In Figure 8 we consider the analysis on the individual node level. We choose the sophisticated Specification 1 as a benchmark.

In the upper panel, the loss differences show how the global underestimation of risk by the naïve management is distributed on the different nodes. The underestimation becomes particularly severe for system 11. This system has the highest degree, ie, the largest number of links, either incoming or outgoing. From a management point of view, this system is critical since a malfunctioning of this system leads to a breakdown in all values produced.

In the lower panel the duration has a maximum deviation from the benchmark not for system 11 but for number 15. Therefore, the duration or recovery of

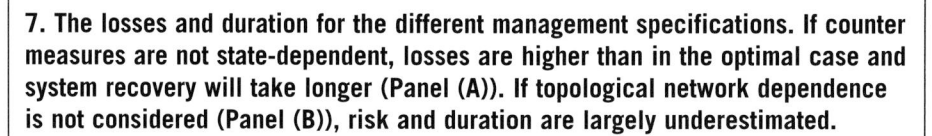

7. The losses and duration for the different management specifications. If counter measures are not state-dependent, losses are higher than in the optimal case and system recovery will take longer (Panel (A)). If topological network dependence is not considered (Panel (B)), risk and duration are largely underestimated.

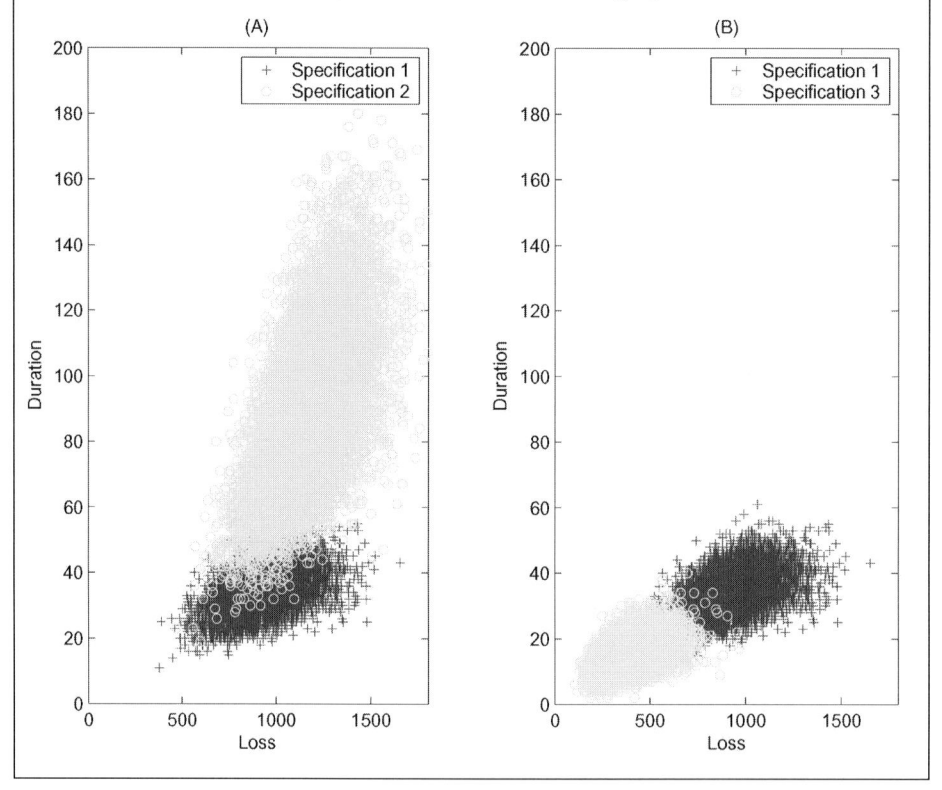

performance becomes a most severe management task not for the system with the highest degree, but for the system with the highest degree following the system with the highest global degree.

Conclusion

In summary, the discussion, which focused on the loss distribution and the duration, showed that some results of the simulation may well be in line with what one expects but others are not. This shows the inherent non-linear nature of operational risk defined properly on a network, where besides the traditional stochastic dependence structure, also a topological dependence holds.

As already noted, risk figures like VAR and Expected Shortfall can be easily derived, as all ingredients are available. What is in our opinion more important than the mere figures is the question which risk measure should one use. As Expected Shortfall and VAR collide for only a very restricted class of distribution functions, and the loss distribution for an IT network does certainly not belong to such a class due to the involved non-linearity and the anti-diversification, one certainly should base decisions such as capital allocation on a coherent risk measure.[7]

To conclude, the three specifications lead to the following insights about profitability. Relative to the sophisticated management, the manager, which considers the dependence structure seriously, but not the way counter-measures affect risk, ends up with a too pessimistic operational risk profile and too high planning costs to maintain the network's performance. Therefore, too much risk capital for operational risk is kept and profitability of the value chain is lower than it could be. The naïve management, which contrary to the sophisticated one neglects the dependence structure, will disclose an unrealistic high profitability. Furthermore, the risk capital will not cover the worst-case losses at the risk acceptance level chosen by the naïve management.

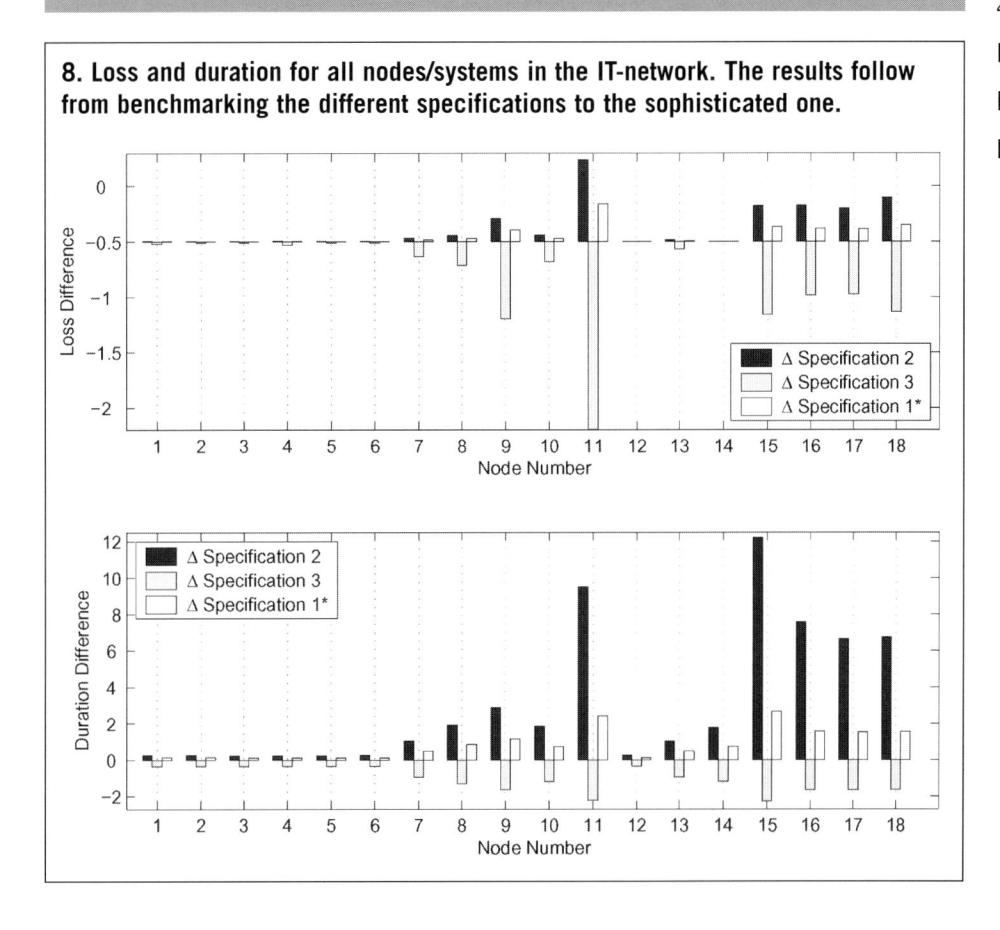

8. Loss and duration for all nodes/systems in the IT-network. The results follow from benchmarking the different specifications to the sophisticated one.

1 *The following article does not reflect the view of the Swiss National Bank.*
2 *The following article does not reflect the view of Zurich Cantonal Bank.*
3 *There seems to be modest increase in operational risk losses in the last years. But given the importance the topic attracts, this increase is more likely a biased perception than an evidence for a true increase in operational risk.*
4 *Broadly speaking, value chains address business processes for planning, design, production, marketing and delivery of the bank's products and services.*
5 *Since the authors assume that a node can be in only two states, ie either running and down, a configuration is then an element of $\{0,1\}^K$ if the states are denoted with 0 and 1, respectively and if there are K nodes affecting the node i (where i is self-affecting by definition).*
6 *If counter-measures are neglected and processes reduced to point objects the example reduces to the model of Kühn and Neu (2002).*
7 *For coherent risk measures and their definition, see Artzner et al. (1999).*

BIBLIOGRAPHY

Artzner, P.H., F. Delbaen, J.-M. Eber and D. Heath, 1999, "Coherent Measures of Risk", *Mathematical Finance* 9, pp. 203–28.

BIS, 2001, Basel Committee on Banking Supervision, "Consultative Document", The New Basel Capital Accord [Available online at: http://www.bis.org.]

BIS, Risk Management Group of the Basel Committee on Banking Supervision, 2001, "Regulatory Treatment of Operational Risk", Working Paper.

BIS, 2003, Basel Committee on Banking Supervision, "3rd Consultative Document", The New Basel Capital Accord.

Ebnöther, S., 2001, "Quantitative Aspects of Operational Risk", Diploma Thesis, ETH Zürich.

Ebnöther, S., P. Vanini, A. McNeil, and P. Antolinez, 2003, "Operational Risk: A Practitioners View", *The Journal of Risk*, 5(3), 1–18.

Ebnöther, S., M. Leippold and P. Vanini, 2003, "Operational Risk: Theory and Application", Preprint.

Embrechts, P., R. Kaufmann, and G. Samorodnitsky, 2002, "Ruin Theory Revisited: Stochastic Models for Operational Risk", Preprint ETH Zurich.

Frachot, A., P. Georges, and T. Roncalli, 2000, "Loss Distribution Approach for Operational Risk", Working Paper, Credit Lyonnais.

Kahnemann, D. and A. Tversky, 1974, "Judgment under uncertainty: Heuristics and Biases", *Science* 185(4157): pp. 1124–31.

Kühn, R. and P. Neu, 2002, "Functional Correlation Approach to Operational Risk in Banking Organizations", forthcoming in Physics Review E.

Nystrom, K. and J. Skoglund, 2002, "Quantitative Operational Risk Management", Preprint.

Rabin, M., 1998, "Psychology and Economics", *Journal of Economic Literature*, XXXVI, 11–46.

16

The Legal and Regulatory View of Operational Risk*

Dermot Turing

Clifford Chance LLP

The proposals issued by the Basel Committee for capital charges for operational risks build on the Committee's recommendations for management of operational risk. It is disappointing, therefore, that the methodology for calculating regulatory capital will give little credit for effective operational risk management procedures. Legal issues pervade the operational issues, which are targeted by Basel for attention by banks. The Basel proposals also require that legal risks are included on the agenda for operational risk management: legal risks raise special issues, which require a tailored approach. Banks will be allowed to use insurance to reduce the operational risk capital charge – and banks will need to be aware of, and avoid, the pitfalls of using insurance as a risk-reduction tool.

Introduction

The Basel Committee on banking supervision has set the agenda for consideration of operational risk by financial institutions. Not only have the Committee issued numerous papers on the subject, but the main influence which changes banks' behaviour – regulatory capital – will include an operational risk capital component once the Basel II capital proposals are brought into force. Changing behaviour by weighting capital so as to minimise credit and market risks is familiar, so why not use the same philosophy in relation to operational risk?

The Basel Committee has listed 10 principles, that summarise best practice for dealing with operational risk, which are directed at financial institutions and their supervisors (see Panel 1 for summary – NB this Panel is a précis rather than the full detail).[1]

These principles prompt the following questions:

❏ What definition of "operational risk" will supervisors use?
❏ How will the Basel II capital requirements implement these principles?
❏ What risk mitigation techniques will be recognised?

Basel has defined operational risk (rather vaguely) as "the risk of loss resulting from inadequate or failed internal processes, people, and systems or from external events". We are also told "The definition includes legal risk but excludes strategic and reputational risk". This, to be brutally frank, is so broad as to be totally unhelpful. There is nothing here to exclude credit or market risk, which clearly fall into other buckets of risk managed separately within the Basel programme. How, for example,

---

* *The views expressed here are those of the author and not those of Clifford Chance.*

THE LEGAL AND REGULATORY VIEW OF OPERATIONAL RISK

> ### PANEL 1
>
> ### THE BASEL COMMITTEE'S 2003 PRINCIPLES
>
> **Risk management environment**
> - The Board of directors should be aware that operational risks need managing as a distinct risk category, and should periodically review the bank's framework for managing operational risk. The framework should set out how operational risk is *identified, assessed, monitored and mitigated/controlled*. The Board should ensure that the framework is internally audited. Internal audit should not be responsible for management of operational risk.
> - Senior management (below the Board) should be accountable for implementing the framework, and develop *policies/processes/procedures* to manage operational risk across the bank's *products, activities, processes and systems*. Staff at all levels should understand their responsibilities as regards operational risk management.
>
> **Identification, assessment, monitoring, mitigation/control**
> - Banks should *identify* and *assess* operational risk in products, activities, processes and systems, particularly new products, etc.
> - Banks should *monitor* operational risk profiles and exposures to losses. Information facilitating proactive operational risk management should be regularly reported to senior management and the Board.
> - Banks should have *policies/processes/procedures* to *control/mitigate* operational risk. Banks should periodically review risk limitation and control strategies.
> - Banks should have contingency and business continuity plans.
>
> **Role of supervisors**
> - Supervisors should require banks to have an effective framework to *identify, assess, monitor, and control/mitigate* operational risk.
> - Supervisors should evaluate a bank's *policies/procedures/practices* in relation to operational risks, and ensure they are apprised of developments.
>
> **Disclosure**
> - Banks should make sufficient public disclosure to allow market participants to assess their approach to operational risk management.

is a borrower default, or a reduction of interest rates in Peru, not an "external event"? Here are some alternative formulations:

- The risk that deficiencies in information systems or internal controls will result in unexpected loss (UL) (an old Basel formulation)
- The risk that a firm will suffer loss as a result of human error or deficiencies in systems or controls (an old International Organisation of Securities Commissions (IOSCO) formulation)
- The risk run by a firm that its internal practices, policies and systems are not rigorous or sophisticated enough to cope with untoward market conditions or human or technological errors (JPMorgan/*Risk* Magazine "Guide to Risk Management")
- Risk of loss resulting from errors in the processing of transactions/breakdown in controls/errors or failures in systems support (Global Association of Risk Professionals – GARP)

THE LEGAL AND REGULATORY VIEW OF OPERATIONAL RISK

> **PANEL 2**
>
> ### THE BASEL COMMITTEE'S LIST OF OPERATIONAL RISK EVENTS WHICH CAN RESULT IN SUBSTANTIAL LOSSES[2]
>
> - *Internal fraud* eg, intentional misreporting of positions, employee theft, and insider trading on an employee's own account.
> - *External fraud* eg, robbery, forgery, cheque kiting, and damage from computer hacking.
> - *Employment practices and workplace safety* eg, workers compensation claims, violation of employee health and safety rules, organised labour activities, discrimination claims, and general liability.
> - *Clients, products and business practices* eg, fiduciary breaches, misuse of confidential customer information, improper trading activities on the bank's account, money laundering, and sale of unauthorised products.
> - *Damage to physical assets* eg, terrorism, vandalism, earthquakes, fires and floods.
> - *Business disruption and system failures* eg, hardware and software failures, telecommunication problems, and utility outages.
> - *Execution, delivery and process management* eg, data entry errors, collateral management failures, incomplete legal documentation, unapproved access given to client accounts, non-client counterparty misperformance, and vendor disputes.

- Everything other than market and credit risk (Basel again – though Basel acknowledge that there has been no universally agreed definition, hence their attempt to stamp their new formula into our collective consciousness).

To be fair to the Basel legislators, there are various key risks that they are trying to encapsulate, which are of course those things that we all recognise to be operational risks (see Panel 2). Plus of course they have changed their mind about the focus of the definition. Legal risk is not explicitly in the list; this is considered later in this chapter.

Operational risk is a collection of concepts that are not amenable to a single policy for management, or indeed reduction of regulatory capital.

How will the Basel Programme be implemented in practice?

The new Basel programme will impose a capital charge on banks for operational risk. There are three ways this may happen:

1. Banks can opt for a "Basic Indicator Approach", under which a bank will have to have capital equating to 15% of its average gross annual income for the previous three years. No recognition will be given for implementing effective operational risk management or controls.
2. Banks can opt for a "Standardised Approach", which sets a different percentage for each of eight business lines, and requires capital equal to the aggregate of [average gross income for the previous three years]*[percentage] for each of the eight business lines. The business lines and percentages are indicated in Table 1.

    No recognition will be given for implementing effective operational risk management or controls. Alarmingly, some business lines are penalised relative to the Basic Indicator Approach.
3. Banks can opt (but once done, cannot go back) for an "Advanced Management Approach" or "AMA". Essentially this requires the bank to have an approved

operational risk measurement model. The qualifying criteria for a model are listed in Panel 3. But once again, no recognition will be given for implementing effective operational risk management or controls unless these manifest themselves in the figures generated by the model. The qualification criteria may be thought to give little credit to techniques used by banks to spot control lapses and rectify errors.

Table 1.

Business Line	%
Corporate finance	18
Trading and sales	18
Retail banking	12
Commercial banking	15
Payment and settlement	18
Agency services	15
Asset management	12
Retail brokerage	12

Banks that wish to opt for the Standardised Approach or AMA will have to satisfy various regulatory requirements. These are additional to the requirements that an acceptable AMA model must satisfy.

a. The bank must have an operational risk management system with clear responsibilities assigned to an operational risk management function. The operational risk management function is responsible for developing strategies to identify, assess, monitor and control/mitigate operational risk; for codifying firm-level policies and procedures concerning operational risk management and controls; for the design and implementation of the firm's operational risk assessment methodology; and for the design and implementation of a risk-reporting system for operational risk.

b. As part of the bank's internal operational risk assessment system, the bank must systematically track relevant operational risk data including material losses by business line. Its operational risk assessment system must be closely integrated into the risk management processes of the bank. Its output must be an integral part of the process of monitoring and controlling the bank operational risk profile. For instance, this information must play a prominent role in risk reporting, management reporting, and risk analysis. The bank must have techniques for creating incentives to improve the management of operational risk throughout the firm.

c. There must be regular reporting of operational risk exposures, including material operational losses, to business unit management, senior management, and to the board of directors. The bank must have procedures for taking appropriate action according to the information within the management reports.

d. The bank's operational risk management system must be well documented. The bank must have a routine in place for ensuring compliance with a documented set of internal policies, controls and procedures concerning the operational risk management system, which must include policies for the treatment of non-compliance issues.

e. The bank's operational risk management processes and assessment system must be subject to validation and regular independent review. These reviews must include both the activities of the business units and of the operational risk management function.

These five precepts also apply where the bank is using an AMA, though the standards under each of them are slightly higher. Where an AMA is used, the bank must also comply with one further standard:

f. The validation of the operational risk measurement system by external auditors and/or supervisory authorities must include the following:
  ❏ Verifying that the internal validation processes are operating in a satisfactory manner; and
  ❏ Making sure that data flows and processes associated with the risk

measurement system are transparent and accessible. In particular, it is necessary that auditors and supervisory authorities be in a position to have easy access, whenever they judge it necessary and under appropriate procedures, to the systems's specifications and parameters.

Quantifying and reducing operational risk

Evidently the starting-point for any bank wishing to reduce the operational risk capital charge under the new Basel regime is to develop a model which satisfies these objectives, at the heart of which will be the capture of quantitative data to measure operational risks. How are we to quantify operational risks? Value at Risk (VAR) techniques do not exist, so old-school banks that still think of "risk management" as the clever stuff with equations done by Black-Scholes pupils in relation to market risk will struggle to see how it is done.

One method is to examine your profit and loss (P&L) account. When an operational risk event occurs it will manifest itself, in some form, as a reduction of profits or a cash loss. The real problem here is capturing the data and reshaping it as a metric for operational risks. For example, if I, as an external lawyer, send a bill to a client for helping them clear up an operational risk problem (such as the consequences of a control failure in relation to a particular product line), that is

---

PANEL 3

QUALIFYING CRITERIA FOR AMA MODELS

1. A bank's operational risk measure must meet a soundness standard comparable to the one year holding period and 99.9% confidence interval standard applicable to credit risk models.
2. The system must be consistent with the scope of operational risk as defined in the Basel definition and the loss event types set out in Panel 2.
3. The regulatory capital requirement is the sum of expected loss (EL) and UL, unless the bank can demonstrate that it is capturing EL in its internal business practices.
4. A bank's risk measurement system must be sufficiently granular to capture the major drivers of operational risk affecting the shape of the tail of the loss estimates.
5. Risk measures for different operational risk estimates must be added. Internally determined correlations may be acceptable subject to additional criteria.
6. Internal data, external data, scenario analysis and business environment/internal control factors must be used. In particular:
   - Internally generated operational risk measures must be based on a minimum five-year observation period of internal loss data (except when a bank first moves to the AMA when a three-year window is acceptable).
   - The bank must have objective criteria for allocating losses to specific business lines and event types.
   - Excluded activities and exposures have to be justified.
   - A *de minimis* (EUR 10,000 is suggested) threshold for small losses that are ignored is required.
   - Qualitative information about the cause of the loss must be captured.
   - Operational risk losses associated with credit risk (eg, collateral management failures) count as credit risk for capital purposes but must be recorded as operational risk.
   - Scenario analysis should be used to assess the impact of deviations from correlation assumptions, and the assessments validated over time by comparison with actual loss experience.

THE LEGAL AND REGULATORY VIEW OF OPERATIONAL RISK

easily seen in the accounts; but I was assisting three internal employees who had been pulled off other tasks to deal with this problem, and there will be at least an opportunity cost to my client for doing so – but there is no specific ledger or journal entry in the accounts which picks this up. Yet, via their salaries, the electricity bill, rent and so forth, this opportunity cost is there in the P&L. Debate continues about which components "count" for the purposes of operational risk management.

To rely on your own historical loss data may be unreliable and also masochistic. Your own loss data may under-represent defects in your controls and fail to bring out latent problems (eg, consider the loss profile of mis-sold pension schemes in the UK during the 1990s). Plus, if you have already suffered a major loss you would be unwise not to have changed your controls to prevent further losses. So historic loss data are an unwieldy tool. To deal with unreliability various providers offer databanks or information that provide benchmarks against which banks can assess their own historic loss profiles, but these are open to the objection that your bank may manage operational risk more cautiously than others.

But beware over-reliance on statistical methods of measuring operational risks:

❑ Data sets bought in from other institutions will be unreliable, because the frequency of operational risk events is directly related to the effectiveness of that institution's controls (or rather the absence of them). Industry averages may be helpful but they are rough guides only.

❑ Data sets from a single institution are unlikely to be large enough to be statistically significant. To get enough data you probably have to go back over many years. Can you be sure that the data-capture is good enough, and that the same thing has been measured over the whole sample period (eg, that controls did not change)?

❑ Few fat-tail operational risks are sufficiently frequent to be susceptible to this quasi-statistical approach.

❑ Choosing which parameters to quantify and correlate is almost as hard as getting reliable data sets.

Reducing operational risk and the capital charge

At the time of writing, it appears as if the new Basel programme looks, on this basis, to be fairly hostile to traditional methods of managing operational risk. What credit does a bank get for managing its operational risks in accordance with best practice? The bank's capital will be determined (on the Basic Indicator Approach or the Standardised Approach) in an arbitrary manner, or (on the AMA) by reference to historical events, which the bank has put behind it. Of course some external events are not amenable to controls, but surely some regulatory capital benefit should follow if controls are in place and properly policed by internal audit?

Two further features of the new Basel programme may reduce this criticism, though both apply only to the AMA.

❑ Key business environment and internal control factors, which can change a bank's operational risk profile, will be recognised as risk reducing. To qualify for regulatory capital purposes, the use of controls and business factors must meet certain standards. These relate to relevance, quantifiability, and sensitivity to change, audit and validation. Because of the focus on quantification, the "factors" may not, depending on how local supervisors interpret the Basel guidance, allow for reduction of capital charges where a bank feels that a newly introduced control system is effective.

❑ Insurance will also be recognised as risk reducing for up to 20% of the total operational risk capital charge. To qualify for regulatory capital purposes, insurance must be:

- provided from at least a single-A rated unaffiliated provider;

- for a term of at least a year or the risk-reduction will itself be reduced proportionately;
- explicitly mapped to the operational risk loss exposure of the bank; and
- disclosed.

There are also various contractual requirements that qualifying insurance policies must satisfy:

- a minimum notice period for cancellation; and
- no exclusions or limitations based on regulatory action or insolvency affecting the bank.

Insurance raises a number of particular issues of which operational risk managers should be aware: these are considered later in this chapter.

Finally, because banks may not be able to implement an AMA across all business lines immediately, banks can use an AMA for some lines and the Basic Indicator Approach or Standardised Approach for the rest.

Capital adequacy is, however, only one of the tools commended by the Basel Committee, and Basel do expect supervisors to exercise regulatory power in other ways. Pillar 2 of the new Basel Accord ("Supervisory Review") is a series of guiding principles for supervisors to assess the risk profiles of banks more generally. Bank regulators are therefore likely to have regard to the Basel Committee's "Sound Practices for the Management and Supervision of Operational Risk", which include evaluation of banks' risk management processes, control environment, monitoring and reporting systems, audit, risk mitigation techniques (including insurance), disaster recovery plans, and so forth.

The business issues that consistently feature in regulatory papers on operational risk each have legal and regulatory aspects in regard to risk mitigation or raise points of legal and regulatory risk.

BUSINESS CONTINUITY

The events of 11 September 2001 have drawn particular attention to the importance of business continuity procedures. The legal aspects of this have not been ignored and feature in various studies, including a UK Treasury consultation.[3] Issues to consider are whether market participants should adopt a common policy to whether contracts are to be closed out or treated as in default if deliveries or payments due under them cannot be performed. It may be difficult to know immediately if non-performance is attributable only to the disruption, or whether the disruption has also caused a credit event in relation to the counterparty. Parties may wish to make use of *force majeure* clauses or treat the days of disruption as not amounting to "business days" as defined in their documentation. Moreover, regulatory authorities may have overriding powers to close markets or to impose public holidays at short notice.

OUTSOURCING

In the UK, the Financial Services Authority (FSA) already imposes requirements on banks wishing to outsource critical services to a supplier.[4] These include detailed specifications for service level agreements and a checklist of points to watch (and contract for) in dealing with suppliers.

EMPLOYMENT PRACTICES

Again the FSA imposes a variety of requirements that impact on the HR function, including rules relating to hiring of staff, training, fitness for certain roles, and a set of statutory principles and a code of conduct for "approved persons".[5] These requirements do not lay down terms and conditions for employees or restrict firms' compensation policies; but regulators are aware of the incentives that flow from a bonus culture and may consider these among the "factors" that influence the reduction of the operational risk capital charge.

COLLATERAL
The variety of operational, contractual and legal factors at work in relation to collateral management is well known. On the legal front, there are numerous legal risks, some (but not all) of which will be reduced when the European Union (EU) Collateral Directive is implemented in EU member states with effect from late December 2003. And from a regulatory perspective, there is now a requirement in the UK for collateral arrangements that are relied on to reduce credit-related capital charges to be supported by legal opinions stating that the collateral arrangements are well-founded in all relevant jurisdictions.[6]

MERGERS
Integration of business practices involves choosing between rival systems, including use of historic documentation that might no longer be compatible with the way business is done. Added to this are factors related to the complex legal structure of groups of companies: a merger may affect the regulatory licensing requirements of different subsidiaries whose business lines are to be integrated, requiring not just systems and personnel changes but a root and branch re-evaluation of everything that the merged institutions do and how they do it.

IT RESOURCES
Although in one sense doing business using computers is no different from dealing by any other means – people did not have to re-evaluate their operational risks when fax replaced telex – there are some particular issues to consider. Remote access brings security and authentication issues. Data protection laws restrict the information that may be held or transmitted across borders. Banks are dependent on suppliers of equipment, software, and facilities maintenance services for the services they themselves supply. All of these matters require management, often through the use of effective documentation.

Legal risk
The new Basel regime will include legal risk within the definition of operational risk. Fitting legal risk within the new Basel framework poses special challenges. Legal risks may not parcel up readily into the business lines laid down by the Basel Committee.

Legal risk is the risk that one is unable to enforce rights against, or rely on obligations incurred by, a counterparty in the event of a default or a dispute. An old Basel/IOSCO definition states it slightly differently, namely, the risk that contracts are not legally enforceable or documented correctly. This is a useful formulation because it highlights a common problem, namely that personnel responsible for the business line believe contractual rights and obligations to be such-and-such, whereas in practice they are not. This may be attributed to a variety of causes:

❏ There may have been no effective agreement with the other party – eg "headline" terms may have been agreed, but there may have been no agreement on the detail. For example, what precisely was envisaged when they said they'd sell the "swaps business"? Misunderstandings and communications failures are key – and avoidance of them is why legal negotiations take so long and legal documents are rarely a fun read.

❏ There may have been a documentation failure – in that key terms were not recorded, or that documentation lags behind trade execution (a problem to which the International Swaps and Derivatives Association (ISDA) has drawn attention).[7]

❏ The contract may be challengeable because the counterparty was misled in entering into it. The "suitability" problem where banks sold mysteriously structured swaps to customers that had unsophisticated treasury departments, and were met by defences when they tried to claim their gains, is an example.
❏ The contract terms may not actually work, or may not work in specified circumstances. The causes of unenforceability are many, but examples include:
  (a) because the counterparty does not have capacity to enter into the obligation, such as, eg, the notorious UK Local Authority swaps cases of the 1980s;
  (b) because there is a statutory rule invalidating the clause, such as "exclusion clauses", are deemed unenforceable under certain conditions under the Unfair Contract Terms Act 1977;
  (c) because the rights are not recognised in the place where the rights are valuable; and
  (d) because of supervening events such as insolvency, which affects the ability to rely on or enforce contractual rights.
❏ The contract terms as written down may be fine in themselves but other terms may be "implied" into the agreement, which have the effect of changing the balance of rights and obligations.

One further point to remember about legal risk is that focusing on contractual rights and obligations is good, but only part of the story. Other legal rights and obligations that should come into the analysis are property rights (do I own it?), duties and obligations under tort or statute (eg, obligations not to damage other people's property, or to mimic their products, or to libel them, or to injure them in the workplace), and the criminal law (eg, non-compliance with anti-money-laundering requirements).

The purpose of a document is to manage the risks. Points to consider in contracts include:

Obligations. Which party shall do what, when and how. (It is no good saying "The company shall be entitled to receive US$1 million" unless the payer is identified. It does not always follow that the other party is the payer, and some agreements have many parties.)

What-ifs. Imagine the worst. (If all goes well, you may never look at the document again, which implies that you will only need it if all goes badly. So the careful draftsman has to consider the things that may go wrong and their implications.) This means more obligations, or at least invocation of remedies.

Remedies. No obligation is worth anything unless you are prepared to stand up for yourself in the event of non-performance. A counterparty who will discuss remedies should not be thought of as a counterparty who is getting ready to renege. Consider the options: non-inception ("condition precedent"); termination; damages; non-renewal; forget the whole thing and start again ("rescission"); special arrangements agreed between the parties. Courts rarely award injunctions or specific performance (ie, compel a party to perform) where damages would be an adequate remedy.

Clauses that don't always work. Sometimes one wants to achieve a particular result (a three-way set-off, for example) where it is known that there are circumstances where the courts would not give effect to the contract term needed. This can make people reluctant to include the clause. But it is quite rare for courts to strike down the whole agreement simply because you included a clause that doesn't always work, for example, if the offensive part can be cut out without leaving the remainder meaningless. If the clause is central to the agreement so that there is nothing of substance left, then the whole contract may fail.

THE LEGAL AND REGULATORY VIEW OF OPERATIONAL RISK

Governing law clauses. Cross-border problems can often be simplified by using a governing law clause: this will identify the legal system by which the rights and liabilities of the parties will be determined and the contract will be interpreted. However, an express choice of law does not fix all cross-border legal problems. By choosing the law of X you do not cause all legal problems to be sorted by the law of X. So a choice of law clause cannot relocate property in jurisdiction X, cause the parties to be incorporated in jurisdiction X, or require the performance of the contractual obligation in jurisdiction X and all these places may be just as relevant in order to obtain enforceable rights under the contract. Further, courts may consider that a system of law was chosen improperly if it has nothing to do with the parties or the subject matter of the contract and the effect of the choice is to evade some rule of law which apply if a more relevant system had been chosen. Courts may also override the chosen system of law in other cases, eg, where insolvency strikes, or for policy reasons.

Master agreements – Failure to agree (and sign, as evidence of agreement including approval at the appropriate level of authority) master agreements may distort the firm's exposure to counterparties, since netting may not be effective without an agreement. Including words such as "subject to the terms of the ISDA master agreement" in a confirmation gives some legal protection, but not much. Agreeing some, but not all, of the terms may not be good enough, eg, failure to agree the parts of an ISDA schedule which require an election between alternatives to be made may leave the agreement unenforceable under a relevant legal system.

Confirmations – Failure to generate a confirmation may, in some legal systems, mean that there is no enforceable agreement. Written confirmations may therefore be of more than evidential value. But even evidence is useful, albeit tedious to compile. Written confirmations and automatic matching systems also help the control process, enabling errors and limit breaches to be detected. Quantitative measures of exposures and risks are no more reliable than the records on which they are based. Disputed confirmations can lead to mis-reporting or even non-reporting.

The new Basel programme probably goes further than documentation risk. Other issues to consider are how to measure legal risk, and how to impose controls or other strategies for reducing risk.

Identifying historical losses arising from legal risk events may be achievable. The most readily identifiable losses will be those that connect to cash payments made when a dispute arose and the firm lost. Simply looking at judgement awards or out-of-court settlement payments made will often be misleading, though cases are frequently settled because of their "nuisance value" rather than because of true legal vulnerability, and legal risks arise in cases where there is no dispute or adverse judgement. It seems likely that regulators will consider nuisance-value settlements to be part and parcel of everyday operational risk, and will not enquire too closely whether the losses are "legal risk" or some other sub-species of operational risk. The more subtle forms of legal risk losses are those where danger was spotted and averted, at some cost (re-negotiating a transaction, for example).

Controls and reduction strategies for legal risk are in place in most banks, but they are hardly quantitative in nature. Insofar as the new Basel programme recognises only quantitative risk-reduction techniques, lawyers responsible for legal risk management will face significant challenges. Lawyers hate to quantify risks; lawyers and numbers rarely mix well. New transactions requiring "legal sign-off" are, however, often treated as black-and-white judgements, where the deal is either completely safe or completely unsafe. Is a more graduated approach to legal risk management feasible?

It is becoming more common for lawyers to sift risks more finely than the traditional yes-or-no boxes: low, medium and high risk for example. But lawyers would still rather list the factors at work and leave it to the business line to assess the likelihood of the potential problems they have identified coming to light. Lawyers can help assess the general legal environment in different countries – legal risks are often higher in countries with less well-developed legal systems or where political risk is high.

Legal opinions may also help in the process of assessing legal risk. The traditional reason for a legal opinion is to identify (rather than erase) legal risks, but it is unlikely to control them. The controls have to come elsewhere (restructure or reprice the deal, or don't do it at all). Some firms regard the legal opinion as the solution to legal risks – they are credit-enhancing the deal with a lawyer's sign-off.

The structure of a formal legal opinion differs according to its author. But, hidden amongst the verbiage, these features will normally be present:

❏ *Terms of reference*. These set out the background against which counsel have been asked to opine, eg, a description of the transaction or (where a generic opinion on a standard form document is required but counsel does not know the identity of the parties) the reasons for producing the opinion.
❏ *Assumptions*. Assumptions emasculate opinions. The opinion does not apply if the actual fact-pattern is not covered by the assumptions. Counsel will therefore assume all sorts of things to stop themselves getting into trouble. Some assumptions are hardly going to cause alarm unless fraud is going on (eg, that the copy documents conform to originals or that the signatures are genuine). Others are more important (eg, that the documents work under some other system of law). Assumptions should always be points of fact or foreign law. If counsel is uncertain on a point of their own law, the point should generally be dealt with as a qualification not an assumption.
❏ *The opinion itself*. Counsel will keep this short and vague. Clients will want it long and thorough.
❏ *Qualifications or reservations*. There will be various circumstances in which the opinion might be unreliable. There may also be particular legal risks mentioned by the client which counsel has been asked to address even though counsel considers that the risks do not arise. These points are generally addressed in qualifications. Qualifications are most helpful if they set out in full what the problem is, how serious it is and what steps can be taken to minimise the risk. Look out for bankruptcy qualifications (eg, "this opinion is subject to laws relating to insolvency, winding-up etc" or "the rights of the parties may be affected if bankruptcy occurs"). Counsel traditionally used to include one of these in anything they wrote about. But opinions needed for counterparty and credit risk management purposes are useless with a bankruptcy qualification. You are most likely to need to enforce certain types of agreement (eg, collateral arrangements) when a bankruptcy event occurs. Counsel dislike giving bankruptcy-proof opinions because contractual obligations are in danger of being invalidated for a whole range of reasons on bankruptcy.

Legal opinions are far from comforting. They identify risks. What they rarely do is rank risks in categories of seriousness. Legal risks may not be deal-breakers. If counsel has identified a risk they can usually be pushed to indicate how serious a risk it is, even if they won't do so in the opinion. Ask counsel for an advisory side-letter on the manner of mitigating the risk (or confirmation of their advice that the risk is slender.) Counsel rarely have historical statistics so it is often pointless to ask them "is it a 50 or a 5% chance?". But counsel do have information about the types of case that go before the court and should be willing to say "to the best of our information there are no reported cases in this jurisdiction in which this argument has been raised".

This may make the process of using external counsel and legal opinions as a "factor" for reducing the operational risk capital charge a difficult one. In current practice, legal opinions are used to alter the capital consequences of different credit risk management techniques (eg, supporting netting or collateral). The process is approximately as follows: counsel produces an opinion; the risks identified in the "qualifications" section of the opinion are assessed, usually by internal counsel working with the business line concerned; if those risks are assessed to be of negligible practical impact (essentially low probability risk events) the arrangement is deemed to "work"; and the capital benefit is obtained. With operational risks, the range of matters on which counsel may be asked to opine may become wider, and it may be much harder to assign risk events to negligible probability buckets. The extent to which regulators find legal opinions a useful "factor" remains to be worked out when the new Basel programme becomes bedded down.

Insurance

Insurance companies can measure some operational risks much better than individual firms, because they see the effects of risk events over a large number of institutions and can therefore aggregate data and calculate probabilities more realistically. Individual institutions, unless they are very large and have very good data capture facilities, are unlikely to be able to do so. Larger institutions may prefer to self-insure against some operational risks. Some of the drawbacks include:

❏ Added bureaucracy in gathering information internally about risk events and losses: without data capture you cannot be said to be "managing" the risk at all and no effective control strategy can be devised;
❏ Staff reluctance to discuss operational failings may be less apparent where some outsider appears to pick up the bill – reporting to an outsider may be perceived by individuals to be less damaging;
❏ Insurance premiums may be priced arbitrarily or competitively and outside insurance may therefore be cheaper for some risks or across a portfolio of risks.

Insurance is one means of managing various types of operational risks, in particular risks of external origin over which the firm may have little control. Some firms shy away from purchasing insurance for risks that are within their control – there is perhaps something disreputable about suggesting that the risk is not fully controlled? Where the risk arises in the course of a business activity that is central to the firm's profitability, this feeling will be particularly strong. But some risks (in particular, perpetrators of fraud) will find a way round all controls. A second line of defence may be prudence rather than admission of failure. Where one-off risks are involved, rather than recurrent risks, insurance can smooth the effect on the P & L account.

On the other hand, insurance may not be the right answer for the business, even if it helps manage regulatory capital. It may be better risk management to have a contingency plan as well as, or instead of, insurance. Bomb damage recovery is better done with immediate off-site back-up than a fat payout two years after the event. It is not possible to eliminate all business risk through insurance.

There are particular legal issues with insurance policies, even before the Basel strictures on policy eligibility:

❏ There is a duty to disclose everything to the insurer that the insurer could regard as relevant to the risk he is assuming. Failure to disclose results in an unenforceable policy. And the insurer will only start mentioning non-disclosures when he investigates a claim. Where group policies are concerned, who is responsible for disclosures and who has the information that ought to be disclosed?
❏ Unless special arrangements are made, insurers who pay up on liability insurance

policies have the right to defend claims bought by third parties. This includes the right to fight or achieve a settlement regardless of the firm's wishes or the reputational cost involved.
- ❏ The insured is not saved from the obligation to mitigate losses if a risk event occurs. Only the loss that reasonably flowed from the event will be recoverable, so failure to mitigate will reduce the amount of the claim as well as complicate and delay the payout by the insurer. Insurance policies are not like performance bonds or letters of credit – there is no practice of immediate payment against documents in the insurance market.
- ❏ Where there is more than one policy covering the same loss:
  - Both policies could be inapplicable, because of a term to that effect in each of them; and
  - If both insurers are liable there will be delay and a dispute as to which should pay.
- ❏ Policy wording is sometimes arcane, old-fashioned and inapplicable to the risks that you are trying to manage.
- ❏ Exclusions from policies can cover a wide range of issues but can include: losses caused by fraud and malice; personal injury and death; fines; remuneration claims; deliberate breaches of contract by the firm; lost or damaged property; advice; and loss in value of investments.

Insurance is a means of converting operational risk into credit risk; and this is a risk that itself should be managed. Investment banks are offering products that perform economically in a similar way to insurance. In those cases there would be no question about assessing the credit status of the counterparty. Insurers should be treated similarly; where a Lloyd's policy is involved, the availability of Lloyd's default backing should be checked. Likewise consider whether any credit risk on the *broker* is involved – to whom are the premiums paid and through whom are claims submitted and paid?

Conclusions

The new Basel programme for operational risk capital charges will make the regulator's view of operational risk management a main driver in every bank from now on. As well as detailed regulatory rules, there are legal issues to consider affecting all operational issues considered important by Basel. Unfortunately, the legal component of operational risk remains vaguely expressed at present, and it is difficult to gauge the impact that legal risk management will have in the framework. Banks can expect a certain degree of interpretation to overlay the new Basel Accord when regulators transpose the Accord into regulatory rules.

In particular, it is uncertain how much credit against the new capital charge for operational risk will be given to banks that have rigorous and effective internal controls. This of course is nothing new: the existing Basel Accord measures credit risk crudely and gives little in the way of benefits to banks that manage credit risk effectively. In practice banks manage credit risk independently of the rules, but use the rules relating to capital proactively but as a separate exercise. The lesson that emerges is that the new capital rules for operational risk will require a process of adjustment, but once they settle in then banks will live with them but not feel compelled to change their operational risk management practices unless a significant capital benefit follows.

1 *Basel Committee on Banking Supervision, 2003, "Sound Practices for the Management and Supervision of Operational Risk", Bank for International Settlements paper No. 96, February.*
2 *Basel Committee on Banking Supervision, 2003, "Sound Practices for the*

Management and Supervision of Operational Risk", Bank for International Settlements paper No. 96, February.

3 H M Treasury, 2003, "The financial system and major operational disruption", Green Paper, February.

4 Financial Services Authority, Handbook of Rules and Guidance, Interim Prudential Sourcebook for Banks, chapter OS.

5 Financial Services Authority, Handbook of Rules and Guidance, Systems and Controls, Supervision, Training and Competence, and Approved Persons Sourcebooks.

6 Financial Services Authority, Handbook of Rules and Guidance, Interim Prudential Sourcebook for Banks, chapter NE.

7 "Derivatives Settlement", 1998, International Swaps and Derivatives Association.

INDEX

A
accounting practices 215–16
activity-based management 16
adequacy and appropriateness 233
advanced management approach 256
Advanced Measurement Approach (AMA) 32, 73, 80, 89, 152, 169
 qualifying for 161–2
Air France 226
Allied Irish Banks 146
allocation of capital 198
alternative standardised approach (ASA) 152
AMA models 257
American Banker 212–13
American Bankers Association (2001) 139
American Banking Association 95
Amram, M. and N. Kulatilaka (1999) 91
Anderson, S. (2001) 137
anti-diversification 249
ANZ case study 5
Aon Risk Services 223, 224
Arthur Andersen 209, 223
Asey, M.R. *et al* (1993) 189
asset allocation 180
asset returns, effects of errors in modeling 186–8
Australian Prudential Regulatory Authority (APRA) (2001) 140

B
bad press 211
Bank 24 123
Bank for International Settlements (BIS) 218
Bank Management Principles for Electronic Banking 218
bankers' blanket bond 45
Bankers Trust 84
BankFirst Corporation 65–6, 69
banking, and operational risk 59–60
banks
 differences and the decision to insure 50–51
 Moody's analytical framework for operational risk management 227–38
Barclays Stockbrokers 123
Barings 47, 179
Basel Capital Accord 227
Basel Committee on Banking Supervision 239, 18, 31, 40, 43, 50
 (1998) 59, 148
 (2000) 47
 (2001) 51, 56, 121, 124, 131, 141
 (2002) 121
 (2003) 59, 122, 129, 131, 132, 133, 139, 140, 141, 147, 150
 Advance Measurement Approach reverse 32, 73, 80, 89
 draft Capital Adequacy Directive (CAD 3) reverse this 18, 21
 New Capital Accord 138–41, 145, 239
 Standardised Approach 32, 80, 97
 statement on insurance 44
 ten principles 253–4
basic indicator approach 30, 97, 151–2, 255
basket insurance products 43
 using 52–3
 views on 53
"bathtub" shape 125
BB&T Corporation, acquisition of BankFirst Corporation 65–6, 69
BBA/ISDA/Robert Morris Associates report (1999) 199
behaviour-based management 15–16
Bennis and Ward Biederman 212
Bethell-Jones, R. (2001) 60
Birge, J.R. (1995) 186
BIS
 (1988) 95
 (1996) 96
 (2001) 95, 96, 101, 102
Blount, E. (2001) 60
board of directors 232
bootstrapping 185–6
Boyle, P.P. and E.S. Schwartz (1977) 180, 193
Boyle, P.P. *et al* (1997) 186
Brennan, M.J. and E.S. Schwartz (1976) 180, 193
British Airways 226
British Bankers Association 11, 50, 197
 (1997) 100
 (2001) 96, 138, 140
Brotzen, D. (2000) 210
Bugalla, J. 224
business activities 235
business continuity 259
business process maps 155
business risk 151
business units 23, 162, 233
 and functional units 24
 functional units and operational risk 24
Butler, D. (2000) 47, 53

INDEX

C
capital, allocation 198
capital adequacy 16
capital asset pricing model 5
capital attribution, for operational risk 162, 164–5
capital charge 96, 258–9
capital-at-risk 12
catastrophes 224
catastrophic losses, insurance against 166
cause-based classification 31
CEO, role in crisis management 224
certainty equivalent excess return on equity (CEexROE) 181, 182, 186, 189, 190, 193
change management 20
Chase and Citibank 123
clustering 132–3
collateral 260
collateral damage 224
committees 25
compliance 20
component reliability under stress 126
Consiglio, A., D. Saunder and S.A. Zenios (2003) 180
Consiglio, E., F. Cocco and S.A. Zenios, (2001a) 180, 181, 191, 194
Consiglio, E., F. Cocco and S.A. Zenios (2001b) 180, 181
contingency planning 233
continuous time models 186
corporate reputation 223–6
cost containment 36
cost-to-fix 149
credibility 40
Credit Risk Modelling Conference 95
crisis management, role of CEO 224
Cruz, M.
  (1999) 55
  (2000) 109
  (2001) 114, 118
  (2002) 121, 133, 136
Cruz, M. et al (1998) 109
Cruz, M. and J. Carroll (2000) 109
Culp (2001) 45
cultural drivers 35–6
culture and ethics 234
Cumming, C.M. and B.J. Hirtle (2001) 60

D
data 4–5, 9–10
  and insurance 49–50
  quantification and modelling 235–7
  for quantification and risk assessment 51–2
data access 10–11
data management 11–12
data pools 11
Davison, A. (1983) 111
de minimis limits 132
depositor protection schemes 46
Dhillon, B.S. and Singh, C. (1981) 125, 130, 136
directors and officers' liability 45–6
directors and senior managers 234
disaggregation 31
disclosure 254
disclosure and reporting 216
discriminatory treatment 216
divergence, assessment 27
Doherty, N. (2000) 47, 49, 51
Doherty and Smith (1993) 48, 51
Dowd, K. (1998) 57
draft Capital Adequacy Directive (CAD 3) 18, 21
Drenick's theorem 126
Drucker, P.F. (1992) 136, 137
Deutsche Bank 41

E
E-risk 218
earnings, stability and quality 227, 228
Ebnother, S. et al (2003) 246
Ebnother, S., M. Leippold and P. Vanini (2003) 241
economic pricing models 5
economic and regulatory capital 34
economics of Operational risk 240–41
The Economist 221
education and training 37–9
  divisions of the internal market for 38
Egg 122
electronic computer crime 45
embedded minimum guarantee option 180
embedded options, pricing 180
Embrechts, P.
  (2000) 107
  (2002) 243
Embrechts, P., C. Klüppelberg and T. Mikosch (1997) 104, 111
employee liability 153
employee relations 217
employment practices 260
employment practices liability 45, 46
Enron 209, 225
enterprise-wide risk management 179–94
ETI (Extract-Transform-Load) process 12
EU Commission 18
European Strategic Account Management Group 223
event (loss) analysis 14
event (loss) database 13–14
evolutionary approach 153
EVT, in operational VAR model 109–19
EVT techniques, application to operational risk database 113–16
expected loss models 5
expert knowledge 246, 246
expert opinions 29
exposure indicator (EI) 153
exposure indicators (EIs) 139
external loss data 11
external risks 4
external solution to operational risk 14–15
extreme value theory (EVT) 109, 110–11, 112
  view of operational risk 89

F
failure, impact of 234
failure events 131
Fidelity blanket bond 45
financial planning, for scenario properties 185
finite risk plans 55
Ford 226
fraud 255
fraud, corruption and financial crime 150, 153, 234
fraud models 12
Frechet, Gumbel and Weibull 110

INDEX

Freeman and Kunreuther (1996) 48
frequency models 116–18
FS 9000 136, 137, 138
FSA (2002) 121
functional units 20, 32
  and business units 24
  operational risk and business units 24
  and risk owners 23–6

G

Gaussian hypothesis 109
generalised extreme value (GEV) distribution 110, 111, 115
generalised Pareto distribution (GPD) 111
Giraldi, C. et al (2000) 180
Global Association of Risk Professionals 254
GOLD (Global Operational Loss Database) 11, 19, 197, 198
  business lines in 205
  data fields 203–4
  impact/effect categories 202
  loss categories 200
Gollier, C. and H. Schlesinger (1995) 51
Gordy, M. (2001) 100
governance 216
granularity 78
Grillet (1992) 48
Grosen, A. and P.I. Jorgensen (2000) 180, 193
Grosen and Jorgensen (2000) 190
group risk function 232–3
Group of Thirty (1993) 148
"group workshop" approach 10
guarantees, modelling 180–81
"Guide to Risk Management" 254
Guiliani, R.W. 224

H

Hadjiemmanuil (1996) 46
hedging 14, 29, 145
Herath, H.S.B. and J.S. Jahera Jr. (2002) 60
Hill (1975) 113
Hill (shape parameter) plot 114
Hiller, F.S. and G.J. Lieberman (1990) 123, 134
Hines, W.W. and D.C. Montgomery (1980) 125
Hoffman, D. (2003) 137
Hoffman, D. and M. Johnson (1996) 127
Holderness (1990) 48
holistic risk management 90
Hosking, J.M.R. et al (1985) 115
Hosking, J.M.R. and J. Wallis (1987) 111
Hull, J. (1989) 123
human reliability under stress 130
human resources 84

I

implementation process 6–7
Industry Technical Working Group (ITWG) 89
information
  dimensions of 31–2
  types of 28–31
information technology 233
innovation 17
insurance 14, 29, 43–57, 264–5
  against catastrophic losses 166
  alternatives to 55
  and the Basel statement 44
  monitoring role 48
  in risk management 45–6
  service efficiencies 48
insurance policies with guarantees 179–94
integrated data requirements framework 32–4
  building or buying 34
integrated risk capital framework 100–101
  model 101–5
integrated risk management 103
integration, risk management 105–6
integrative asset and liability modelling 180–3
  sources of model error 183–4
internal capital calculation 87–9
internal event/loss data 11
internal investment funds 14
internal measurement approach 97–9
internal process limits 132
International Institute of Finance 89
International Swaps and Derivatives Association (ISDA) 197, 261
ISO 9000 standard 137
IT resources 260
IWG 55

J

Japan 224
Jobst, N.J. and S.A. Zenios (2001) 184
Johnson and Johnson 226
Jorion, P. (1997) 123, 134, 136

K

Kahnemann, D. and A. Tversky (1974) 246
Kang, P. and S.A. Zenios (1997) 189
Karels and McClatchey (1999) 46
Katzman (1985) 48
Kececioglu, D. (1991) 125, 126
key risk indicators (KRIs) 7, 13, 83–5
  tracking 85
Klüppelberg and Mikosch (1997) 107
knock-on effect 224
knowledge management 16
Kopp, G. (2003) 136, 137
Kuhn, R. and P. Neu (2003) 243
Kyriacou, M.N. and E.A. Medova (2001) 89

L

Leadbetter, M.R., G. Lindgren and H. Rootzen (1983) 104
legal risk 260–64
Lepus Growing Importance of Operational Risk (2003) 90
liability modelling 188–90
liability risk 188–90
Long Term Capital Management (LTCM) 95, 179, 180
"longevity risk" 188
loss data 31–2
Loss Data Collection Exercise (LDCE) 131
loss databases 32–3, 50, 79–83
loss distribution approach 153
loss event monitoring 13–14
loss events 8
loss giving events (LGEs) 153
loss reporting
  local vs hierarchical 82
  simplifying 81

INDEX

losses
  classification by type 150–51
  classification/categorisation 200
  estimation 131–4

M

McConnell, P.J. (1998) 131, 134
McDonough, W. (1998) 95, 96
Main (1982) 48
management 162
  quality 228, 230
management oversight 235
managerial flexibility, value in acquisitions 64–8
managing operational risk 17–42
marketing 84
Markowitz, H.M. (1991) 123
maximum domain of attraction (MDA) 111
maximum likelihood estimation (MLE) 12
Mayers and Smith (1982) 48, 51
mean time to repair 134
mean variance surplus organisation models 180
measurement of operational risk 258
measurements of quality 136–8
measuring operational risk 124
media damage 212
media headlines 211
Medova, E.A. (2000) 103, 104
Medova, E.A. and M.N. Kyriacou
  (2000) 103, 104
  (2001) 106
mergers 260
mergers and acquisitions 60–61
Miller (1998) 47
Minimum Regulatory Capital (MRC) 121
Minneapolis Star Tribune 209
mis-selling 216
Mittelstaedt, R.E. Jr. 224
model error 179–94
model framework, for an IT network 247–9
model frameworks 243
  calibration and data issues 246
model selection, for operational risk 145–77
modelling, guarantees 180–81
modelling operational risk 241–2
models
  implementation 155–65
  long-term aspects 158–9
  short-term aspects 158
money launderers 216
Monte Carlo simulations 12, 123, 136
Moody's analytical framework for operational risk management of banks 227–38
  definition and boundaries of Oprisk 229
  driving forces and limitations 229–30
  key operational risks 231
  management 230
  methodology 229
  OpRisk profile document, reports and indicators 231–2
  stages of development and organisational structure 230–31
Moody's Investor Service 224
moral hazard, and basket insurance products 52
MorExchange 50
multi-peril basket insurance products 44–53
  advantages 47–9
  data and risk classification 49–50
  diversification benefits 48–9
  lack of critical mass 49
mutual self-insurance pools 55

N

National Criminal Intelligence Service 234
NatWest Bank 123
New Capital Accord, Basel Committee on Banking Supervision 138–41
new issues 7
Nissan Mutual 179
normal, establishing the 102
Nornes, R. 223, 224, 225
Nostro Breaks 83, 85

O

Ong, M.K. (1999) 99
operation processes, aggregation 130–31
operational data 11
operational failure, types 157
operational loss, versus operations loss 199–200
operational loss database
  anonymity 198–9
  auditability 206
  building and running 197–207
  business activity 204
  cause/event versus impact/event 201–2
  classification/categorisation of losses 200–201
  completeness of reporting 206–7
  confidentiality 198
  consistency 199
  contingent losses 201
  drivers to develop 197–8
  flexibility/evolution 199
  hard losses 201
  limitations 206
  modelling 111–13
  near misses 201
  purpose 207
  reporting 206
  reporting threshold 202
  scaling 202–3
  soft losses 201, 204
  threshold levels 206
  trust between participants 199
operational losses, firm-wide matrix 100
operational processes, defining 129
operational research and risk 123
operational risk
  and banking 59–60
  see also Moody's analytical framework for operational risk management of banks
  building blocks 79
  business units and functional units 24
  definitions 4, 43, 96, 102, 121, 145
  examples 122–4
  extreme value theory (EVT) 89
  internal and external 147
  key considerations 228
  loss types 112
  managing 17–42
  measuring 124
  ownership of 21–2

INDEX

process solution 5–6
taxonomy for 4
in a transaction process 149
typology 148–9
"Operational Risk - The Next Frontier" 39
operational risk database, applying EVT techniques to 113–16
operational risk exposure 156
operational risk framework acceptance 75
  managing establishing 74, 74–9
    expectation 75–7
    senior management buy-in 74
    organisation structure 76–8
    terminology 78–9
operational risk insurance for banks 43–57
operational risk management
  activities at group level 22–3
  benchmarking and improving 197–8
  granularity 78
  guidelines 19–21
  roles and responsibilities 18–19
  style 18
operational risk membrane 77
operational risk metrics 155
operational risk mitigation 165–6
operational risk nodes 242–3
operational risk policy 155
operational VAR 109–10
  calculating 117–18
operational VAR model, using EVT 109–19
OpVAR 154, 158, 159, 160–61, 167, 174
  comparison by business 168
  comparison by loss type 168
  comparison by regulatory approach 168–9
  implementing 156
organisation, establishing 6
organisational structure 76–8
  for risk management 232
Organizing Genius – The Secrets of Creative Collaborations 212
ORX pool 11

outsourcing 14–15, 235, 259
ownership of operational risk 21–2
Oxford metrica 225

P

parameter estimation, and threshold choice 106
partners/suppliers/outsourcers 217
peaks over threshold (POT) model 104, 111
people risks 4
people solution to operational risk 8–9
  job factors 9
  organisational factors 9
  personal factors 9
performance, auditing and reviewing 8
performance measurement 7–8, 40, 105
performance tracking 13
Perry, D.J. and R.E. Knight 225
Pezier, J. (2002) 139, 141
Pickands, J. (1975) 111
Poisson distribution 116, 117, 121
policies, procedures and systems 235
policy, setting 5–6
pre claim settlement cash advances 43, 53–5
privacy 217
probability weighted moments (PWM) method 114
process risks 4
process solution, to operational risk 5–8
professional indemnity 45
Punjabi, S. (1998) 105

Q

QQ-Plot 115–16
quality, measurements of 136–8
quality management systems (QMS) 137–8
quantifying and reducing operational risk 257
quantitative analysis and modelling 198
"quasi-Monte Carlo" algorithm 186
Quick, J. 43

R

Rabin, M. (1998) 246
RAROC (risk-adjusted return on capital) 23, 35, 158

Real Options - Managing Strategic Investment in an Uncertain World 91
Real Options and Energy Management 91
real options market 61–4, 91
regulation 3, 16, 18, 35, 39
  operational risk insurance 56
regulatory approach to risk models 151–5
regulatory capital 86–90
regulatory scrutiny, reputational risk 214–19
reinsurance 54
  and securitisation 166–8
reliability theory 121–44
  aggregation of operation processes 130–31
  defining operational processes 129
  estimating losses 131–3
  learning period 127–9
  reliability function 125–7
    applying 127–9
  saw tooth pattern 129
reliability-centred management 15
reporting exposure 156
reports and results 237
result presentation 12–13
representativeness heuristic 246
reputational impairment, impact of 225–6
reputational risk 209–22
  analysts' assessments 212–13
  anticipation 219–21
  areas for financial services institutions 215
  bad press 211
  causes 224
  control and detection mechanisms 218, 220
  crisis management plan 220–21
  definition 210
  guiding principles 221
  impact 210–11
  regulatory scrutiny 214–19
  visibility of outcomes 212–14
  weighting 219–20
resolution 149
retrocessions 167
reviews, frequency and independence 234
risk analysis 12
risk analysis tools 156
"risk appetite" 17, 22, 23

INDEX

risk assessment 26, 85–6
risk assessment workshops 34
Risk Cockpit 9, 10, 11
risk committee 232
risk control/mitigation 26
  assuming risk 27
  avoiding risk 26
  reducing risk 26
  transferring risk 26
risk identification 155
risk indicators 33
risk management, integration 105–6
risk management cycle 25
  iteration 27–8
risk management plan, developing 224–5
risk management process 25–6
risk maps 10, 14, 15
risk owners, and functional units 23–6
risk process and environment 7
risk profile document 237–8
risk profile index (RPI) 139
risk transfer 223
risk-adjusted return on Investment (RAROI) 241
risks
  definition and review 6
  self-assessment of 9, 198
RMA, BBA and ISDA and Pricewaterhouse Coopers (1999) 43
Roberts, S. (2000) 46
Rogue traders 146–7

S

sales force 216
Sarbanes-Oxley Act 223, 238
SAS Institute 9
scenario analysis/subjective loss estimate models 5
scenario modelling of asset returns 184–6
scenario optimisation model 191–4
scenario properties, for financial planning 185
scenario-based optimisation model 180
  sources of error 180–81
Schrand and Unal (1998) 51
scorecards 33
securitisation 43, 55–6
  and reinsurance 166–8
"segmented transaction value chain" 32
self-assessment of risks 9
self-assessment workshops 29–30
service 217
service level agreement 244
settlement failure 31
shareholders 17
Six Sigma 137, 138
Skipper (1998) 57
Skogh (1989) 48
Skogh (1991) 48
Smith, R.I.
  (1985) 104
  (1987) 104
  (1990) 104
"Sound Practices for the Management and Supervision of Operational Risk" 18
sponsors 40
stability and quality of earnings 227, 228
standardised approach 152, 255
  Basel Committee on Banking Supervision 32
statistical modelling 186
statistical models 145
statistical quality control (SQC) 136
strategic actions and mitigation 7
subsidiaries/affiliates 217
supervisors, role 254
systems and procedures 233
SYSTRUST scheme 138

T

tax 20
taxonomy for operational risk 4
technology 147
technology risks 4
technology solution to operational risk 9–14
threshold choice, and parameter estimation 106
thresholds 104
Tomski, R. (2001) 123
tools 36–7
total capital charge reconciliation 106
transaction process, in operational risk 149, 150
transaction-processing risk, calculating 169, 170–73
transparency 174, 228, 238
Trigeorgis, L. (1996) 69

U

UBS 123
unauthorised trading insurance 45, 46
universal risk indicator 30

V

ValueReaction model 225
VAR 28, 29, 96, 101, 109, 134–5, 147, 148
  calculation for a portfolio of processes 135
  see also operational VAR; OpVAR
Vinod, R.S. and K.B. Hendricks (1998) 137
Visa fraud 154, 160
Vose, D. (1996) 136

W

Wall Street Journal 216, 218
Waring, A. and I. Glendon (1998) 50
WEBTRUST system 138
Wharton's Aresty Institute of Executive Education 224
Williams, Smith and Young (1998) 50, 55
WorldCom 209

Y

Young, B. (2000) 50

Also published by Risk Books

The Basel Handbook
A Guide for Financial Practitioners
Edited by Michael K. Ong
ISBN 1 904339 15 8

Operational Risk and Financial Institutions
"The most useful publication on operational risk...a book containing 'the 10 commandments' of operational risk. It will certainly become an operational risk bible."
Paul Dorey, Barclays Bank
ISBN 1 899332 04 9

Credit Ratings
Methodologies, Rationale and Default Risk
Edited by Michael K. Ong
"I expect this volume to become a standard, highly-quoted reference."
Didier Cossin, Professor of Finance and Director, Institute of Banking and Finance, HEC, University of Lausanne
ISBN 1 899332 69 3

Model Risk
Concepts, Calibration and Pricing
Edited by Professor Rajna Gibson
ISBN 1 899332 98 8

Internal Modelling and CAD II
Qualifying and Quantifying Risk within a Financial Institution
Published in Association with the British Bankers Association
ISBN 1 899332 29 4

For more information on these as well as the entire range of books published by Risk Books, please visit our website
www.riskbooks.com